Story & Art by Shouko A

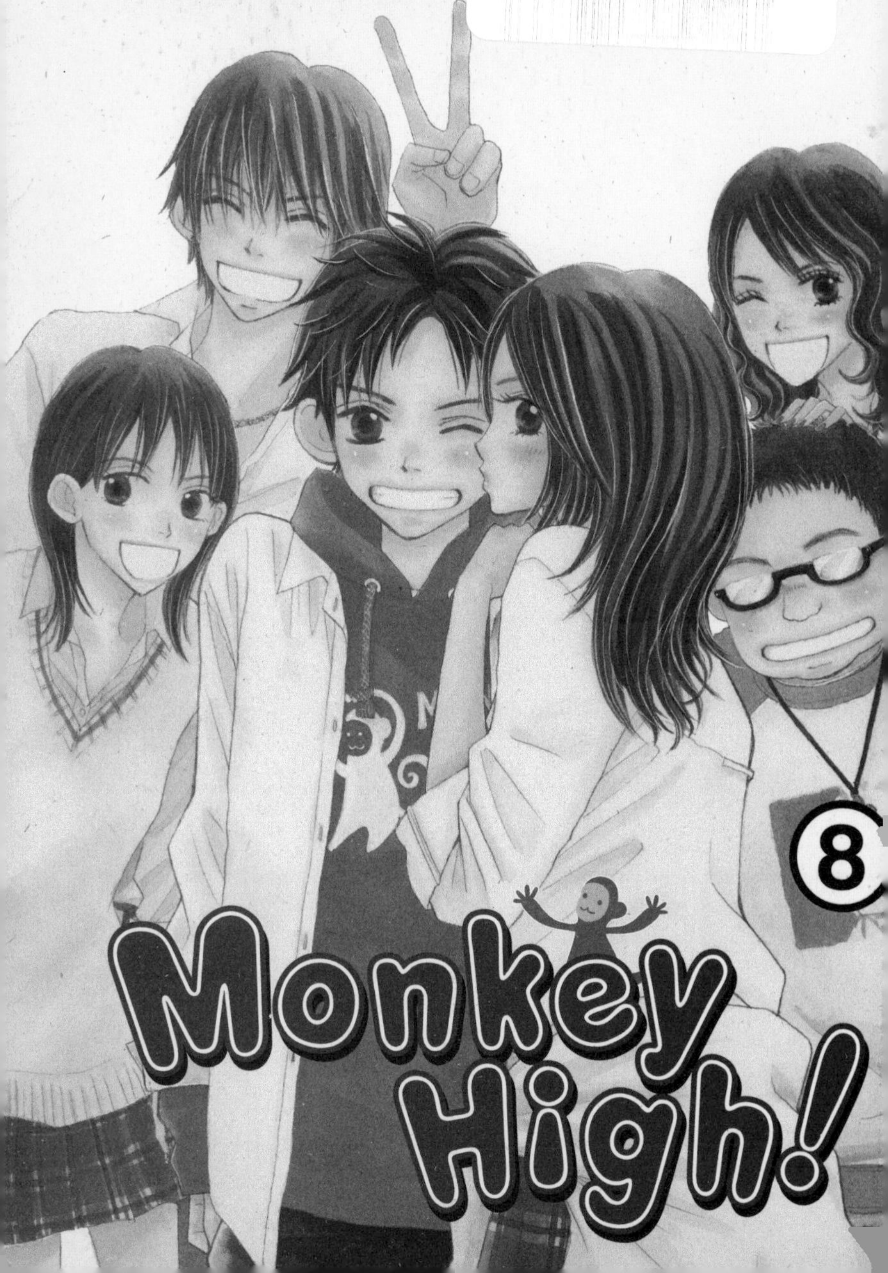
8
Monkey
High!

Monkey High!

⑧
CONTENTS

Story Thus Far

Masaru Yamashita
(Nickname: Macharu)

It's been two years since Haruna started going out with the monkey-like Macharu. Now as third-years, everyone is in the midst of studying for university entrance exams, and even Macharu begins to feel the pressure. Concerns about the future create a divide between the couple, but the two also confirm their strong feelings for each other. Haruna follows Macharu to Nagano, and…?!

Haruna Aizawa

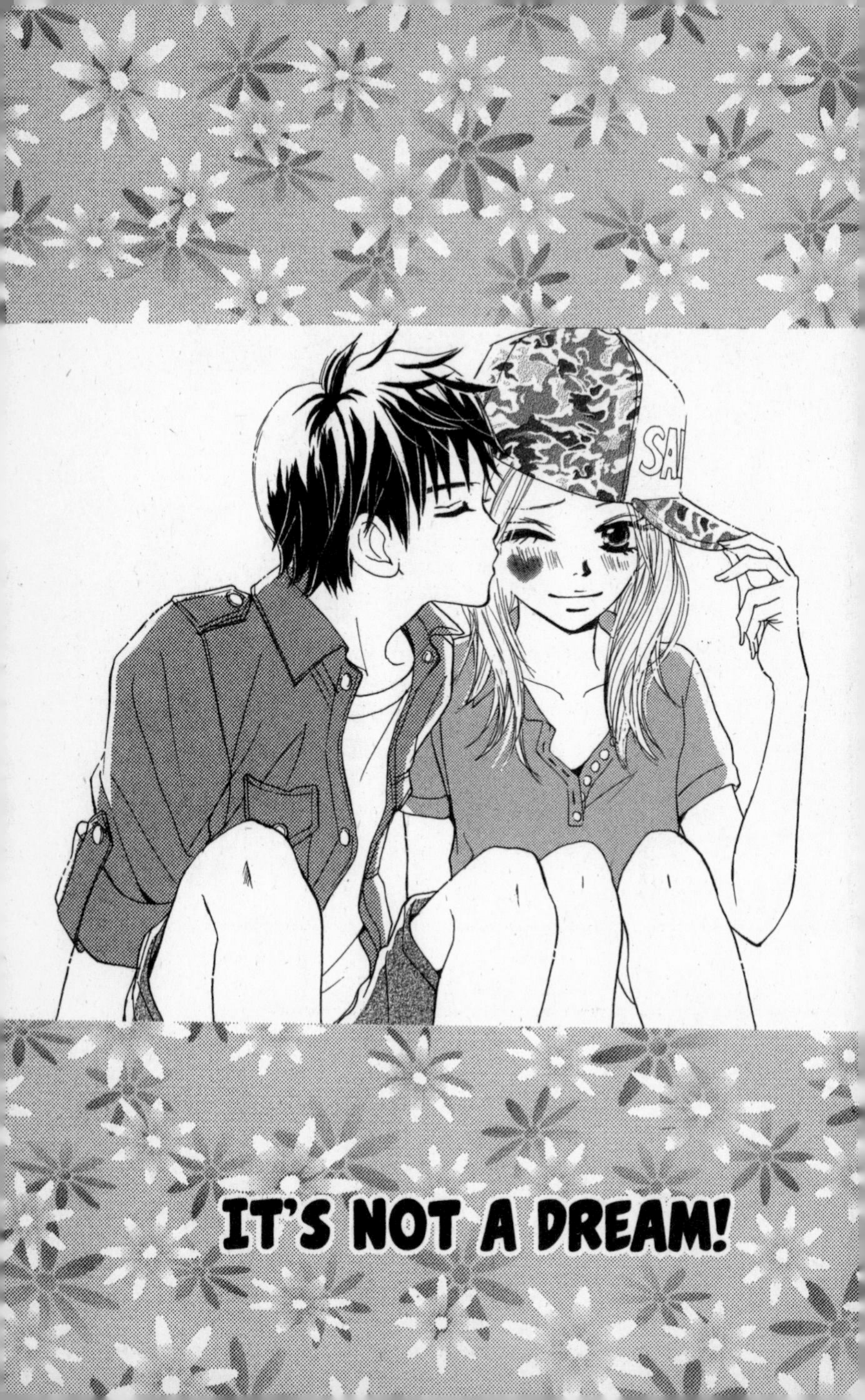

IT'S NOT A DREAM!

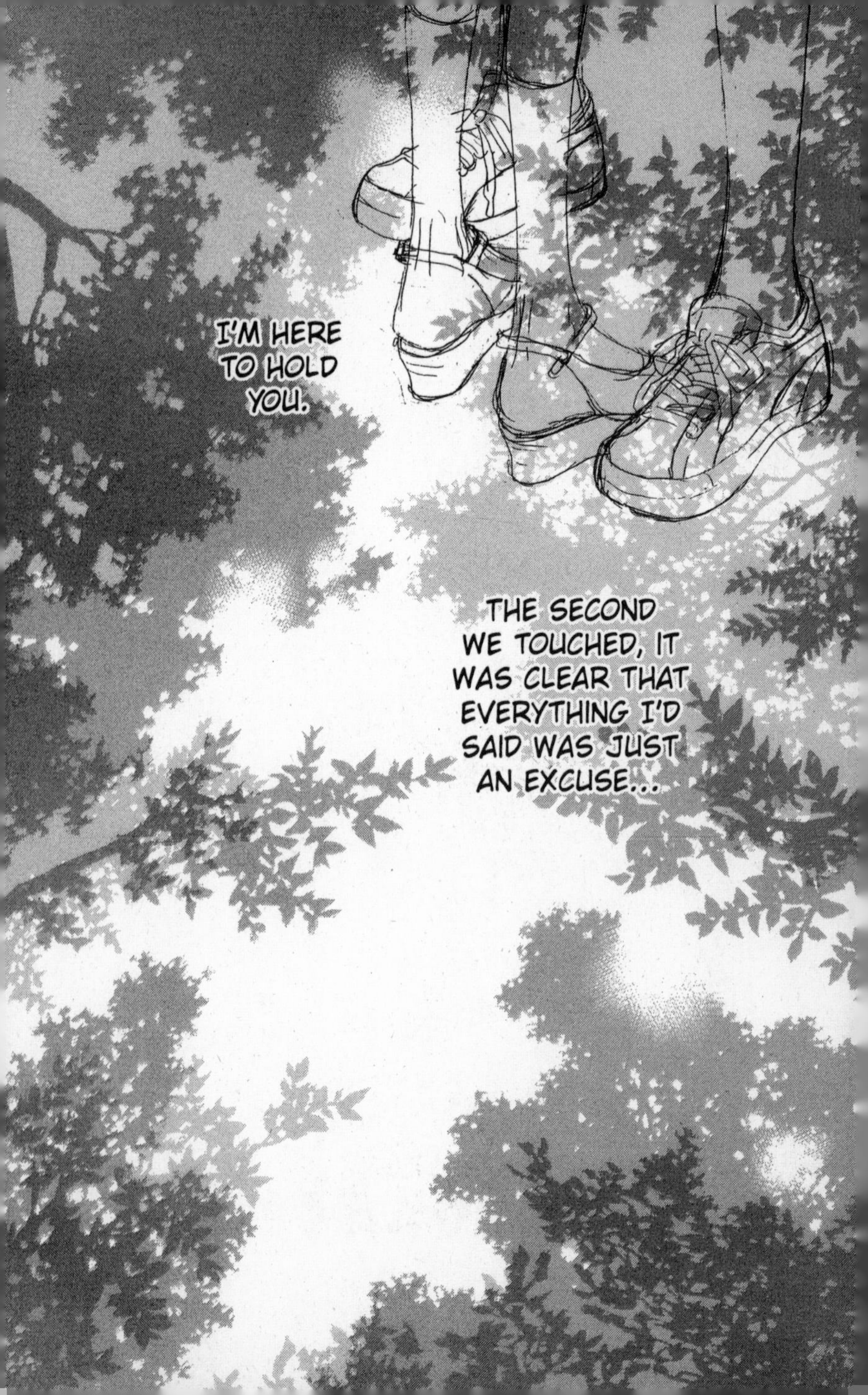
I'M HERE TO HOLD YOU.
THE SECOND WE TOUCHED, IT WAS CLEAR THAT EVERYTHING I'D SAID WAS JUST AN EXCUSE...

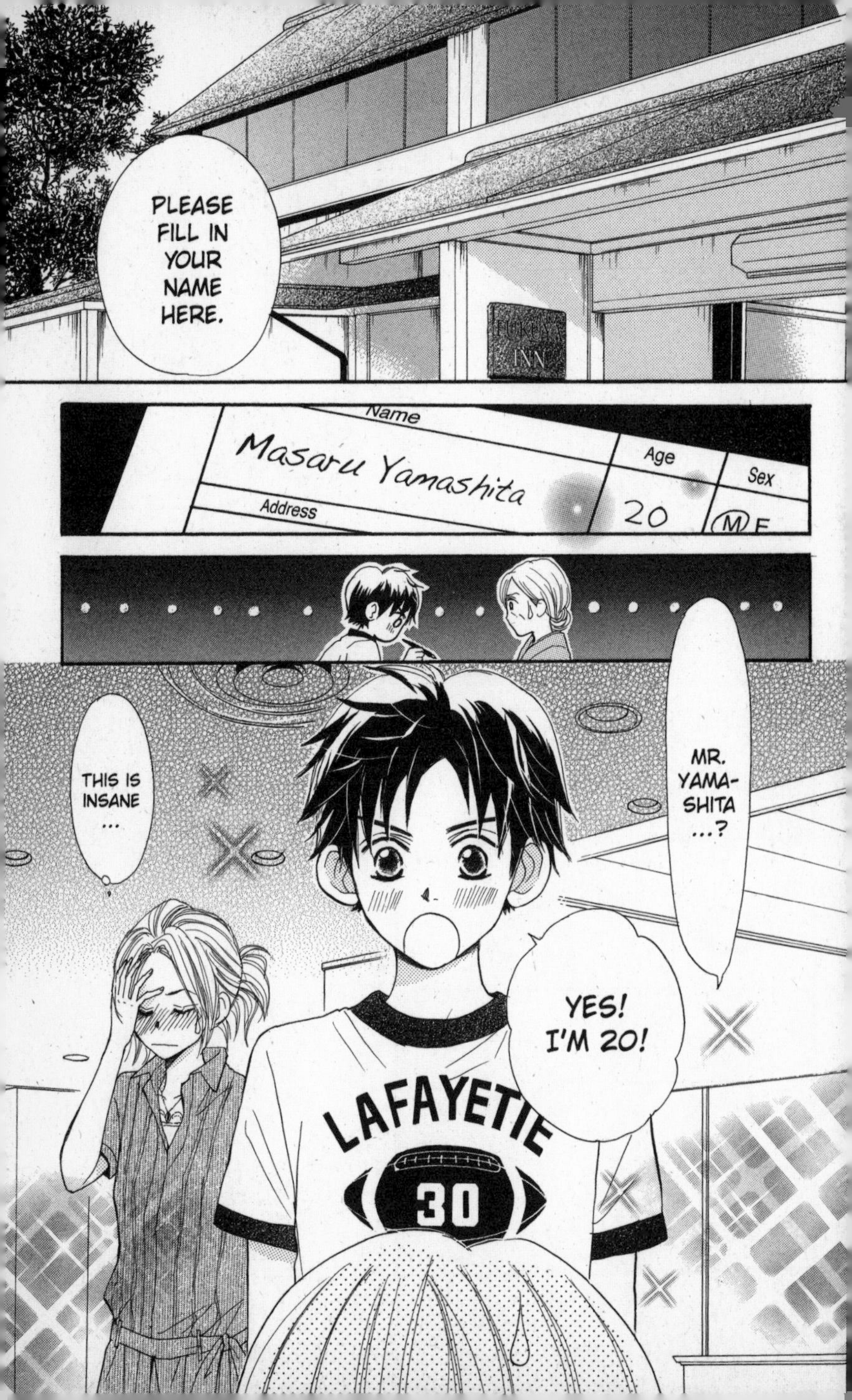
PLEASE FILL IN YOUR NAME HERE.
Name
Masaru Yamashita
Age
20
Sex
M F
Address
MR. YAMA-SHITA ...?
YES! I'M 20!
LAFAYETIE 30
THIS IS INSANE ...

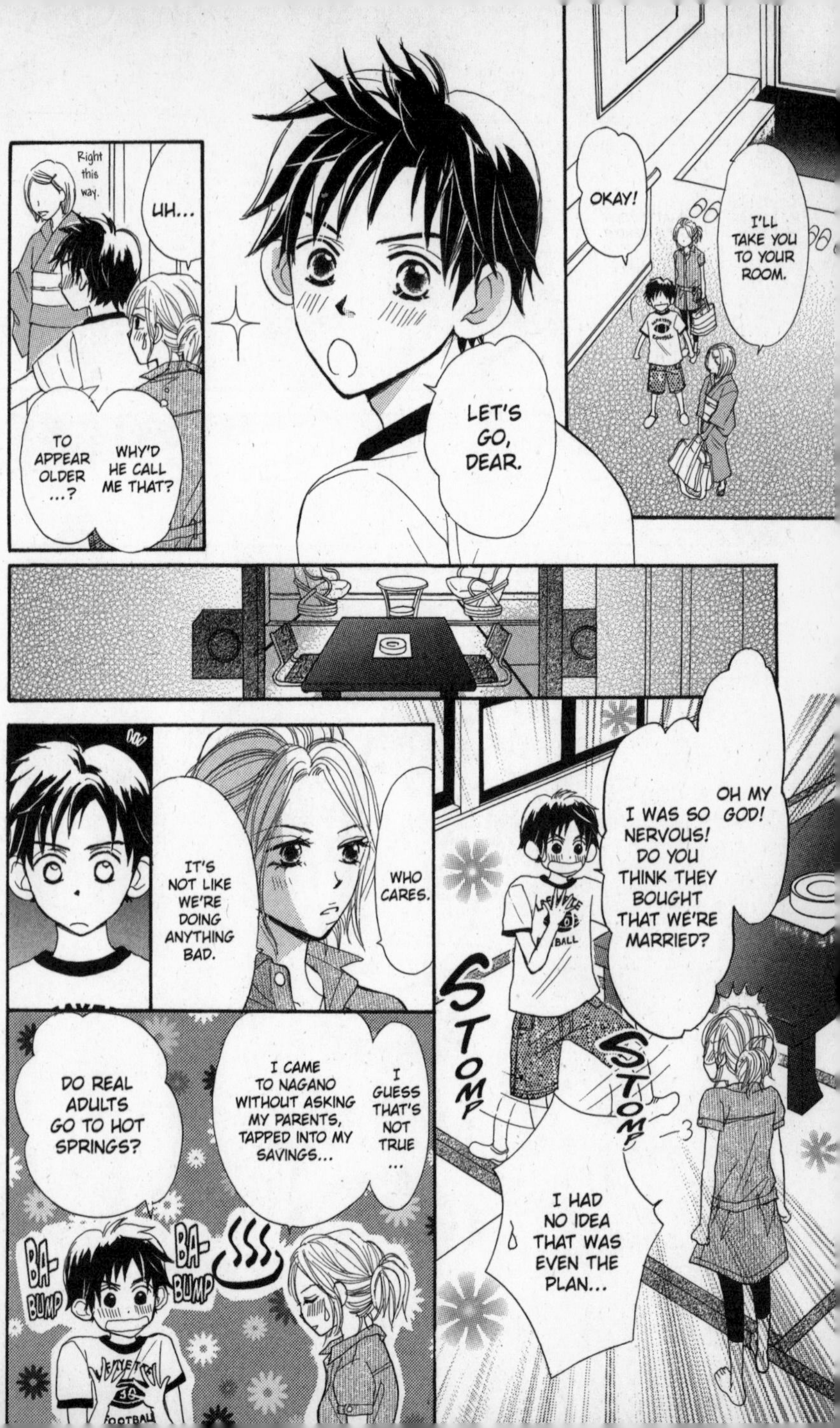
I'LL TAKE YOU TO YOUR ROOM.
OKAY!
LET'S GO, DEAR.
Right this way.
UH...
WHY'D HE CALL ME THAT?
TO APPEAR OLDER ...?
OH MY GOD!
I WAS SO NERVOUS! DO YOU THINK THEY BOUGHT THAT WE'RE MARRIED?
STOMP
STOMP
I HAD NO IDEA THAT WAS EVEN THE PLAN...
WHO CARES.
IT'S NOT LIKE WE'RE DOING ANYTHING BAD.
I GUESS THAT'S NOT TRUE ...
I CAME TO NAGANO WITHOUT ASKING MY PARENTS, TAPPED INTO MY SAVINGS...
DO REAL ADULTS GO TO HOT SPRINGS?
BA-BUMP
BA-BUMP

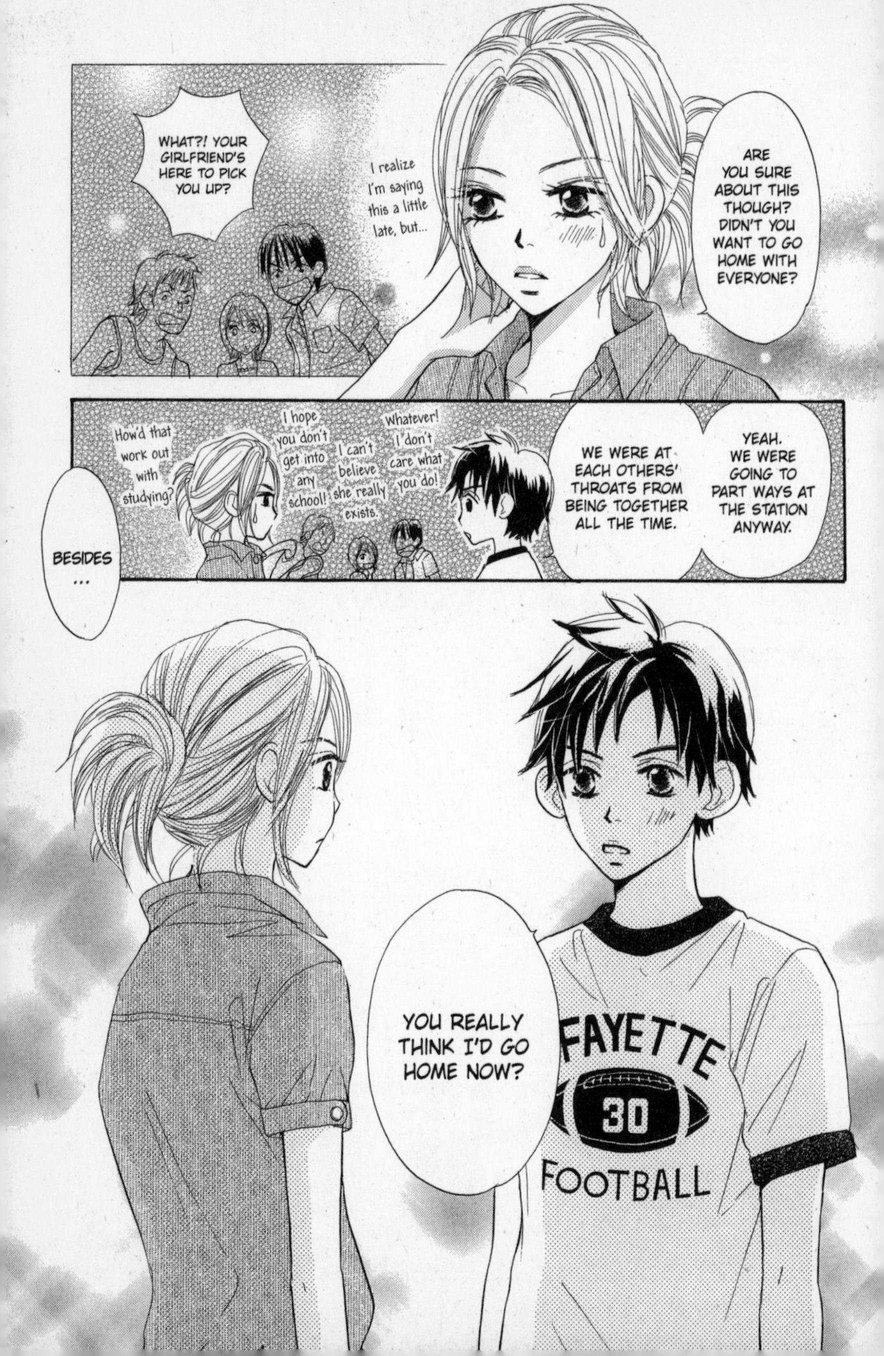
I realize I'm saying this a little late, but...
ARE YOU SURE ABOUT THIS THOUGH? DIDN'T YOU WANT TO GO HOME WITH EVERYONE?
WHAT?! YOUR GIRLFRIEND'S HERE TO PICK YOU UP?
YEAH. WE WERE GOING TO PART WAYS AT THE STATION ANYWAY.
WE WERE AT EACH OTHERS' THROATS FROM BEING TOGETHER ALL THE TIME.
Whatever! I don't care what you do!
I can't believe she really exists.
I hope you don't get into any school!
How'd that work out with studying?
BESIDES...
YOU REALLY THINK I'D GO HOME NOW?
FAYETTE
30
FOOTBALL

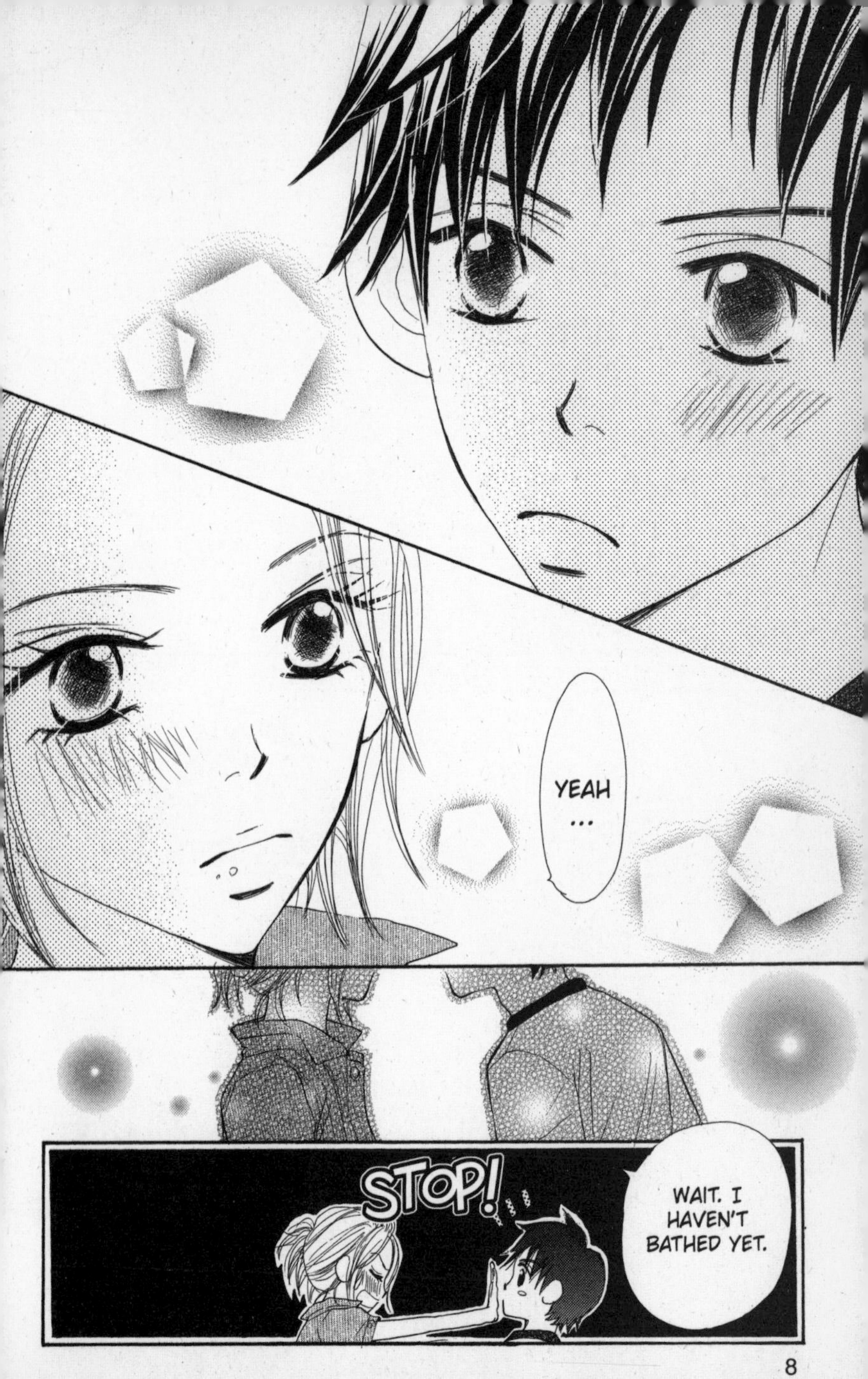
YEAH ...
STOP!
WAIT. I HAVEN'T BATHED YET.

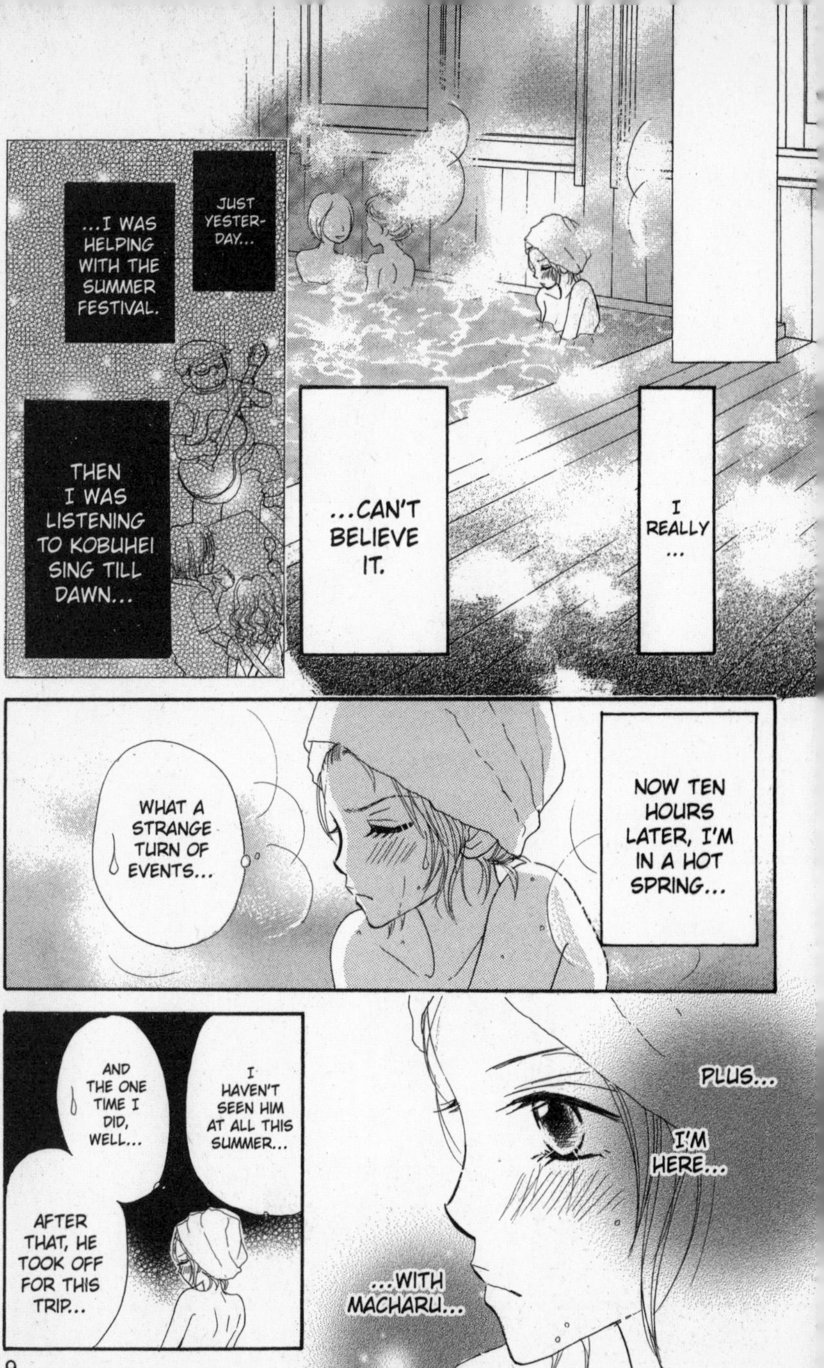
I REALLY...
...CAN'T BELIEVE IT.
JUST YESTER-DAY...
...I WAS HELPING WITH THE SUMMER FESTIVAL.
THEN I WAS LISTENING TO KOBUHEI SING TILL DAWN...
NOW TEN HOURS LATER, I'M IN A HOT SPRING...
WHAT A STRANGE TURN OF EVENTS...
PLUS...
I'M HERE...
...WITH MACHARU...
I HAVEN'T SEEN HIM AT ALL THIS SUMMER...
AND THE ONE TIME I DID, WELL...
AFTER THAT, HE TOOK OFF FOR THIS TRIP...

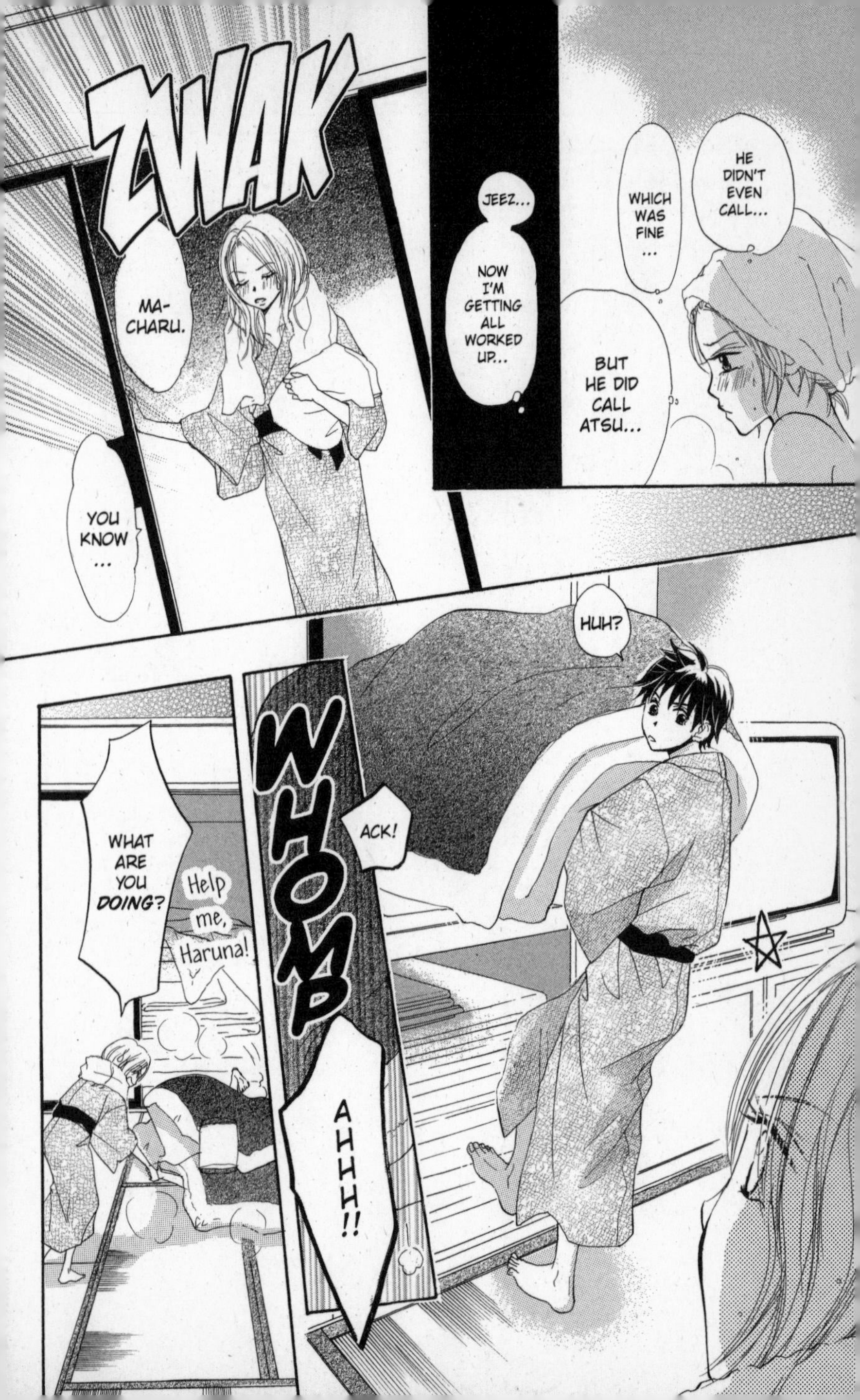
HE DIDN'T EVEN CALL...
WHICH WAS FINE...
BUT HE DID CALL ATSU...
JEEZ...
NOW I'M GETTING ALL WORKED UP...
ZWAK
MA-CHARU.
YOU KNOW...
HUH?
ACK!
WHOMP
AHHHH!!
WHAT ARE YOU DOING?
Help me, Haruna!

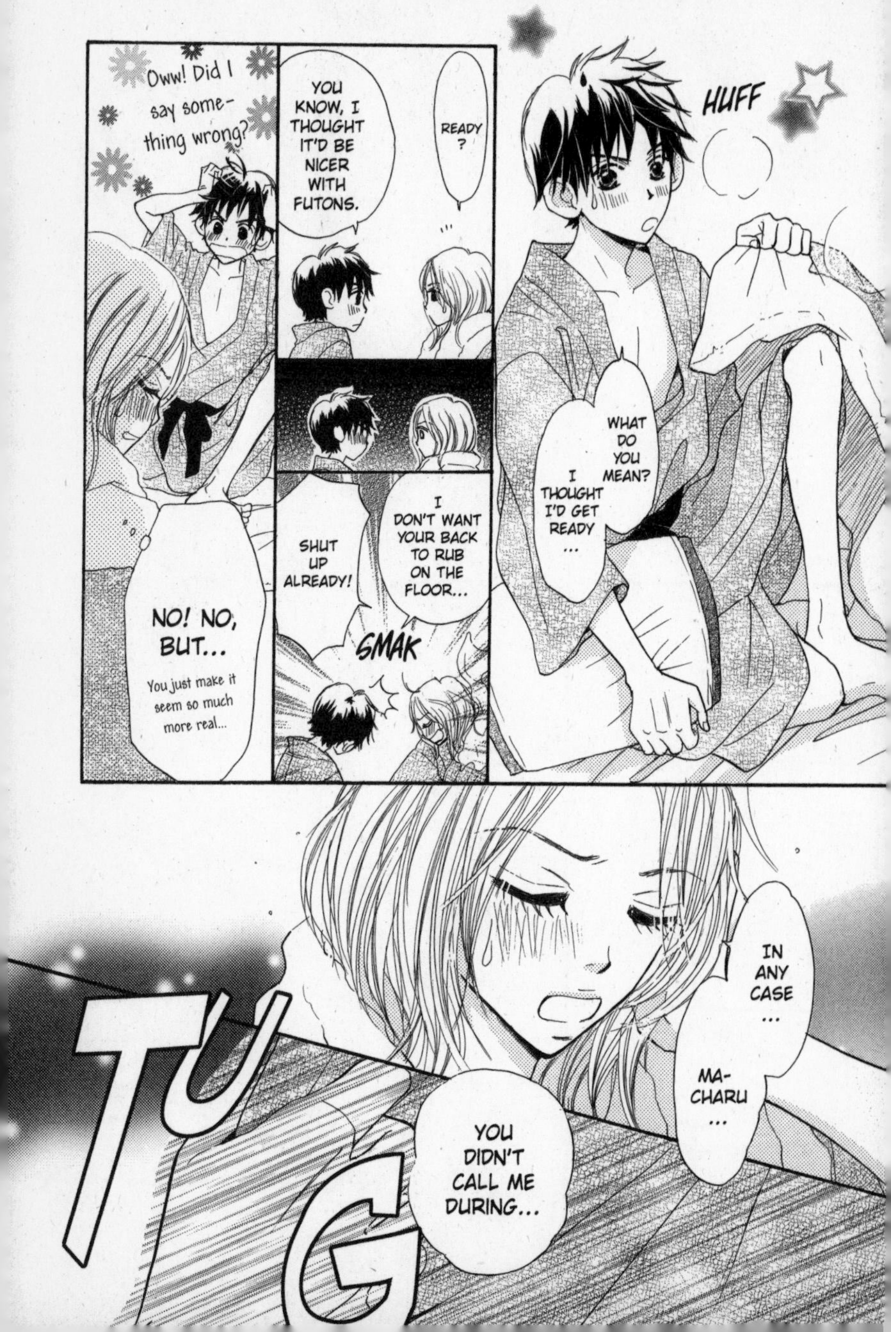
HUFF
WHAT DO YOU MEAN?
I THOUGHT I'D GET READY ...
READY ?
...
YOU KNOW, I THOUGHT IT'D BE NICER WITH FUTONS.
I DON'T WANT YOUR BACK TO RUB ON THE FLOOR...
SHUT UP ALREADY!
SMAK
Oww! Did I say some-thing wrong?
NO! NO, BUT...
You just make it seem so much more real...
IN ANY CASE ...
MA-CHARU ...
YOU DIDN'T CALL ME DURING...
TUG

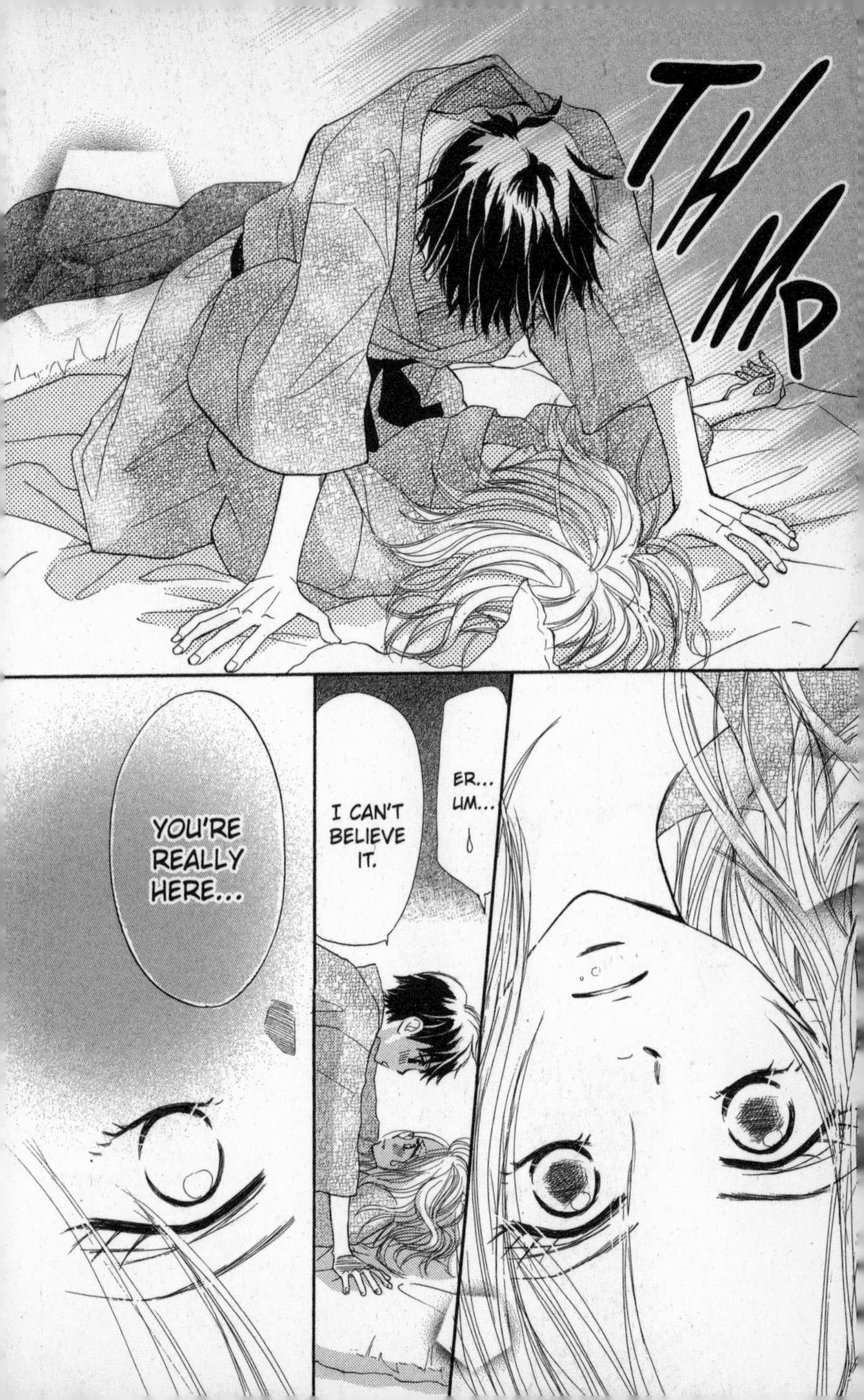
THMP
ER... UM...
I CAN'T BELIEVE IT.
YOU'RE REALLY HERE...

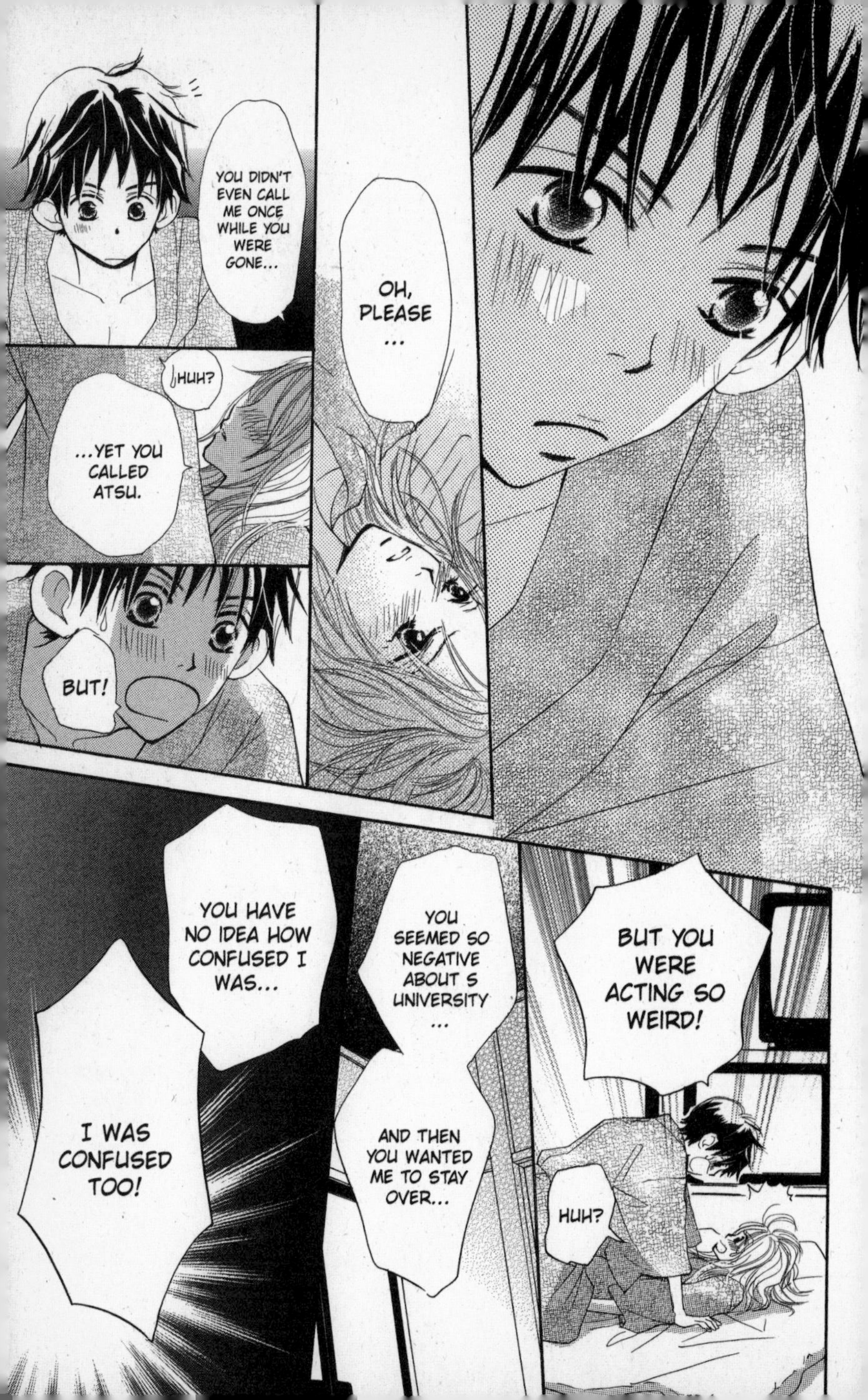
OH, PLEASE ...
YOU DIDN'T EVEN CALL ME ONCE WHILE YOU WERE GONE...
HUH?
...YET YOU CALLED ATSU.
BUT!
BUT YOU WERE ACTING SO WEIRD!
HUH?
YOU SEEMED SO NEGATIVE ABOUT S UNIVERSITY ...
AND THEN YOU WANTED ME TO STAY OVER...
YOU HAVE NO IDEA HOW CONFUSED I WAS...
I WAS CONFUSED TOO!

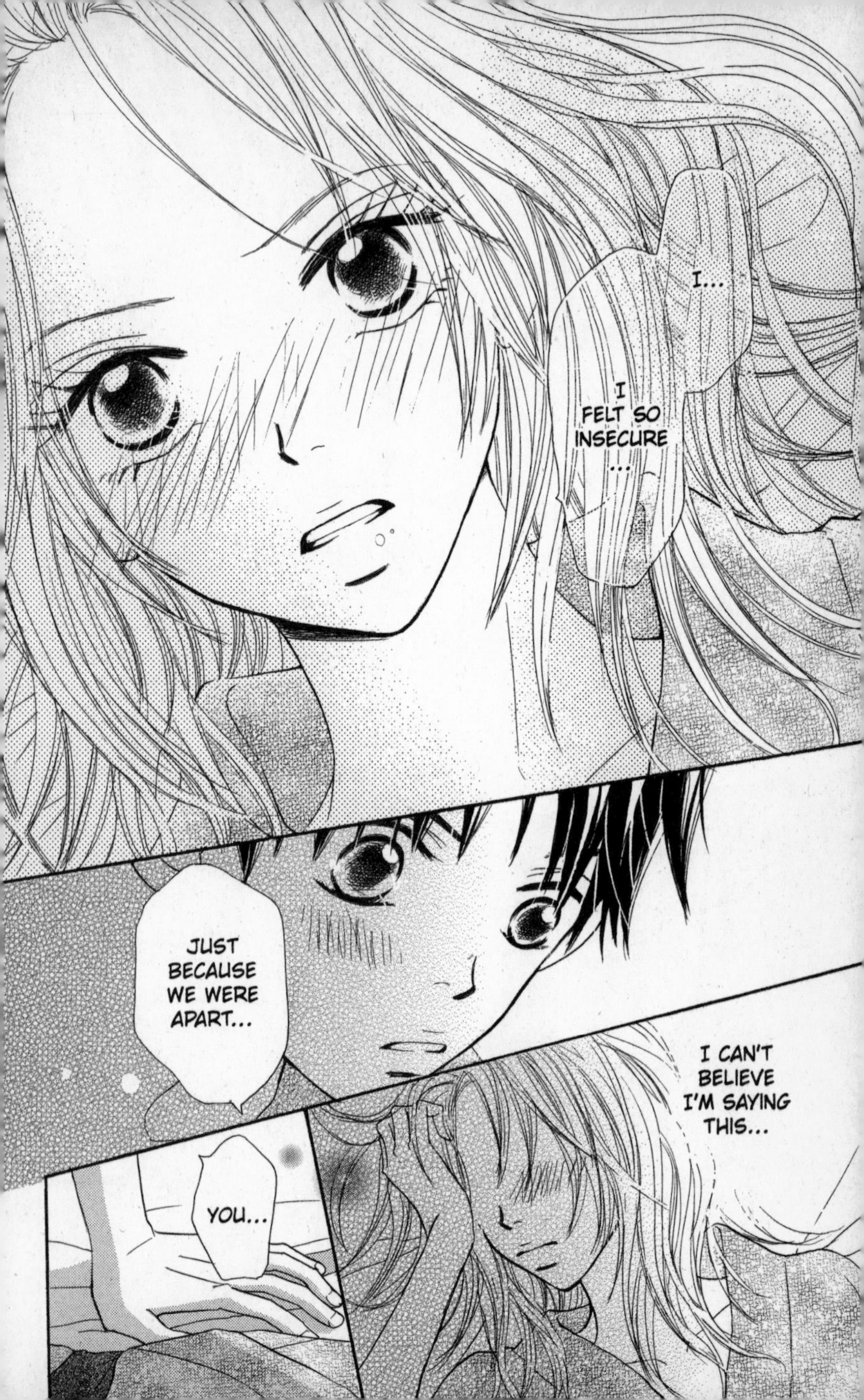
I...
I FELT SO INSECURE...
JUST BECAUSE WE WERE APART...
I CAN'T BELIEVE I'M SAYING THIS...
YOU...

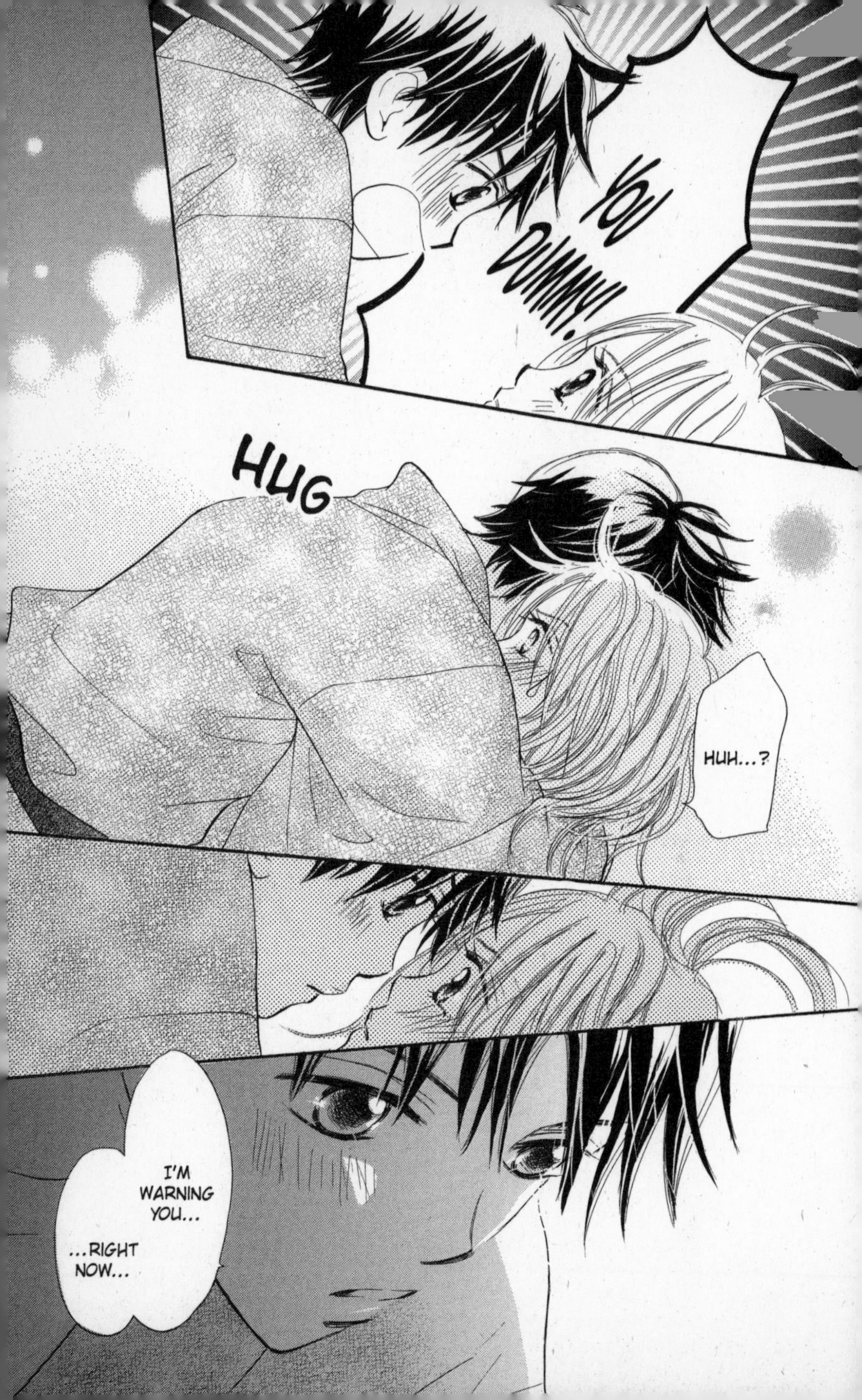
YOU DUMMY!!
HUG
HUH...?
I'M WARNING YOU...
...RIGHT NOW...

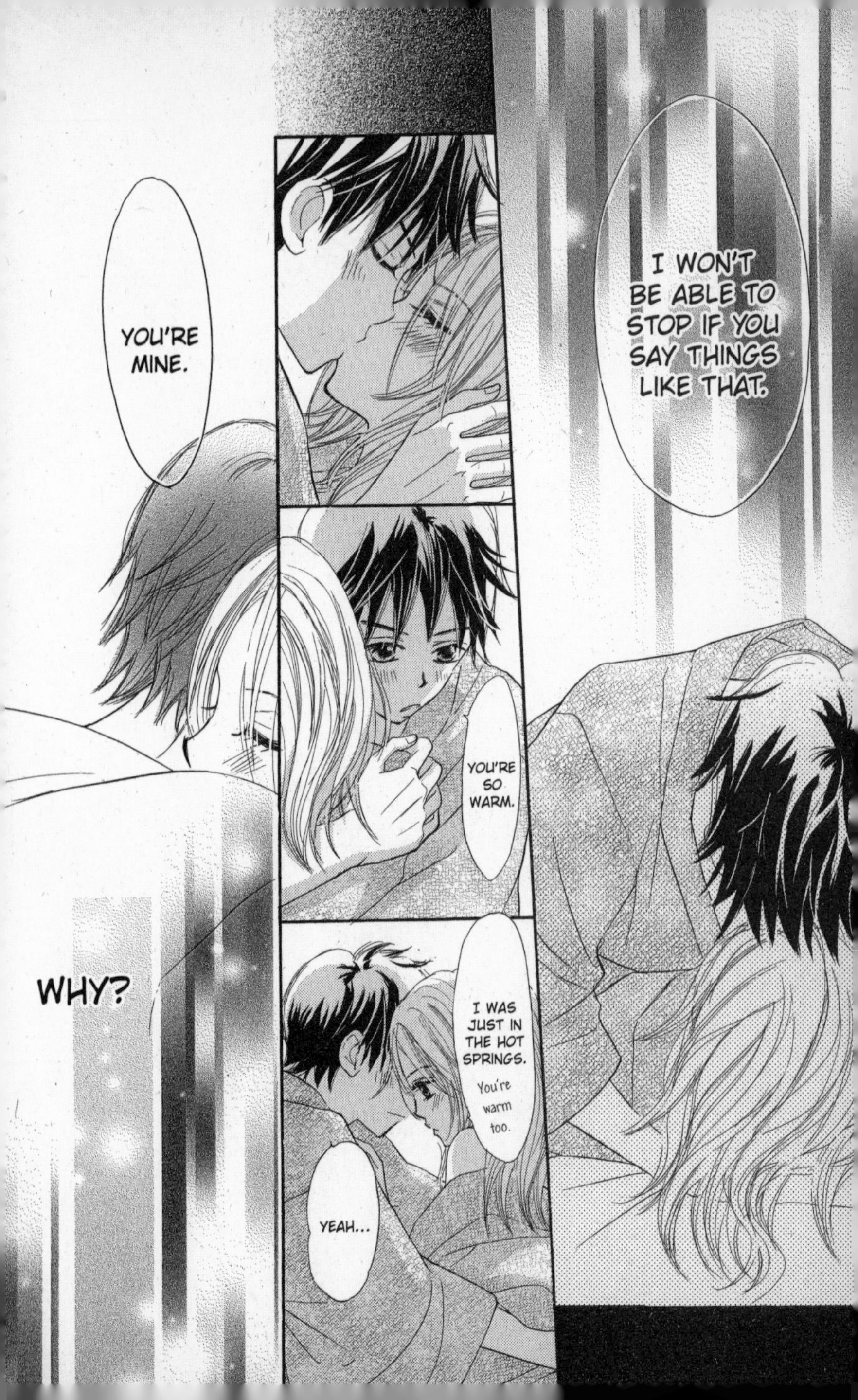
I WON'T BE ABLE TO STOP IF YOU SAY THINGS LIKE THAT.
YOU'RE SO WARM.
I WAS JUST IN THE HOT SPRINGS.
You're warm too.
YEAH...
YOU'RE MINE.
WHY?

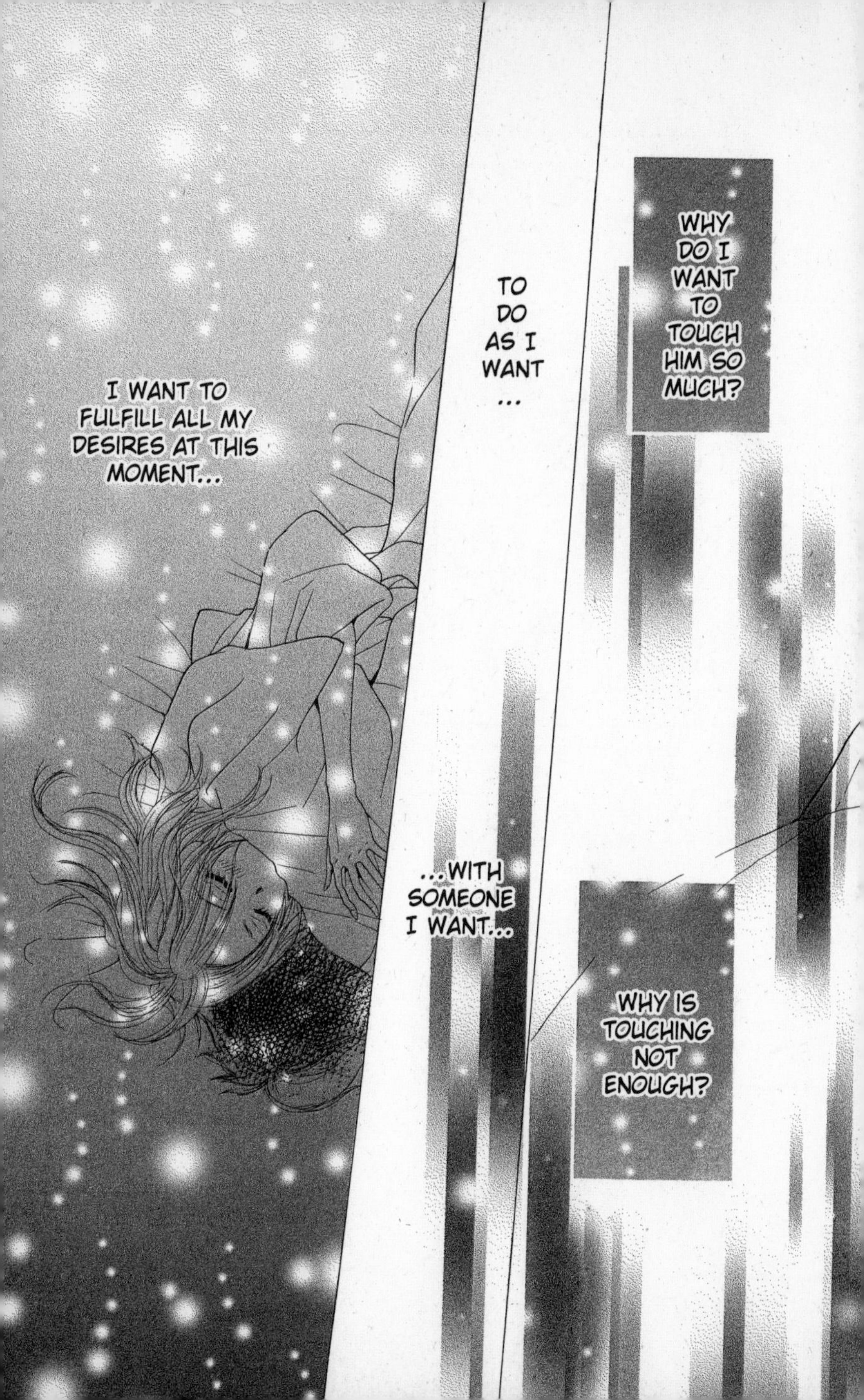
WHY DO I WANT TO TOUCH HIM SO MUCH?
WHY IS TOUCHING NOT ENOUGH?
TO DO AS I WANT...
...WITH SOMEONE I WANT...
I WANT TO FULFILL ALL MY DESIRES AT THIS MOMENT...

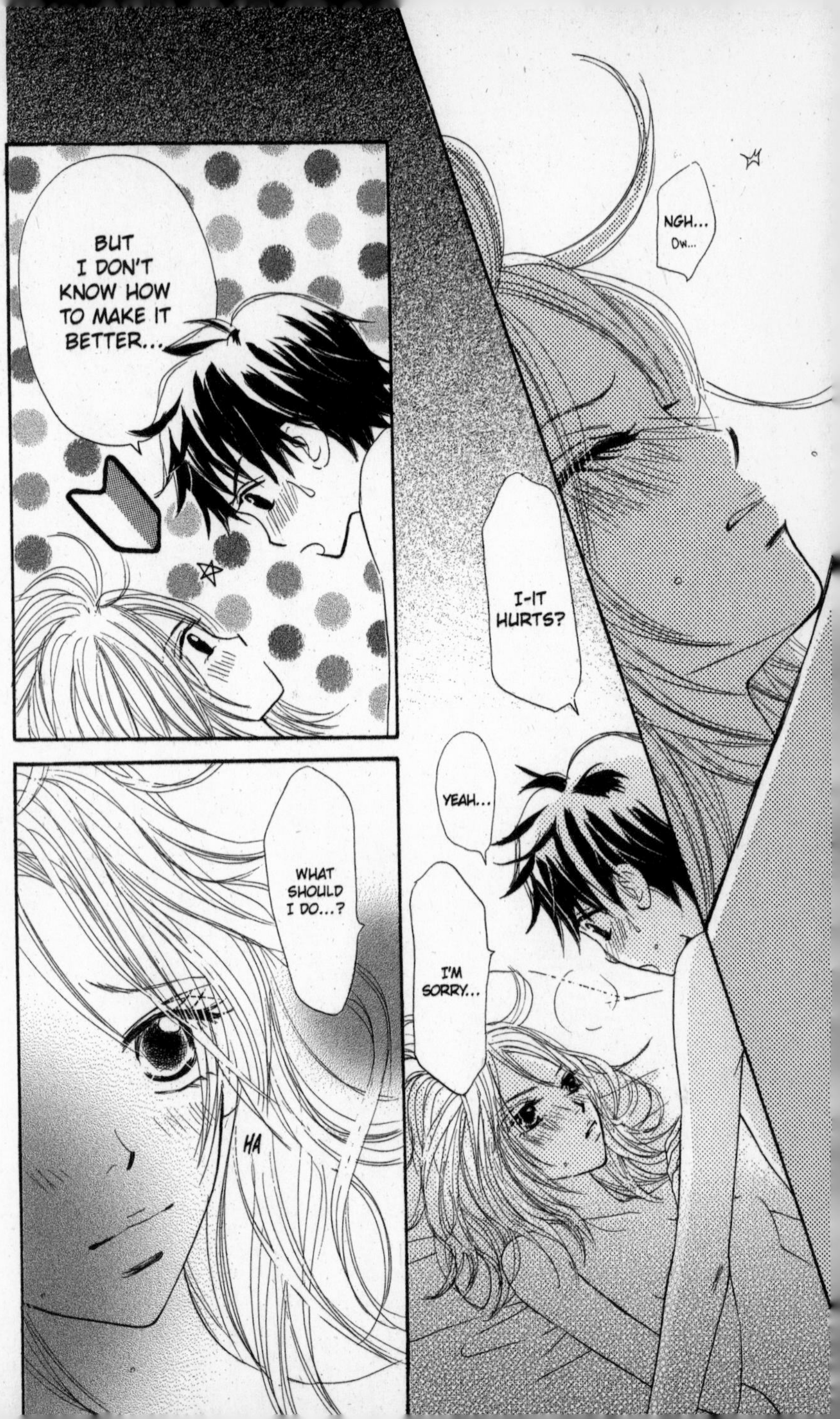
NGH... OW...
I-IT HURTS?
YEAH...
I'M SORRY...
BUT I DON'T KNOW HOW TO MAKE IT BETTER...
WHAT SHOULD I DO...?
HA

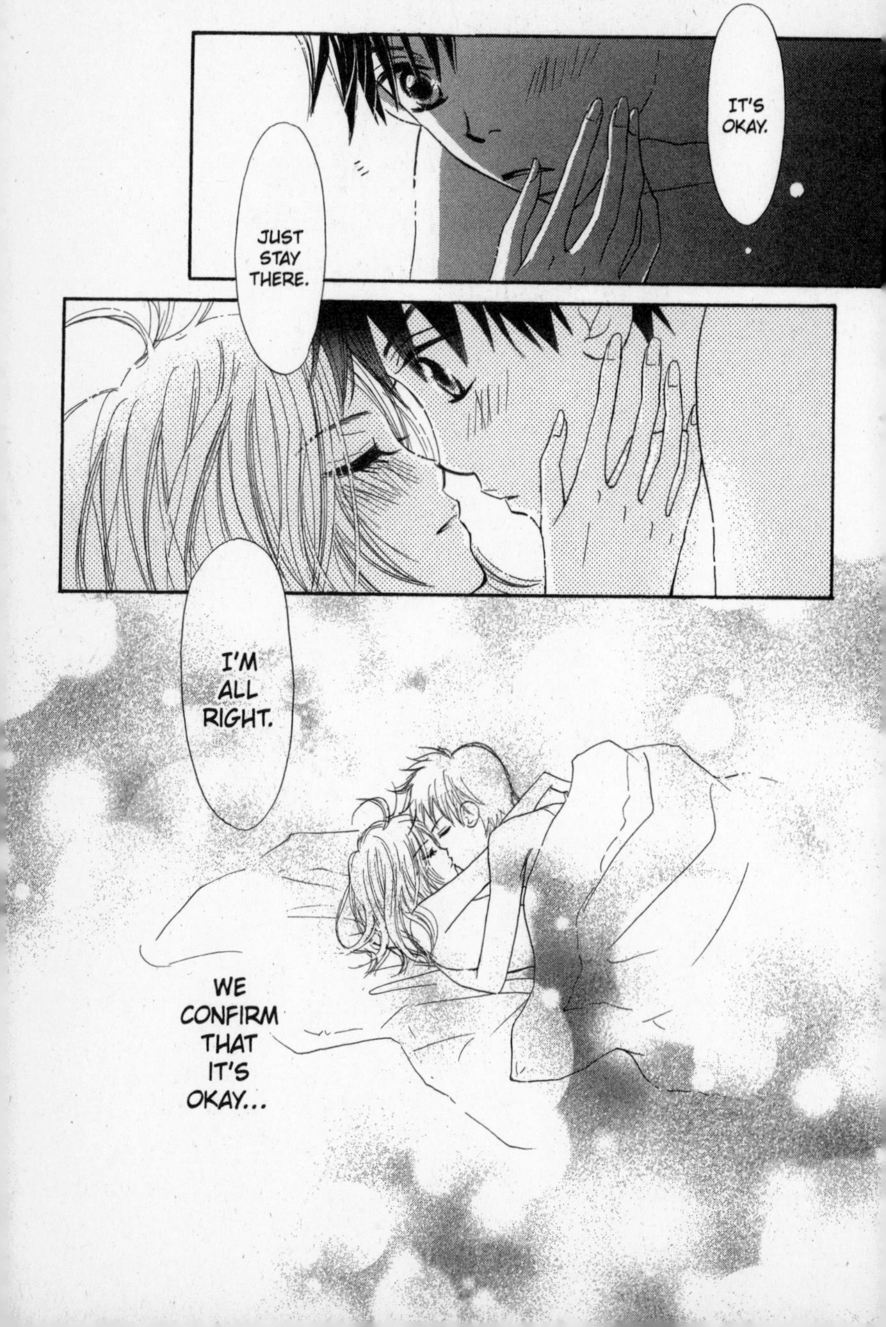

IT'S OKAY.
JUST STAY THERE.
I'M ALL RIGHT.
WE CONFIRM THAT IT'S OKAY...

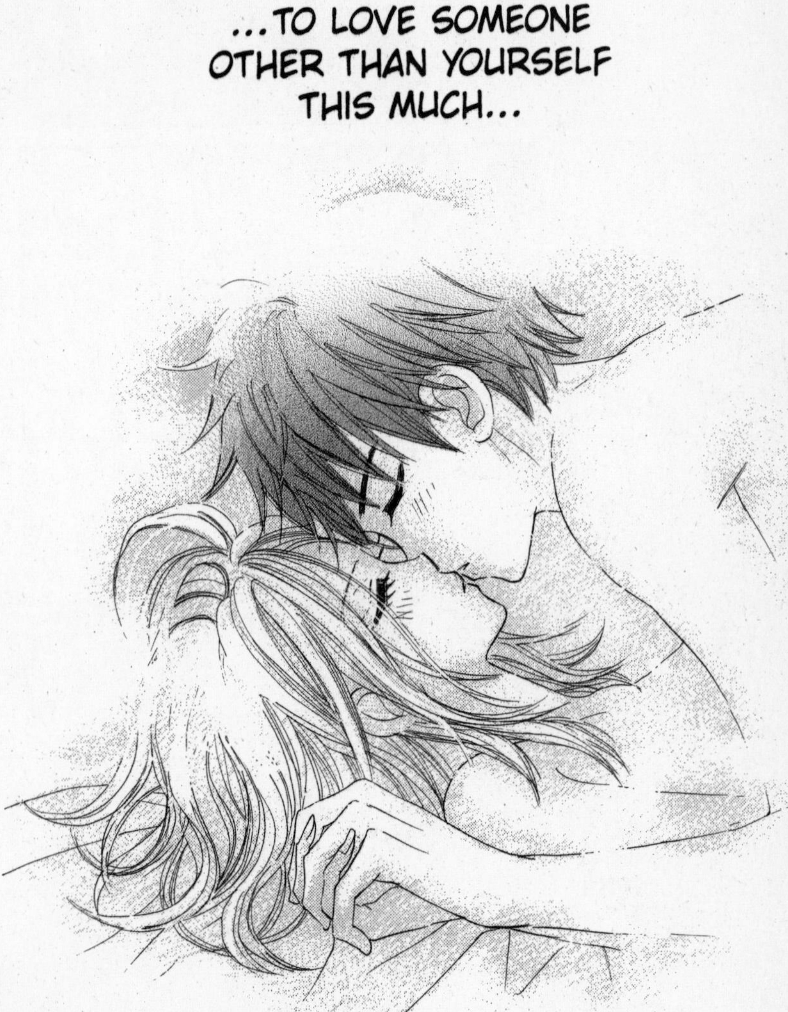
...TO LOVE SOMEONE OTHER THAN YOURSELF THIS MUCH...

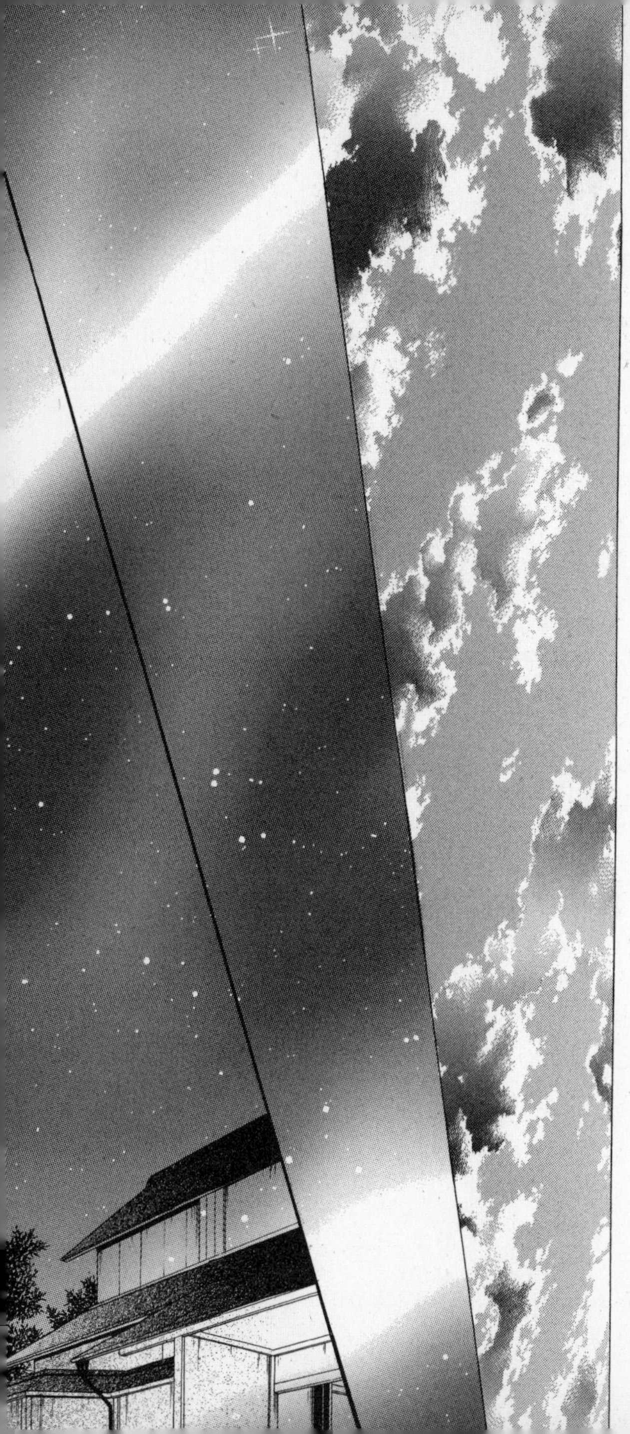

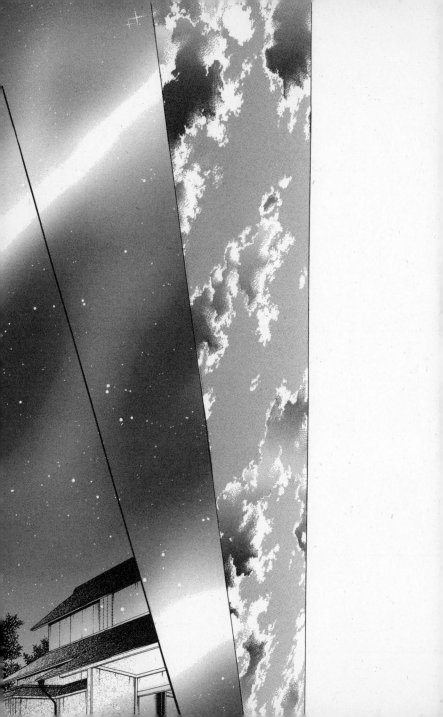

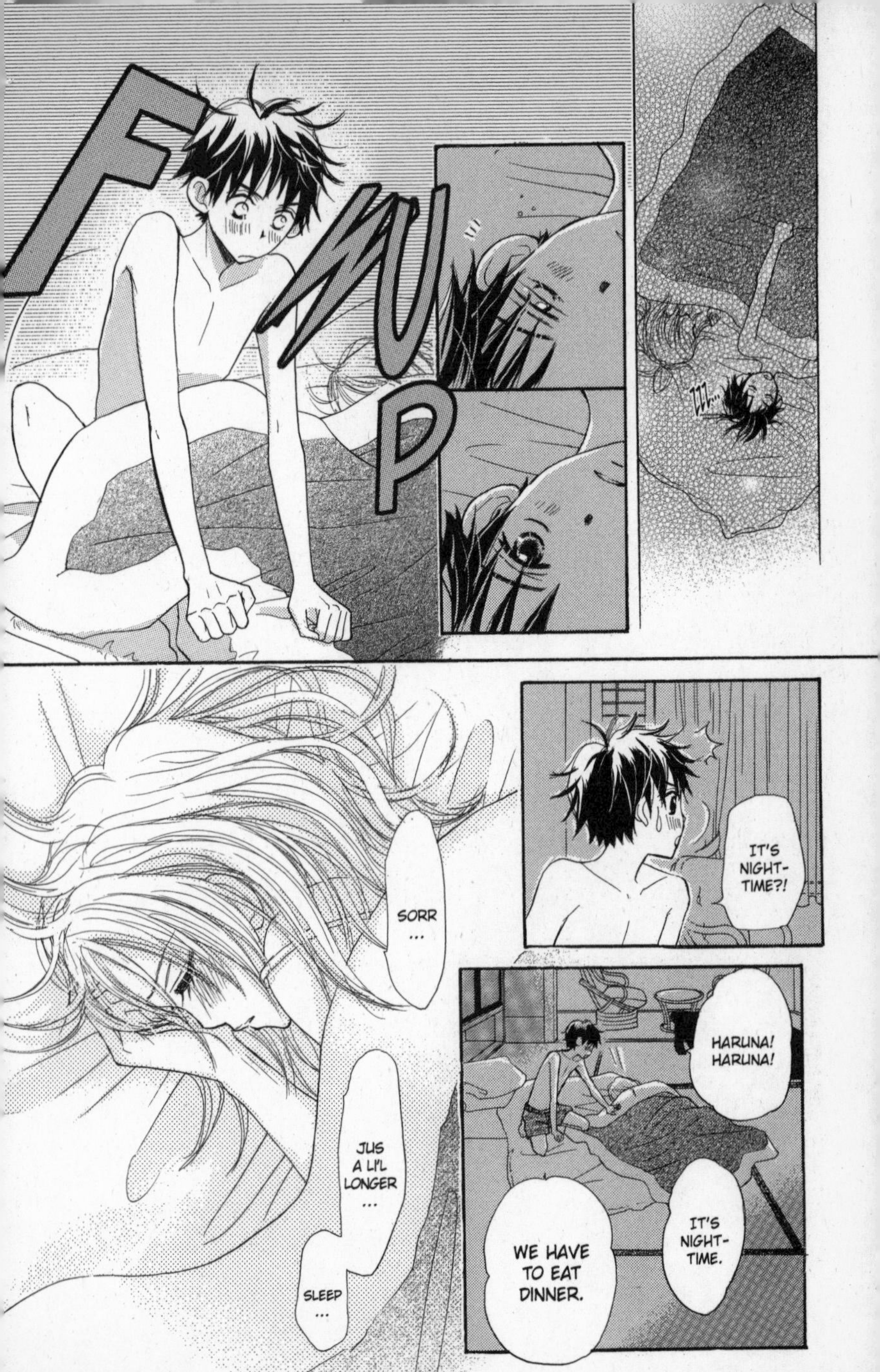
ZZZ...
FWUMP
IT'S NIGHT-TIME?!
HARUNA! HARUNA!
IT'S NIGHT-TIME.
WE HAVE TO EAT DINNER.
SORR ...
JUS A LI'L LONGER ...
SLEEP ...

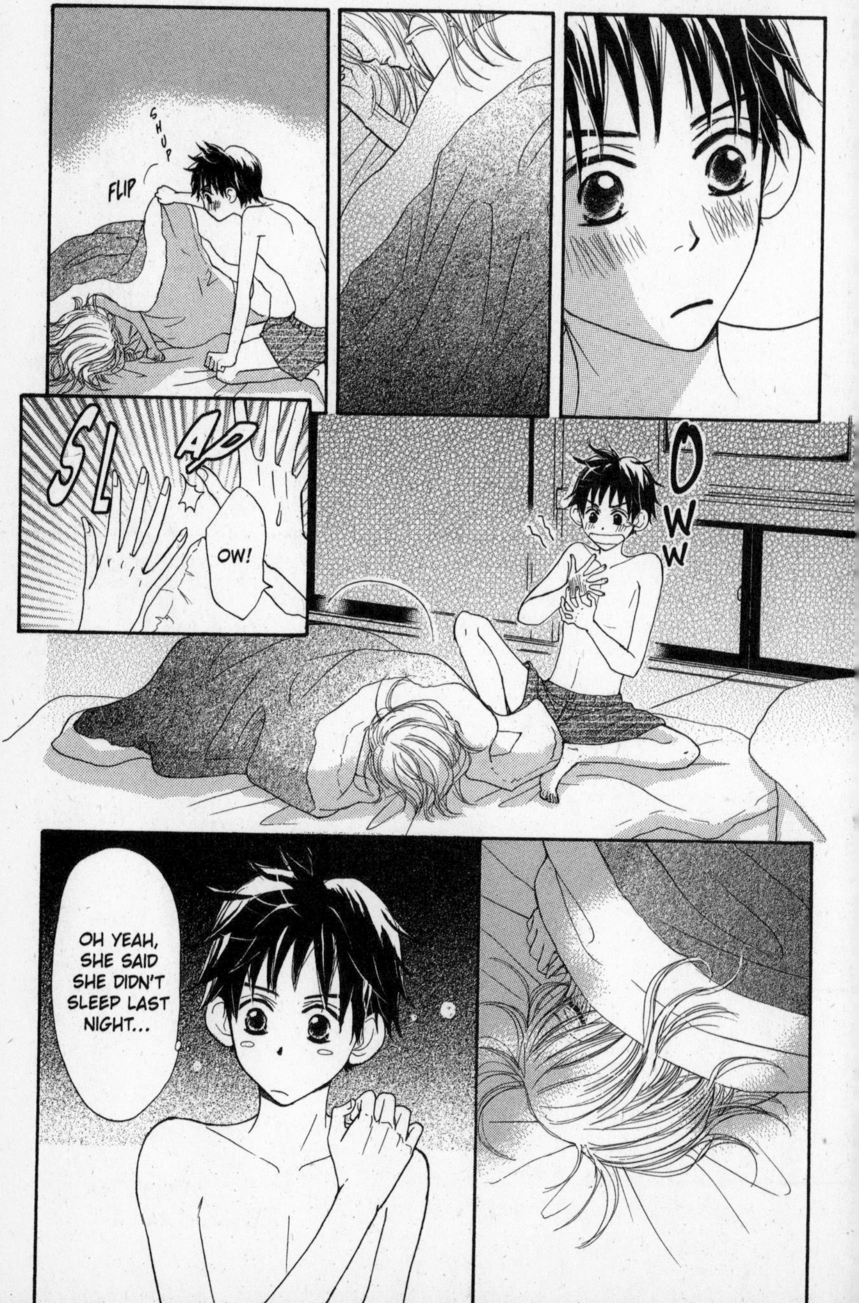
SHUP
FLIP
OWWW
SLAP
OW!
OH YEAH, SHE SAID SHE DIDN'T SLEEP LAST NIGHT...

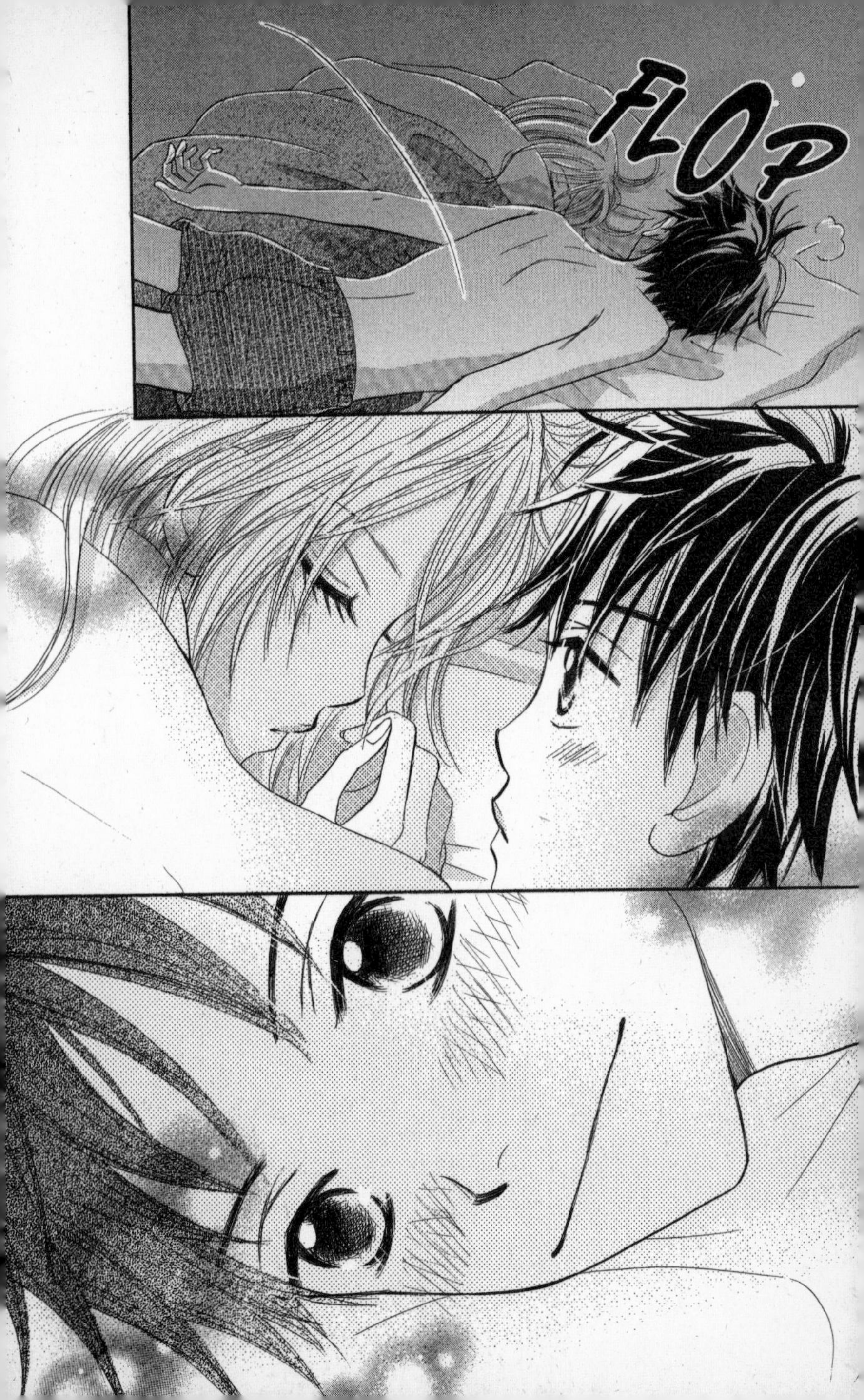
FLOP

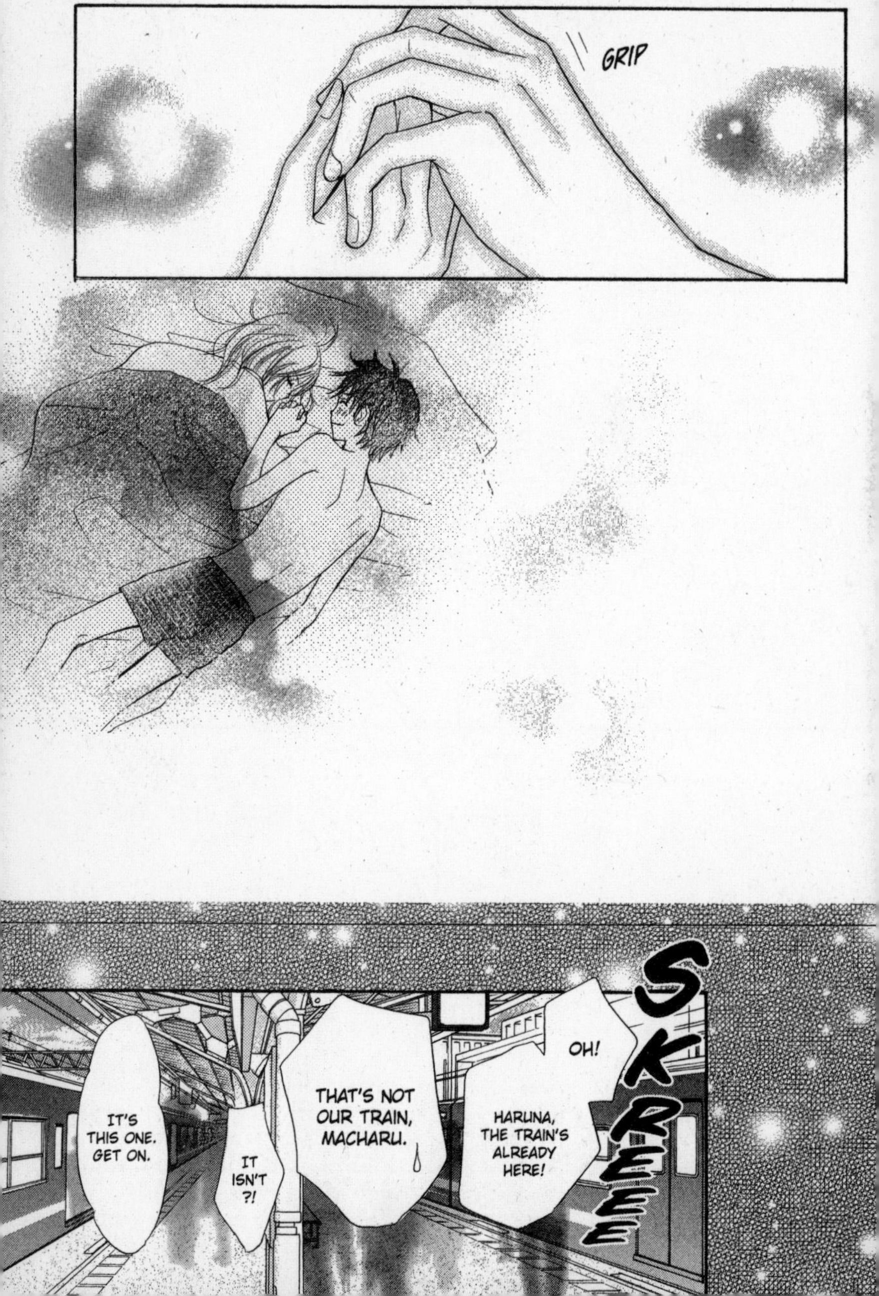
GRIP
SKREEE
OH!
HARUNA, THE TRAIN'S ALREADY HERE!
THAT'S NOT OUR TRAIN, MACHARU.
IT ISN'T ?!
IT'S THIS ONE. GET ON.

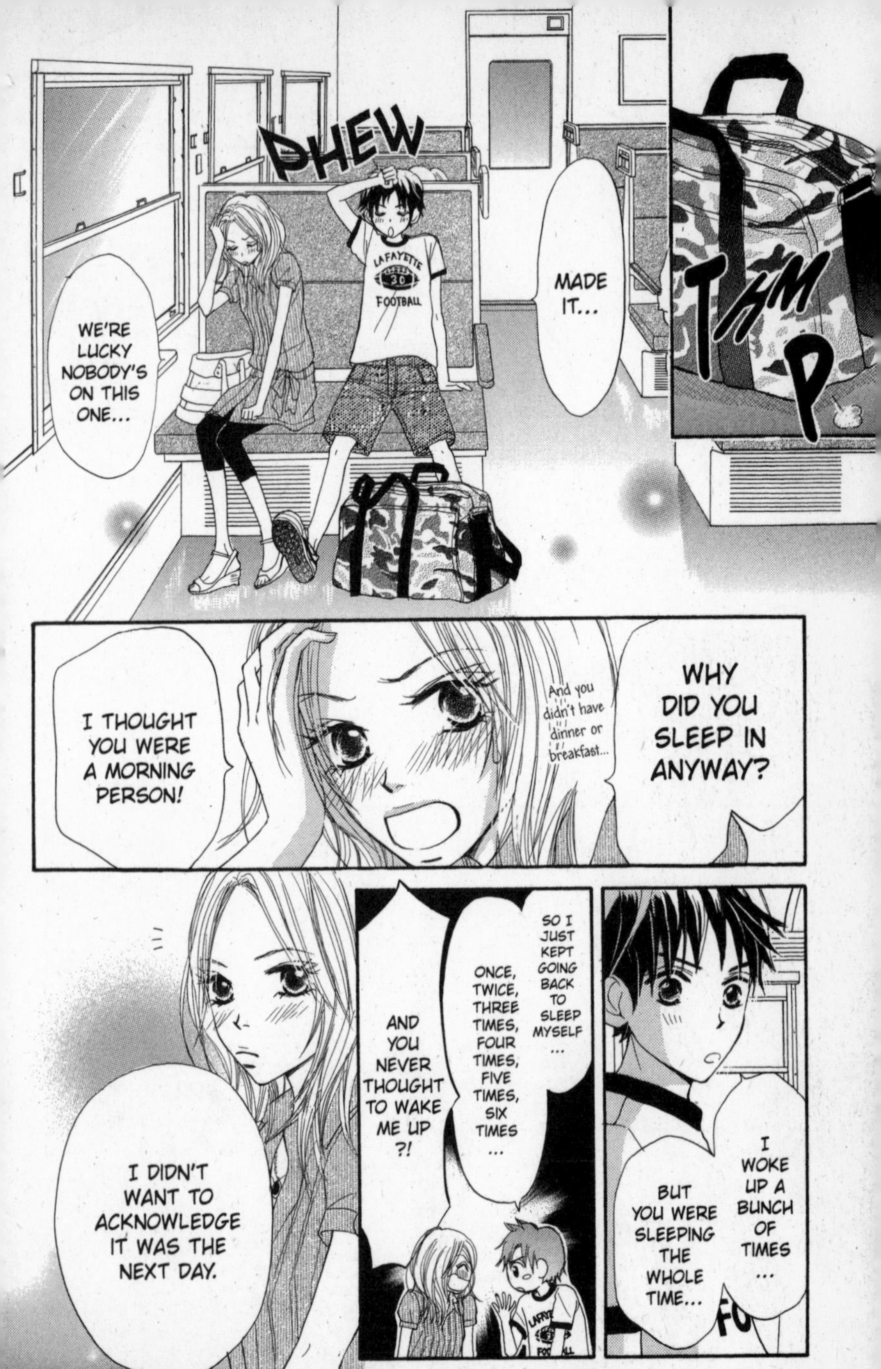

TMP
PHEW
MADE IT...
LAFAYETTE 30 FOOTBALL
WE'RE LUCKY NOBODY'S ON THIS ONE...
WHY DID YOU SLEEP IN ANYWAY?
And you didn't have dinner or breakfast...
I THOUGHT YOU WERE A MORNING PERSON!
I WOKE UP A BUNCH OF TIMES...
BUT YOU WERE SLEEPING THE WHOLE TIME...
SO I JUST KEPT GOING BACK TO SLEEP MYSELF...
ONCE, TWICE, THREE TIMES, FOUR TIMES, FIVE TIMES, SIX TIMES...
AND YOU NEVER THOUGHT TO WAKE ME UP?!
I DIDN'T WANT TO ACKNOWLEDGE IT WAS THE NEXT DAY.

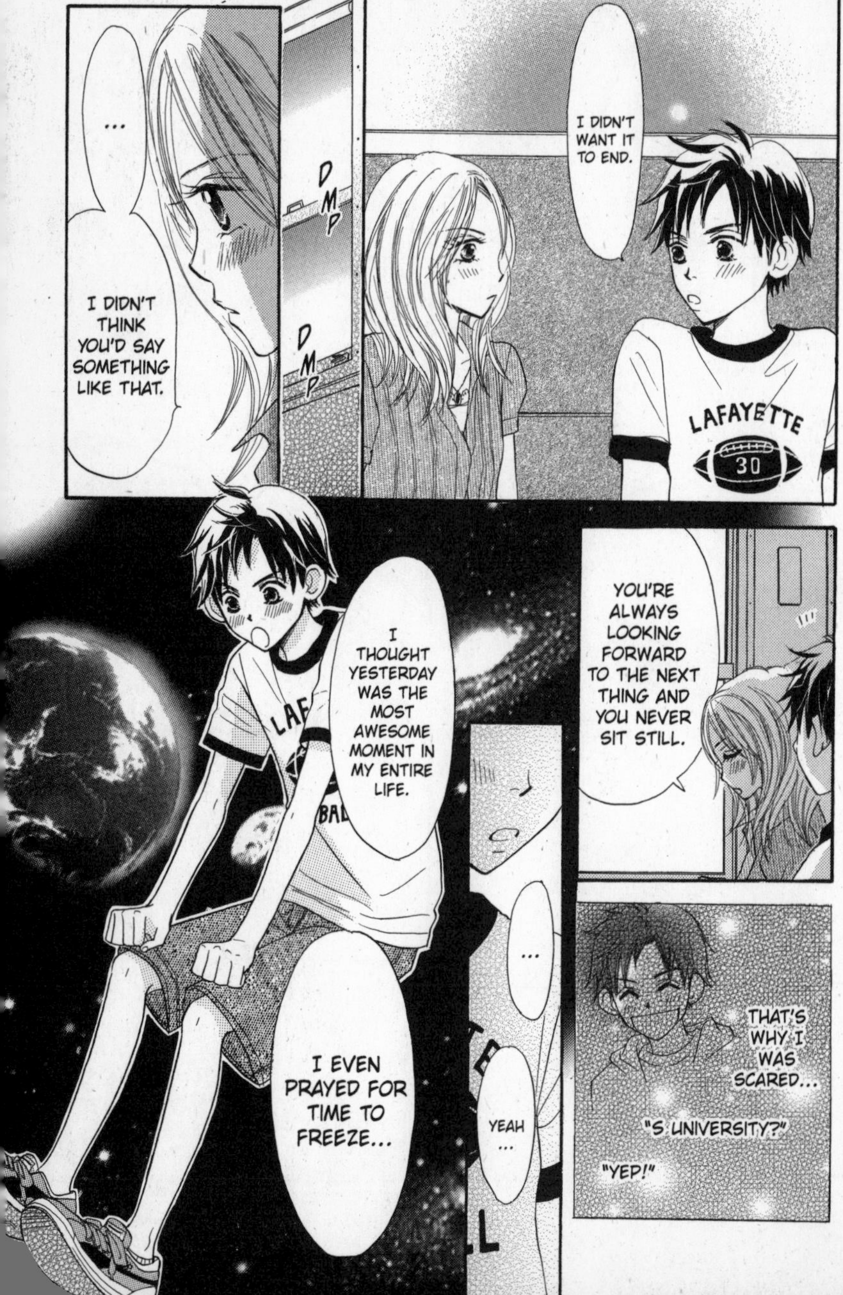
I DIDN'T WANT IT TO END.
...
I DIDN'T THINK YOU'D SAY SOMETHING LIKE THAT.
DMP
DMP
YOU'RE ALWAYS LOOKING FORWARD TO THE NEXT THING AND YOU NEVER SIT STILL.
THAT'S WHY I WAS SCARED...
"S UNIVERSITY?"
"YEP!"
...
YEAH...
I THOUGHT YESTERDAY WAS THE MOST AWESOME MOMENT IN MY ENTIRE LIFE.
I EVEN PRAYED FOR TIME TO FREEZE...

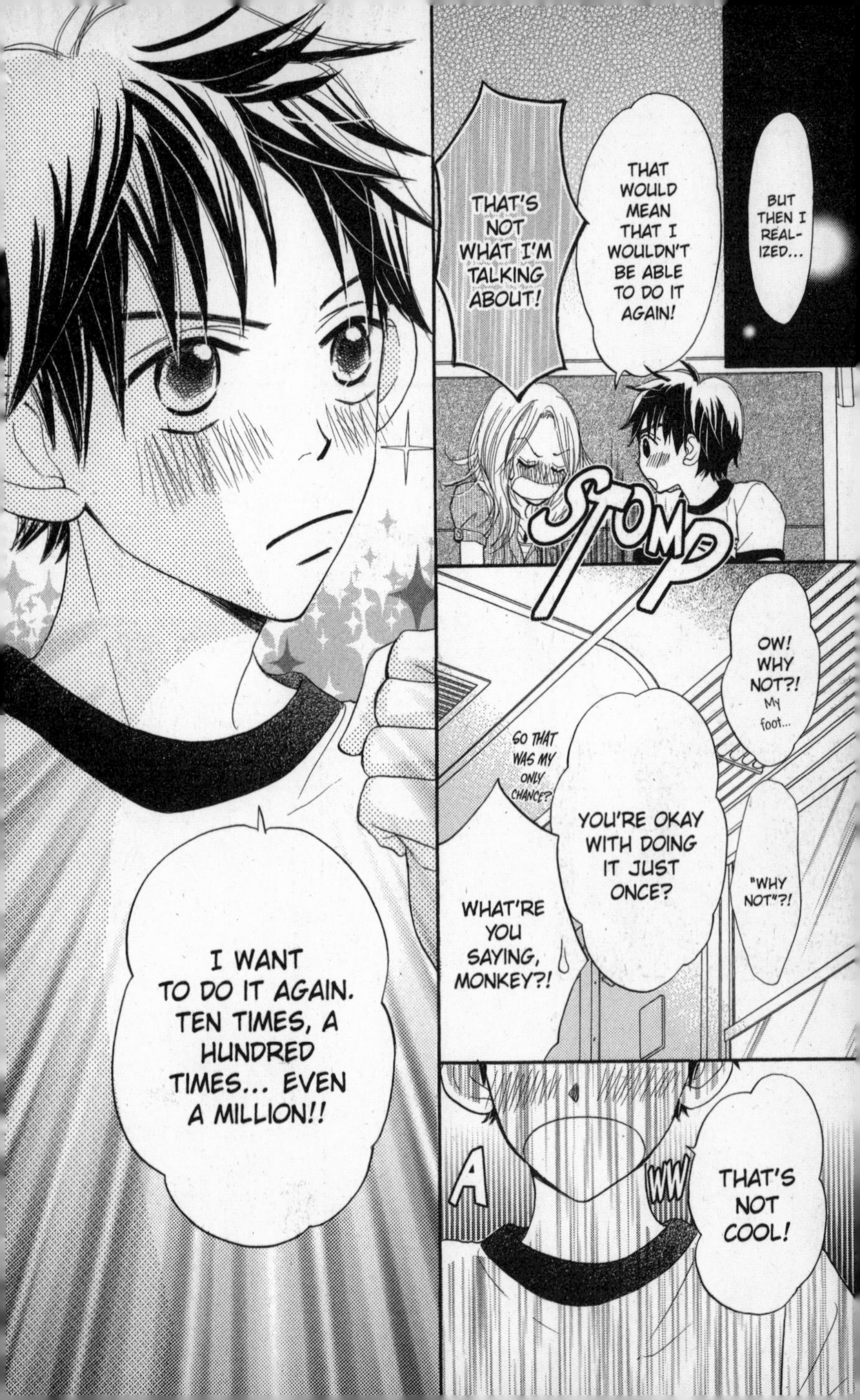
BUT THEN I REALIZED...
THAT WOULD MEAN THAT I WOULDN'T BE ABLE TO DO IT AGAIN!
THAT'S NOT WHAT I'M TALKING ABOUT!
STOMP
OW! WHY NOT?! My foot...
"WHY NOT"?!
YOU'RE OKAY WITH DOING IT JUST ONCE?
SO THAT WAS MY ONLY CHANCE?
WHAT'RE YOU SAYING, MONKEY?!
THAT'S NOT COOL!
AWW
I WANT TO DO IT AGAIN. TEN TIMES, A HUNDRED TIMES... EVEN A MILLION!!

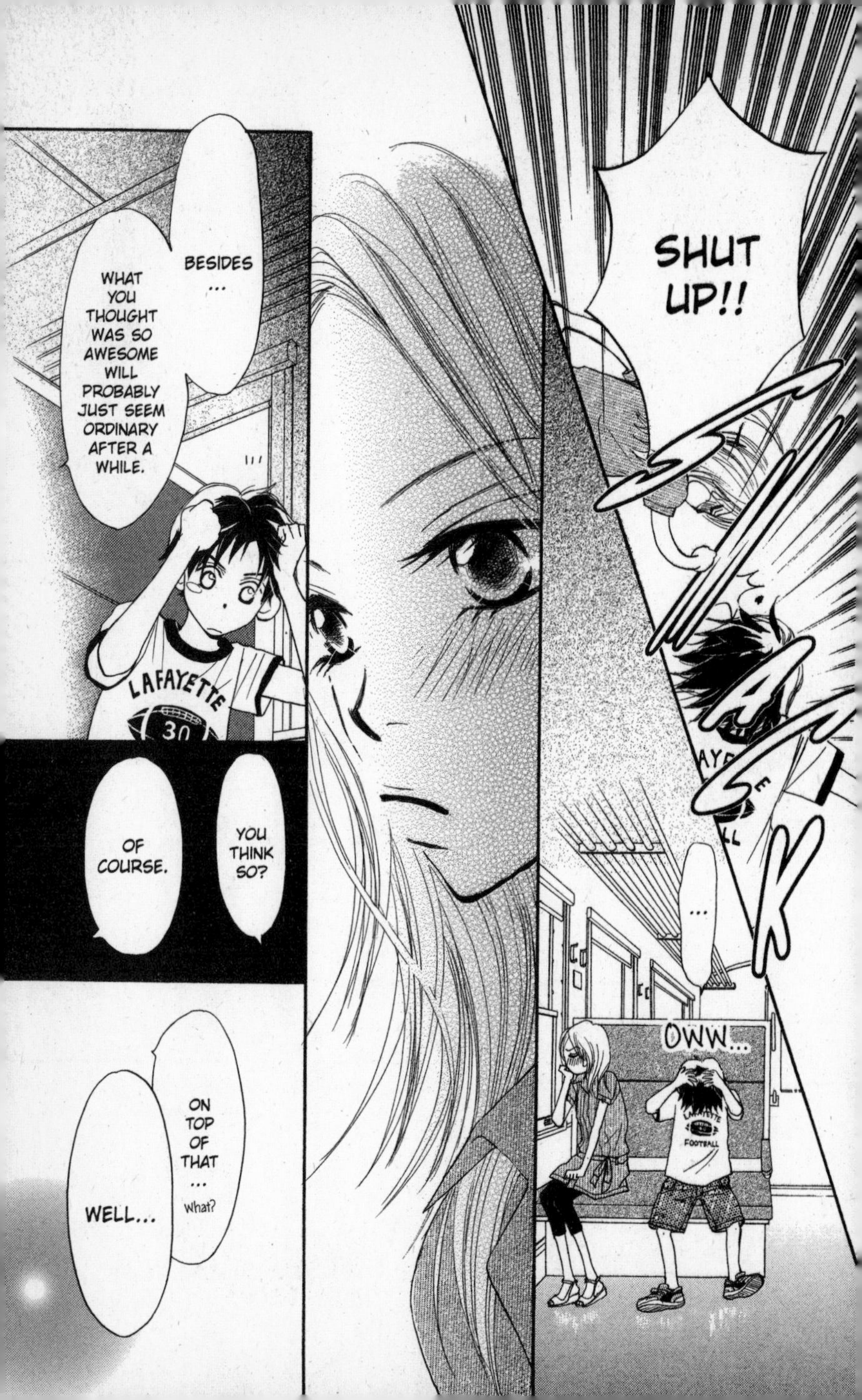
SHUT UP!!
...
OWW...
BESIDES ...
WHAT YOU THOUGHT WAS SO AWESOME WILL PROBABLY JUST SEEM ORDINARY AFTER A WHILE.
YOU THINK SO?
OF COURSE.
ON TOP OF THAT ...
What?
WELL...

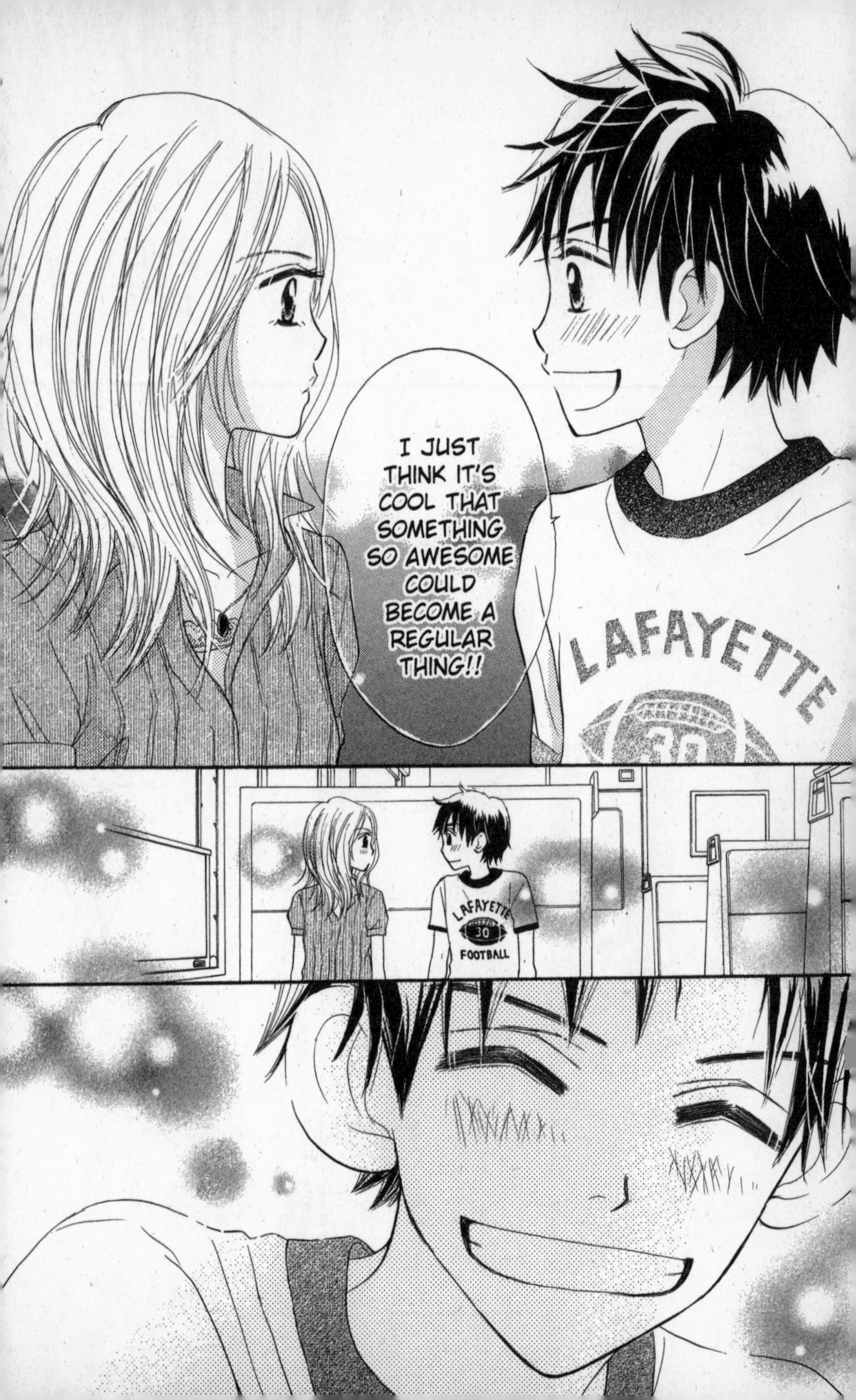
I JUST THINK IT'S COOL THAT SOMETHING SO AWESOME COULD BECOME A REGULAR THING!!
LAFAYETTE
LAFAYETTE
30
FOOTBALL

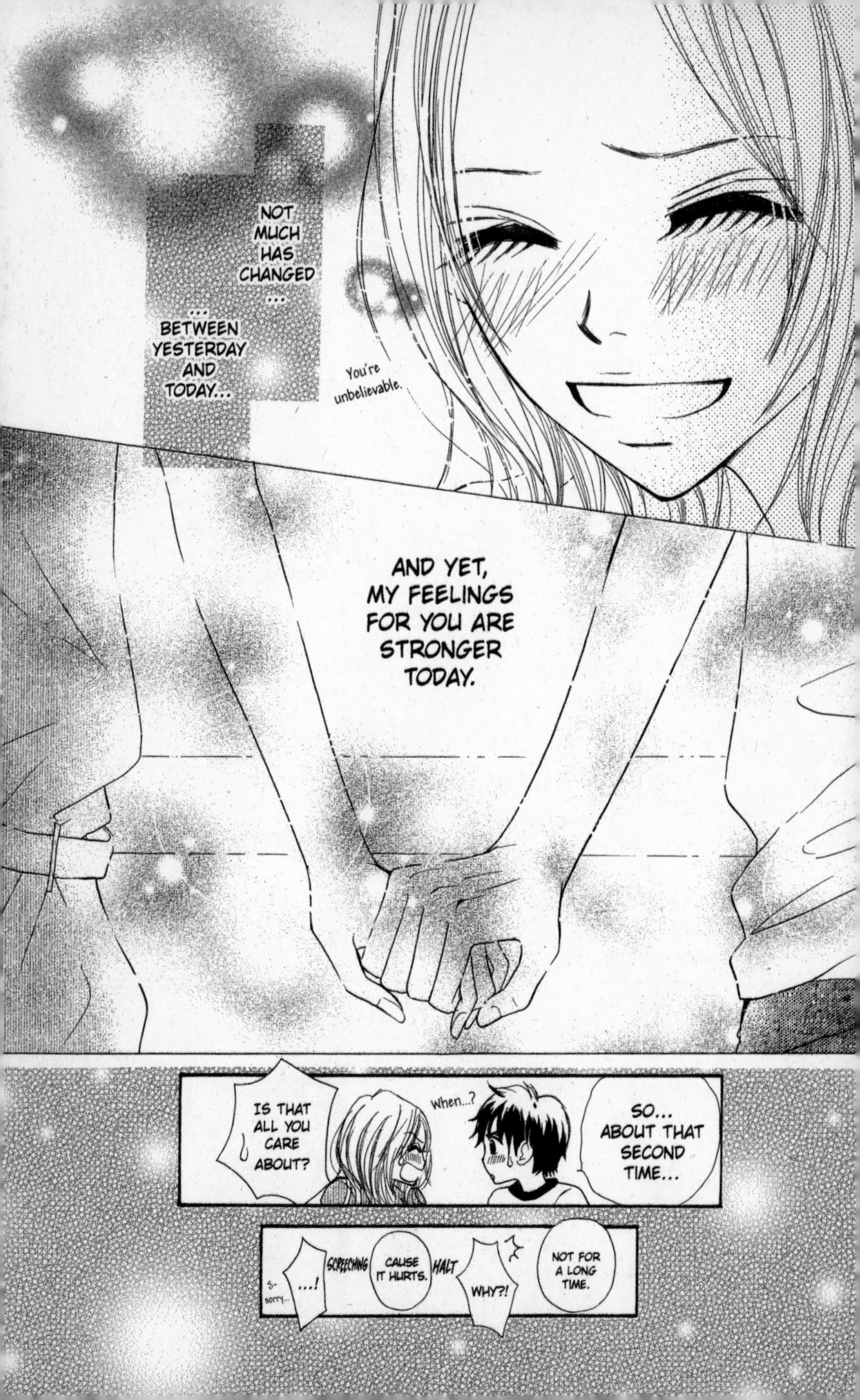
You're unbelievable.
NOT MUCH HAS CHANGED...
...BETWEEN YESTERDAY AND TODAY...
AND YET, MY FEELINGS FOR YOU ARE STRONGER TODAY.
SO... ABOUT THAT SECOND TIME...
When...?
IS THAT ALL YOU CARE ABOUT?
NOT FOR A LONG TIME.
WHY?!
HALT
CAUSE IT HURTS.
SCREECHING
...!
S-sorry...

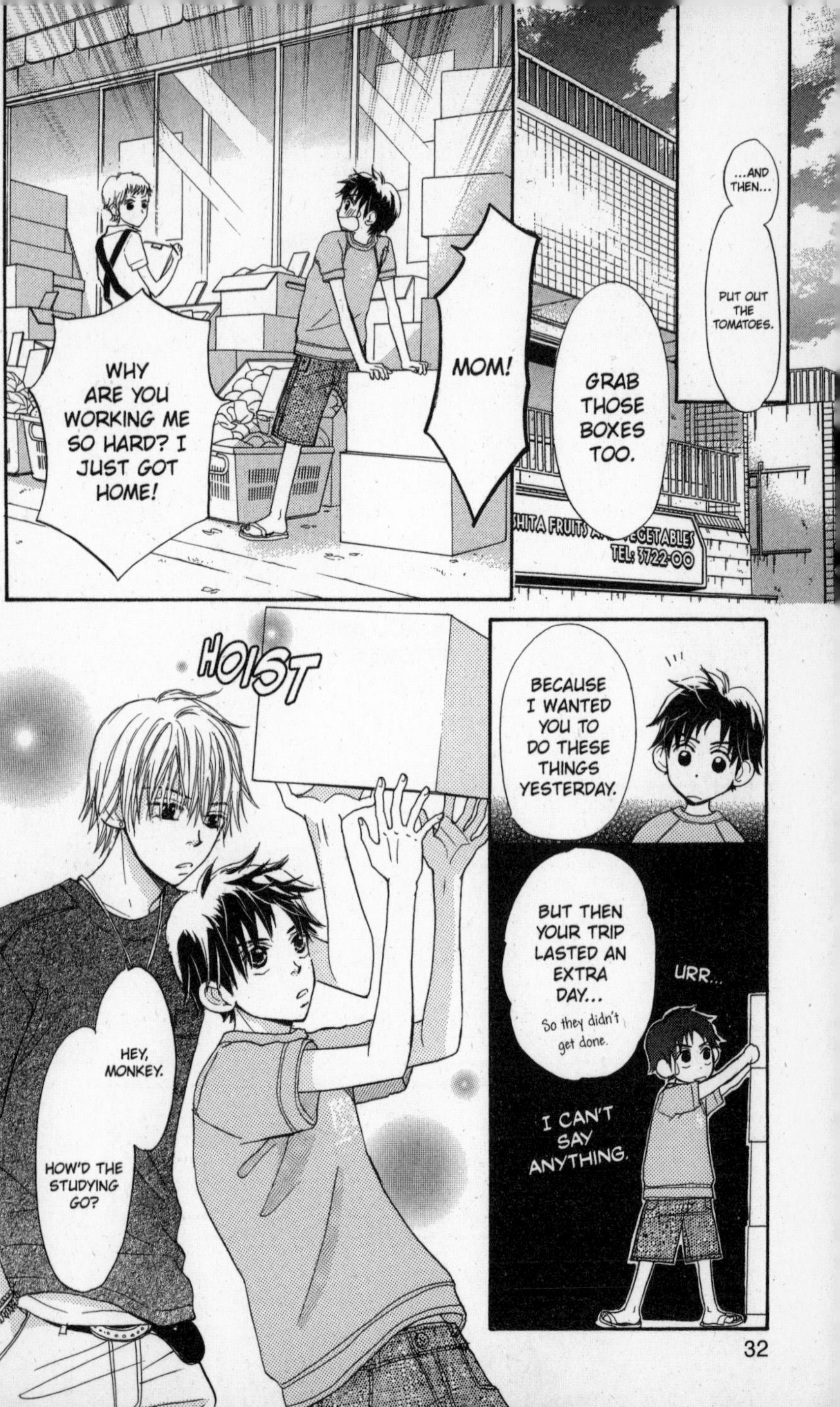
...AND THEN...
PUT OUT THE TOMATOES.
GRAB THOSE BOXES TOO.
MOM!
WHY ARE YOU WORKING ME SO HARD? I JUST GOT HOME!
BECAUSE I WANTED YOU TO DO THESE THINGS YESTERDAY.
BUT THEN YOUR TRIP LASTED AN EXTRA DAY...
So they didn't get done.
URR...
I CAN'T SAY ANYTHING.
HOIST
HEY, MONKEY.
HOW'D THE STUDYING GO?

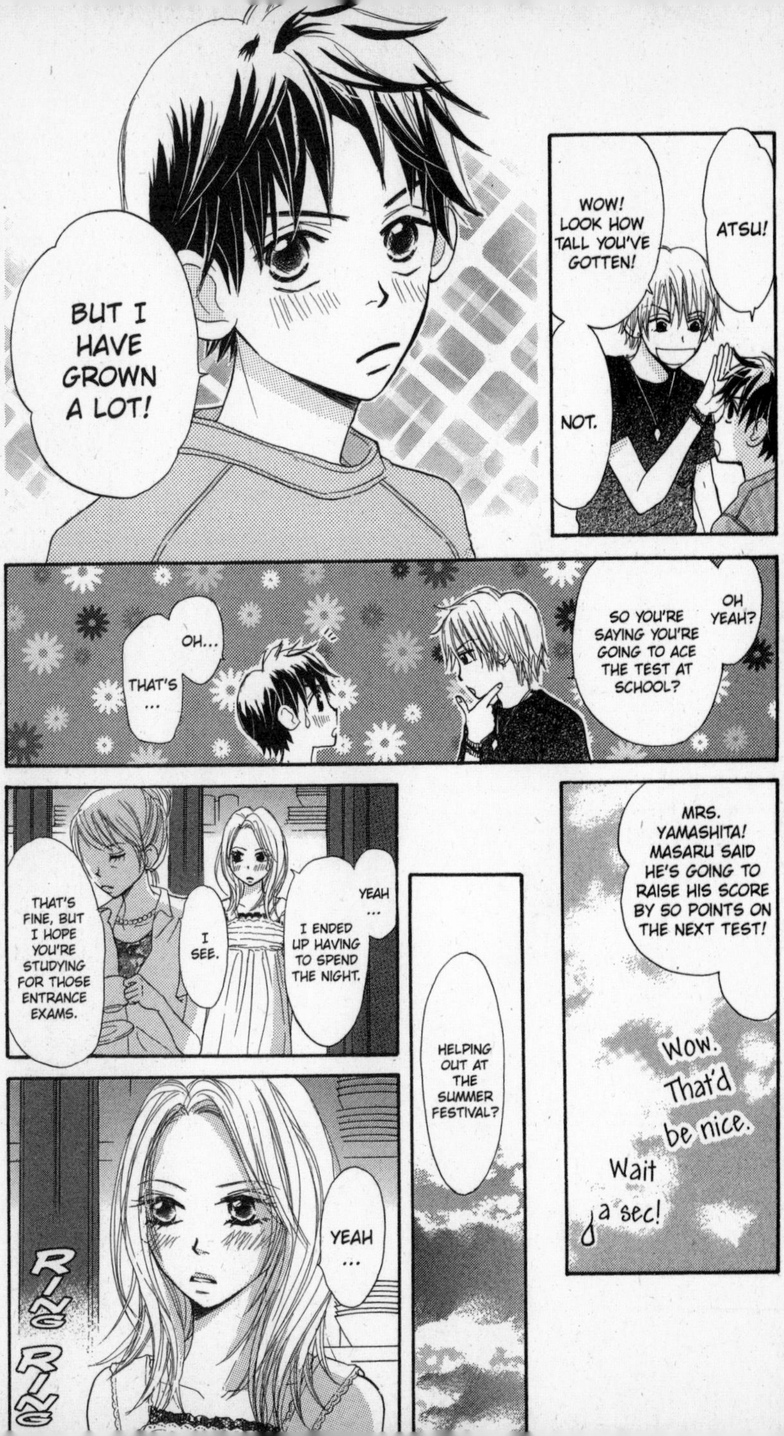
ATSU!
WOW! LOOK HOW TALL YOU'VE GOTTEN!
NOT.
BUT I HAVE GROWN A LOT!
OH YEAH?
SO YOU'RE SAYING YOU'RE GOING TO ACE THE TEST AT SCHOOL?
OH...
THAT'S ...
MRS. YAMASHITA! MASARU SAID HE'S GOING TO RAISE HIS SCORE BY 50 POINTS ON THE NEXT TEST!
Wow. That'd be nice.
Wait a sec!
HELPING OUT AT THE SUMMER FESTIVAL?
YEAH ...
I ENDED UP HAVING TO SPEND THE NIGHT.
I SEE.
THAT'S FINE, BUT I HOPE YOU'RE STUDYING FOR THOSE ENTRANCE EXAMS.
YEAH ...
RING RING

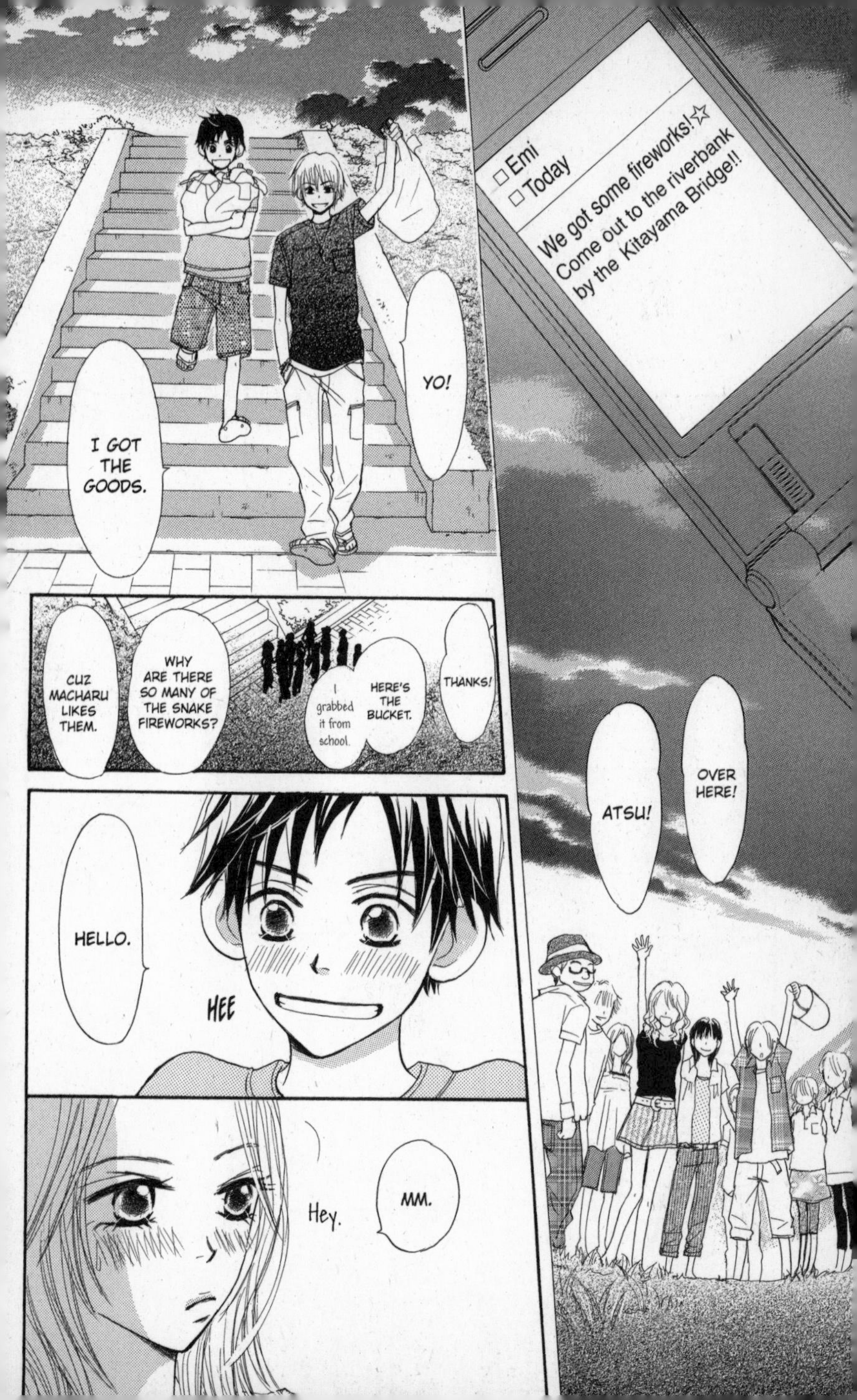
□ Emi
□ Today
We got some fireworks!☆
Come out to the riverbank
by the Kitayama Bridge!!
OVER HERE!
ATSU!
YO!
I GOT THE GOODS.
THANKS!
HERE'S THE BUCKET.
I grabbed it from school.
WHY ARE THERE SO MANY OF THE SNAKE FIREWORKS?
CUZ MACHARU LIKES THEM.
HEE
HELLO.
MM.
Hey.

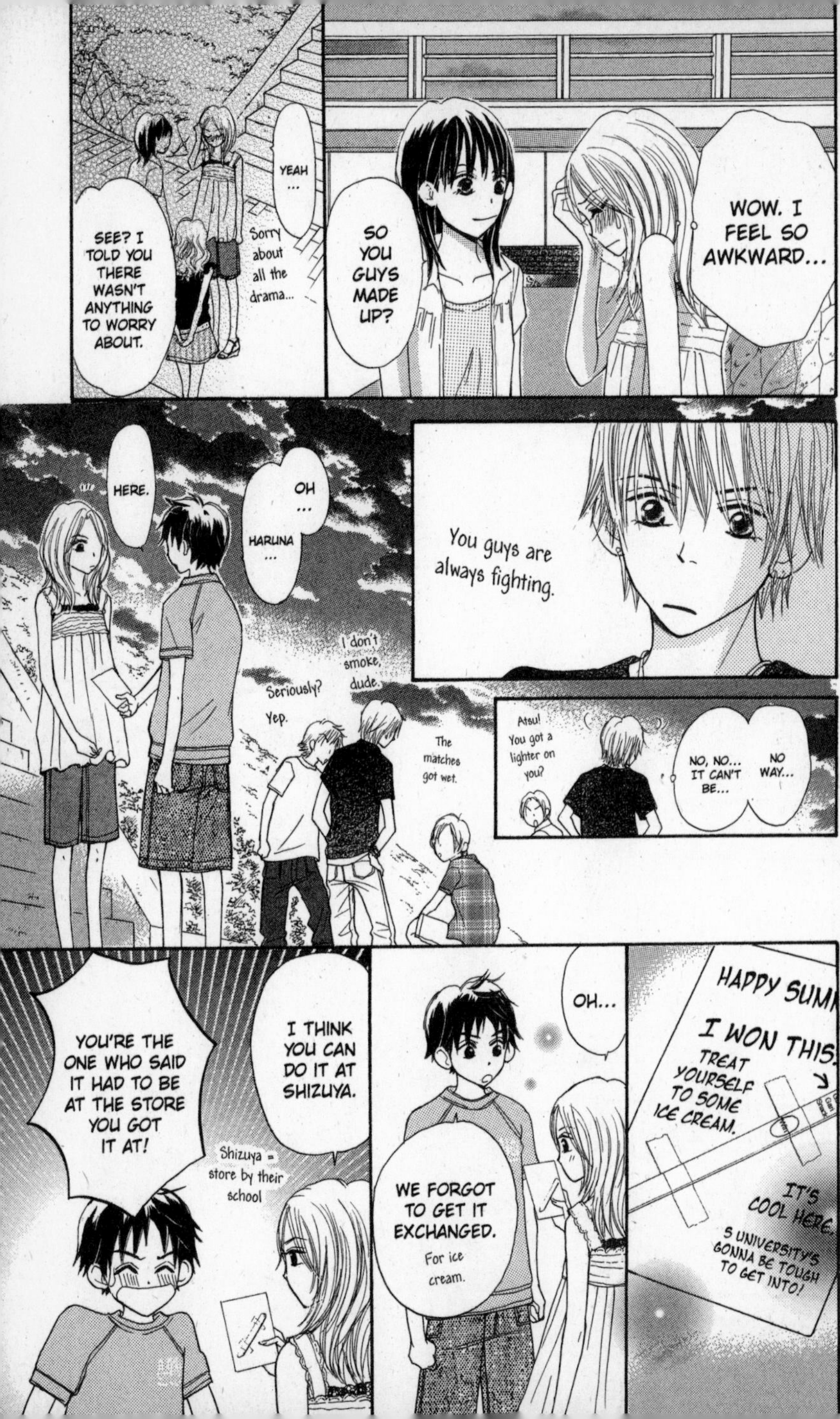
WOW. I FEEL SO AWKWARD...
SO YOU GUYS MADE UP?
YEAH ...
Sorry about all the drama...
SEE? I TOLD YOU THERE WASN'T ANYTHING TO WORRY ABOUT.
You guys are always fighting.
NO WAY...
NO, NO... IT CAN'T BE...
Atsu! You got a lighter on you?
OH ... HARUNA ...
HERE.
I don't smoke, dude.
The matches got wet.
Seriously?
Yep.
HAPPY SUM
I WON THIS.
TREAT YOURSELF TO SOME ICE CREAM.
IT'S COOL HERE.
S UNIVERSITY'S GONNA BE TOUGH TO GET INTO!
OH...
WE FORGOT TO GET IT EXCHANGED.
For ice cream.
I THINK YOU CAN DO IT AT SHIZUYA.
Shizuya = store by their school
YOU'RE THE ONE WHO SAID IT HAD TO BE AT THE STORE YOU GOT IT AT!

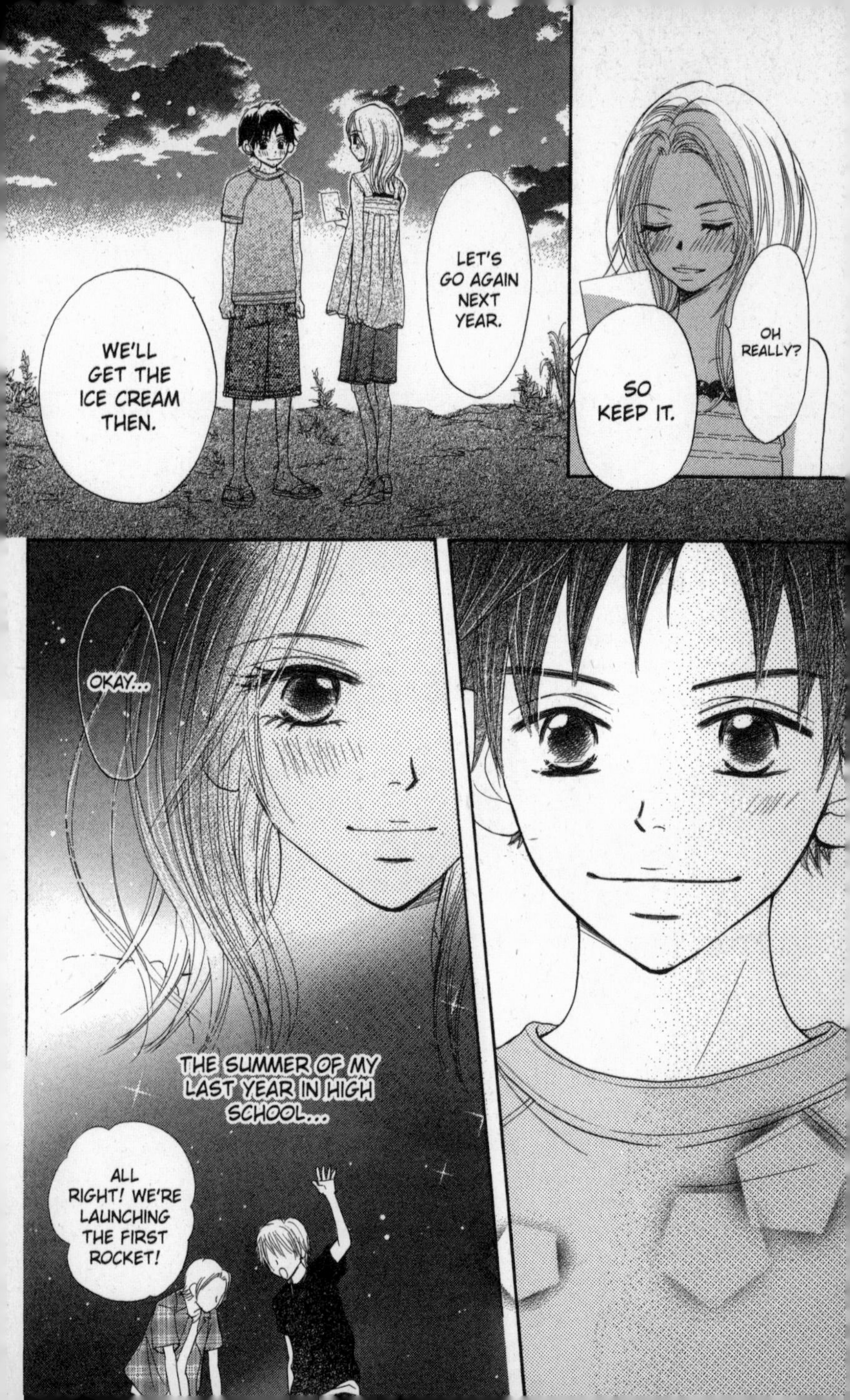
OH REALLY?
SO KEEP IT.
LET'S GO AGAIN NEXT YEAR.
WE'LL GET THE ICE CREAM THEN.
OKAY...
THE SUMMER OF MY LAST YEAR IN HIGH SCHOOL...
ALL RIGHT! WE'RE LAUNCHING THE FIRST ROCKET!

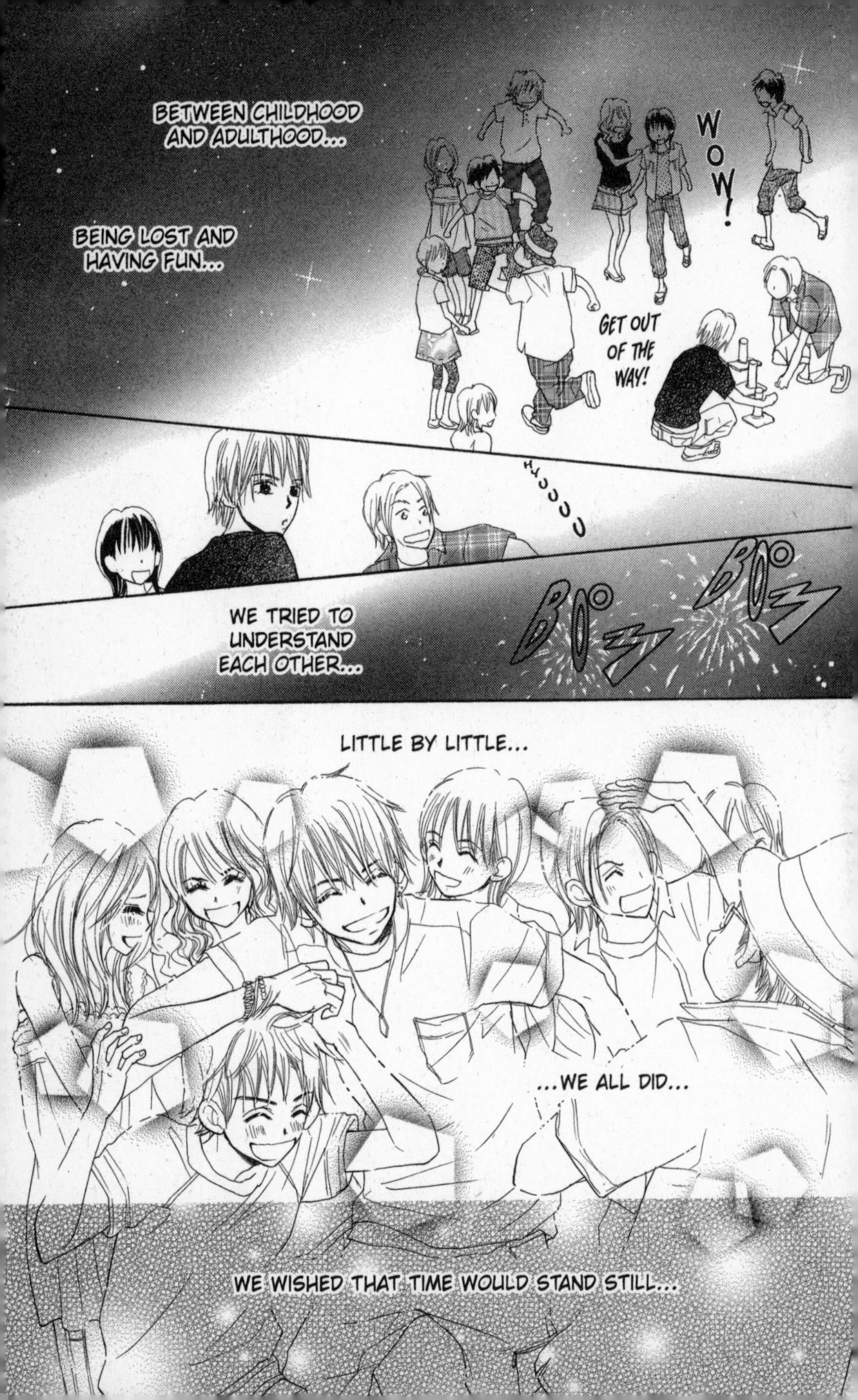
WOW!
BETWEEN CHILDHOOD AND ADULTHOOD...
BEING LOST AND HAVING FUN...
GET OUT OF THE WAY!
HYUUUUU
BOOM
BOOM
WE TRIED TO UNDERSTAND EACH OTHER...
LITTLE BY LITTLE...
...WE ALL DID...
WE WISHED THAT TIME WOULD STAND STILL...

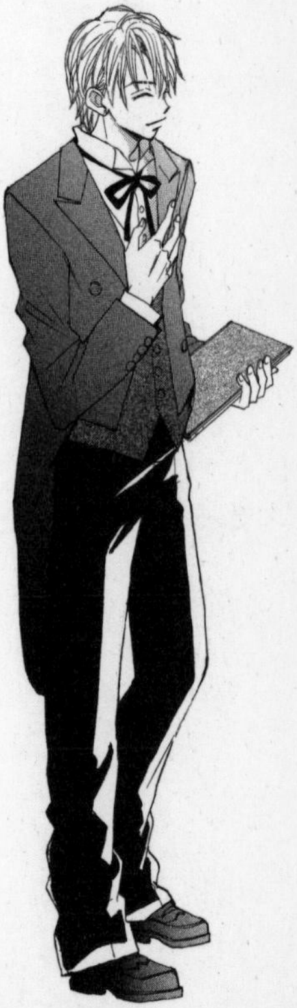

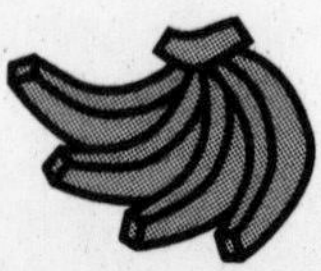

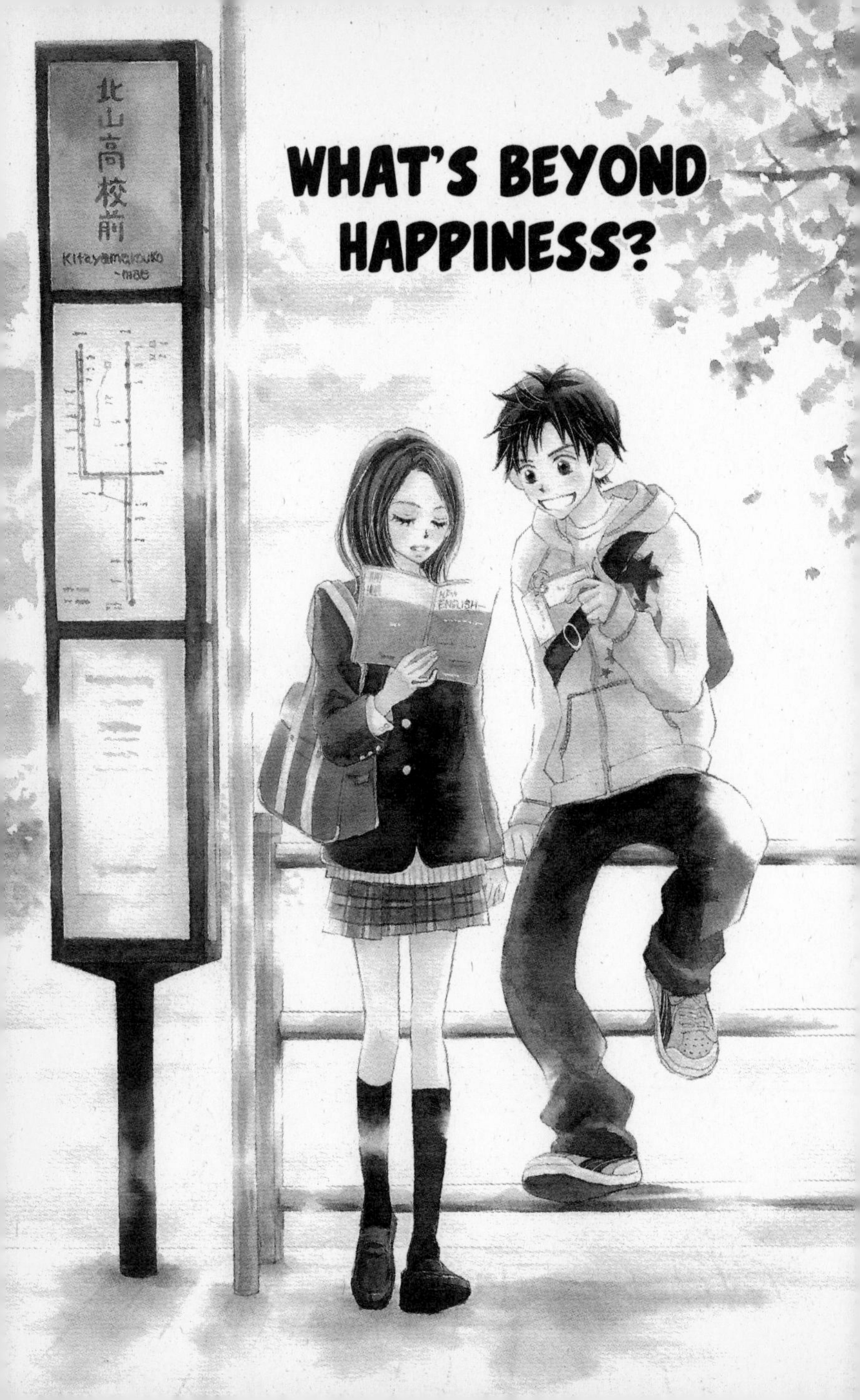
WHAT'S BEYOND HAPPINESS?
北山高校前
Kitayamakouko
-mae
ENGLISH

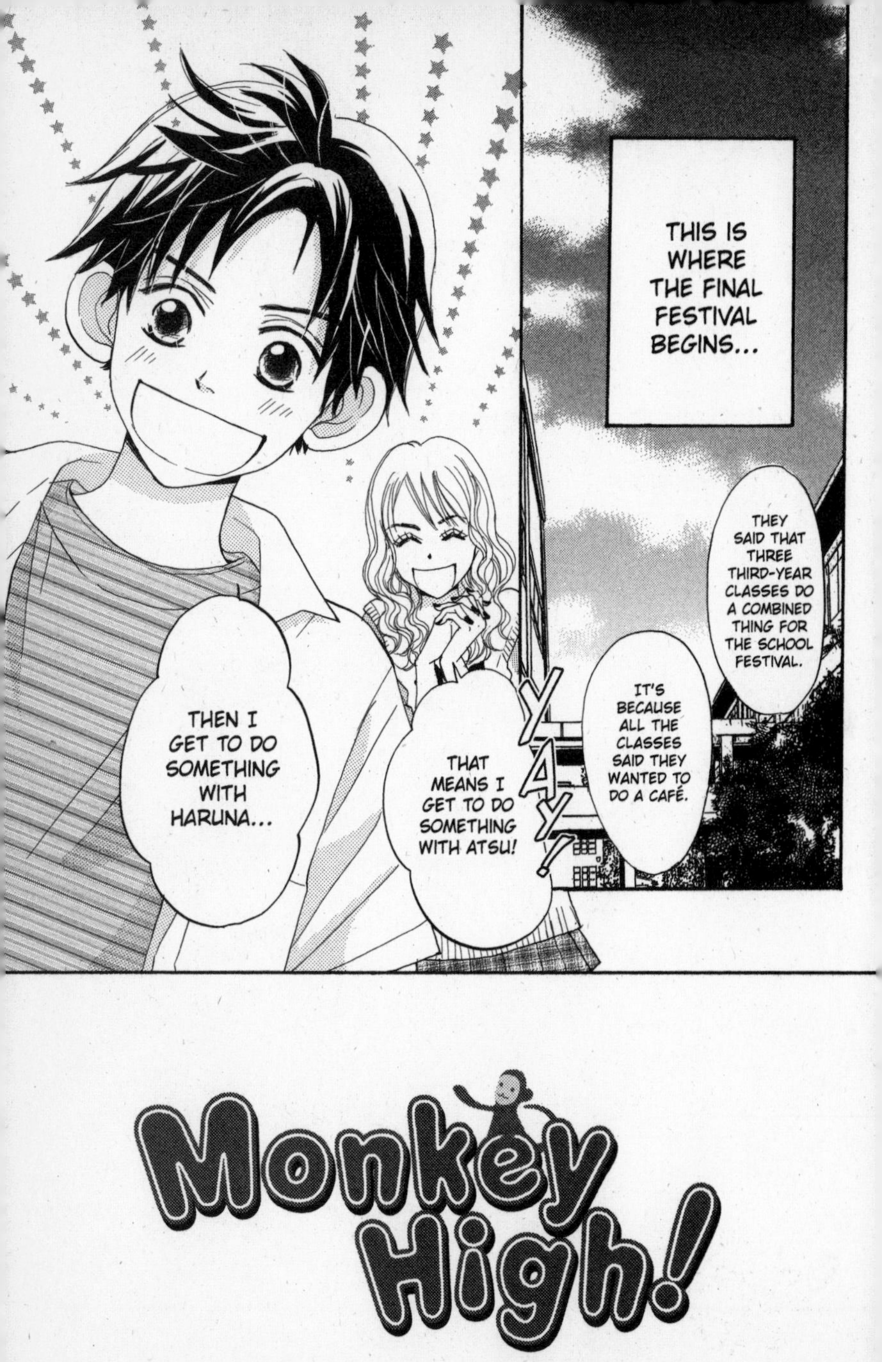
THIS IS WHERE THE FINAL FESTIVAL BEGINS...
THEY SAID THAT THREE THIRD-YEAR CLASSES DO A COMBINED THING FOR THE SCHOOL FESTIVAL.
IT'S BECAUSE ALL THE CLASSES SAID THEY WANTED TO DO A CAFÉ.
YAY!
THAT MEANS I GET TO DO SOMETHING WITH ATSU!
THEN I GET TO DO SOMETHING WITH HARUNA...

Monkey High!

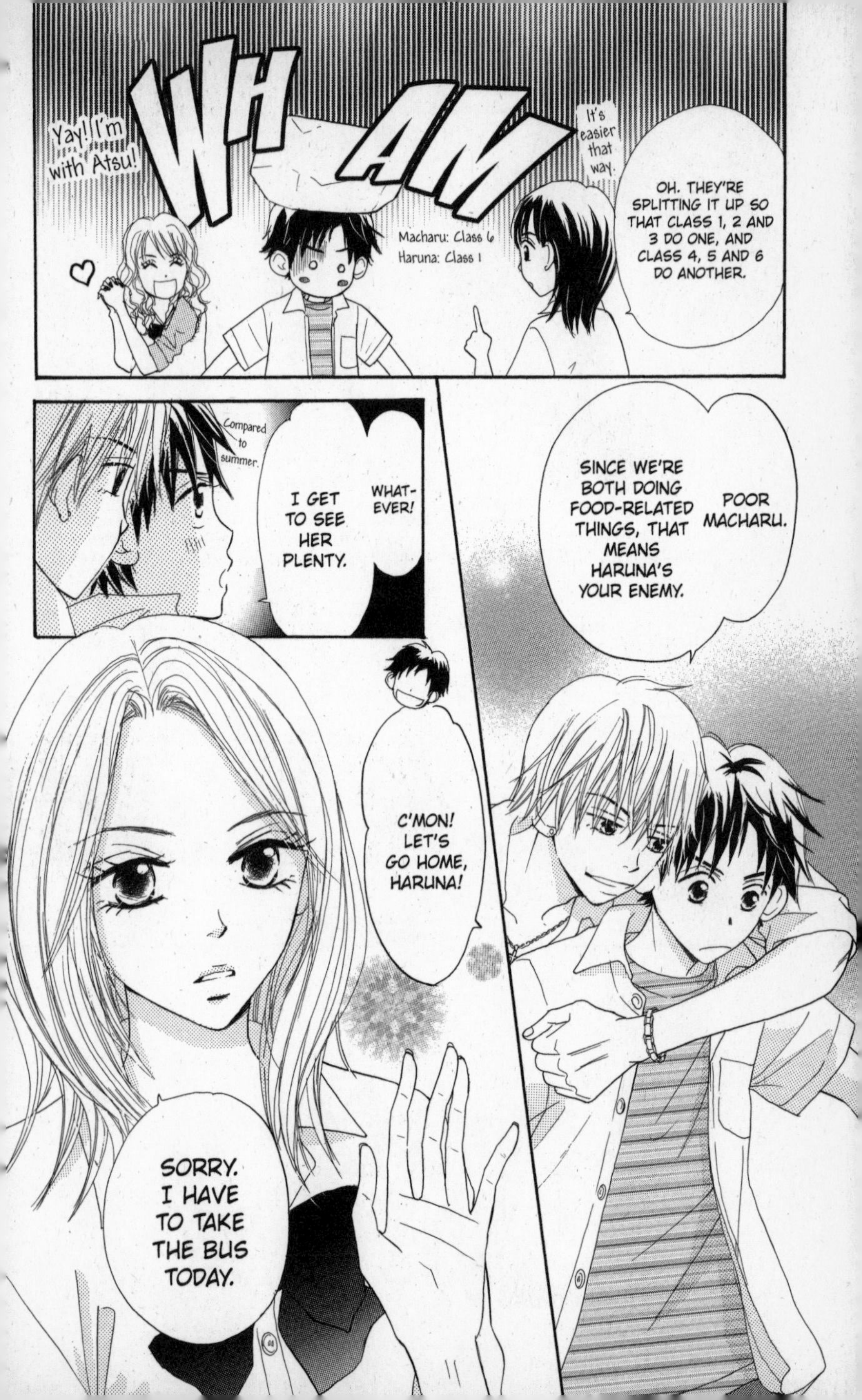
OH. THEY'RE SPLITTING IT UP SO THAT CLASS 1, 2 AND 3 DO ONE, AND CLASS 4, 5 AND 6 DO ANOTHER.
It's easier that way.
WHAM
Yay! I'm with Atsu!
Macharu: Class 6
Haruna: Class 1
POOR MACHARU.
SINCE WE'RE BOTH DOING FOOD-RELATED THINGS, THAT MEANS HARUNA'S YOUR ENEMY.
WHAT-EVER!
I GET TO SEE HER PLENTY.
Compared to summer.
C'MON! LET'S GO HOME, HARUNA!
SORRY. I HAVE TO TAKE THE BUS TODAY.

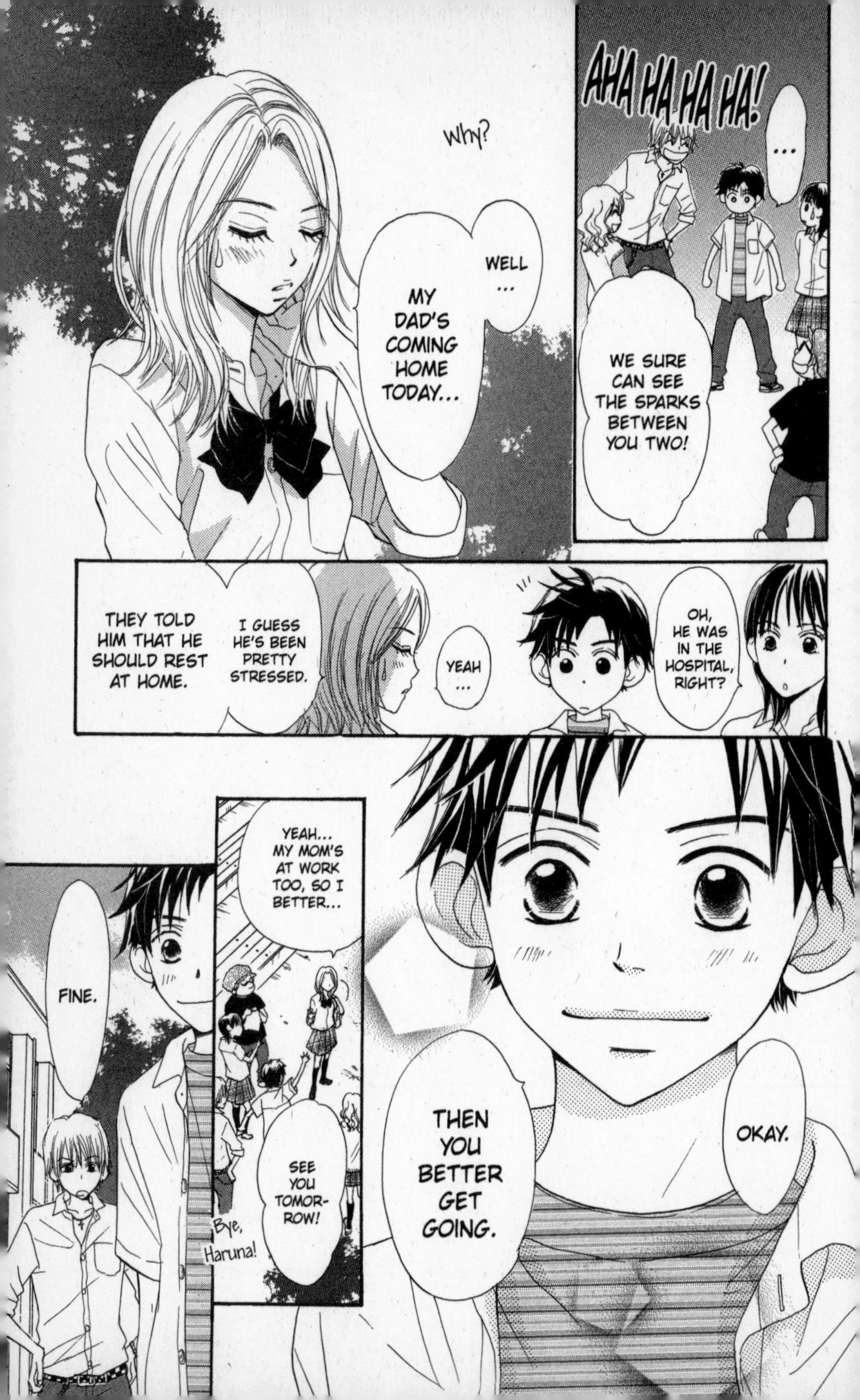
AHA HA HA HA!
...
WE SURE CAN SEE THE SPARKS BETWEEN YOU TWO!
Why?
WELL...
MY DAD'S COMING HOME TODAY...
OH, HE WAS IN THE HOSPITAL, RIGHT?
YEAH...
I GUESS HE'S BEEN PRETTY STRESSED.
THEY TOLD HIM THAT HE SHOULD REST AT HOME.
OKAY.
THEN YOU BETTER GET GOING.
YEAH... MY MOM'S AT WORK TOO, SO I BETTER...
SEE YOU TOMOR-ROW!
Bye, Haruna!
FINE.

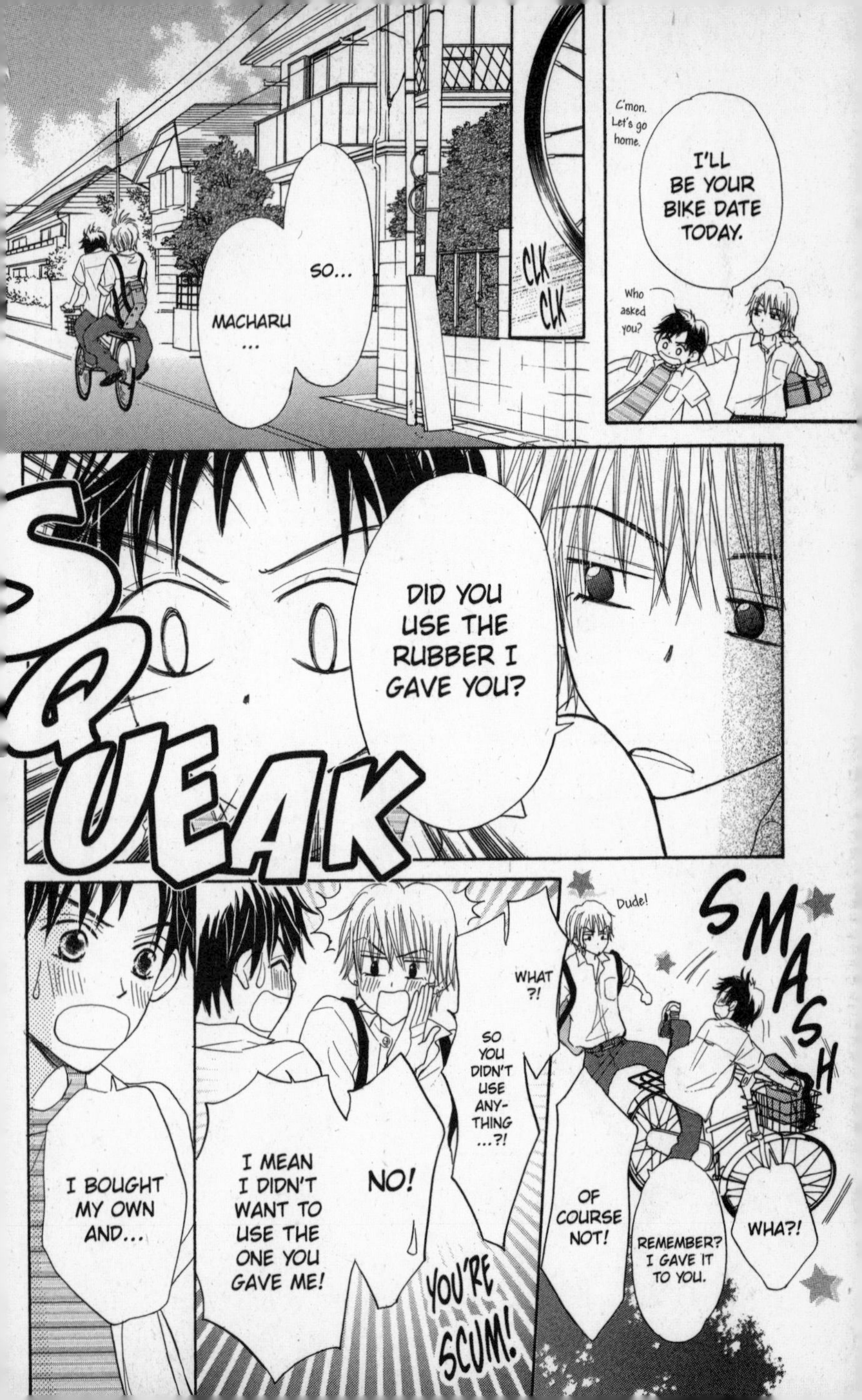
C'mon. Let's go home.
I'LL BE YOUR BIKE DATE TODAY.
Who asked you?
CLK CLK
SO...
MACHARU ...
DID YOU USE THE RUBBER I GAVE YOU?
SQUEAK
SMASH
Dude!
WHAT ?!
WHA?!
REMEMBER? I GAVE IT TO YOU.
OF COURSE NOT!
SO YOU DIDN'T USE ANY-THING ...?!
NO!
I MEAN I DIDN'T WANT TO USE THE ONE YOU GAVE ME!
YOU'RE SCUM!
I BOUGHT MY OWN AND...

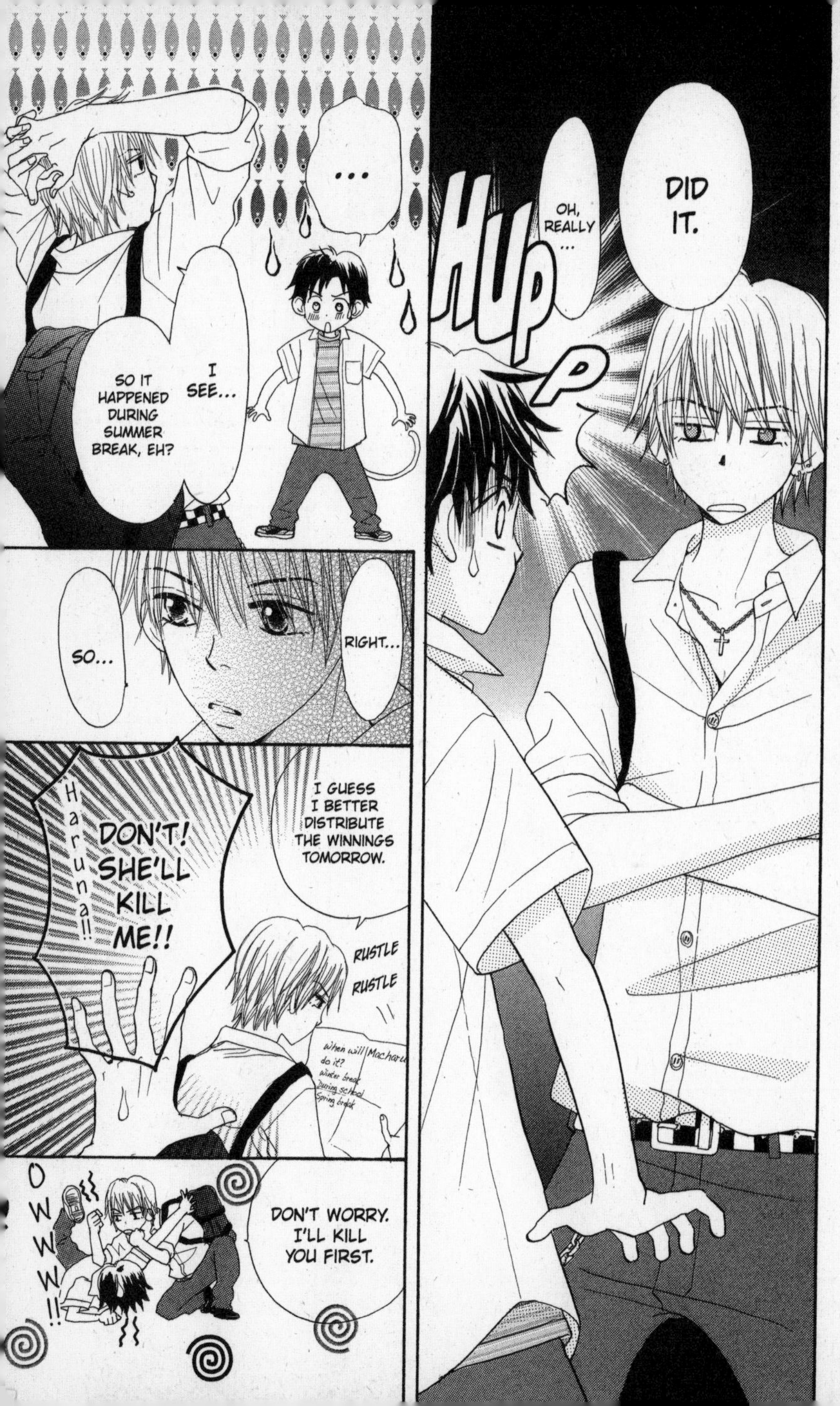
DID IT.
OH, REALLY ...
HUPP
...
I SEE...
SO IT HAPPENED DURING SUMMER BREAK, EH?
RIGHT...
SO...
I GUESS I BETTER DISTRIBUTE THE WINNINGS TOMORROW.
RUSTLE RUSTLE
When will Macharu do it?
Winter break
During school
Spring break
DON'T! SHE'LL KILL ME!!
Haruna!!
DON'T WORRY. I'LL KILL YOU FIRST.
OWWW!!

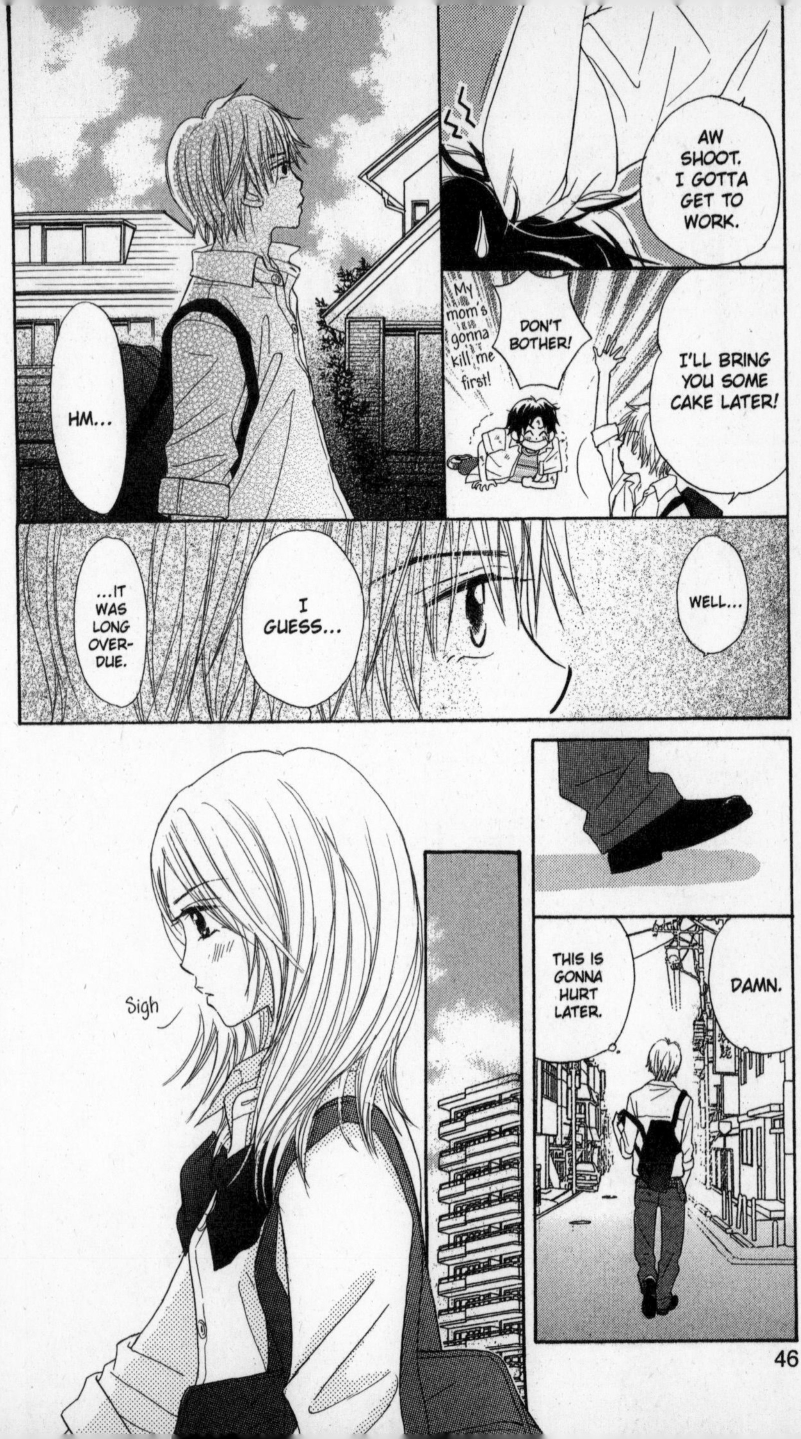
AW SHOOT. I GOTTA GET TO WORK.
I'LL BRING YOU SOME CAKE LATER!
DON'T BOTHER!
My mom's gonna kill me first!
HM...
WELL...
I GUESS...
...IT WAS LONG OVERDUE.
DAMN.
THIS IS GONNA HURT LATER.
Sigh

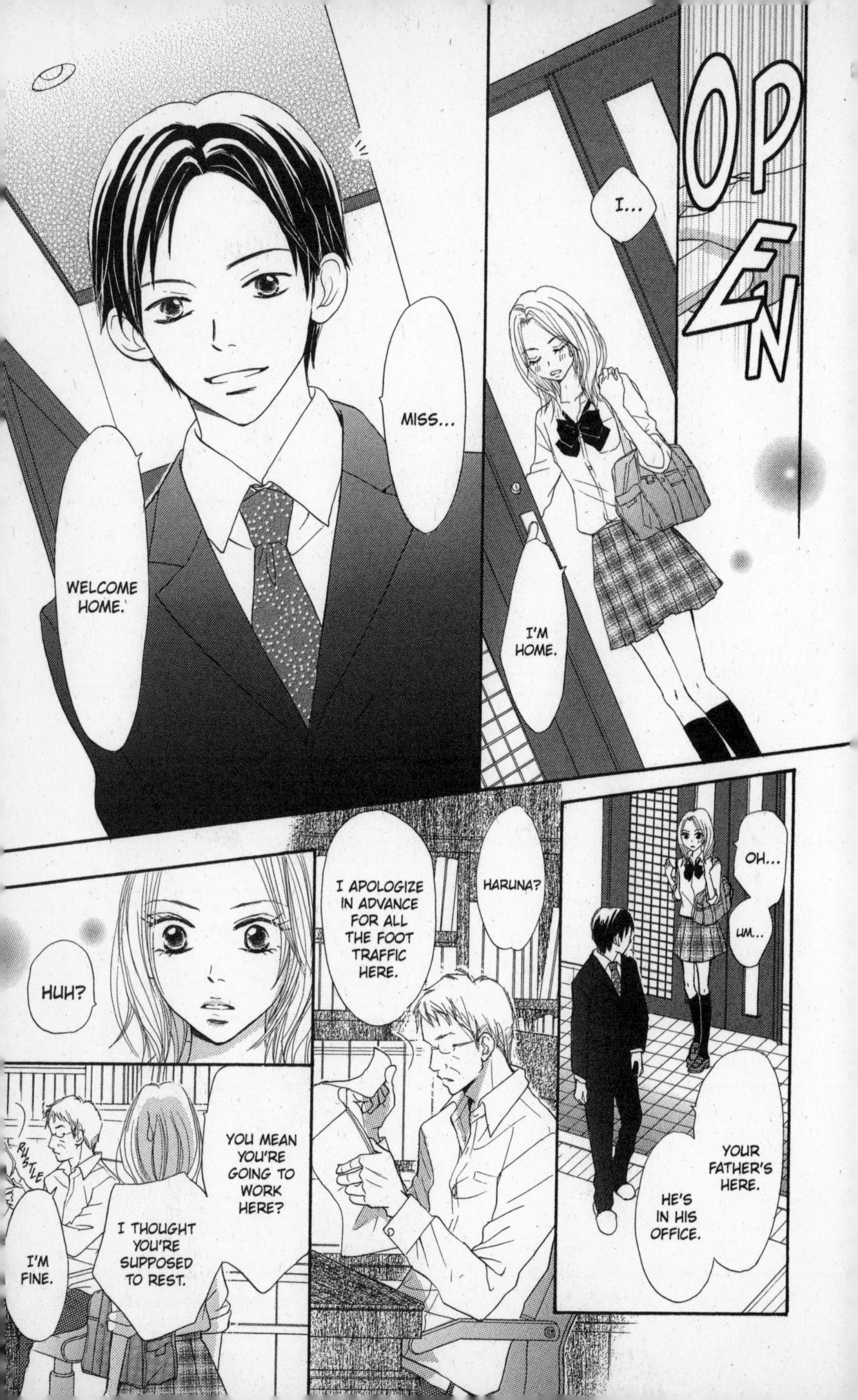
OPEN
I...
I'M HOME.
MISS...
WELCOME HOME.
OH...
UM...
YOUR FATHER'S HERE.
HE'S IN HIS OFFICE.
HARUNA?
I APOLOGIZE IN ADVANCE FOR ALL THE FOOT TRAFFIC HERE.
HUH?
YOU MEAN YOU'RE GOING TO WORK HERE?
I THOUGHT YOU'RE SUPPOSED TO REST.
RUSTLE
I'M FINE.

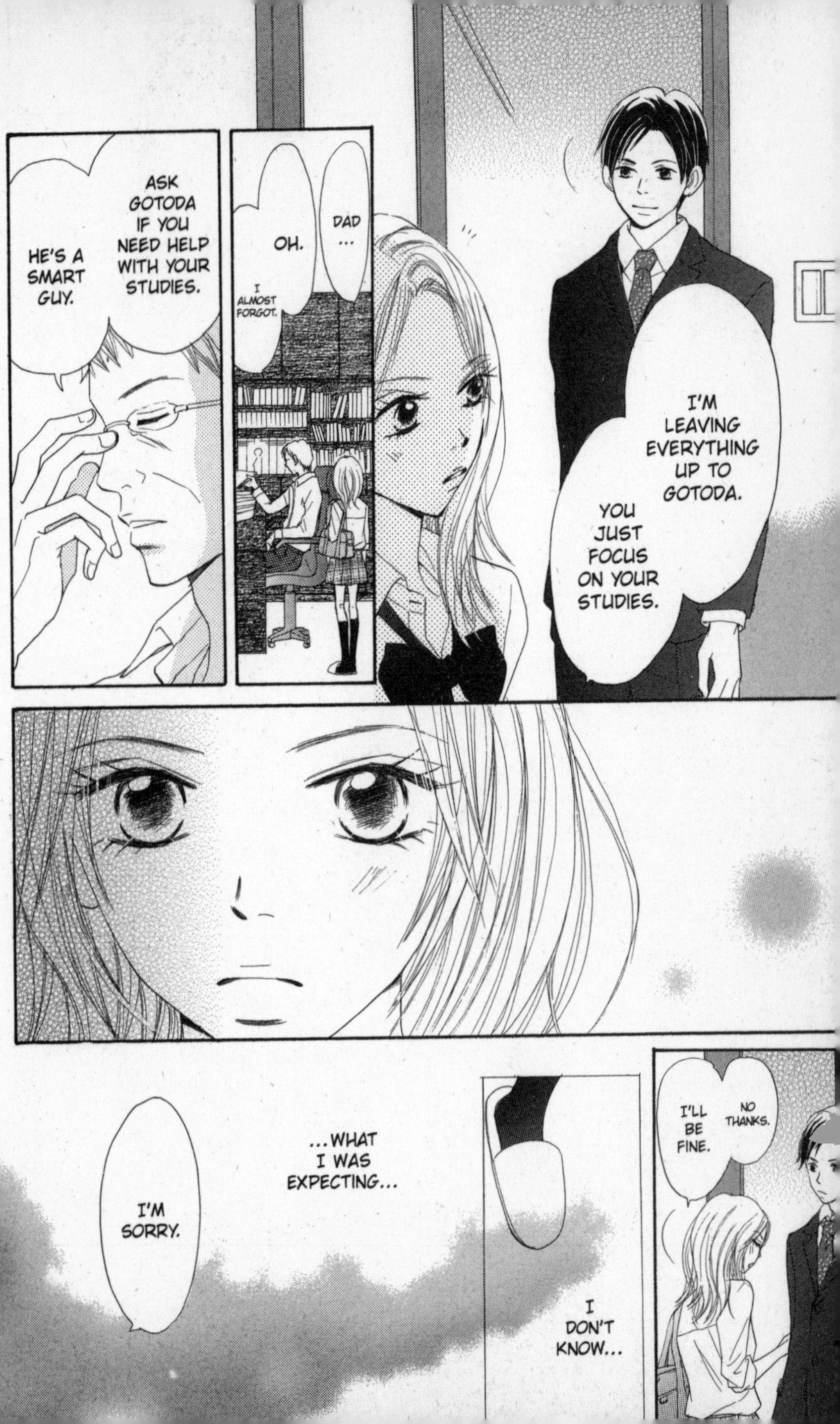
I'M LEAVING EVERYTHING UP TO GOTODA.
YOU JUST FOCUS ON YOUR STUDIES.
DAD...
OH.
I ALMOST FORGOT.
ASK GOTODA IF YOU NEED HELP WITH YOUR STUDIES.
HE'S A SMART GUY.
NO THANKS.
I'LL BE FINE.
I DON'T KNOW...
...WHAT I WAS EXPECTING...
I'M SORRY.

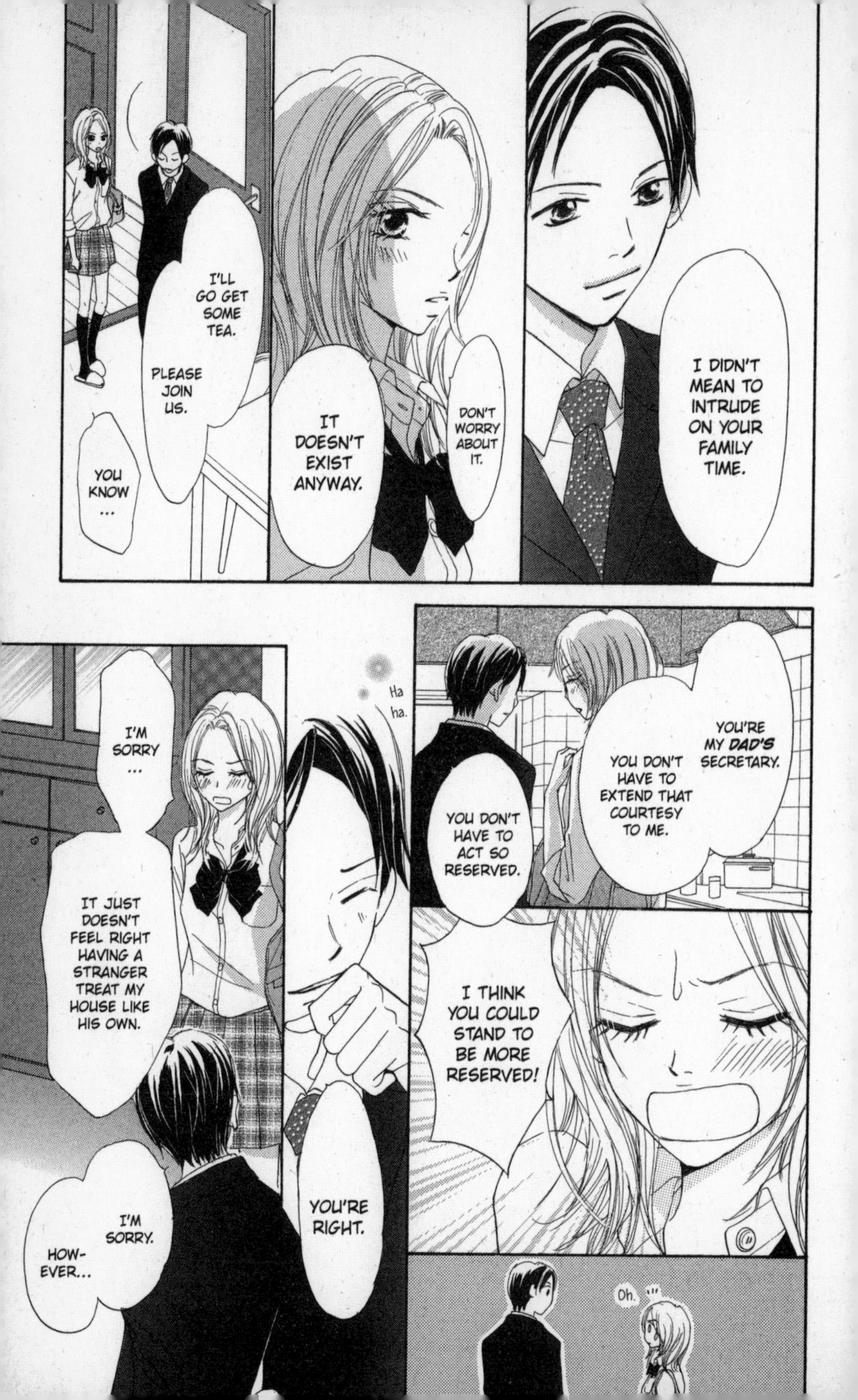
I DIDN'T MEAN TO INTRUDE ON YOUR FAMILY TIME.
DON'T WORRY ABOUT IT.
IT DOESN'T EXIST ANYWAY.
I'LL GO GET SOME TEA.
PLEASE JOIN US.
YOU KNOW...
YOU'RE MY ***DAD'S*** SECRETARY.
YOU DON'T HAVE TO EXTEND THAT COURTESY TO ME.
YOU DON'T HAVE TO ACT SO RESERVED.
I THINK YOU COULD STAND TO BE MORE RESERVED!
Oh.
Ha ha.
YOU'RE RIGHT.
I'M SORRY...
IT JUST DOESN'T FEEL RIGHT HAVING A STRANGER TREAT MY HOUSE LIKE HIS OWN.
I'M SORRY.
HOW-EVER...

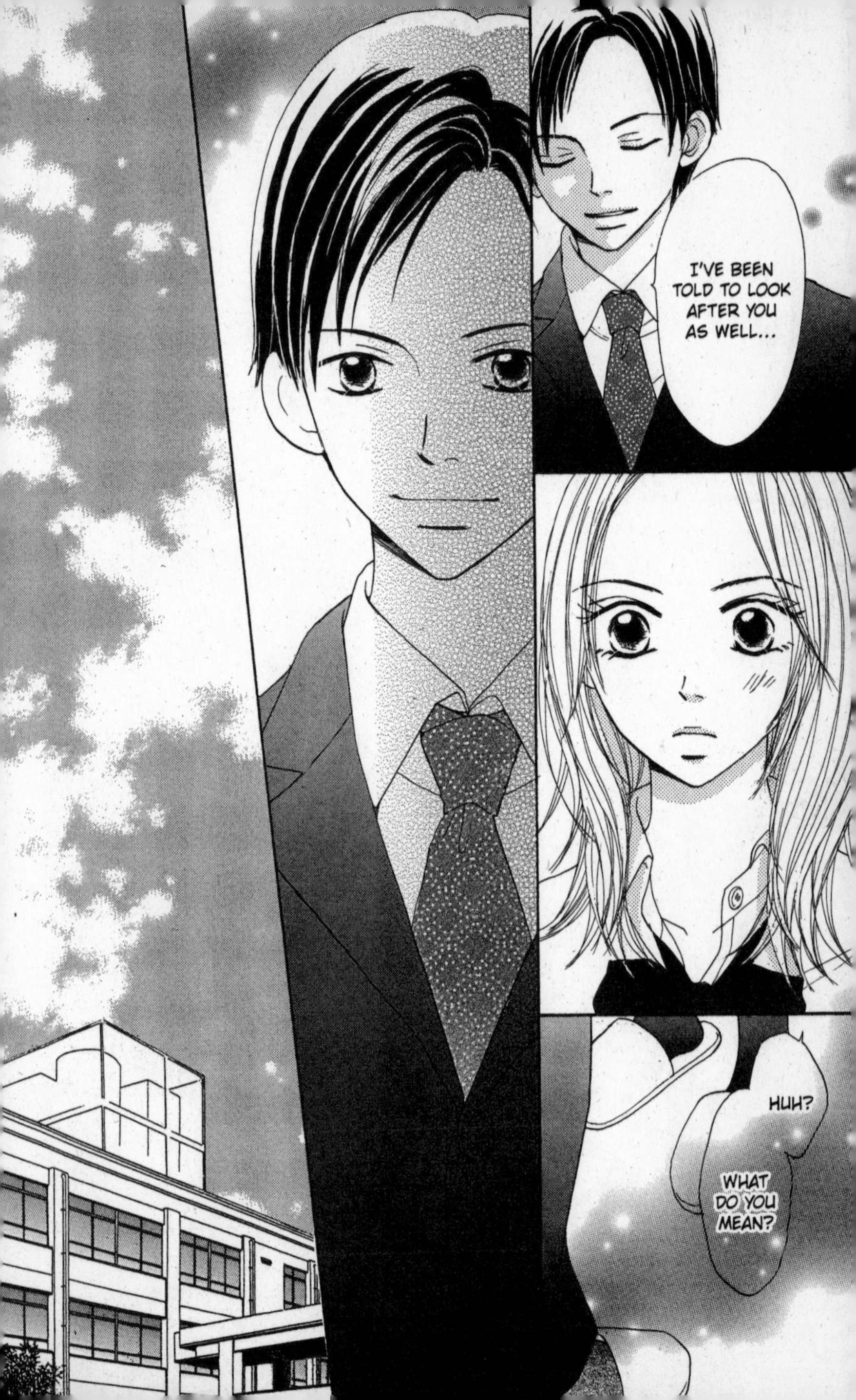
I'VE BEEN TOLD TO LOOK AFTER YOU AS WELL...
HUH?
WHAT DO YOU MEAN?

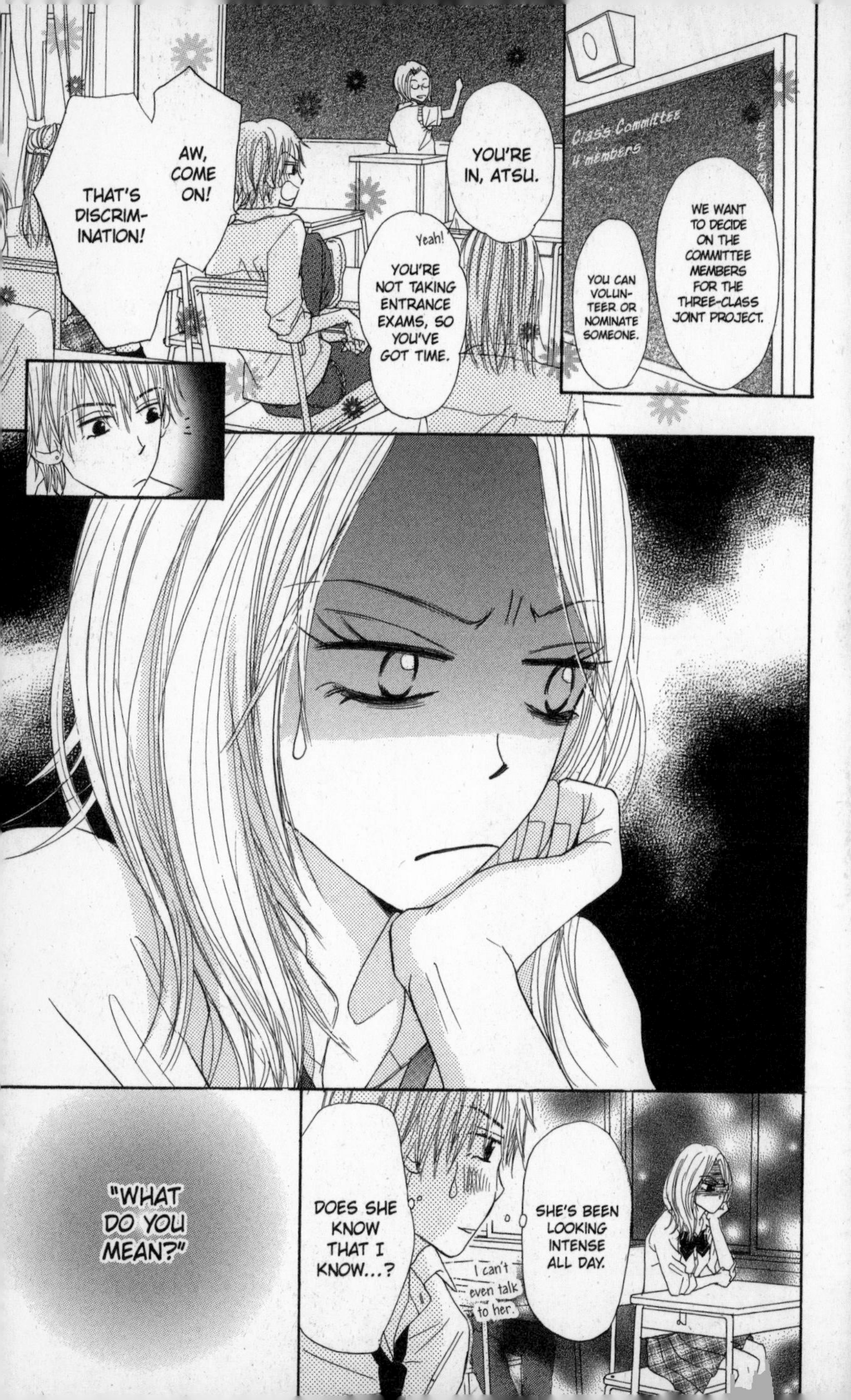
Class Committee
4 members
WE WANT TO DECIDE ON THE COMMITTEE MEMBERS FOR THE THREE-CLASS JOINT PROJECT.
YOU CAN VOLUNTEER OR NOMINATE SOMEONE.
YOU'RE IN, ATSU.
Yeah!
YOU'RE NOT TAKING ENTRANCE EXAMS, SO YOU'VE GOT TIME.
AW, COME ON!
THAT'S DISCRIMINATION!
SHE'S BEEN LOOKING INTENSE ALL DAY.
DOES SHE KNOW THAT I KNOW...?
I can't even talk to her.
"WHAT DO YOU MEAN?"

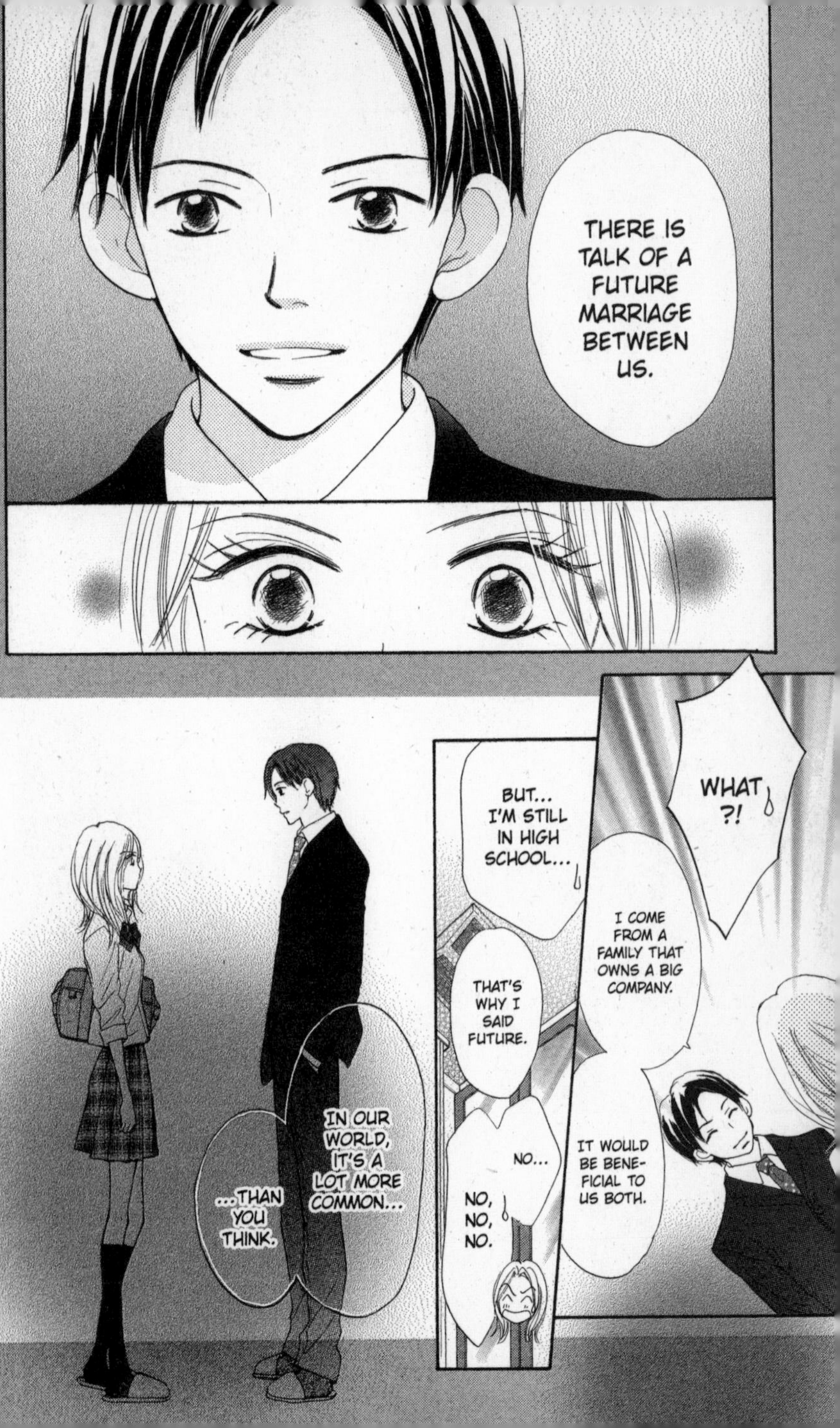
THERE IS TALK OF A FUTURE MARRIAGE BETWEEN US.
WHAT ?!
I COME FROM A FAMILY THAT OWNS A BIG COMPANY.
IT WOULD BE BENE-FICIAL TO US BOTH.
BUT... I'M STILL IN HIGH SCHOOL...
THAT'S WHY I SAID FUTURE.
NO...
NO, NO, NO.
IN OUR WORLD, IT'S A LOT MORE COMMON...
...THAN YOU THINK.

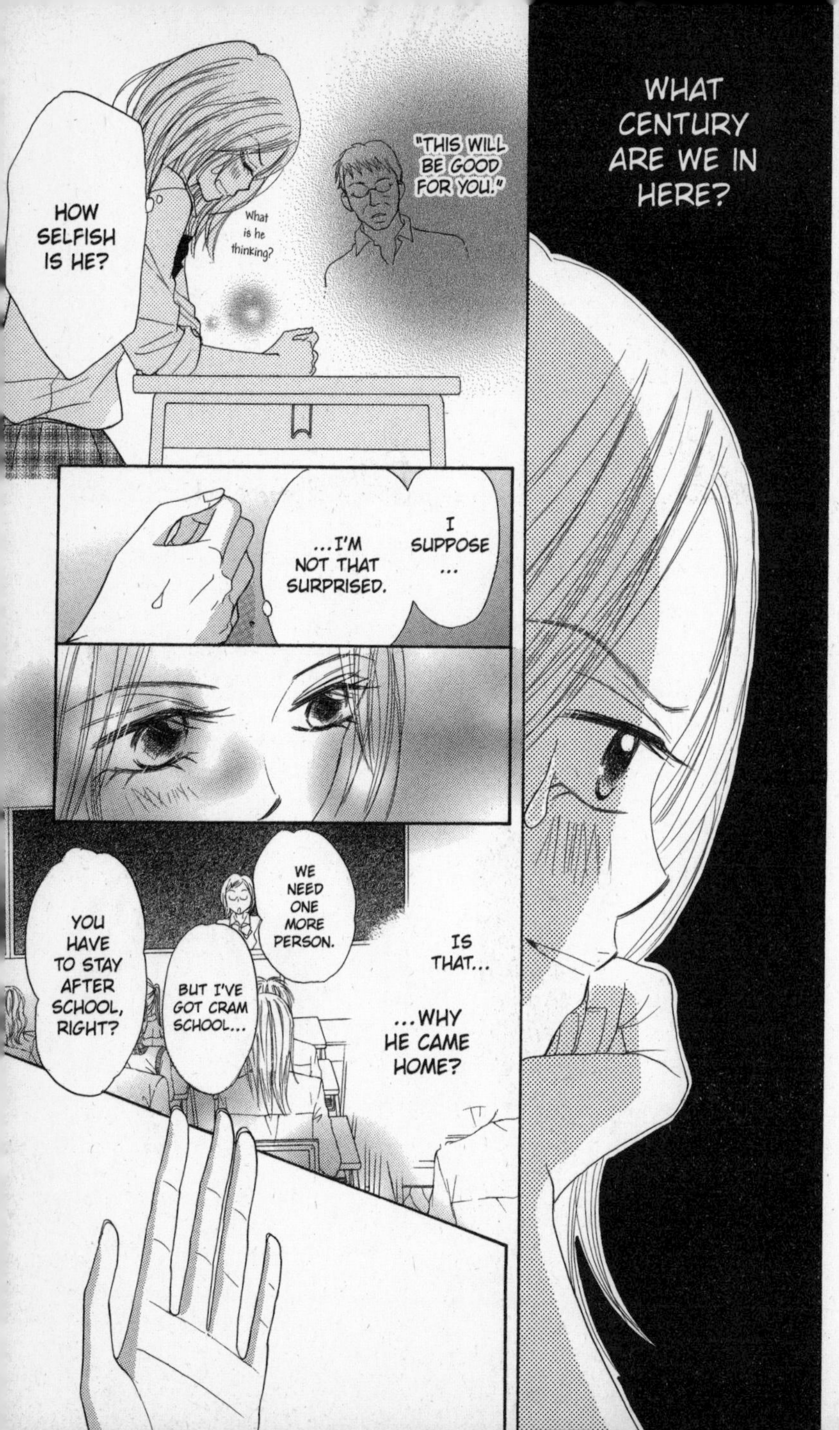
WHAT CENTURY ARE WE IN HERE?
"THIS WILL BE GOOD FOR YOU."
What is he thinking?
HOW SELFISH IS HE?
I SUPPOSE ...
...I'M NOT THAT SURPRISED.
IS THAT...
...WHY HE CAME HOME?
WE NEED ONE MORE PERSON.
BUT I'VE GOT CRAM SCHOOL...
YOU HAVE TO STAY AFTER SCHOOL, RIGHT?

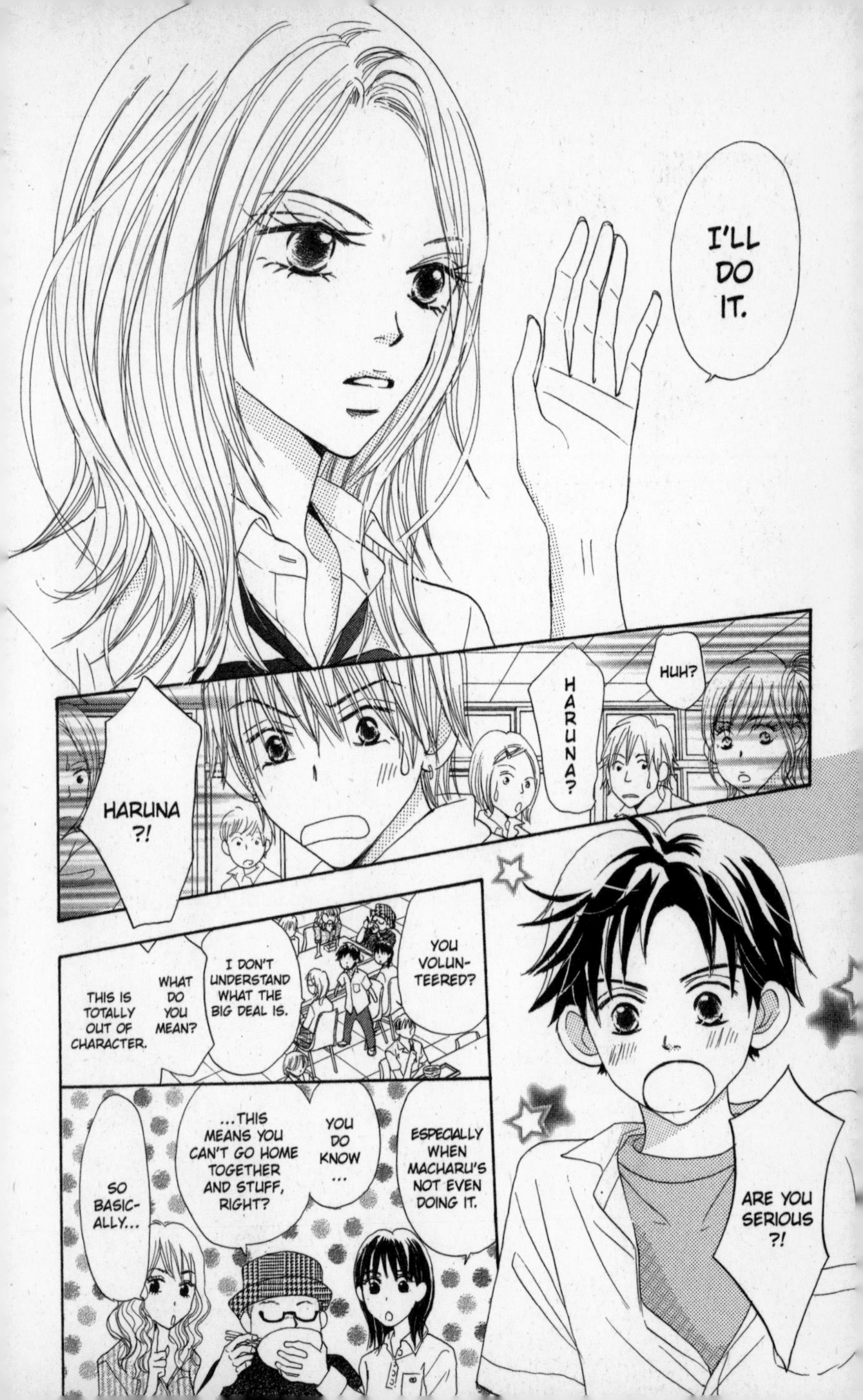
I'LL DO IT.
HUH?
HARUNA?
HARUNA ?!
ARE YOU SERIOUS ?!
YOU VOLUN- TEERED?
I DON'T UNDERSTAND WHAT THE BIG DEAL IS.
WHAT DO YOU MEAN?
THIS IS TOTALLY OUT OF CHARACTER.
ESPECIALLY WHEN MACHARU'S NOT EVEN DOING IT.
YOU DO KNOW ...
...THIS MEANS YOU CAN'T GO HOME TOGETHER AND STUFF, RIGHT?
SO BASIC- ALLY...

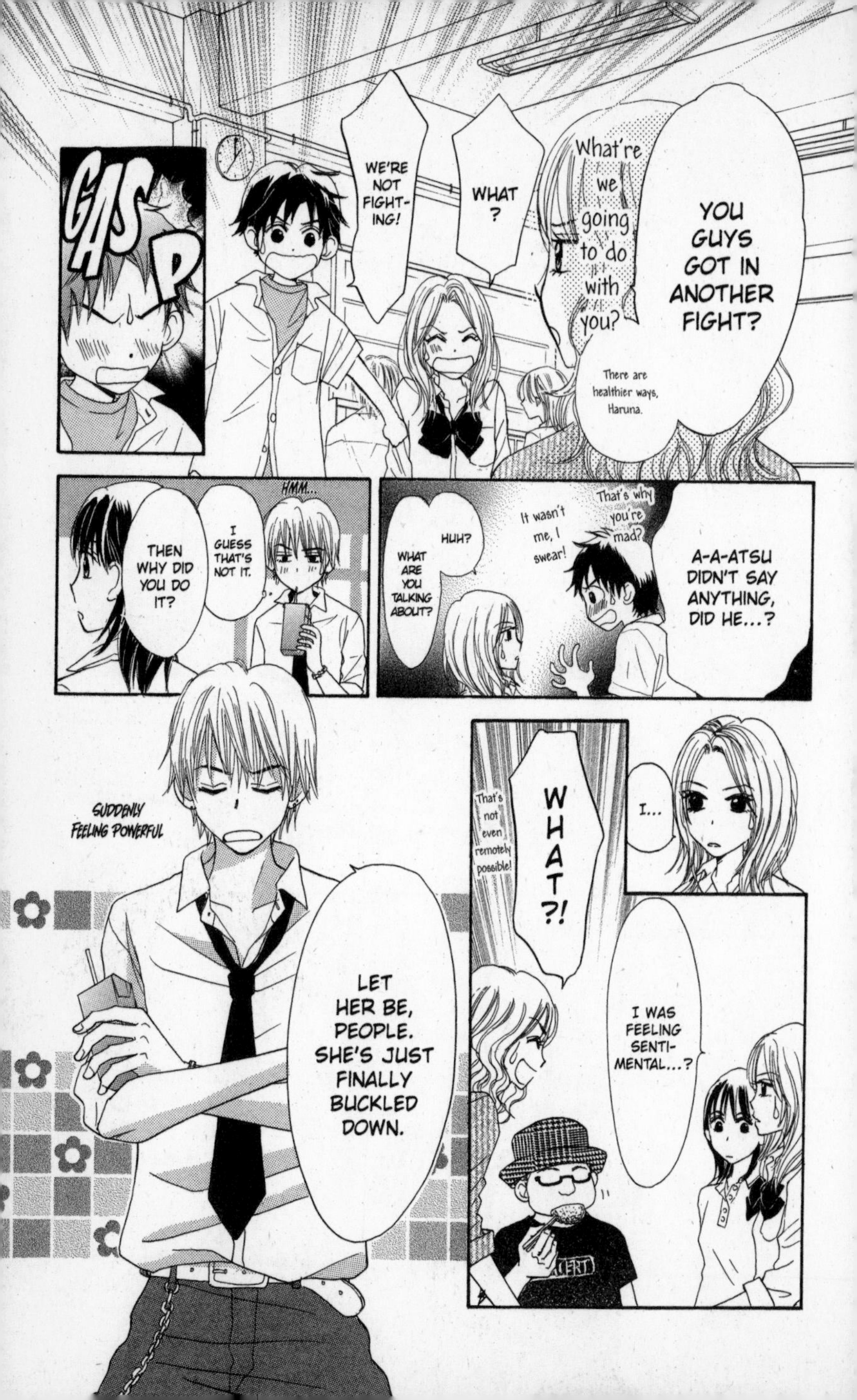
YOU GUYS GOT IN ANOTHER FIGHT?
What're we going to do with you?
There are healthier ways, Haruna.
WHAT?
WE'RE NOT FIGHT-ING!
GASP
A-A-ATSU DIDN'T SAY ANYTHING, DID HE...?
That's why you're mad?
It wasn't me, I swear!
HUH?
WHAT ARE YOU TALKING ABOUT?
HMM...
I GUESS THAT'S NOT IT.
THEN WHY DID YOU DO IT?
I...
WHAT?!
That's not even remotely possible!
I WAS FEELING SENTI-MENTAL...?
LET HER BE, PEOPLE. SHE'S JUST FINALLY BUCKLED DOWN.
SUDDENLY FEELING POWERFUL

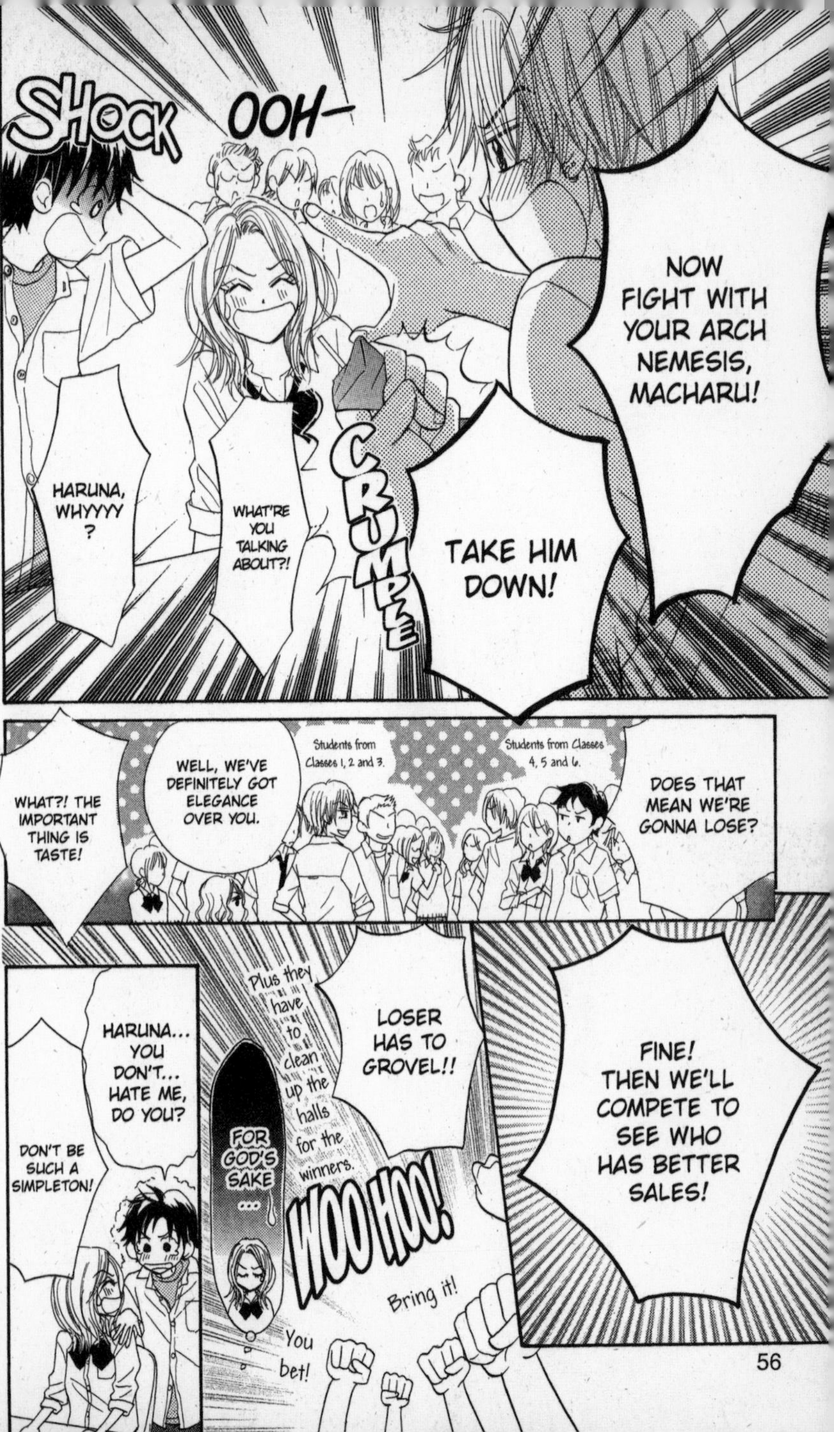
NOW FIGHT WITH YOUR ARCH NEMESIS, MACHARU!
TAKE HIM DOWN!
CRUMPLE
WHAT'RE YOU TALKING ABOUT?!
HARUNA, WHYYYY?
SHOCK
OOH-
DOES THAT MEAN WE'RE GONNA LOSE?
Students from Classes 4, 5 and 6.
Students from Classes 1, 2 and 3.
WELL, WE'VE DEFINITELY GOT ELEGANCE OVER YOU.
WHAT?! THE IMPORTANT THING IS TASTE!
FINE! THEN WE'LL COMPETE TO SEE WHO HAS BETTER SALES!
LOSER HAS TO GROVEL!!
Plus they have to clean up the halls for the winners.
WOO HOO!
Bring it!
You bet!
FOR GOD'S SAKE...
HARUNA... YOU DON'T... HATE ME, DO YOU?
DON'T BE SUCH A SIMPLETON!

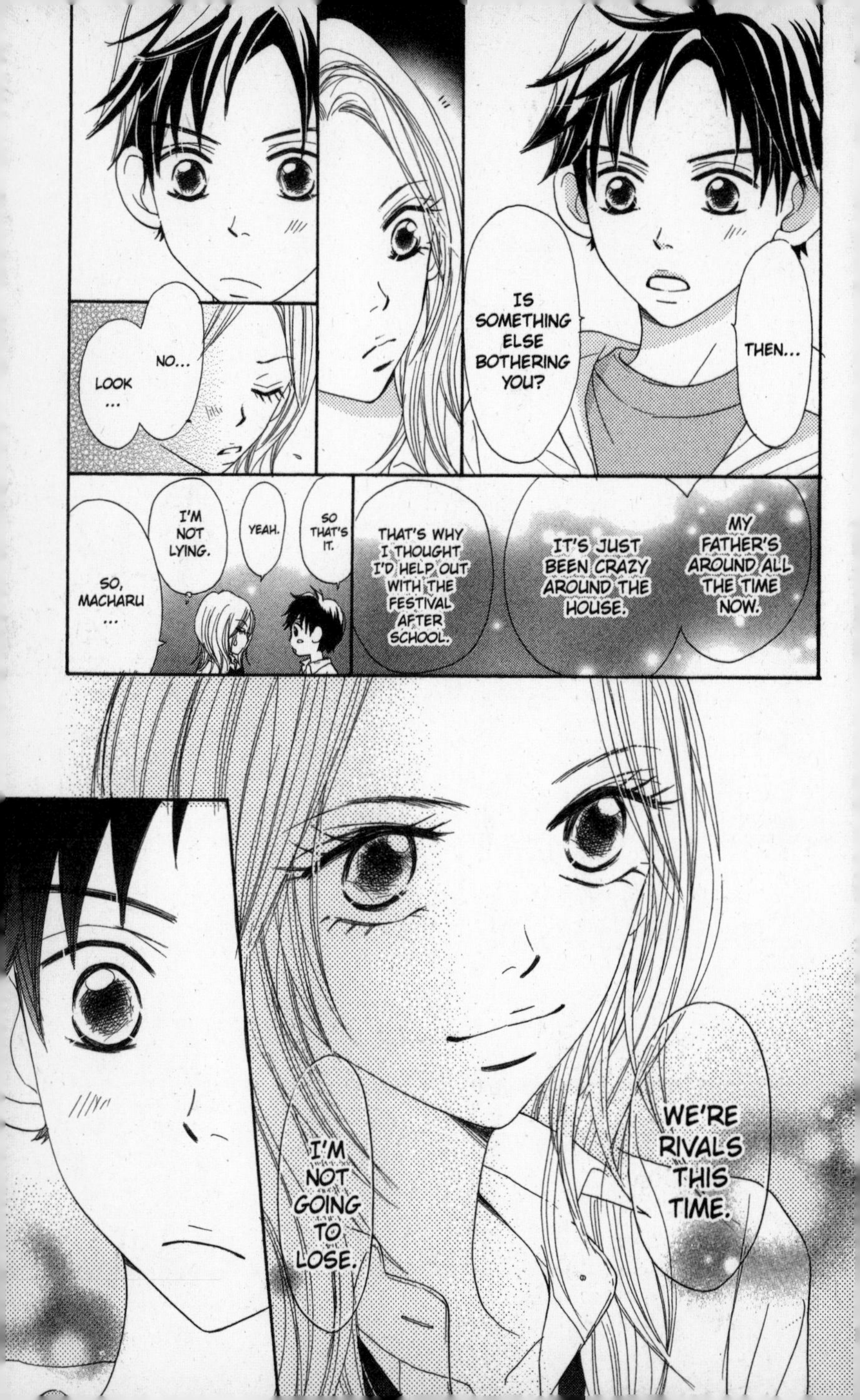
THEN...
IS SOMETHING ELSE BOTHERING YOU?
NO...
LOOK...
MY FATHER'S AROUND ALL THE TIME NOW.
IT'S JUST BEEN CRAZY AROUND THE HOUSE.
THAT'S WHY I THOUGHT I'D HELP OUT WITH THE FESTIVAL AFTER SCHOOL.
SO THAT'S IT.
YEAH.
I'M NOT LYING.
SO, MACHARU...
WE'RE RIVALS THIS TIME.
I'M NOT GOING TO LOSE.

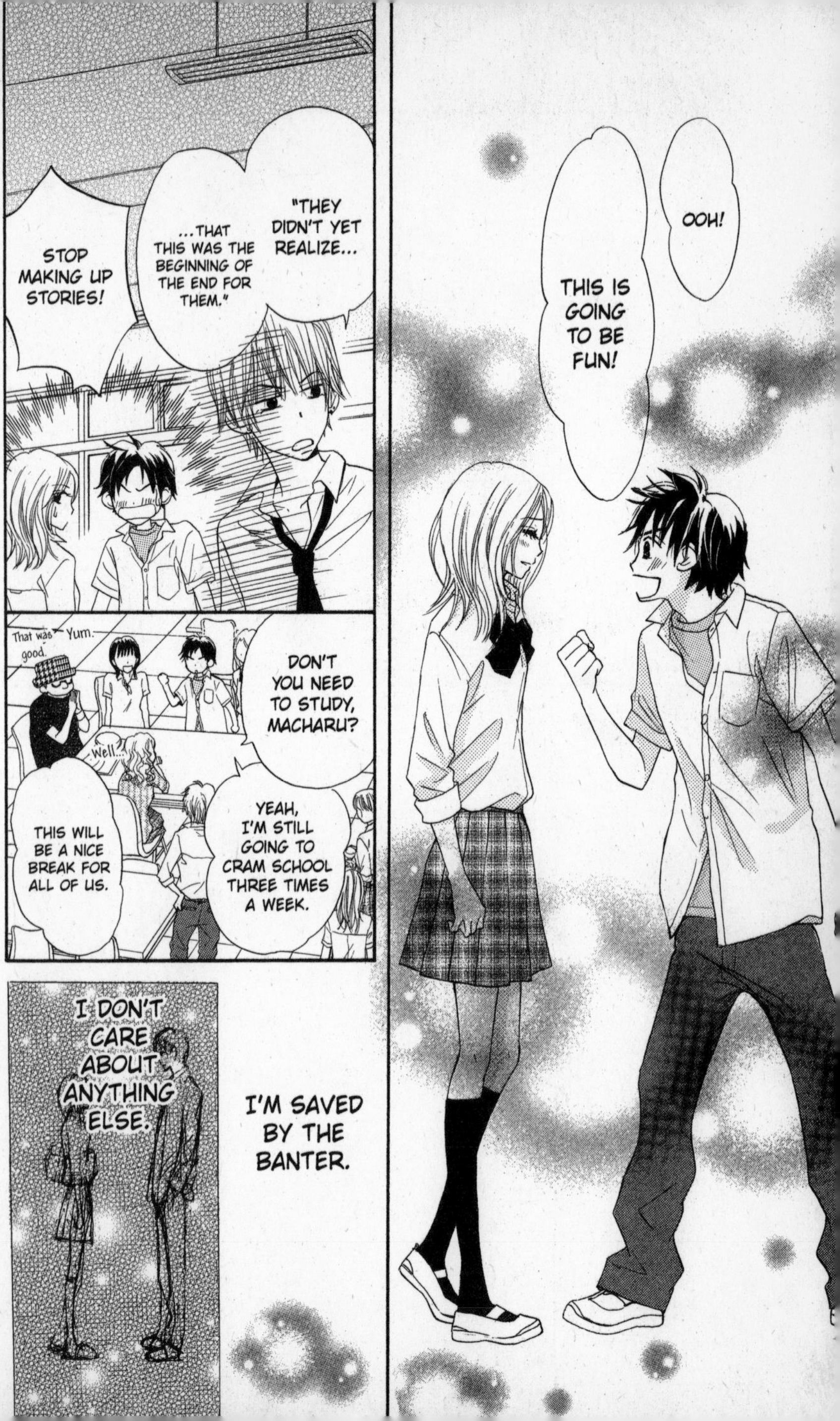
OOH!
THIS IS GOING TO BE FUN!
"THEY DIDN'T YET REALIZE...
...THAT THIS WAS THE BEGINNING OF THE END FOR THEM."
STOP MAKING UP STORIES!
DON'T YOU NEED TO STUDY, MACHARU?
Yum.
That was good.
Well...
YEAH, I'M STILL GOING TO CRAM SCHOOL THREE TIMES A WEEK.
THIS WILL BE A NICE BREAK FOR ALL OF US.
I'M SAVED BY THE BANTER.
I DON'T CARE ABOUT ANYTHING ELSE.

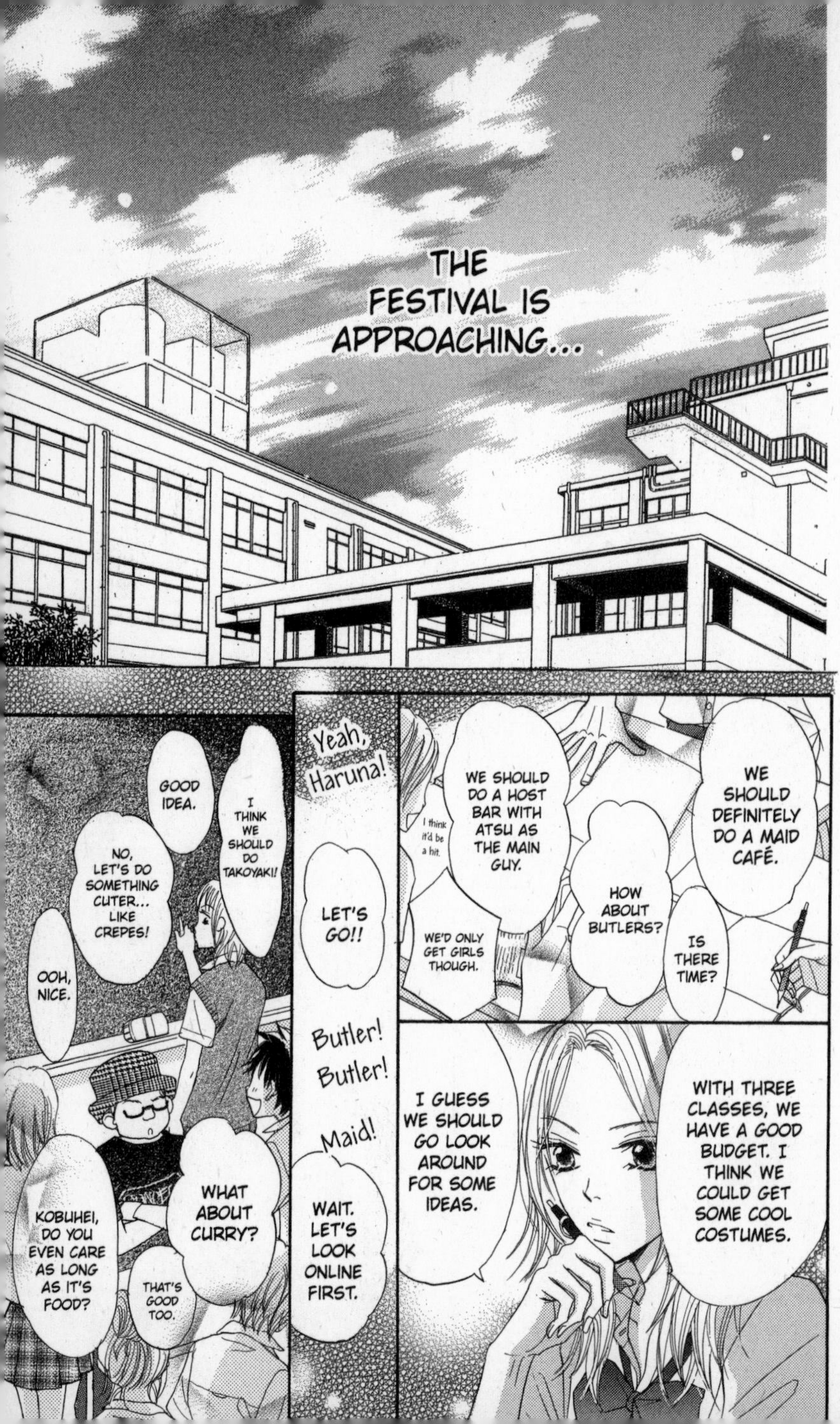
THE FESTIVAL IS APPROACHING...
WE SHOULD DEFINITELY DO A MAID CAFÉ.
IS THERE TIME?
HOW ABOUT BUTLERS?
WE SHOULD DO A HOST BAR WITH ATSU AS THE MAIN GUY.
I think it'd be a hit.
WE'D ONLY GET GIRLS THOUGH.
WITH THREE CLASSES, WE HAVE A GOOD BUDGET. I THINK WE COULD GET SOME COOL COSTUMES.
I GUESS WE SHOULD GO LOOK AROUND FOR SOME IDEAS.
Yeah, Haruna!
LET'S GO!!
Butler! Butler!
Maid!
WAIT. LET'S LOOK ONLINE FIRST.
I THINK WE SHOULD DO TAKOYAKI!
GOOD IDEA.
NO, LET'S DO SOMETHING CUTER... LIKE CREPES!
OOH, NICE.
WHAT ABOUT CURRY?
KOBUHEI, DO YOU EVEN CARE AS LONG AS IT'S FOOD?
THAT'S GOOD TOO.

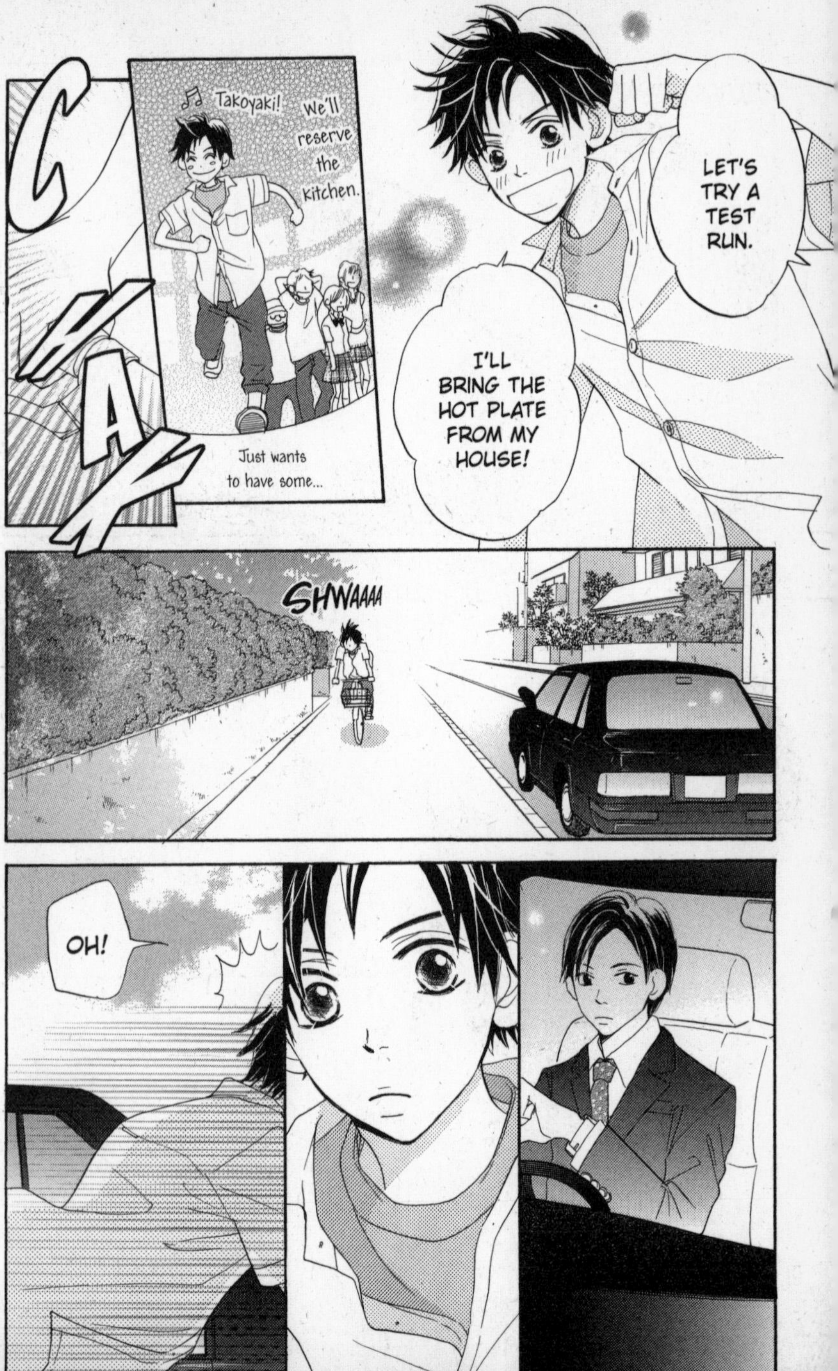
LET'S TRY A TEST RUN.
I'LL BRING THE HOT PLATE FROM MY HOUSE!
We'll reserve the kitchen.
♫ Takoyaki!
Just wants to have some...
CHAK
SHWAAAA
OH!

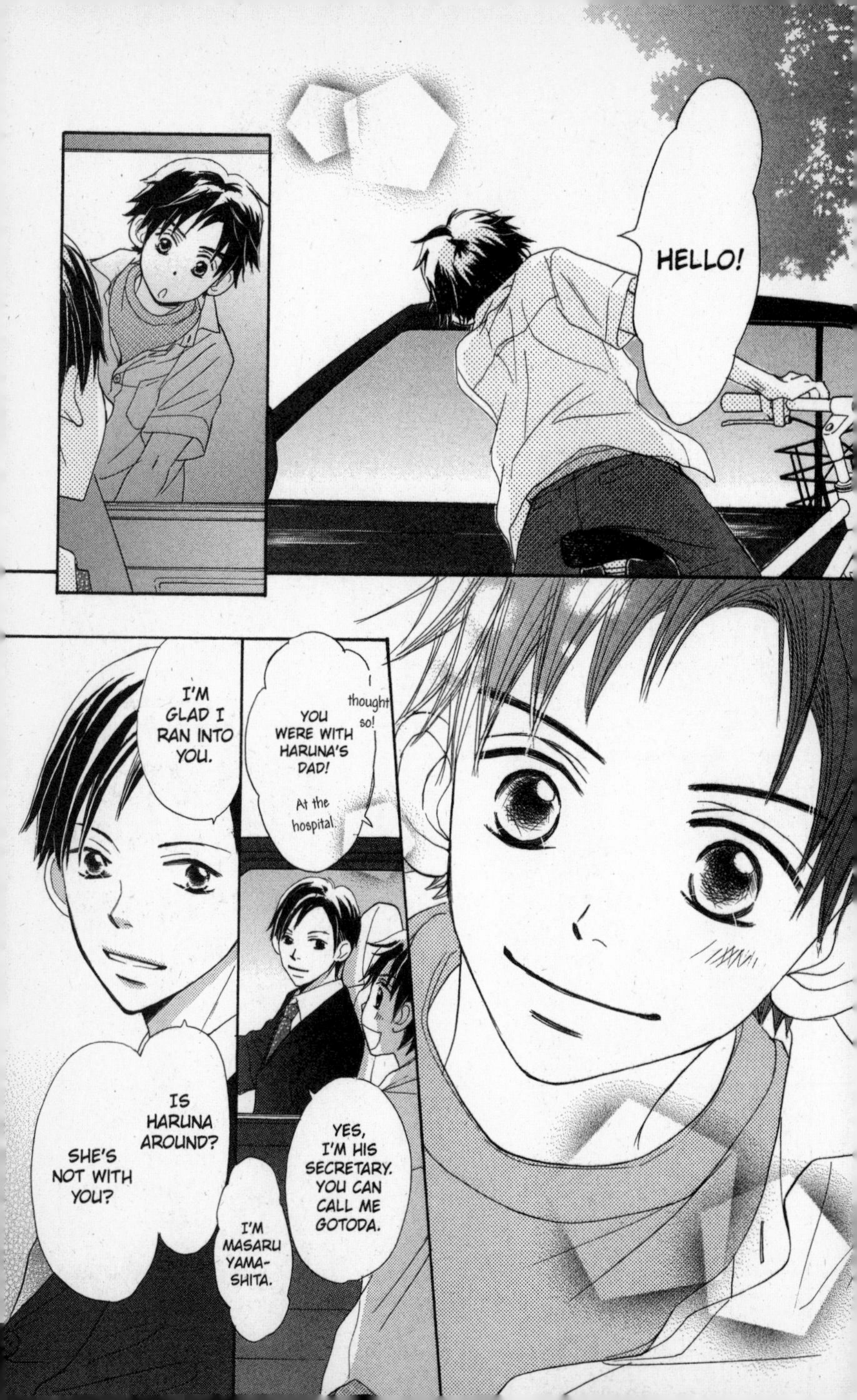
HELLO!
YOU WERE WITH HARUNA'S DAD!
I thought so!
At the hospital.
YES, I'M HIS SECRETARY. YOU CAN CALL ME GOTODA.
I'M MASARU YAMA-SHITA.
I'M GLAD I RAN INTO YOU.
IS HARUNA AROUND?
SHE'S NOT WITH YOU?

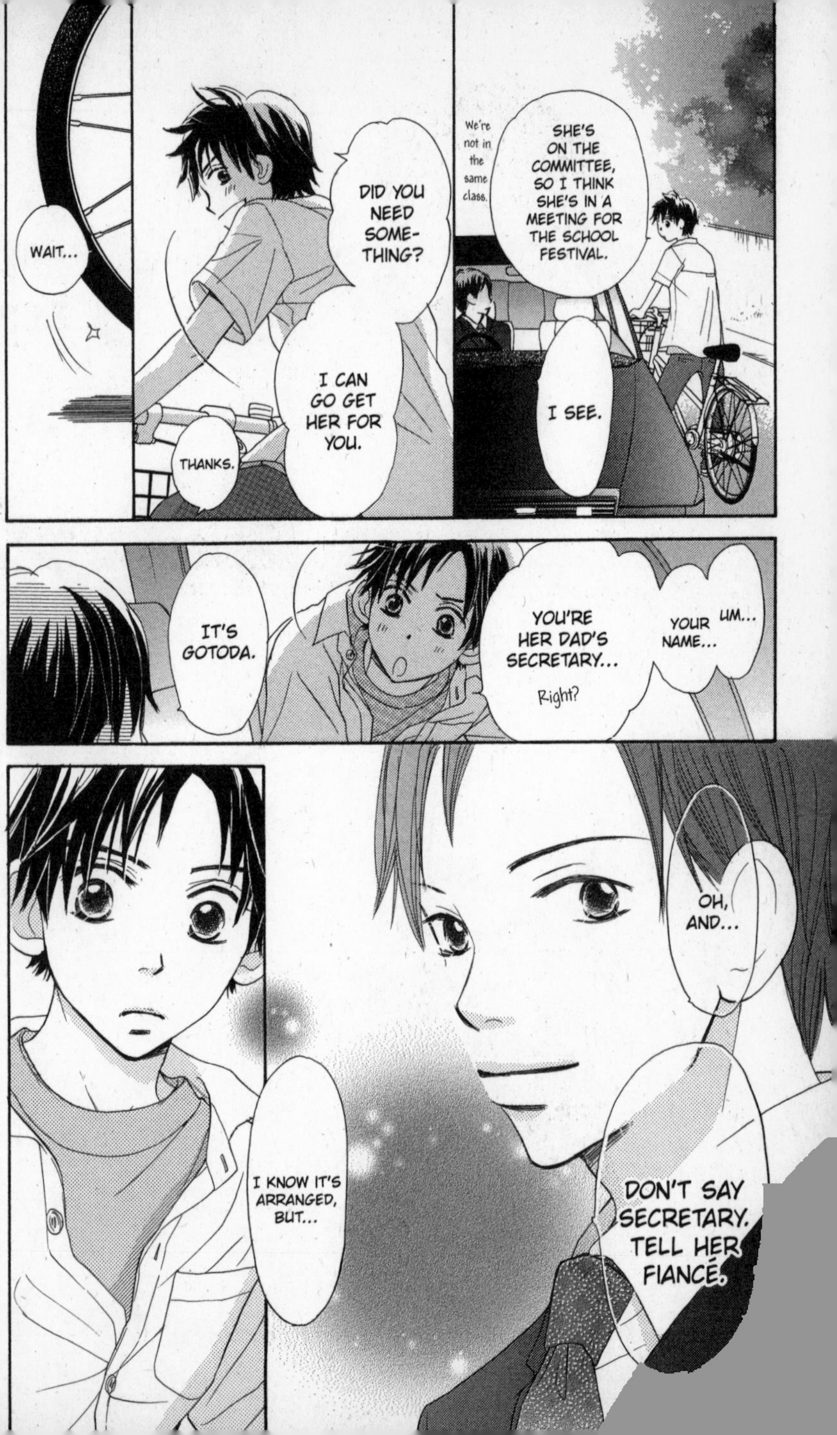
SHE'S ON THE COMMITTEE, SO I THINK SHE'S IN A MEETING FOR THE SCHOOL FESTIVAL.
We're not in the same class.
I SEE.
DID YOU NEED SOMETHING?
I CAN GO GET HER FOR YOU.
THANKS.
WAIT...
UM...
YOUR NAME...
YOU'RE HER DAD'S SECRETARY...
Right?
IT'S GOTODA.
OH, AND...
DON'T SAY SECRETARY. TELL HER FIANCÉ.
I KNOW IT'S ARRANGED, BUT...

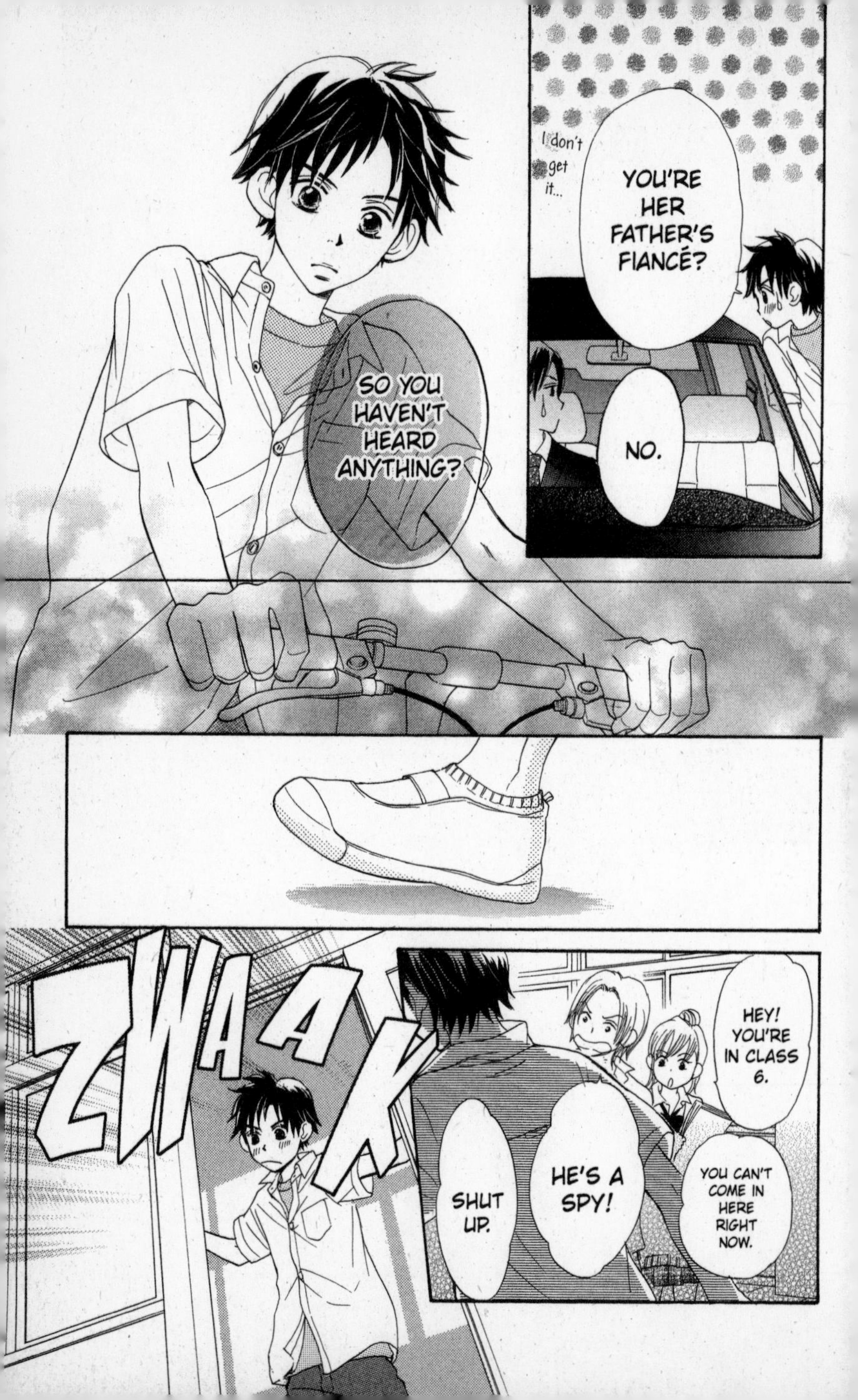
YOU'RE HER FATHER'S FIANCÉ?
I don't get it...
NO.
SO YOU HAVEN'T HEARD ANYTHING?
HEY! YOU'RE IN CLASS 6.
YOU CAN'T COME IN HERE RIGHT NOW.
HE'S A SPY!
SHUT UP.
ZWAAK

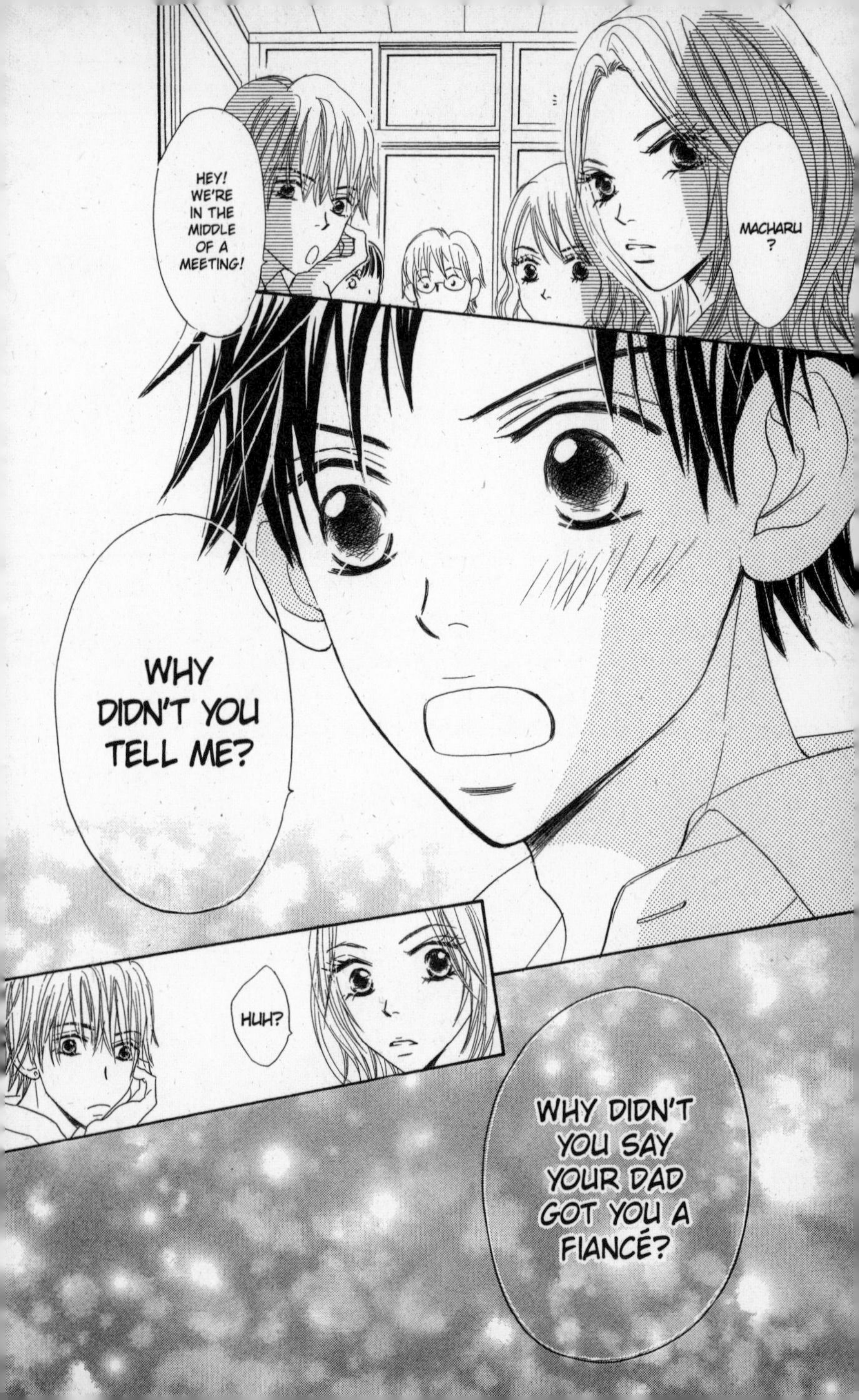
MACHARU?
HEY! WE'RE IN THE MIDDLE OF A MEETING!
WHY DIDN'T YOU TELL ME?
HUH?
WHY DIDN'T YOU SAY YOUR DAD GOT YOU A FIANCÉ?

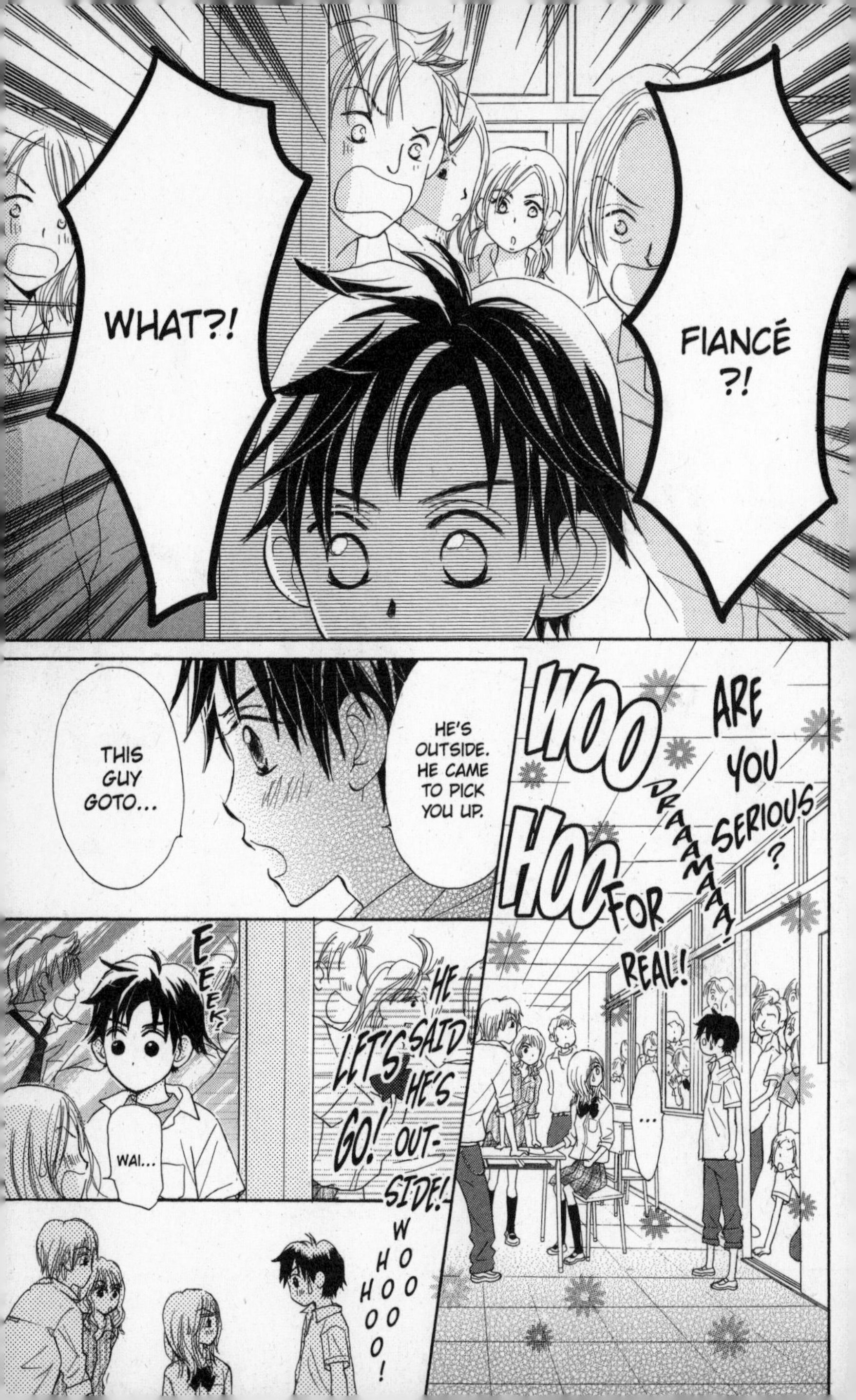
FIANCÉ ?!
WHAT?!
ARE YOU SERIOUS ?
WOO HOO
DRAAAMAAA!
FOR REAL!
...
HE'S OUTSIDE. HE CAME TO PICK YOU UP.
THIS GUY GOTO...
HE SAID HE'S OUTSIDE!
LET'S GO!
EEEK!
WAI...
WOO HOOO HOOO!

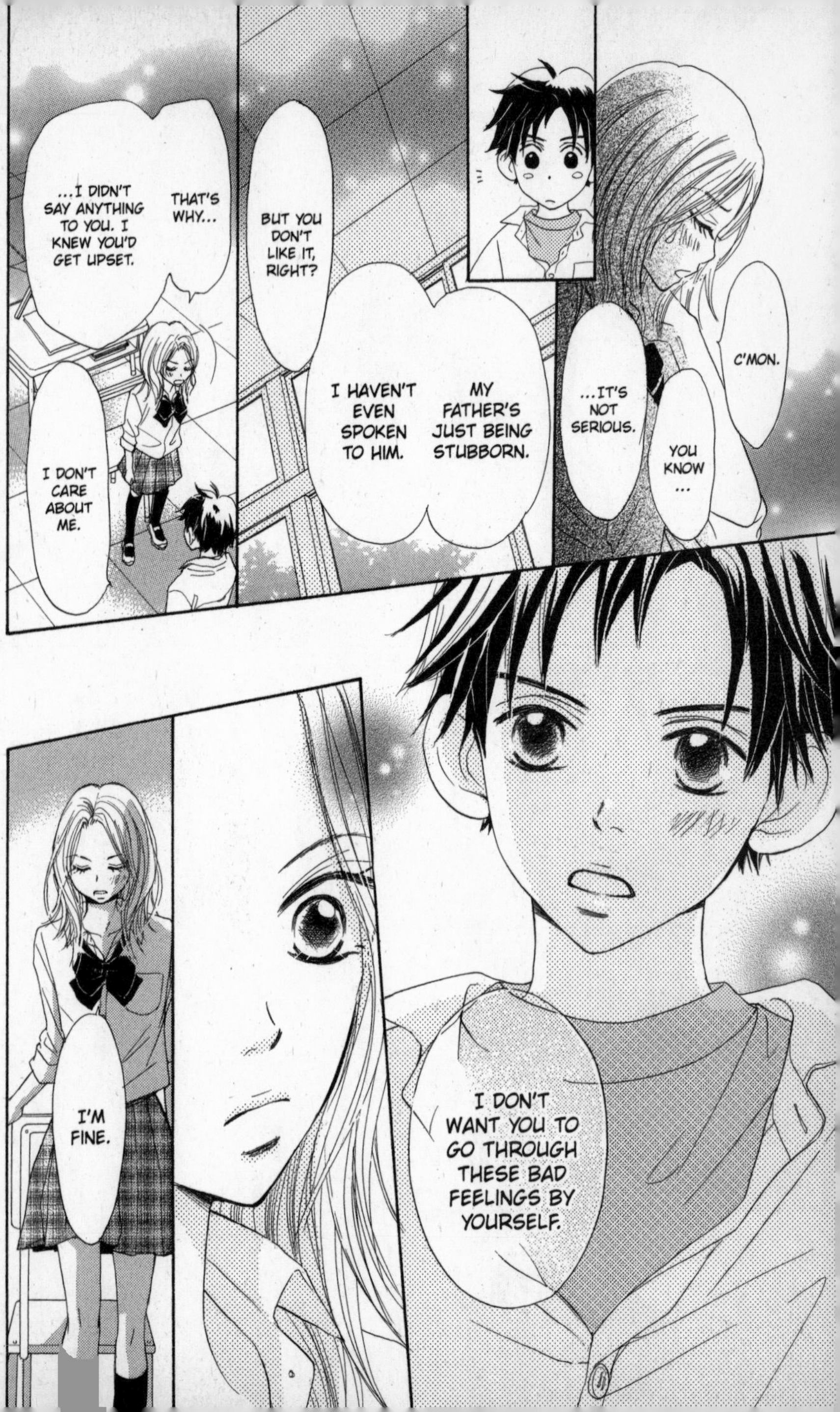
C'MON.
YOU KNOW...
...IT'S NOT SERIOUS.
BUT YOU DON'T LIKE IT, RIGHT?
MY FATHER'S JUST BEING STUBBORN.
I HAVEN'T EVEN SPOKEN TO HIM.
THAT'S WHY...
...I DIDN'T SAY ANYTHING TO YOU. I KNEW YOU'D GET UPSET.
I DON'T CARE ABOUT ME.
I DON'T WANT YOU TO GO THROUGH THESE BAD FEELINGS BY YOURSELF.
I'M FINE.

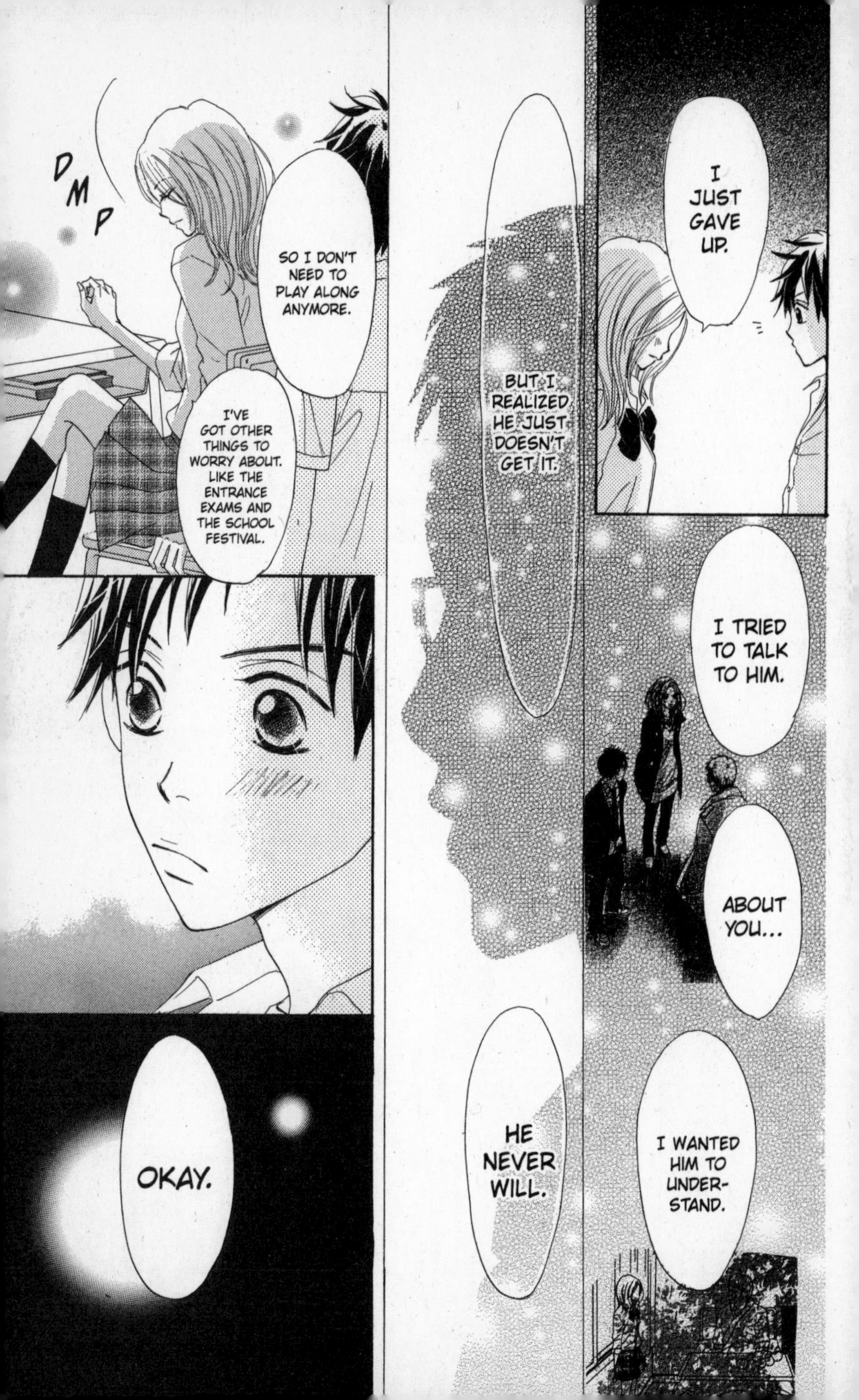

I JUST GAVE UP.
I TRIED TO TALK TO HIM.
ABOUT YOU...
I WANTED HIM TO UNDER-STAND.
BUT I REALIZED HE JUST DOESN'T GET IT.
HE NEVER WILL.
DMP
SO I DON'T NEED TO PLAY ALONG ANYMORE.
I'VE GOT OTHER THINGS TO WORRY ABOUT. LIKE THE ENTRANCE EXAMS AND THE SCHOOL FESTIVAL.
OKAY.

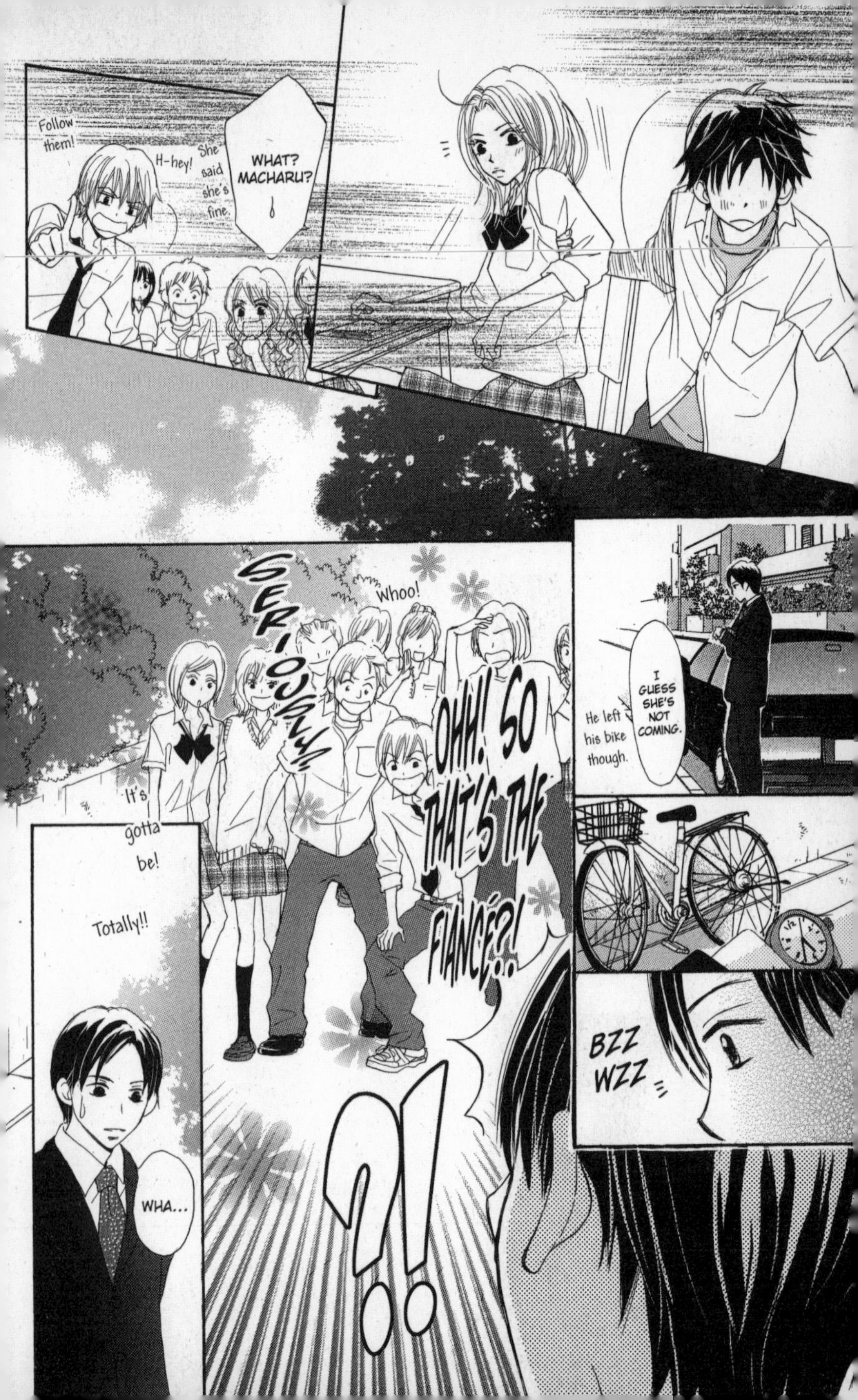
WHAT? MACHARU?
She said she's fine.
H-hey!
Follow them!
I GUESS SHE'S NOT COMING.
He left his bike though.
BZZ WZZ
OHH! SO THAT'S THE FIANCÉ?!
Whoo!
SERIOUSLY?!
It's gotta be!
Totally!!
?!!
WHA...

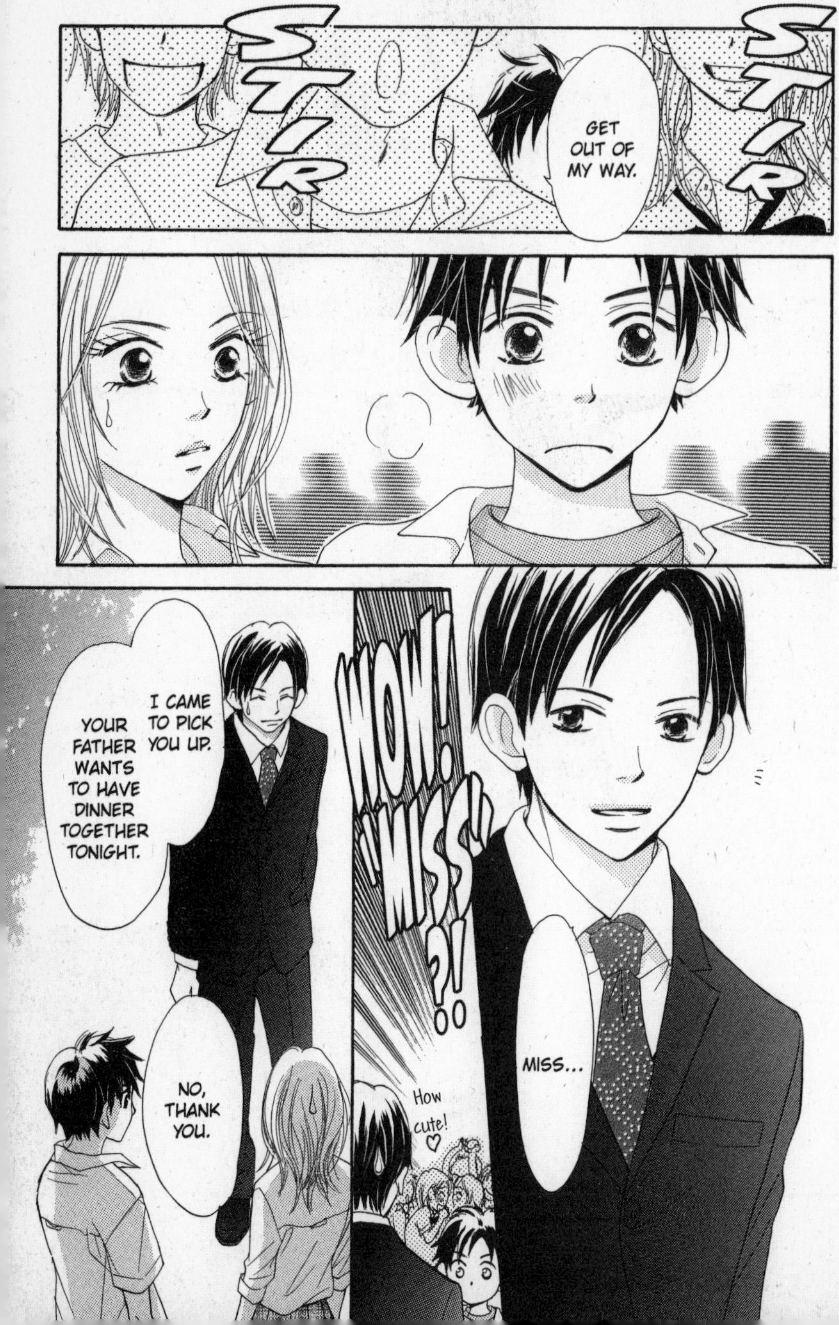
STIR
GET OUT OF MY WAY.
STIR
WOW! "MISS"?!
MISS...
How cute! ♥
I CAME TO PICK YOU UP.
YOUR FATHER WANTS TO HAVE DINNER TOGETHER TONIGHT.
NO, THANK YOU.

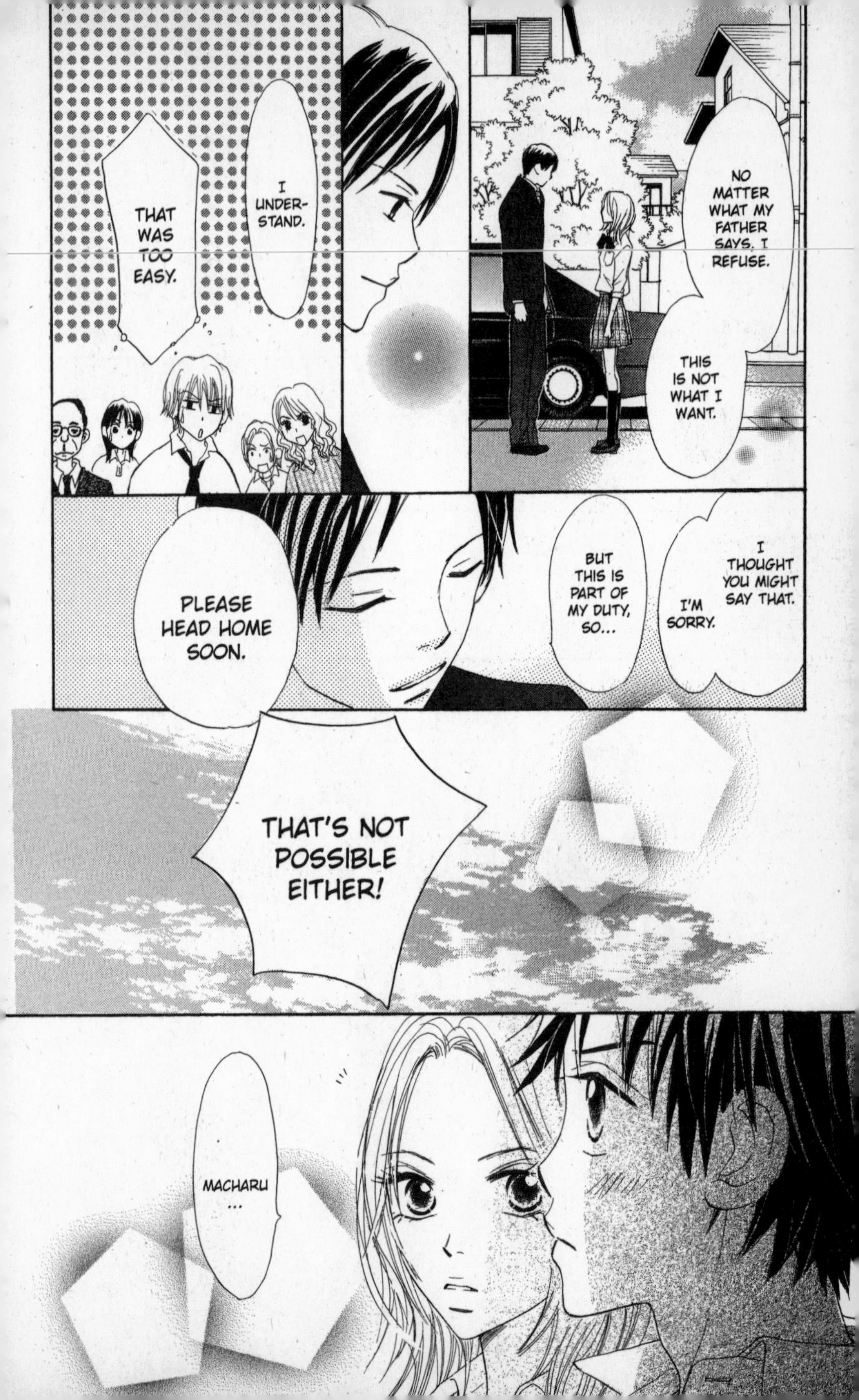
NO MATTER WHAT MY FATHER SAYS. I REFUSE.
THIS IS NOT WHAT I WANT.
I UNDER-STAND.
THAT WAS TOO EASY.
I THOUGHT YOU MIGHT SAY THAT.
I'M SORRY.
BUT THIS IS PART OF MY DUTY, SO...
PLEASE HEAD HOME SOON.
THAT'S NOT POSSIBLE EITHER!
MACHARU ...

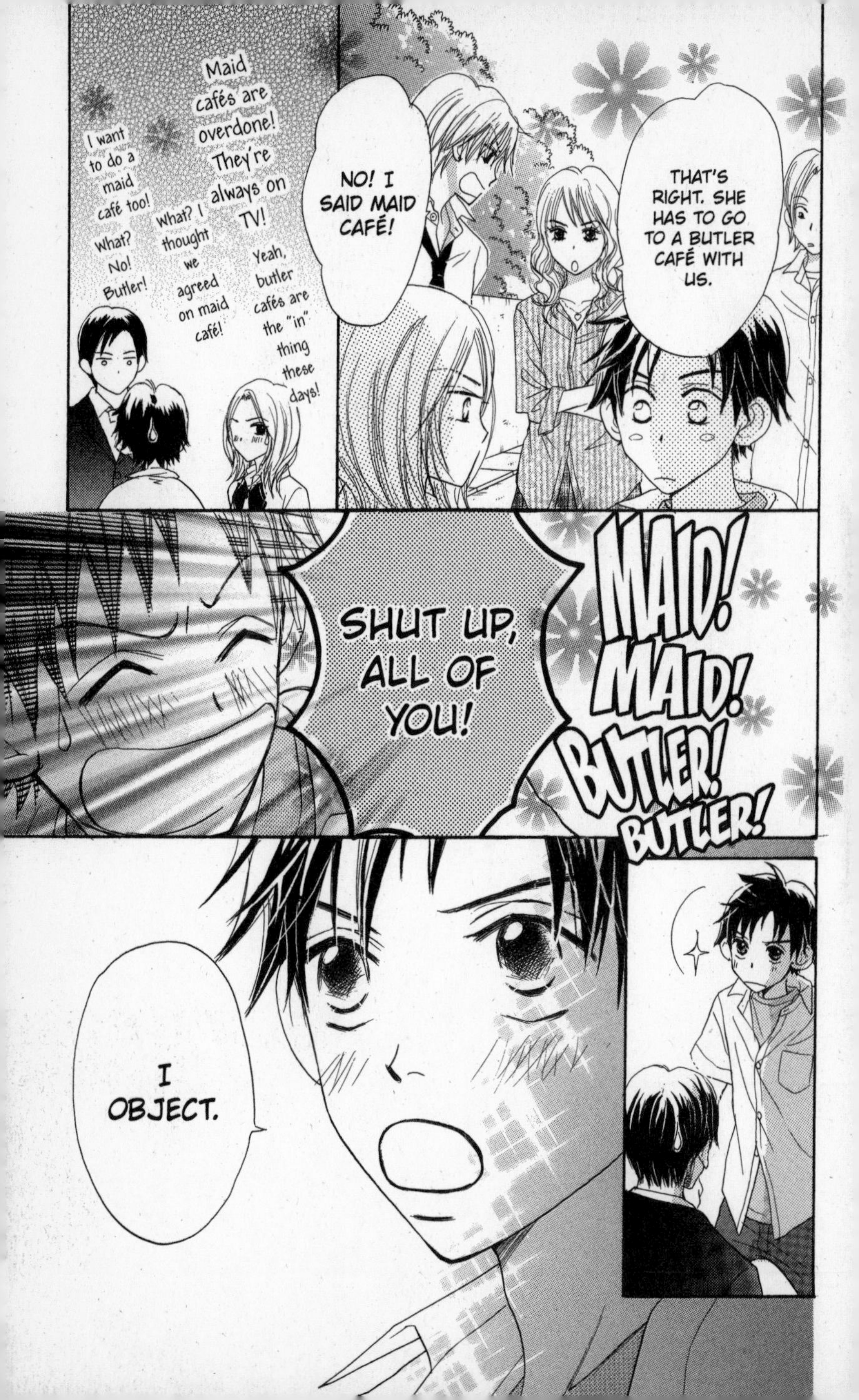
THAT'S RIGHT. SHE HAS TO GO TO A BUTLER CAFÉ WITH US.
NO! I SAID MAID CAFÉ!
Maid cafés are overdone! They're always on TV!
Yeah, butler cafés are the "in" thing these days!
What? I thought we agreed on maid café!
I want to do a maid café too!
What? No! Butler!
MAID! MAID! BUTLER! BUTLER!
SHUT UP, ALL OF YOU!
I OBJECT.

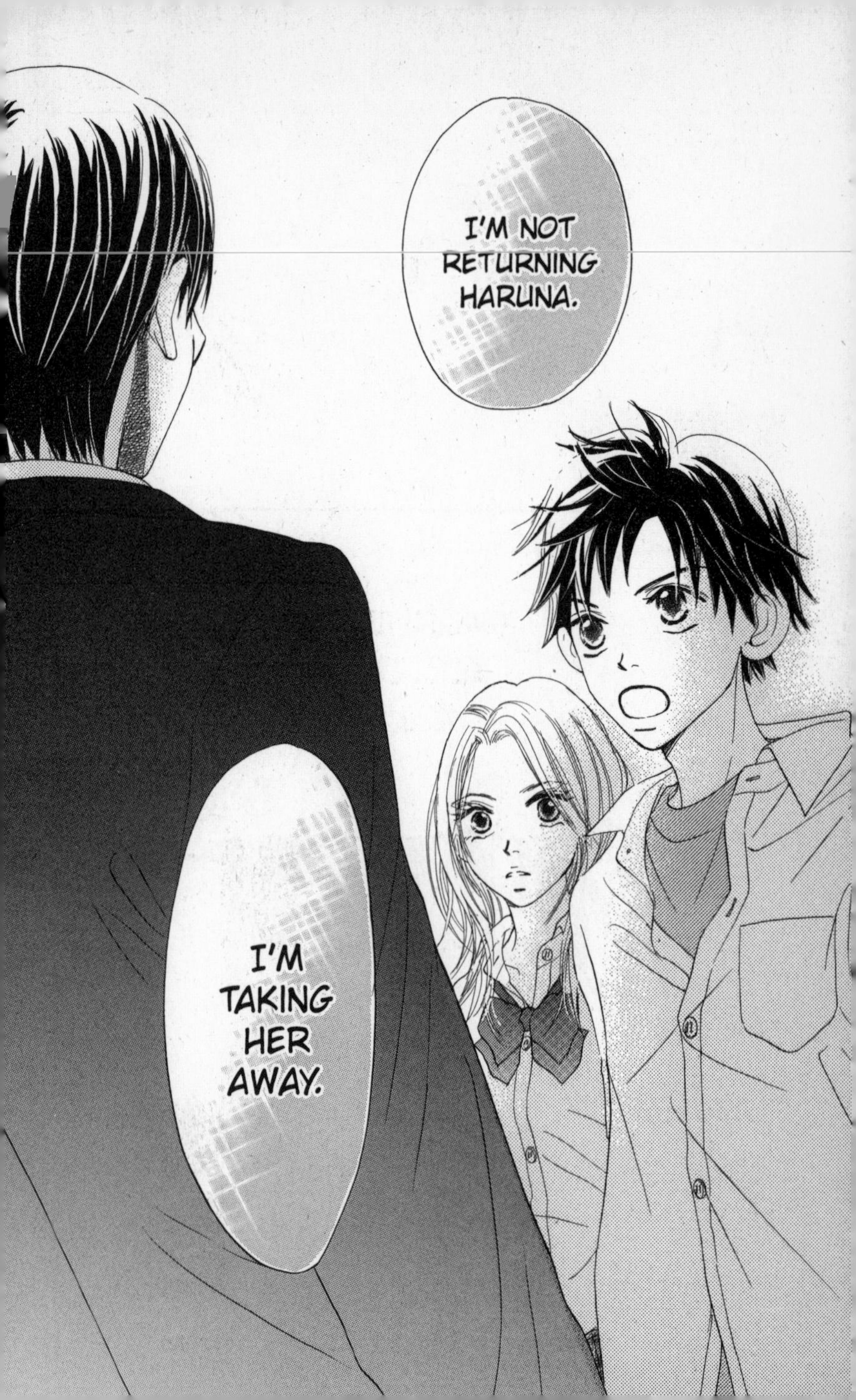
I'M NOT RETURNING HARUNA.
I'M TAKING HER AWAY.

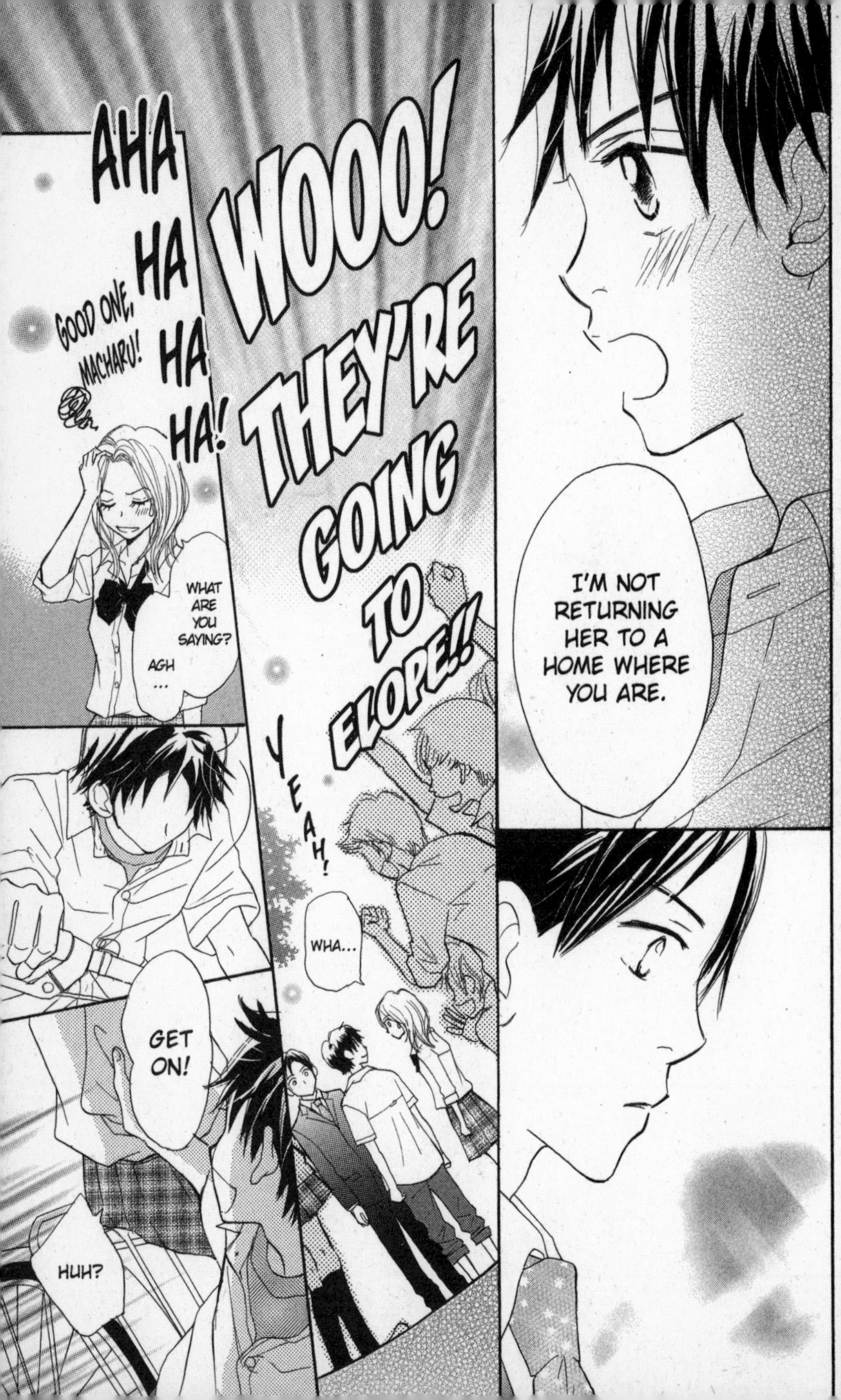
I'M NOT RETURNING HER TO A HOME WHERE YOU ARE.
WOOO! THEY'RE GOING TO ELOPE!!
YEAH!
WHA...
AHA HA HA HA!
GOOD ONE, MACHARU!
WHAT ARE YOU SAYING? AGH...
GET ON!
HUH?

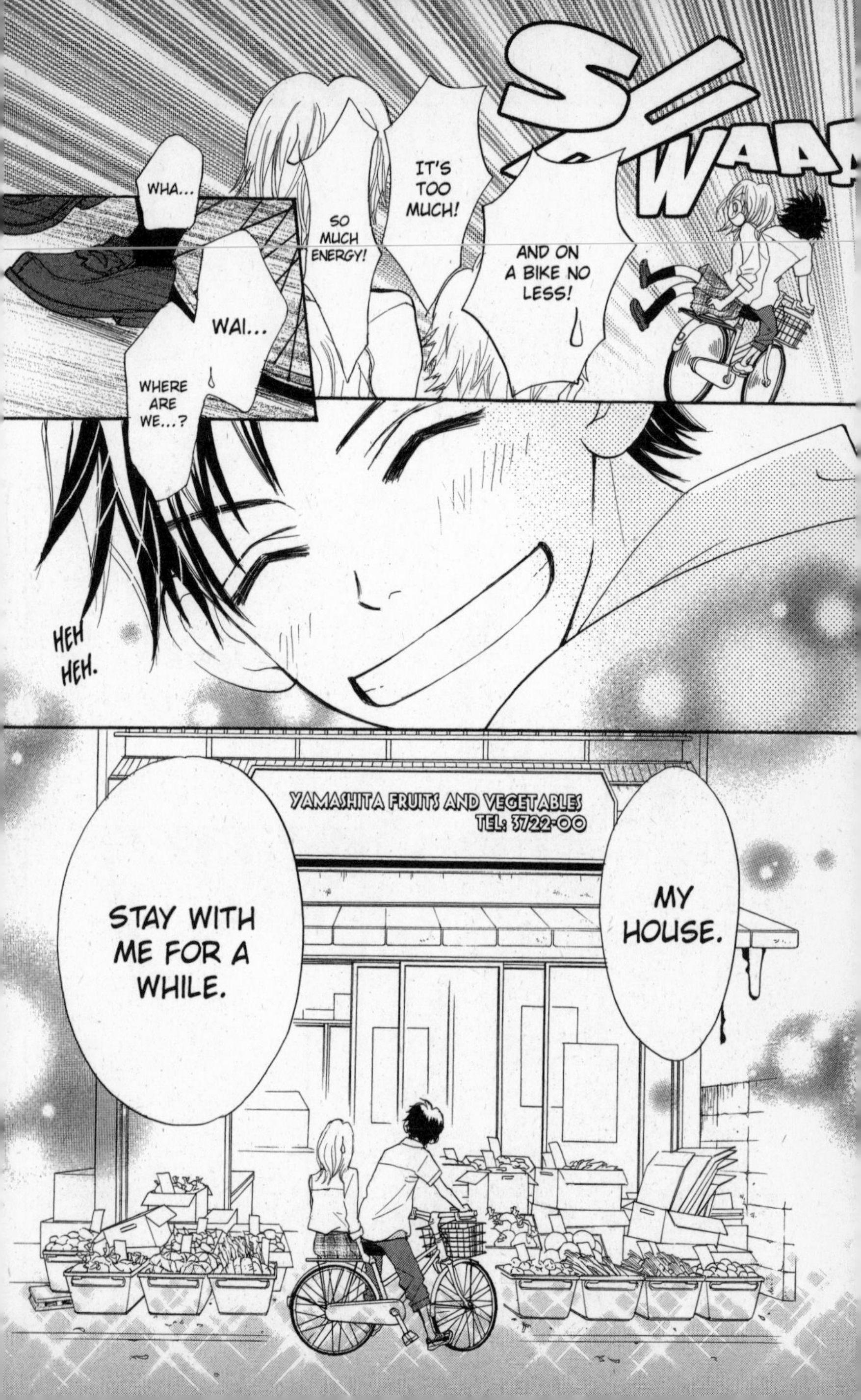
SHWAAA!
AND ON A BIKE NO LESS!
IT'S TOO MUCH!
SO MUCH ENERGY!
WHA...
WAI...
WHERE ARE WE...?
HEH HEH.
YAMASHITA FRUITS AND VEGETABLES
TEL: 3722-00
MY HOUSE.
STAY WITH ME FOR A WHILE.

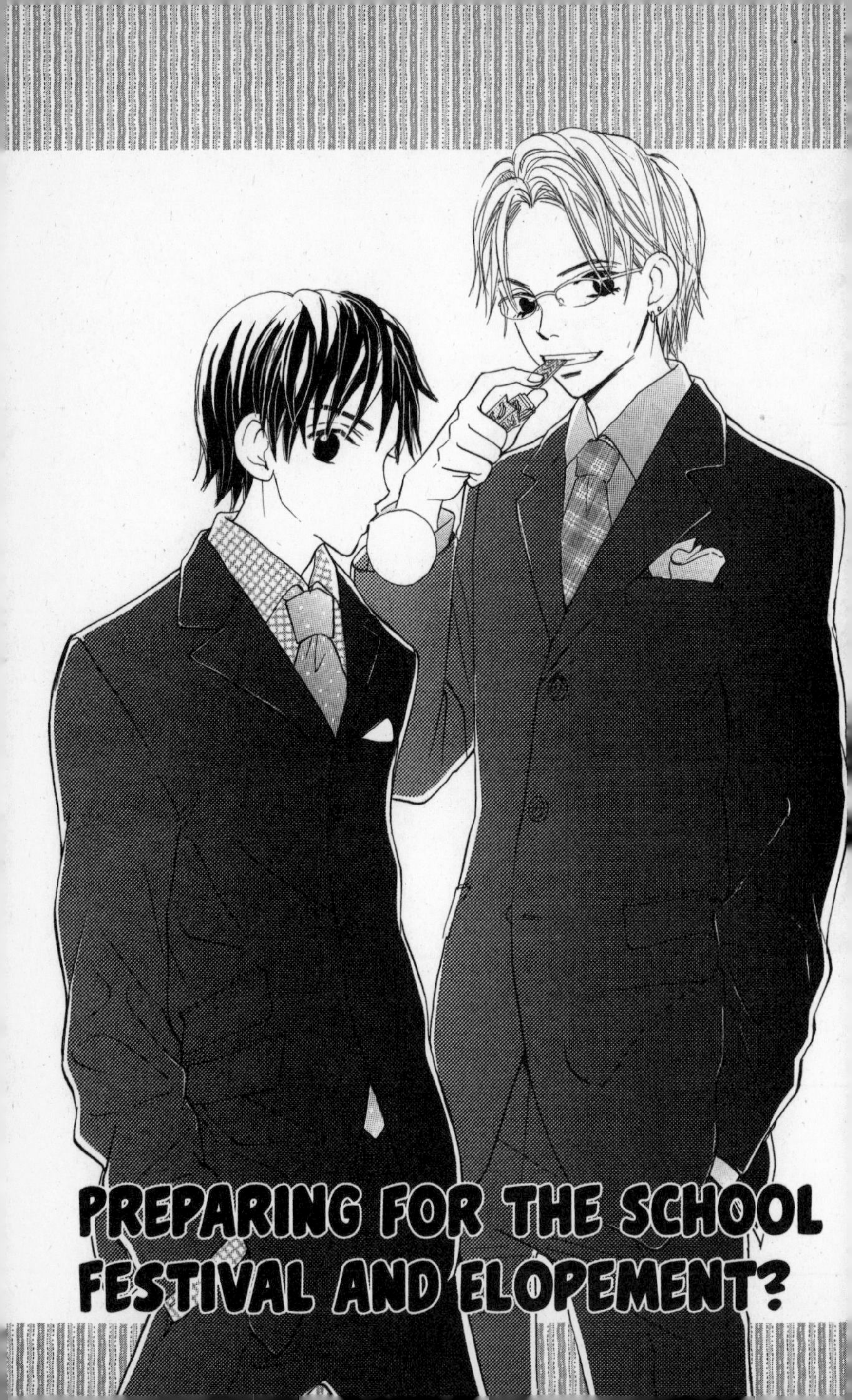

PREPARING FOR THE SCHOOL FESTIVAL AND ELOPEMENT?

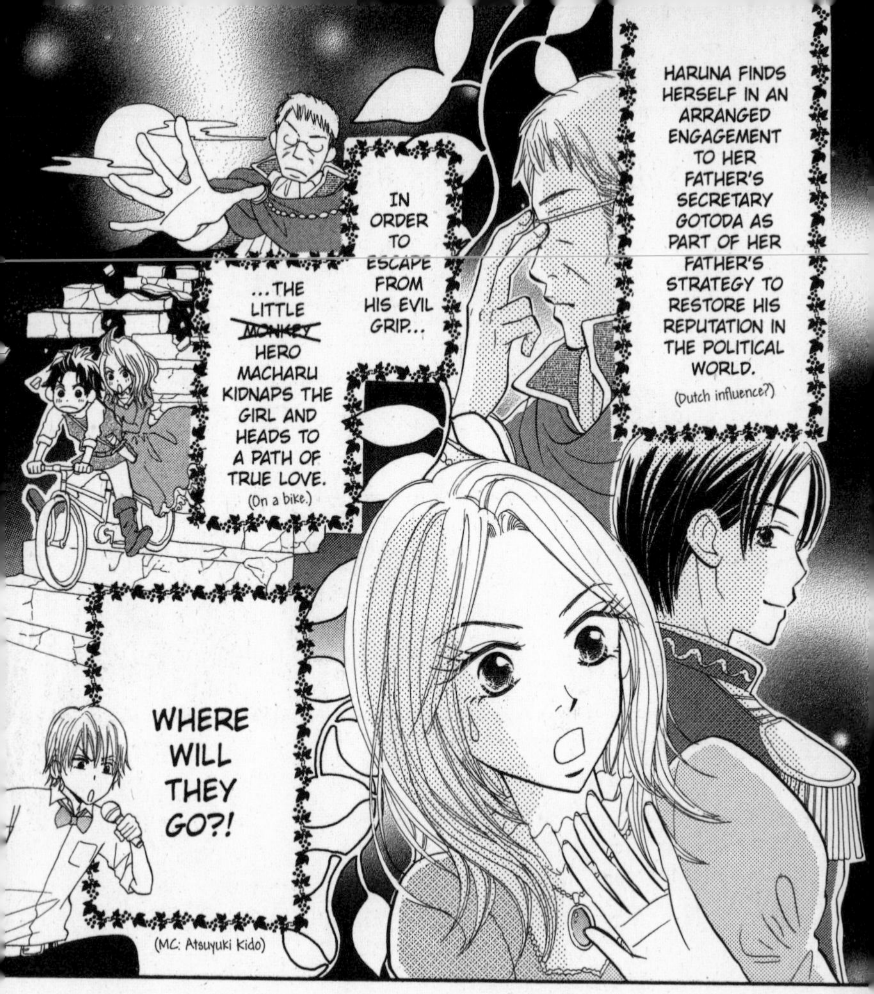
HARUNA FINDS HERSELF IN AN ARRANGED ENGAGEMENT TO HER FATHER'S SECRETARY GOTODA AS PART OF HER FATHER'S STRATEGY TO RESTORE HIS REPUTATION IN THE POLITICAL WORLD.
(Dutch influence?)
IN ORDER TO ESCAPE FROM HIS EVIL GRIP...
...THE LITTLE ~~MONKEY~~ HERO MACHARU KIDNAPS THE GIRL AND HEADS TO A PATH OF TRUE LOVE.
(On a bike.)
WHERE WILL THEY GO?!
(MC: Atsuyuki Kido)

Monkey High!

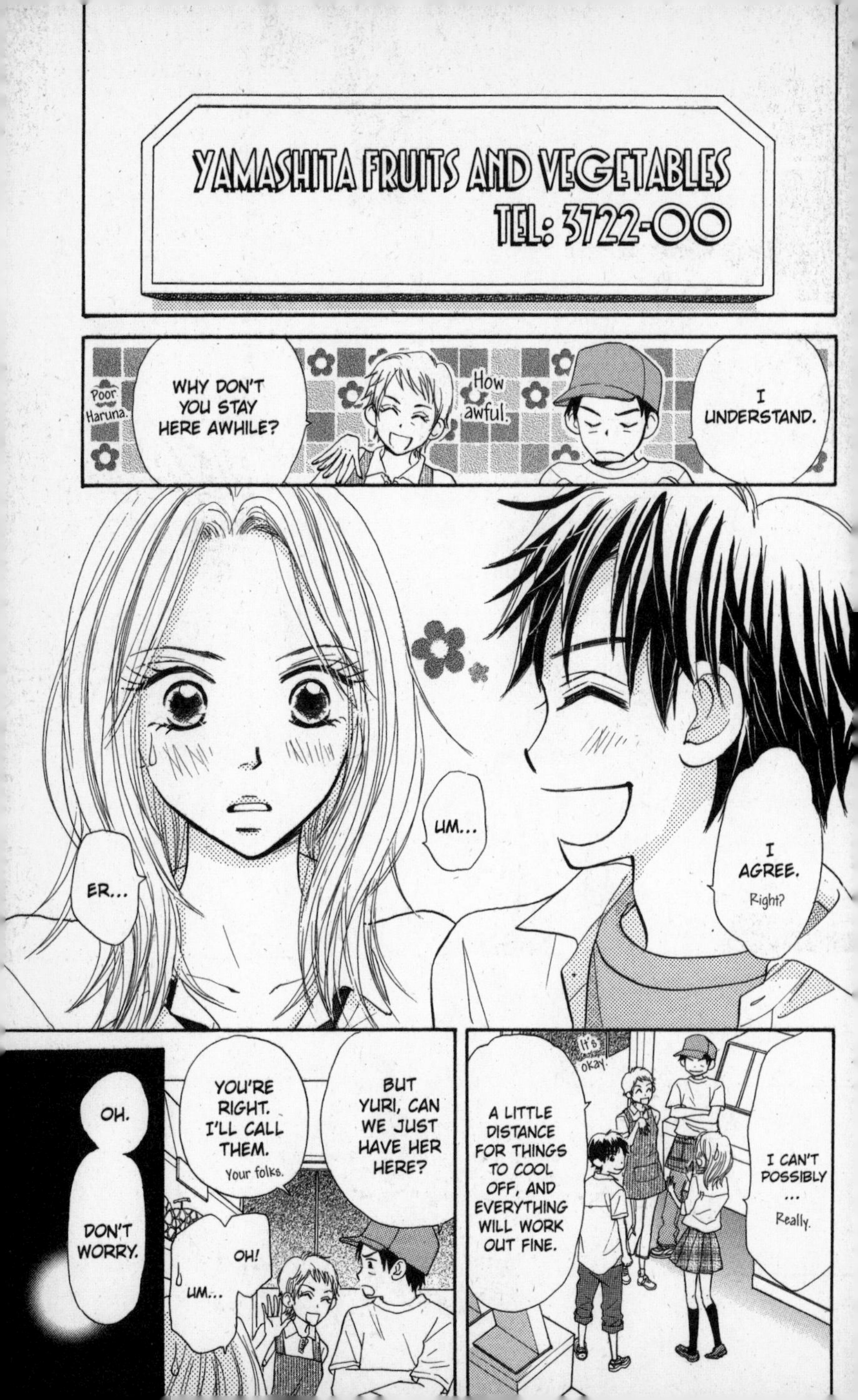
YAMASHITA FRUITS AND VEGETABLES
TEL: 3722-OO
I UNDERSTAND.
How awful.
WHY DON'T YOU STAY HERE AWHILE?
Poor Haruna.
I AGREE.
Right?
UM...
ER...
I CAN'T POSSIBLY...
Really.
A LITTLE DISTANCE FOR THINGS TO COOL OFF, AND EVERYTHING WILL WORK OUT FINE.
It's okay.
BUT YURI, CAN WE JUST HAVE HER HERE?
YOU'RE RIGHT. I'LL CALL THEM.
Your folks.
OH!
UM...
OH.
DON'T WORRY.

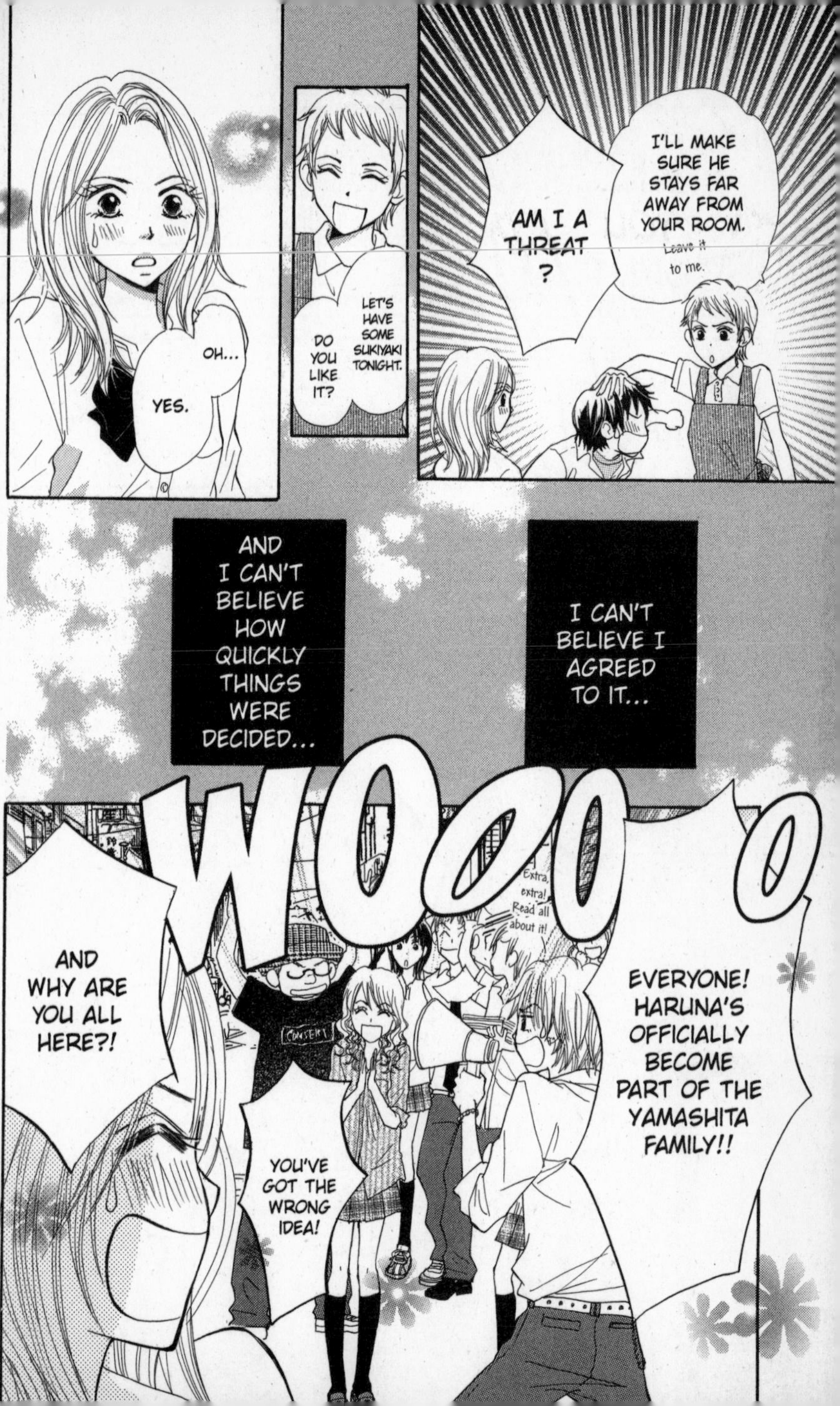
I'LL MAKE SURE HE STAYS FAR AWAY FROM YOUR ROOM.
Leave it to me.
AM I A THREAT ?
LET'S HAVE SOME SUKIYAKI TONIGHT.
DO YOU LIKE IT?
OH...
YES.
I CAN'T BELIEVE I AGREED TO IT...
AND I CAN'T BELIEVE HOW QUICKLY THINGS WERE DECIDED...
WOOO-O
EVERYONE! HARUNA'S OFFICIALLY BECOME PART OF THE YAMASHITA FAMILY!!
Extra, extra! Read all about it!
YOU'VE GOT THE WRONG IDEA!
AND WHY ARE YOU ALL HERE?!

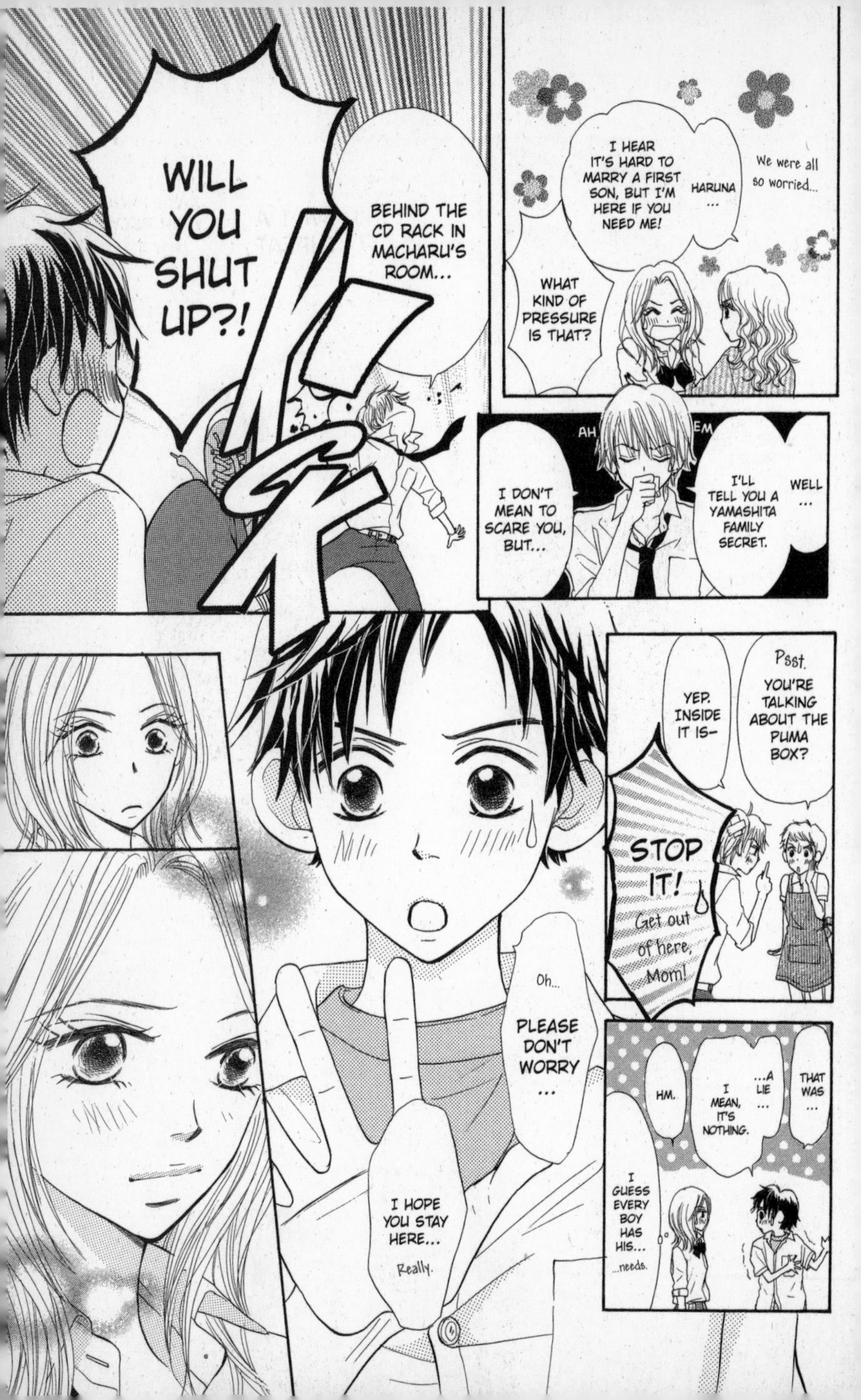
We were all so worried...
HARUNA ...
I HEAR IT'S HARD TO MARRY A FIRST SON, BUT I'M HERE IF YOU NEED ME!
WHAT KIND OF PRESSURE IS THAT?
AH EM
WELL ...
I'LL TELL YOU A YAMASHITA FAMILY SECRET.
I DON'T MEAN TO SCARE YOU, BUT...
BEHIND THE CD RACK IN MACHARU'S ROOM...
WILL YOU SHUT UP?!
Psst.
YOU'RE TALKING ABOUT THE PUMA BOX?
YEP. INSIDE IT IS–
STOP IT!
Get out of here, Mom!
THAT WAS ...
...A LIE ...
I MEAN, IT'S NOTHING.
HM.
I GUESS EVERY BOY HAS HIS...
...needs.
Oh...
PLEASE DON'T WORRY ...
I HOPE YOU STAY HERE...
Really.

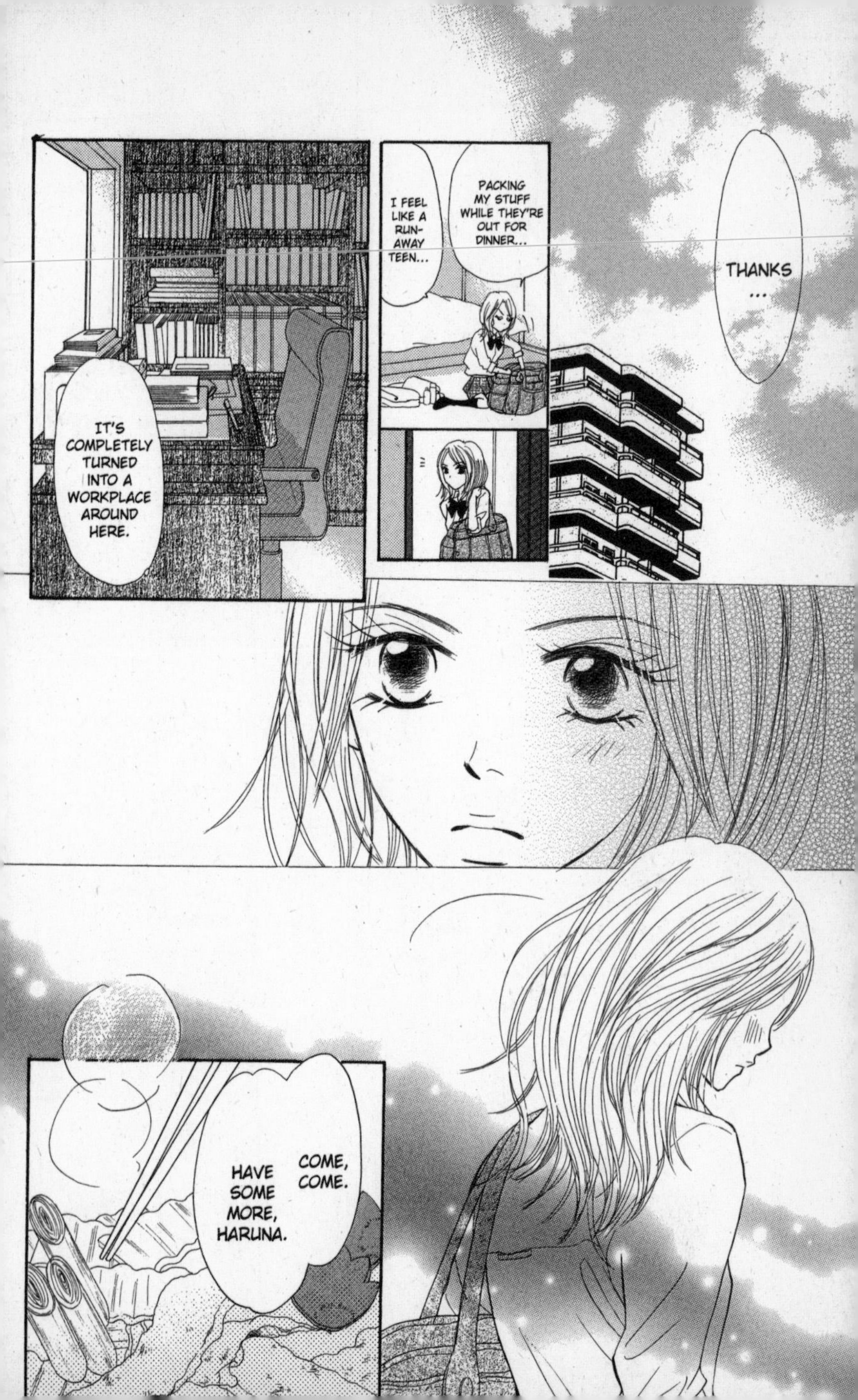
THANKS ...
PACKING MY STUFF WHILE THEY'RE OUT FOR DINNER...
I FEEL LIKE A RUN-AWAY TEEN...
IT'S COMPLETELY TURNED INTO A WORKPLACE AROUND HERE.
COME, COME.
HAVE SOME MORE, HARUNA.

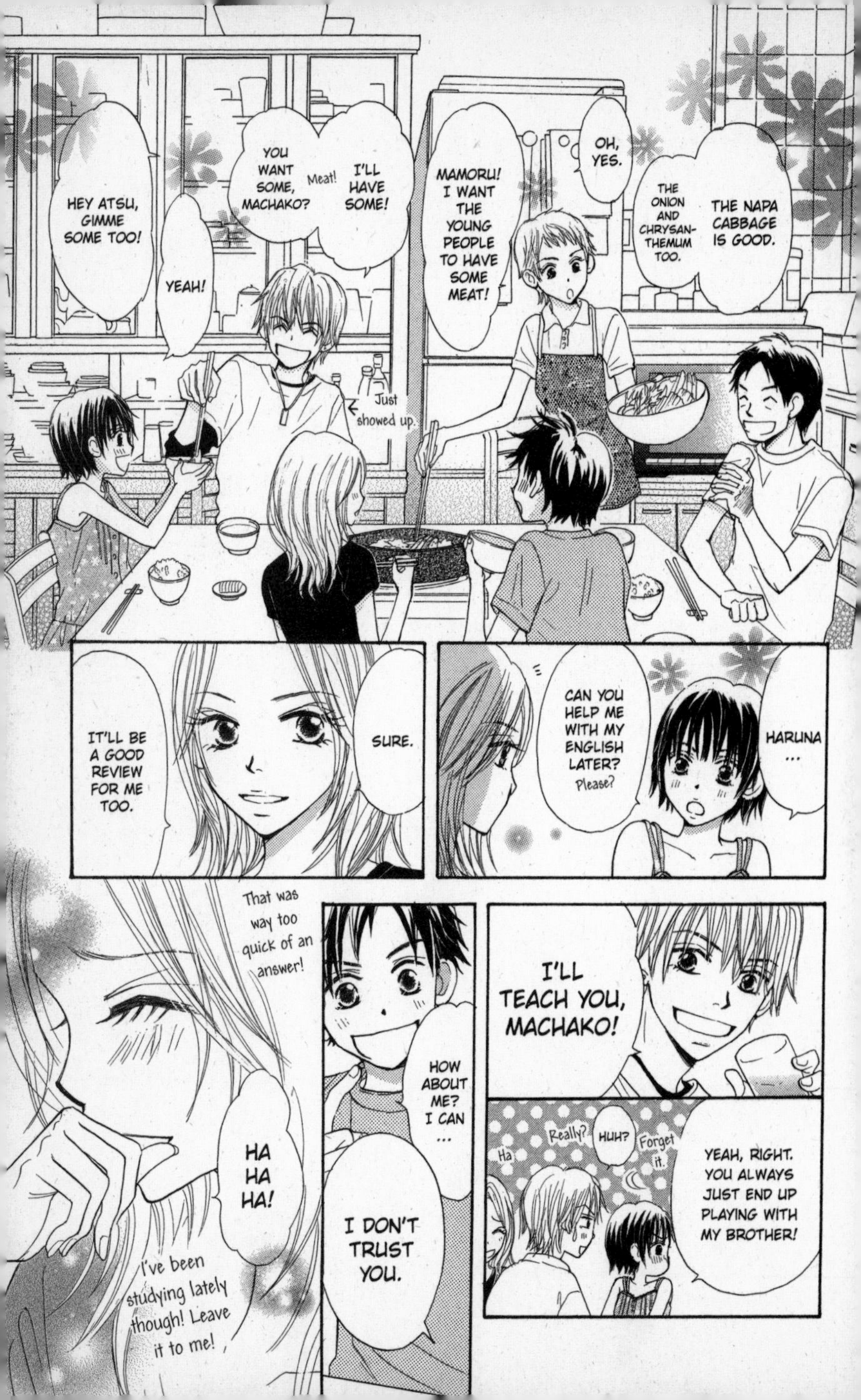
THE NAPA CABBAGE IS GOOD.
THE ONION AND CHRYSAN-THEMUM TOO.
OH, YES.
MAMORU! I WANT THE YOUNG PEOPLE TO HAVE SOME MEAT!
I'LL HAVE SOME!
Meat!
YOU WANT SOME, MACHAKO?
YEAH!
HEY ATSU, GIMME SOME TOO!
Just showed up.
HARUNA ...
CAN YOU HELP ME WITH MY ENGLISH LATER?
Please?
SURE.
IT'LL BE A GOOD REVIEW FOR ME TOO.
I'LL TEACH YOU, MACHAKO!
YEAH, RIGHT. YOU ALWAYS JUST END UP PLAYING WITH MY BROTHER!
Forget it.
HUH?
Really?
Ha
HOW ABOUT ME? I CAN ...
I DON'T TRUST YOU.
That was way too quick of an answer!
HA HA HA!
I've been studying lately though! Leave it to me!

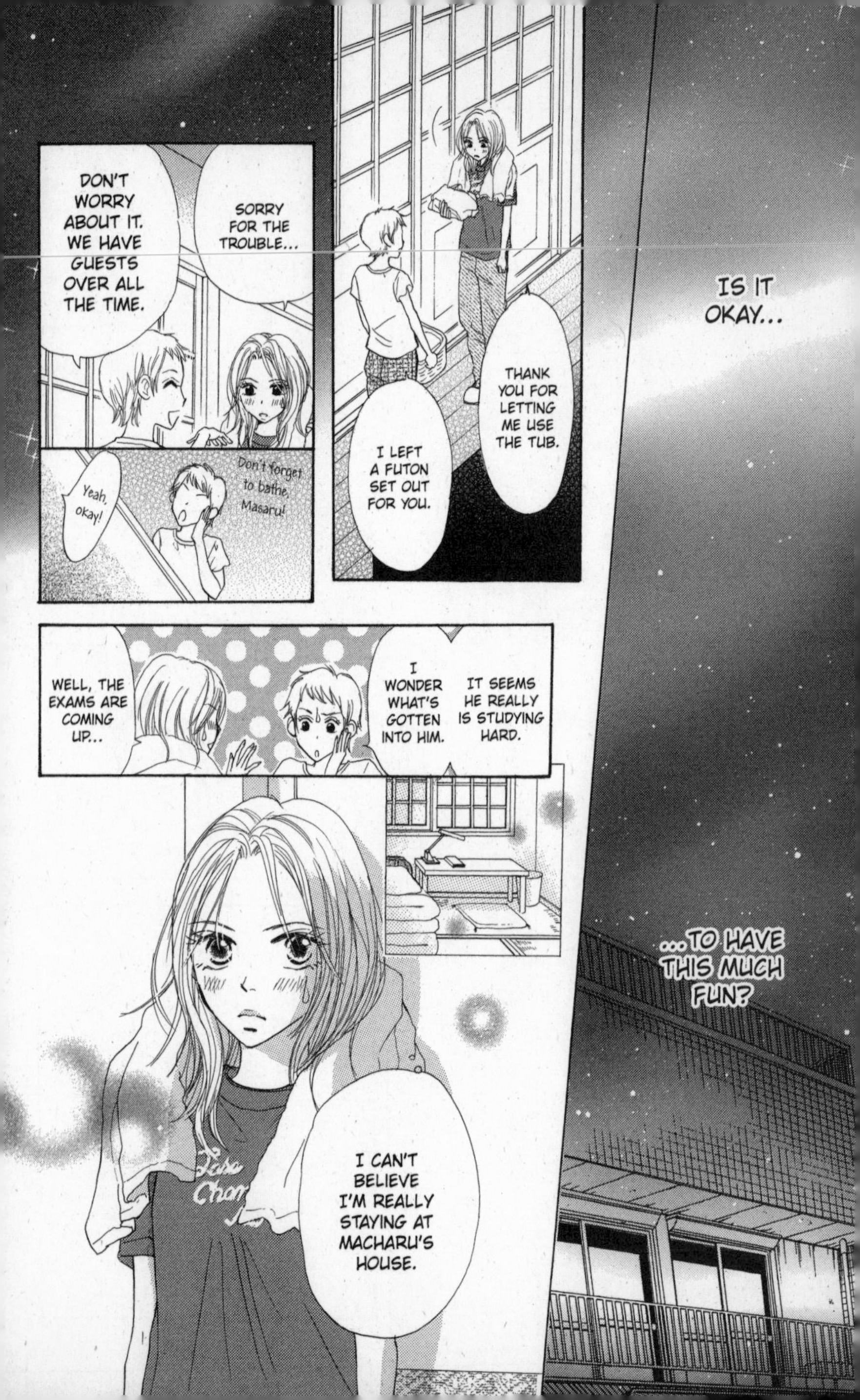
IS IT OKAY...
...TO HAVE THIS MUCH FUN?
THANK YOU FOR LETTING ME USE THE TUB.
I LEFT A FUTON SET OUT FOR YOU.
SORRY FOR THE TROUBLE...
DON'T WORRY ABOUT IT. WE HAVE GUESTS OVER ALL THE TIME.
Don't forget to bathe, Masaru!
Yeah, okay!
IT SEEMS HE REALLY IS STUDYING HARD.
I WONDER WHAT'S GOTTEN INTO HIM.
WELL, THE EXAMS ARE COMING UP...
I CAN'T BELIEVE I'M REALLY STAYING AT MACHARU'S HOUSE.

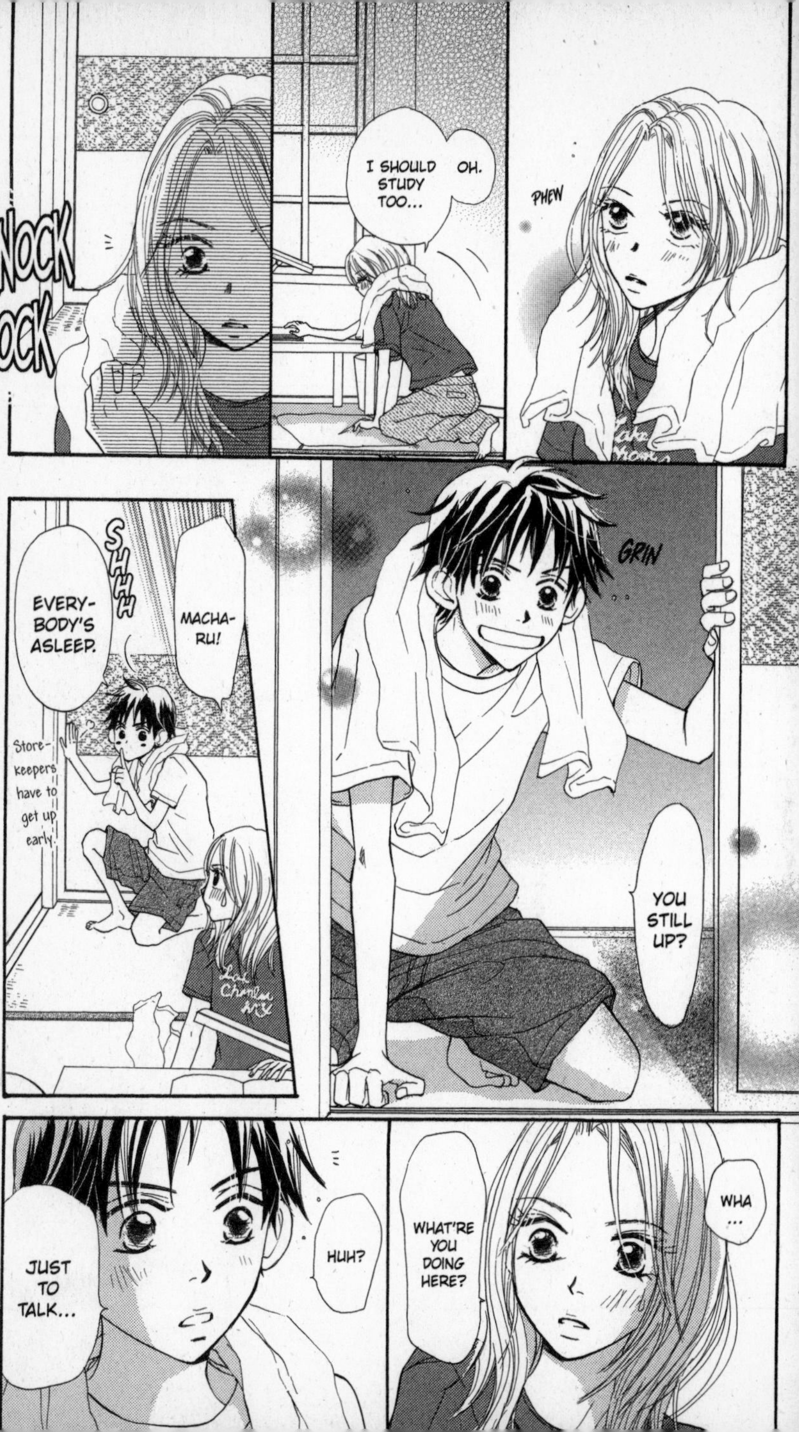
PHEW
OH.
I SHOULD STUDY TOO...
KNOCK KNOCK
GRIN
YOU STILL UP?
MACHA-RU!
EVERY-BODY'S ASLEEP.
SHHH
Store-keepers have to get up early.
WHA...
WHAT'RE YOU DOING HERE?
HUH?
JUST TO TALK...

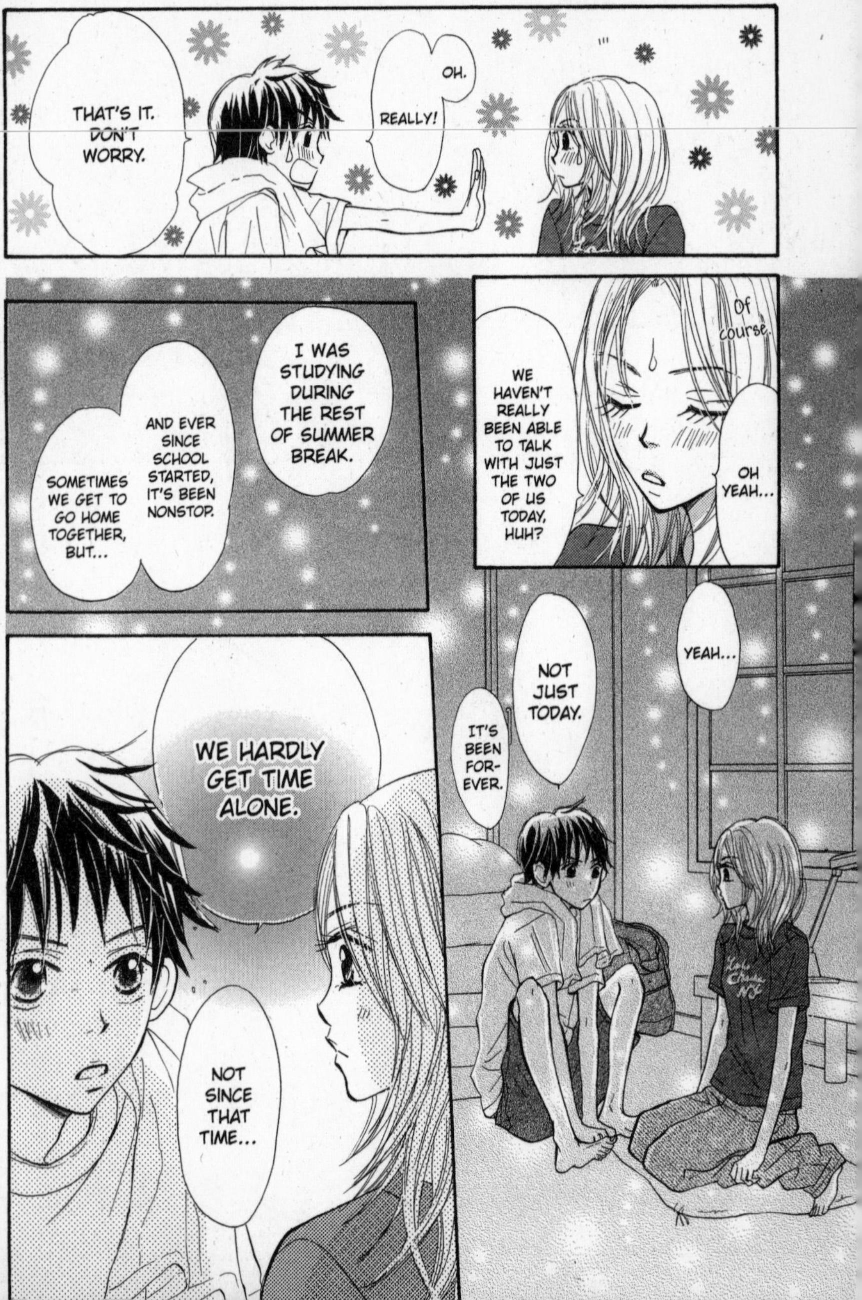
OH.
REALLY!
THAT'S IT. DON'T WORRY.
Of course.
OH YEAH...
WE HAVEN'T REALLY BEEN ABLE TO TALK WITH JUST THE TWO OF US TODAY, HUH?
I WAS STUDYING DURING THE REST OF SUMMER BREAK.
AND EVER SINCE SCHOOL STARTED, IT'S BEEN NONSTOP.
SOMETIMES WE GET TO GO HOME TOGETHER, BUT...
YEAH...
NOT JUST TODAY.
IT'S BEEN FOR-EVER.
WE HARDLY GET TIME ALONE.
NOT SINCE THAT TIME...

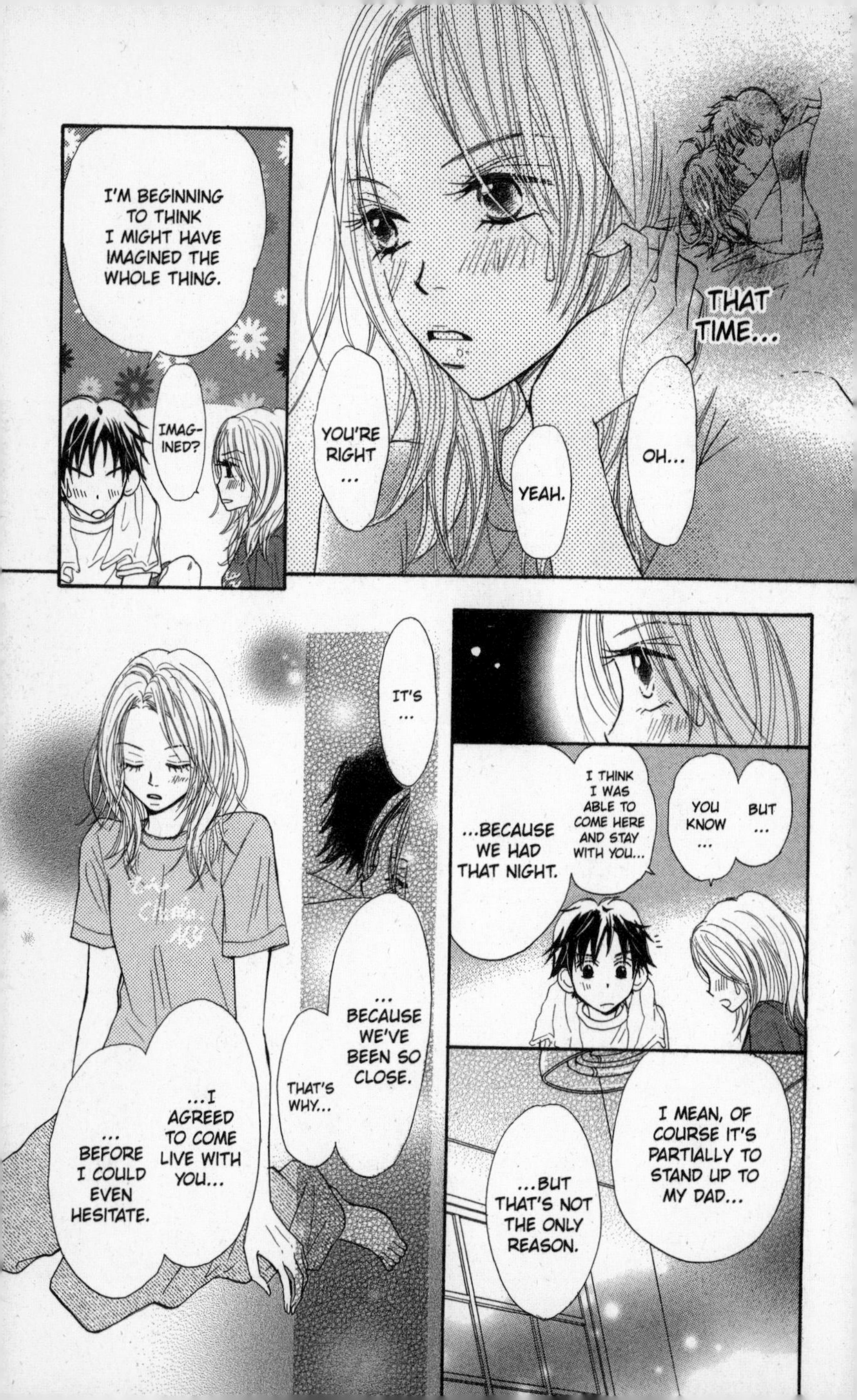
THAT TIME...
OH...
YEAH.
YOU'RE RIGHT...
I'M BEGINNING TO THINK I MIGHT HAVE IMAGINED THE WHOLE THING.
IMAGINED?
BUT...
YOU KNOW...
I THINK I WAS ABLE TO COME HERE AND STAY WITH YOU...
...BECAUSE WE HAD THAT NIGHT.
I MEAN, OF COURSE IT'S PARTIALLY TO STAND UP TO MY DAD...
...BUT THAT'S NOT THE ONLY REASON.
IT'S...
...BECAUSE WE'VE BEEN SO CLOSE.
THAT'S WHY...
...I AGREED TO COME LIVE WITH YOU...
...BEFORE I COULD EVEN HESITATE.

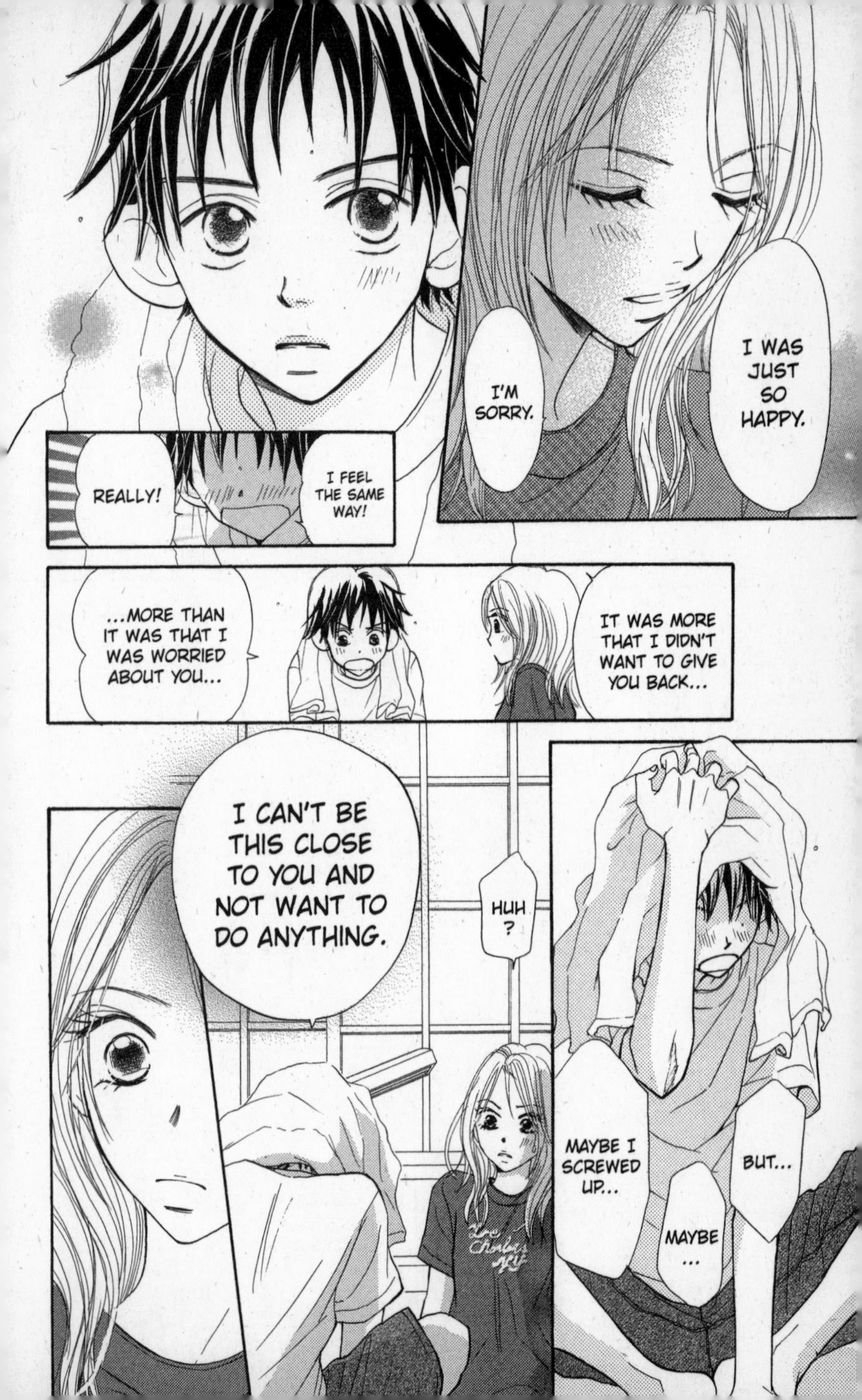
I WAS JUST SO HAPPY.
I'M SORRY.
I FEEL THE SAME WAY!
REALLY!
IT WAS MORE THAT I DIDN'T WANT TO GIVE YOU BACK...
...MORE THAN IT WAS THAT I WAS WORRIED ABOUT YOU...
MAYBE I SCREWED UP...
BUT...
MAYBE ...
I CAN'T BE THIS CLOSE TO YOU AND NOT WANT TO DO ANYTHING.
HUH?

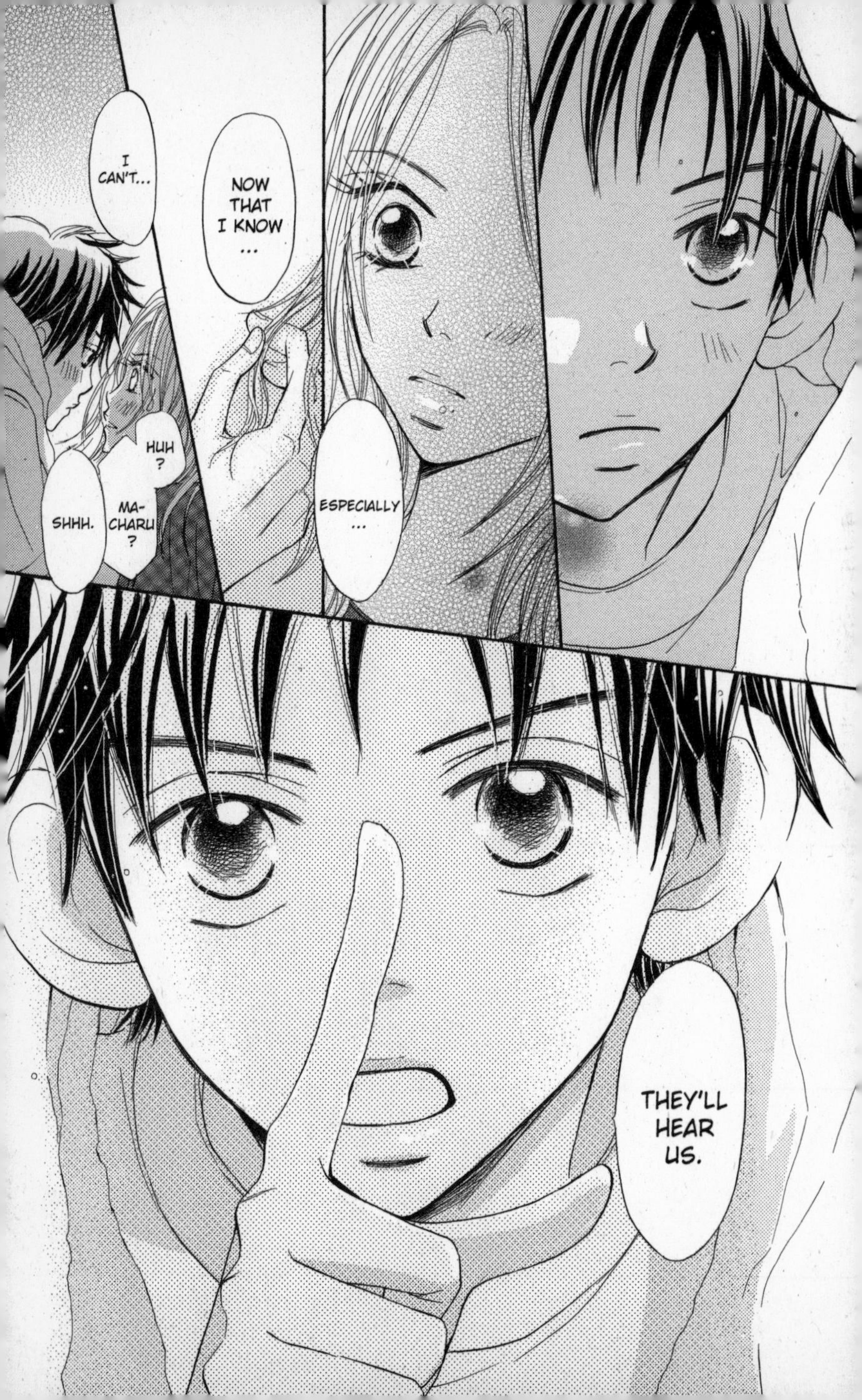
ESPECIALLY ...
NOW THAT I KNOW ...
I CAN'T...
HUH?
MA-CHARU?
SHHH.
THEY'LL HEAR US.

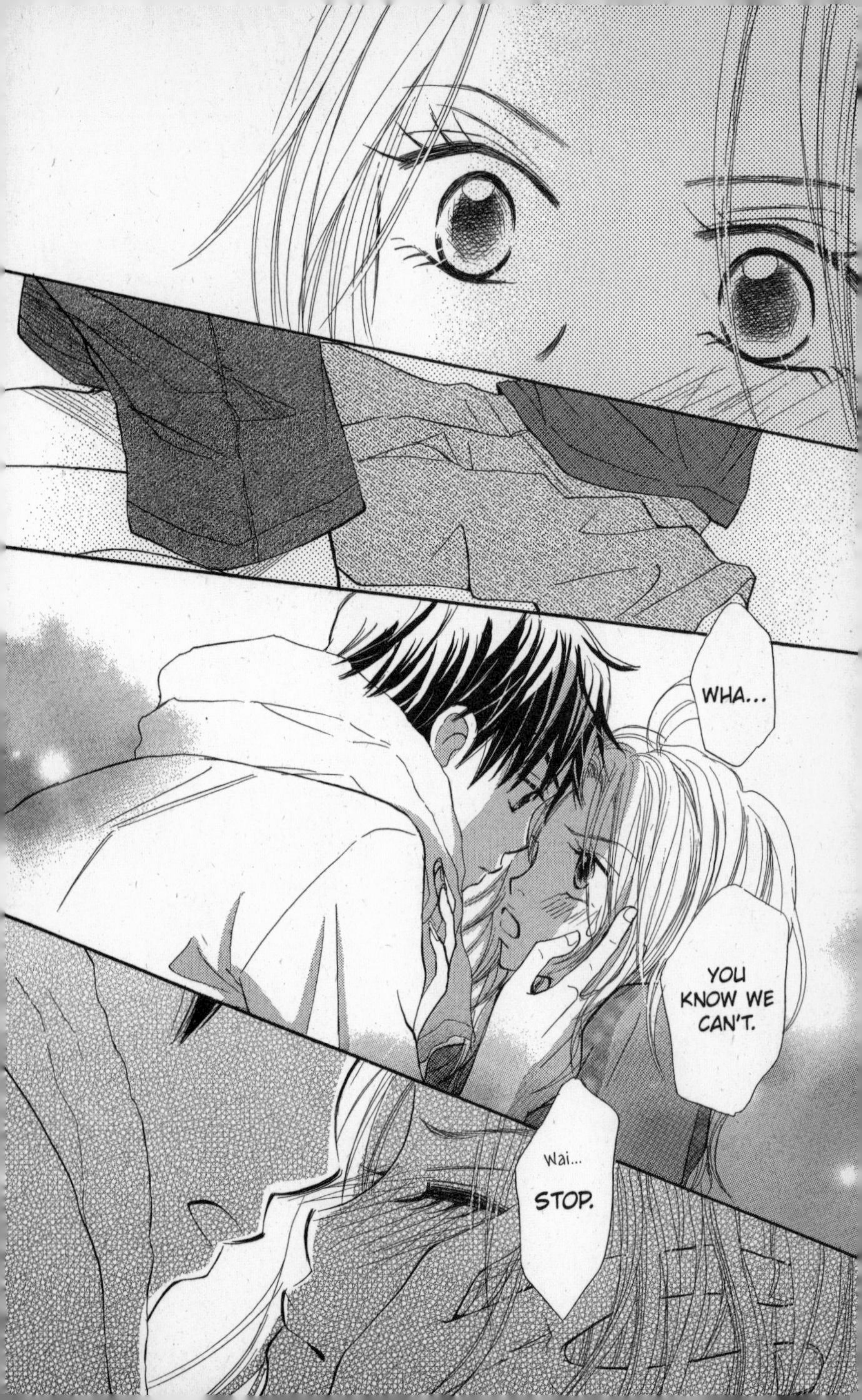
WHA...
YOU KNOW WE CAN'T.
Wai...
STOP.

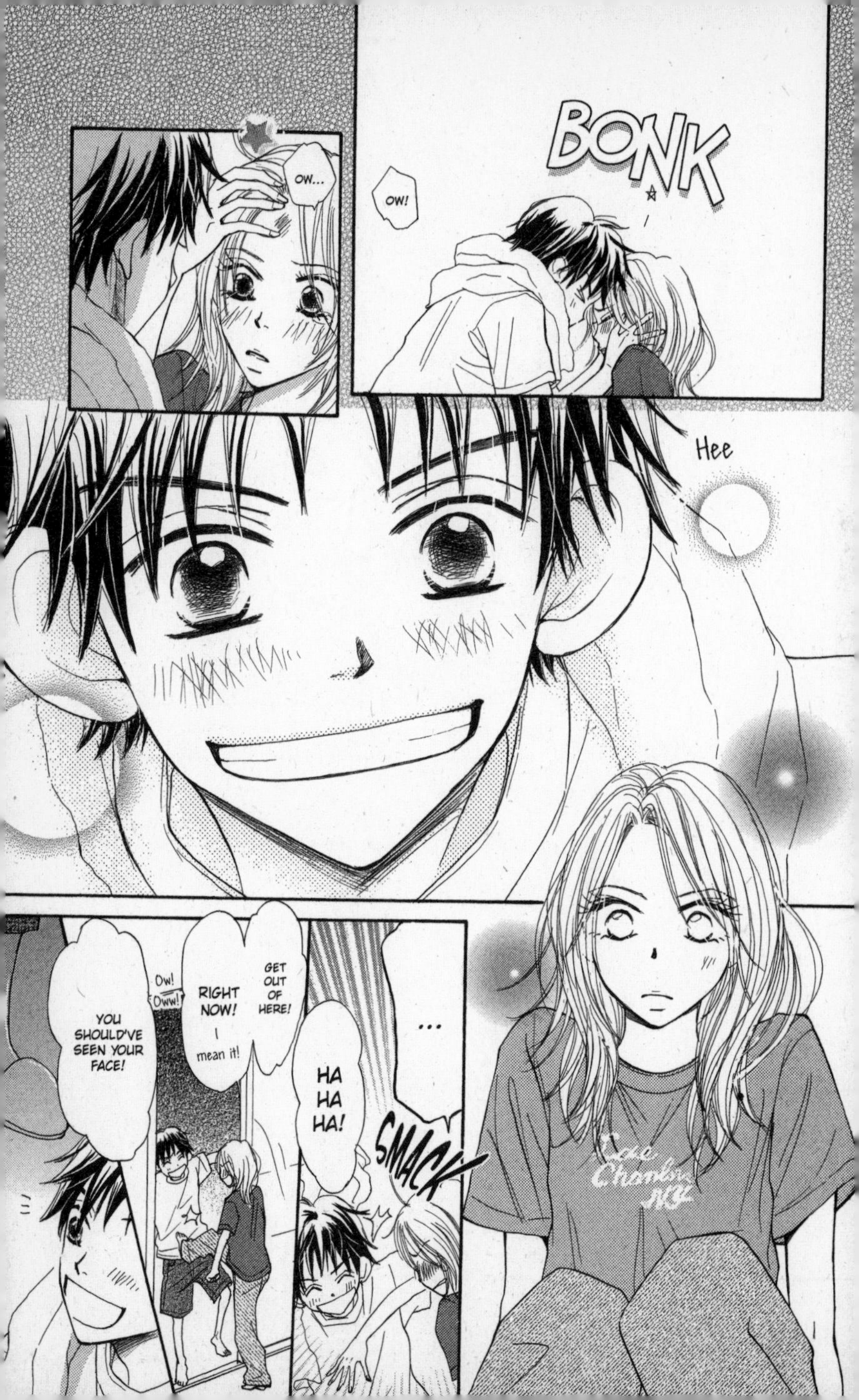
BONK
OW!
OW...
Hee
...
HA HA HA!
SMACK
GET OUT OF HERE!
RIGHT NOW!
I mean it!
Ow!
Oww!
YOU SHOULD'VE SEEN YOUR FACE!

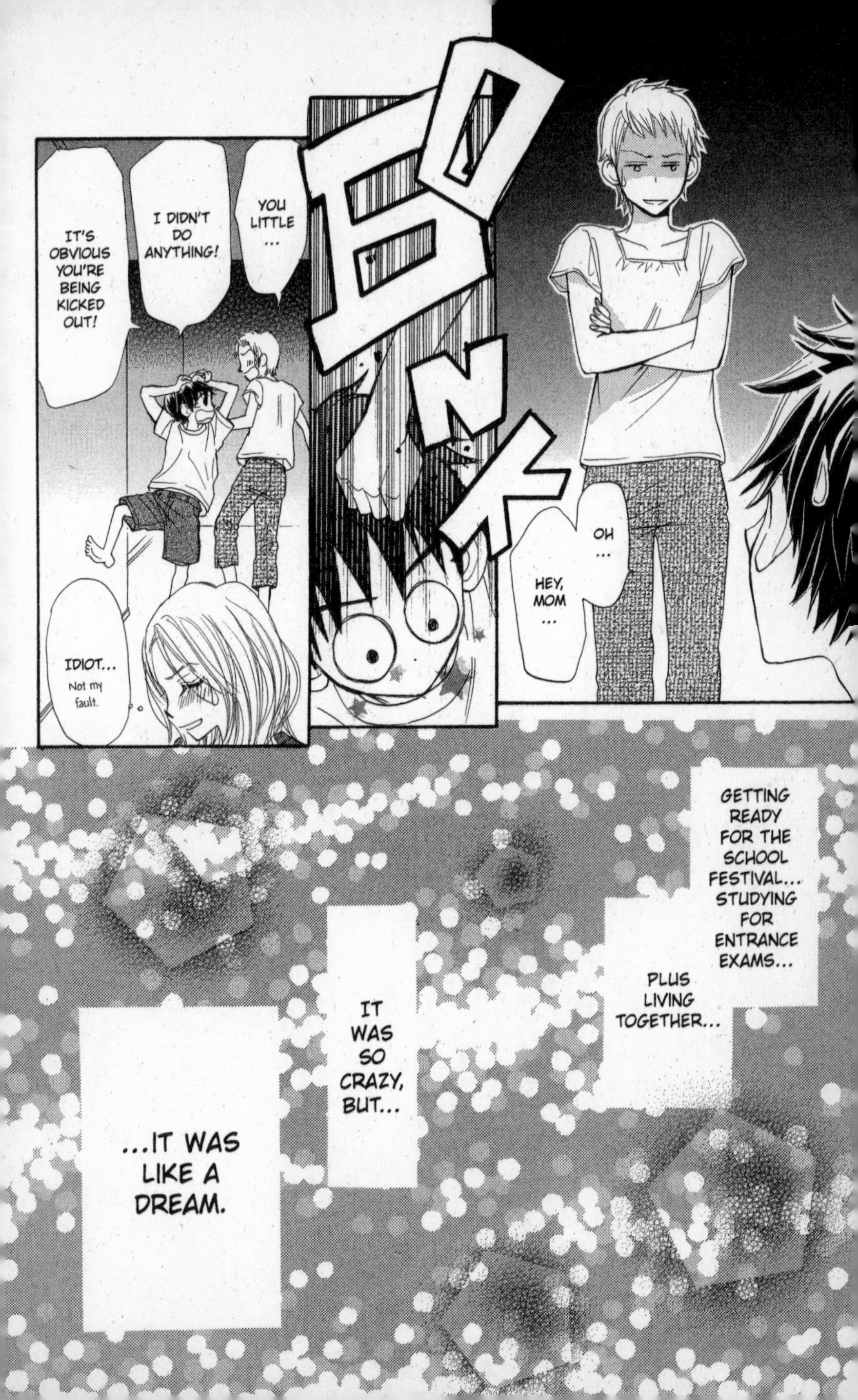
OH... HEY, MOM...
BONK
YOU LITTLE...
I DIDN'T DO ANYTHING!
IT'S OBVIOUS YOU'RE BEING KICKED OUT!
IDIOT...
Not my fault.
GETTING READY FOR THE SCHOOL FESTIVAL... STUDYING FOR ENTRANCE EXAMS...
PLUS LIVING TOGETHER...
IT WAS SO CRAZY, BUT...
...IT WAS LIKE A DREAM.

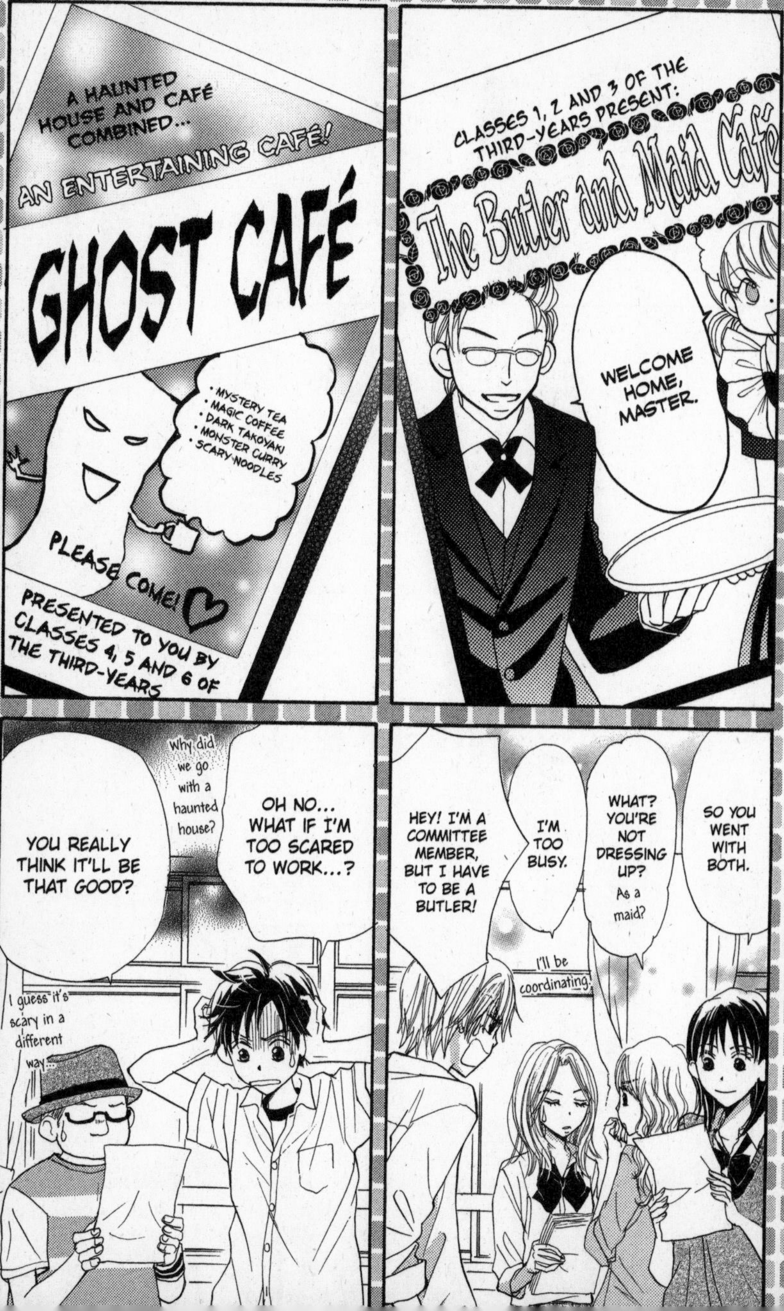

CLASSES 1, 2 AND 3 OF THE THIRD-YEARS PRESENT:
The Butler and Maid Café
WELCOME HOME, MASTER.
A HAUNTED HOUSE AND CAFÉ COMBINED...
AN ENTERTAINING CAFÉ!
GHOST CAFÉ
• MYSTERY TEA • MAGIC COFFEE • DARK TAKOYAKI • MONSTER CURRY • SCARY NOODLES
PLEASE COME! ♡
PRESENTED TO YOU BY CLASSES 4, 5 AND 6 OF THE THIRD-YEARS
SO YOU WENT WITH BOTH.
WHAT? YOU'RE NOT DRESSING UP?
As a maid?
I'M TOO BUSY.
I'll be coordinating.
HEY! I'M A COMMITTEE MEMBER, BUT I HAVE TO BE A BUTLER!
OH NO... WHAT IF I'M TOO SCARED TO WORK...?
Why did we go with a haunted house?
YOU REALLY THINK IT'LL BE THAT GOOD?
I guess it's scary in a different way...

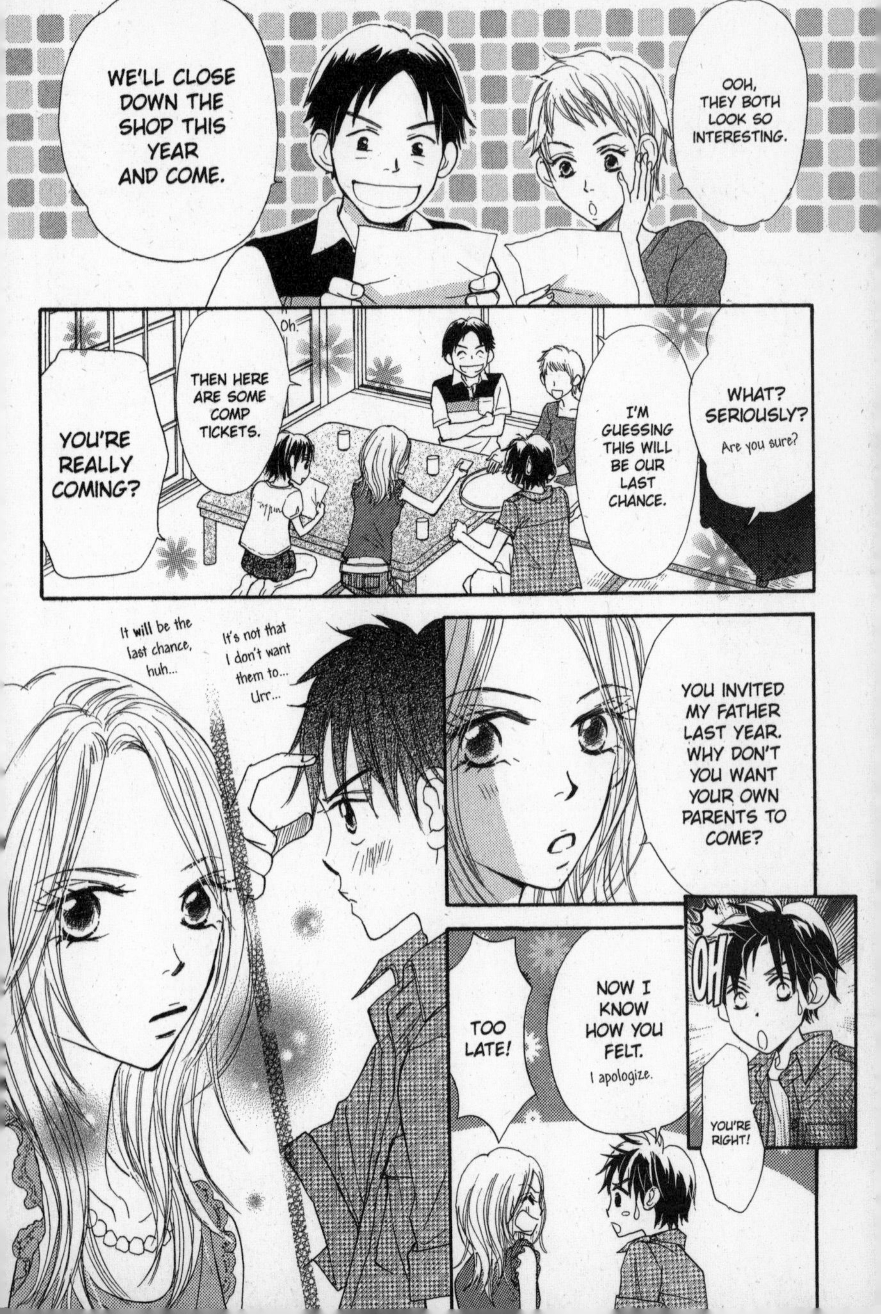
OOH, THEY BOTH LOOK SO INTERESTING.
WE'LL CLOSE DOWN THE SHOP THIS YEAR AND COME.
WHAT? SERIOUSLY?
Are you sure?
I'M GUESSING THIS WILL BE OUR LAST CHANCE.
Oh.
THEN HERE ARE SOME COMP TICKETS.
YOU'RE REALLY COMING?
YOU INVITED MY FATHER LAST YEAR. WHY DON'T YOU WANT YOUR OWN PARENTS TO COME?
OH
YOU'RE RIGHT!
NOW I KNOW HOW YOU FELT.
I apologize.
TOO LATE!
It's not that I don't want them to... Urr...
It will be the last chance, huh...

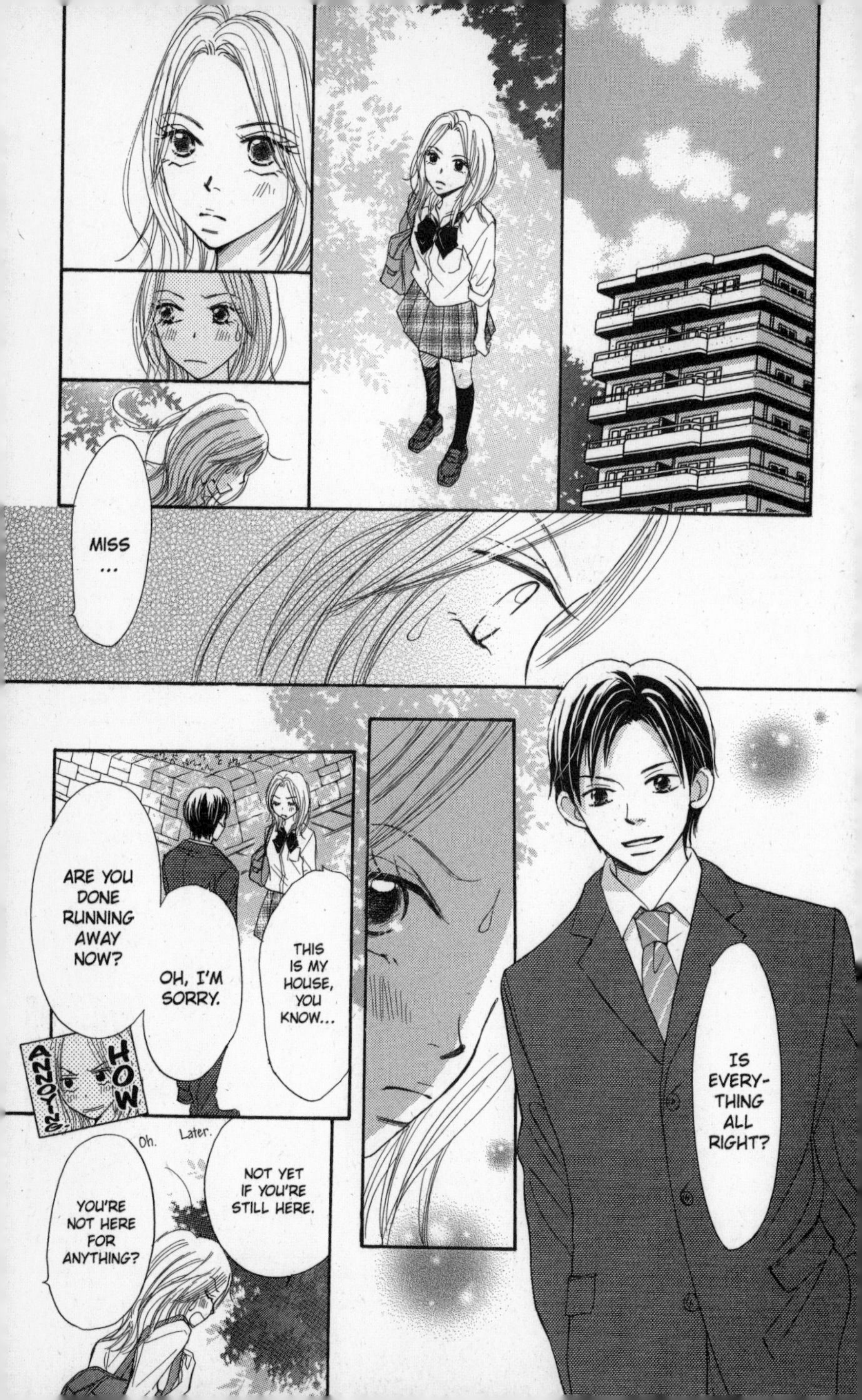
MISS...
IS EVERY-THING ALL RIGHT?
THIS IS MY HOUSE, YOU KNOW...
OH, I'M SORRY.
ARE YOU DONE RUNNING AWAY NOW?
HOW ANNOYING
Later.
NOT YET IF YOU'RE STILL HERE.
Oh.
YOU'RE NOT HERE FOR ANYTHING?

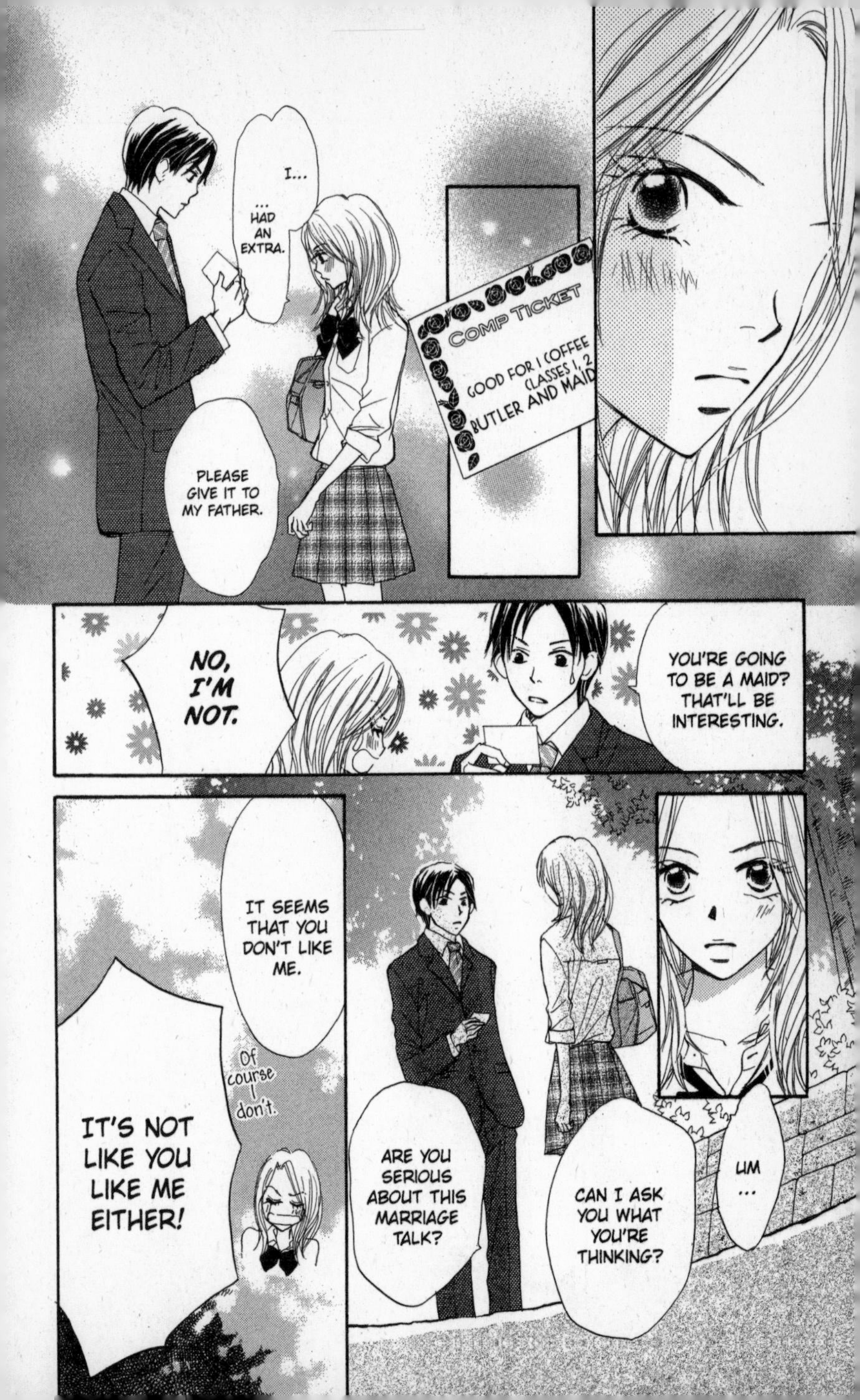
COMP TICKET
GOOD FOR 1 COFFEE
CLASSES 1, 2
BUTLER AND MAID
I...
...HAD AN EXTRA.
PLEASE GIVE IT TO MY FATHER.
YOU'RE GOING TO BE A MAID? THAT'LL BE INTERESTING.
NO, I'M NOT.
UM ...
CAN I ASK YOU WHAT YOU'RE THINKING?
ARE YOU SERIOUS ABOUT THIS MARRIAGE TALK?
IT SEEMS THAT YOU DON'T LIKE ME.
Of course I don't.
IT'S NOT LIKE YOU LIKE ME EITHER!

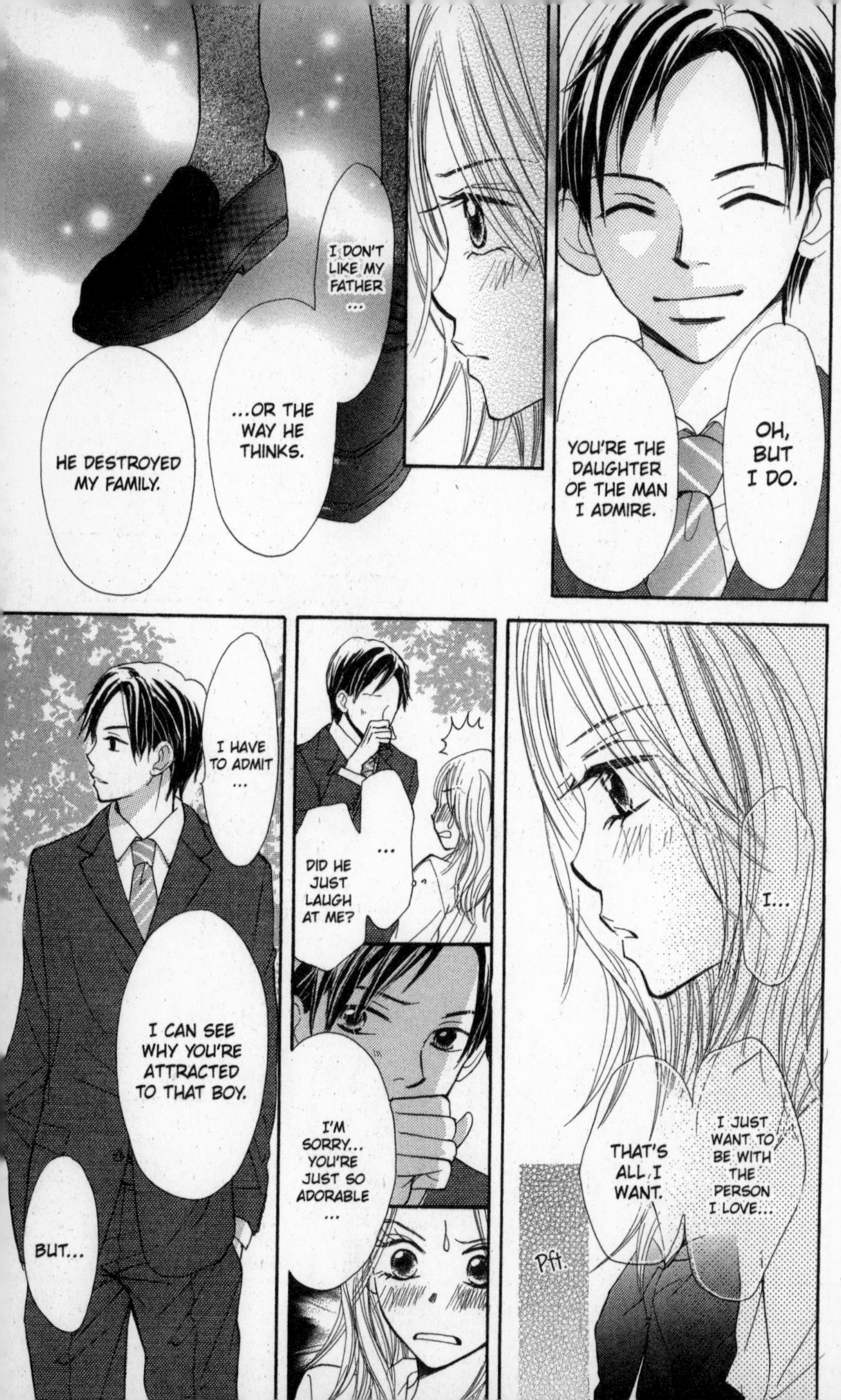
OH, BUT I DO.
YOU'RE THE DAUGHTER OF THE MAN I ADMIRE.
I DON'T LIKE MY FATHER...
...OR THE WAY HE THINKS.
HE DESTROYED MY FAMILY.
I...
I JUST WANT TO BE WITH THE PERSON I LOVE...
THAT'S ALL I WANT.
Pft.
...
DID HE JUST LAUGH AT ME?
I'M SORRY... YOU'RE JUST SO ADORABLE...
I HAVE TO ADMIT...
I CAN SEE WHY YOU'RE ATTRACTED TO THAT BOY.
BUT...

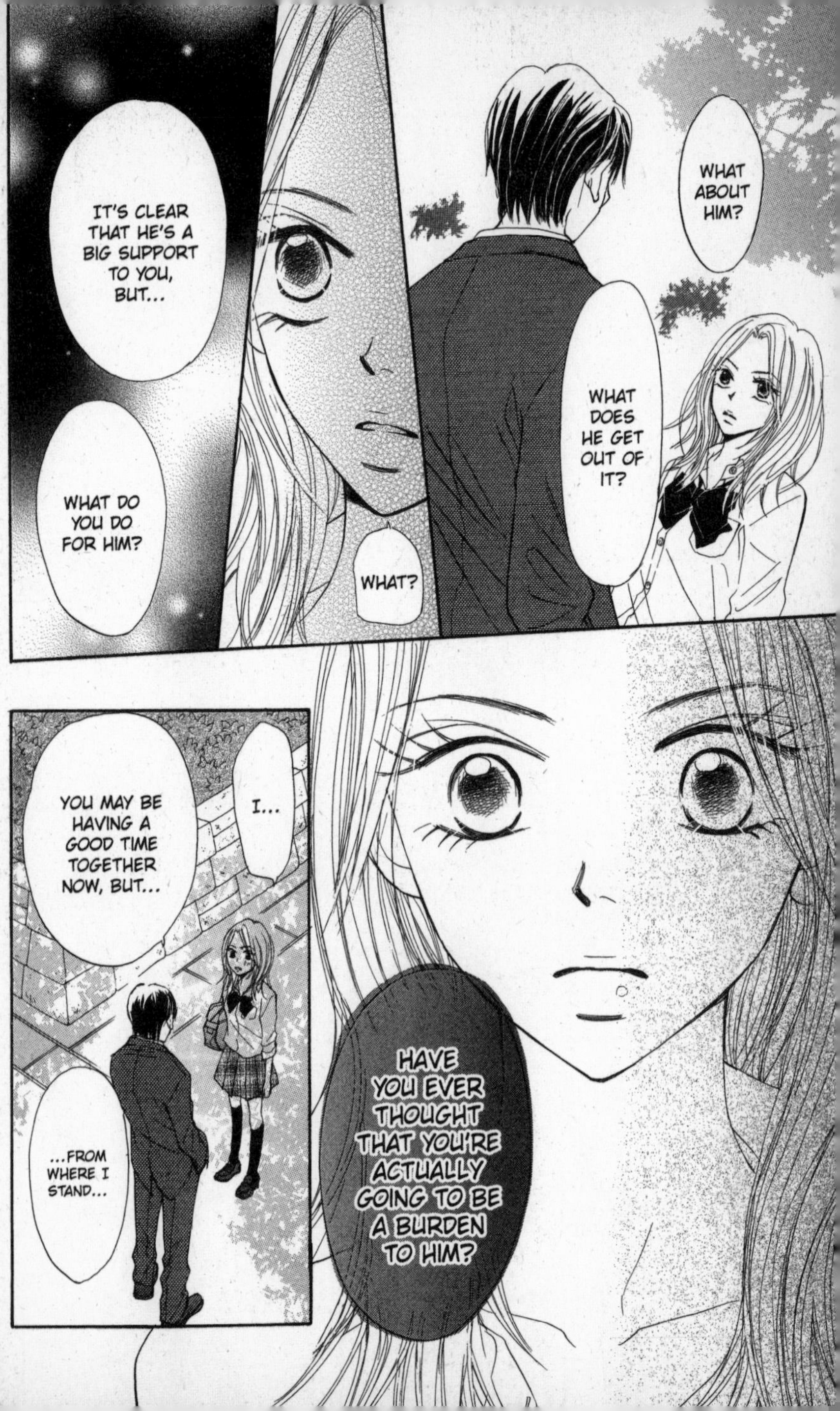
WHAT ABOUT HIM?
WHAT DOES HE GET OUT OF IT?
WHAT?
IT'S CLEAR THAT HE'S A BIG SUPPORT TO YOU, BUT...
WHAT DO YOU DO FOR HIM?
I...
YOU MAY BE HAVING A GOOD TIME TOGETHER NOW, BUT...
...FROM WHERE I STAND...
HAVE YOU EVER THOUGHT THAT YOU'RE ACTUALLY GOING TO BE A BURDEN TO HIM?

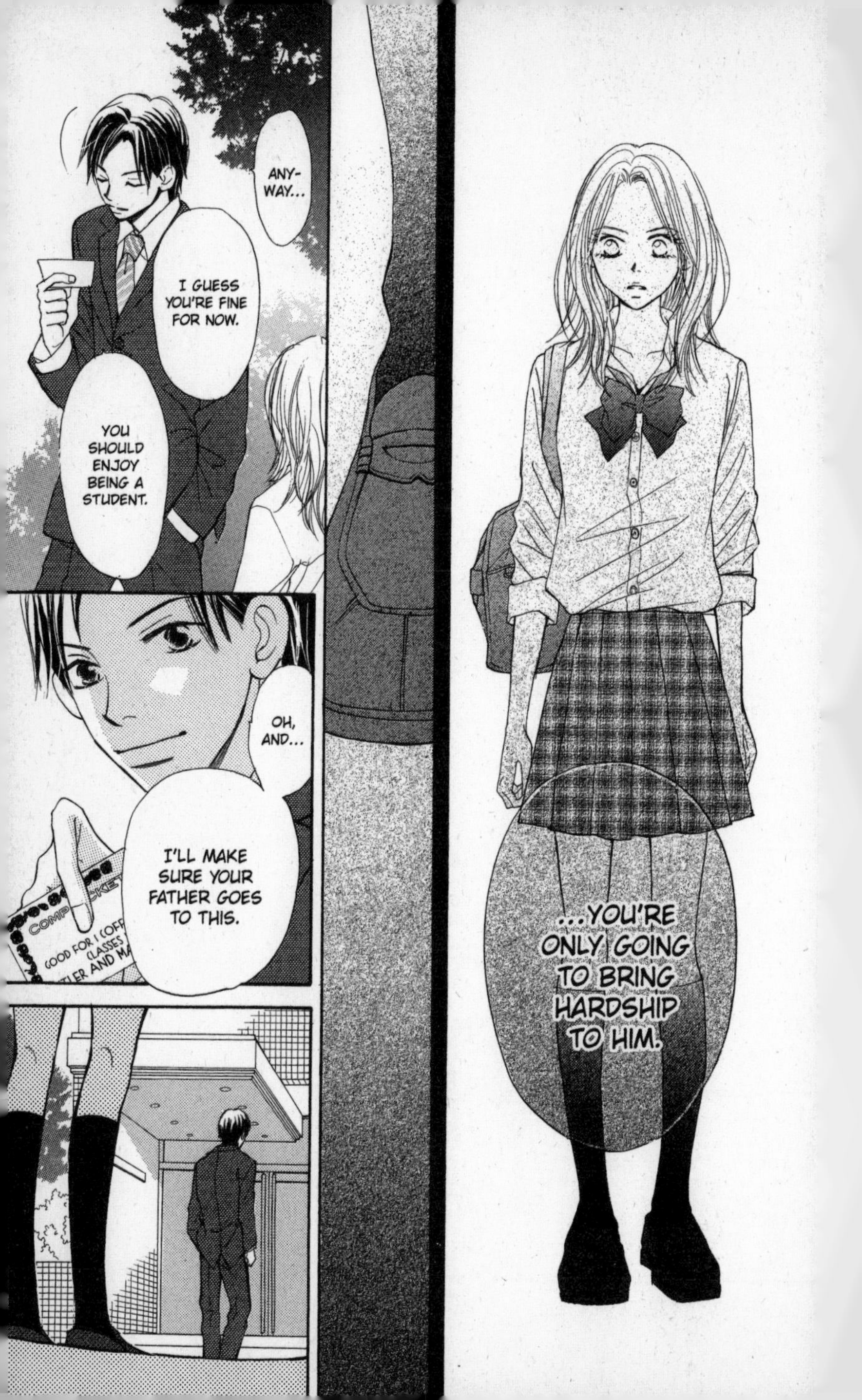
...YOU'RE ONLY GOING TO BRING HARDSHIP TO HIM.
ANY-WAY...
I GUESS YOU'RE FINE FOR NOW.
YOU SHOULD ENJOY BEING A STUDENT.
OH, AND...
I'LL MAKE SURE YOUR FATHER GOES TO THIS.

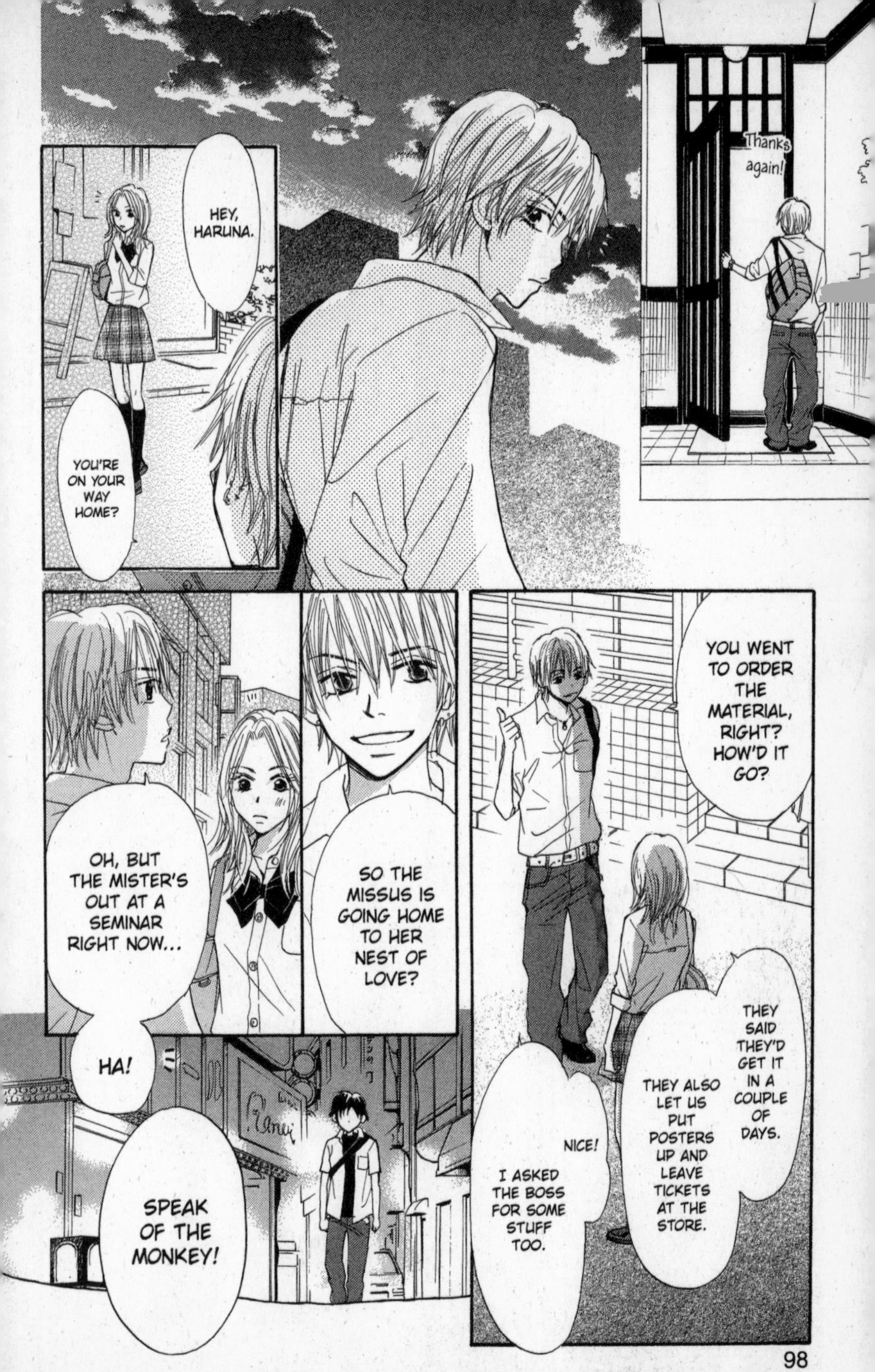

Thanks again!
HEY, HARUNA.
YOU'RE ON YOUR WAY HOME?
YOU WENT TO ORDER THE MATERIAL, RIGHT? HOW'D IT GO?
THEY SAID THEY'D GET IT IN A COUPLE OF DAYS.
THEY ALSO LET US PUT POSTERS UP AND LEAVE TICKETS AT THE STORE.
NICE!
I ASKED THE BOSS FOR SOME STUFF TOO.
SO THE MISSUS IS GOING HOME TO HER NEST OF LOVE?
OH, BUT THE MISTER'S OUT AT A SEMINAR RIGHT NOW...
HA!
SPEAK OF THE MONKEY!

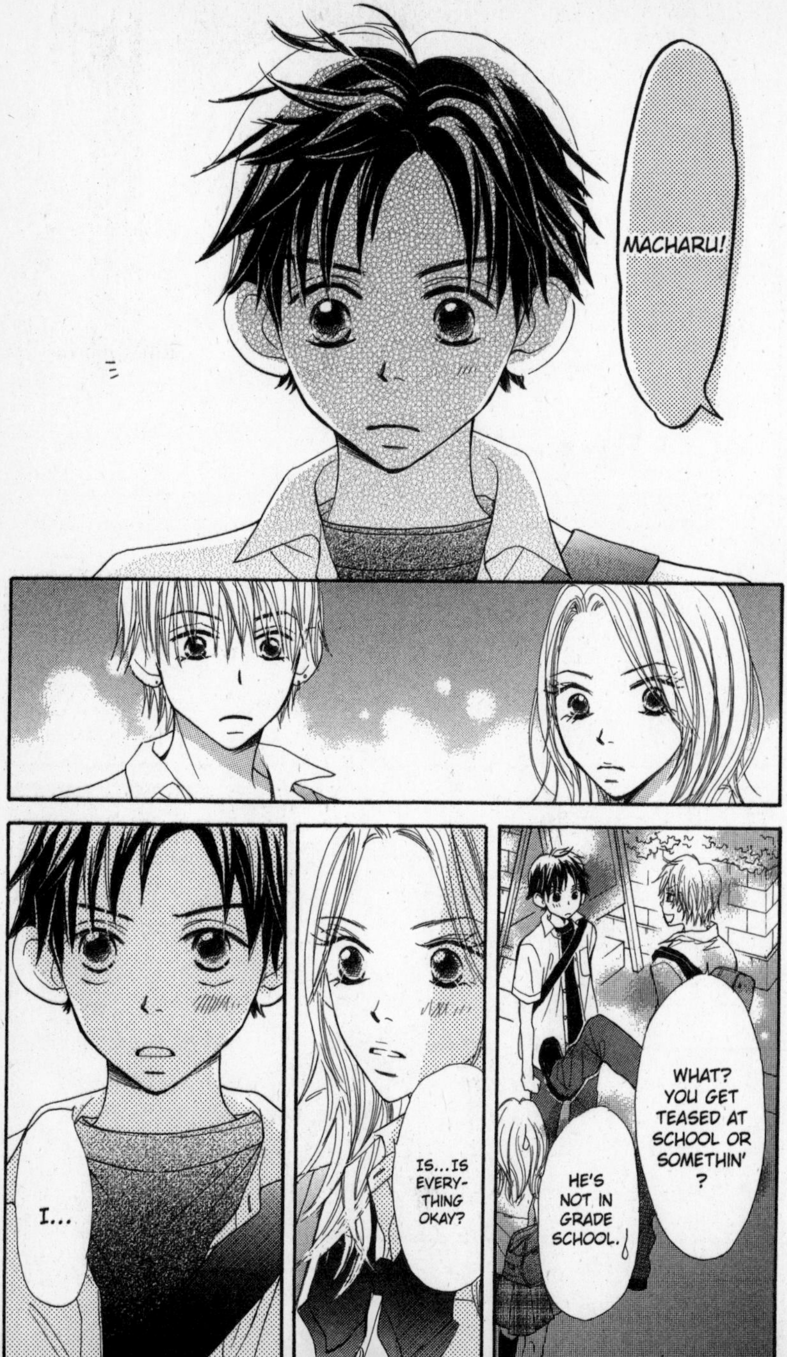
MACHARU!
WHAT? YOU GET TEASED AT SCHOOL OR SOMETHIN'?
HE'S NOT IN GRADE SCHOOL.
IS...IS EVERY-THING OKAY?
I...

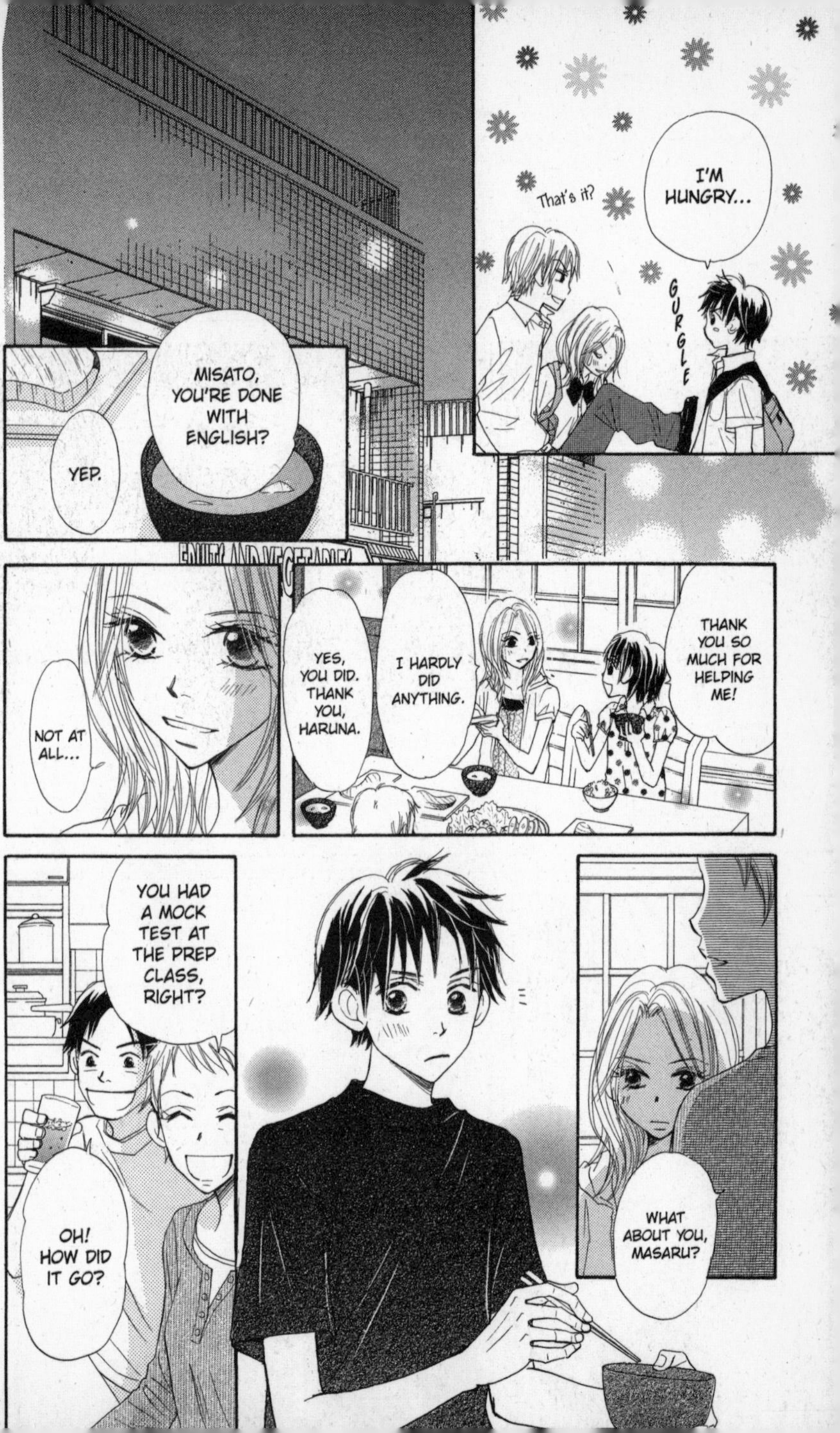
I'M HUNGRY...
GURGLE
That's it?
MISATO, YOU'RE DONE WITH ENGLISH?
YEP.
THANK YOU SO MUCH FOR HELPING ME!
I HARDLY DID ANYTHING.
YES, YOU DID. THANK YOU, HARUNA.
NOT AT ALL...
WHAT ABOUT YOU, MASARU?
YOU HAD A MOCK TEST AT THE PREP CLASS, RIGHT?
OH! HOW DID IT GO?

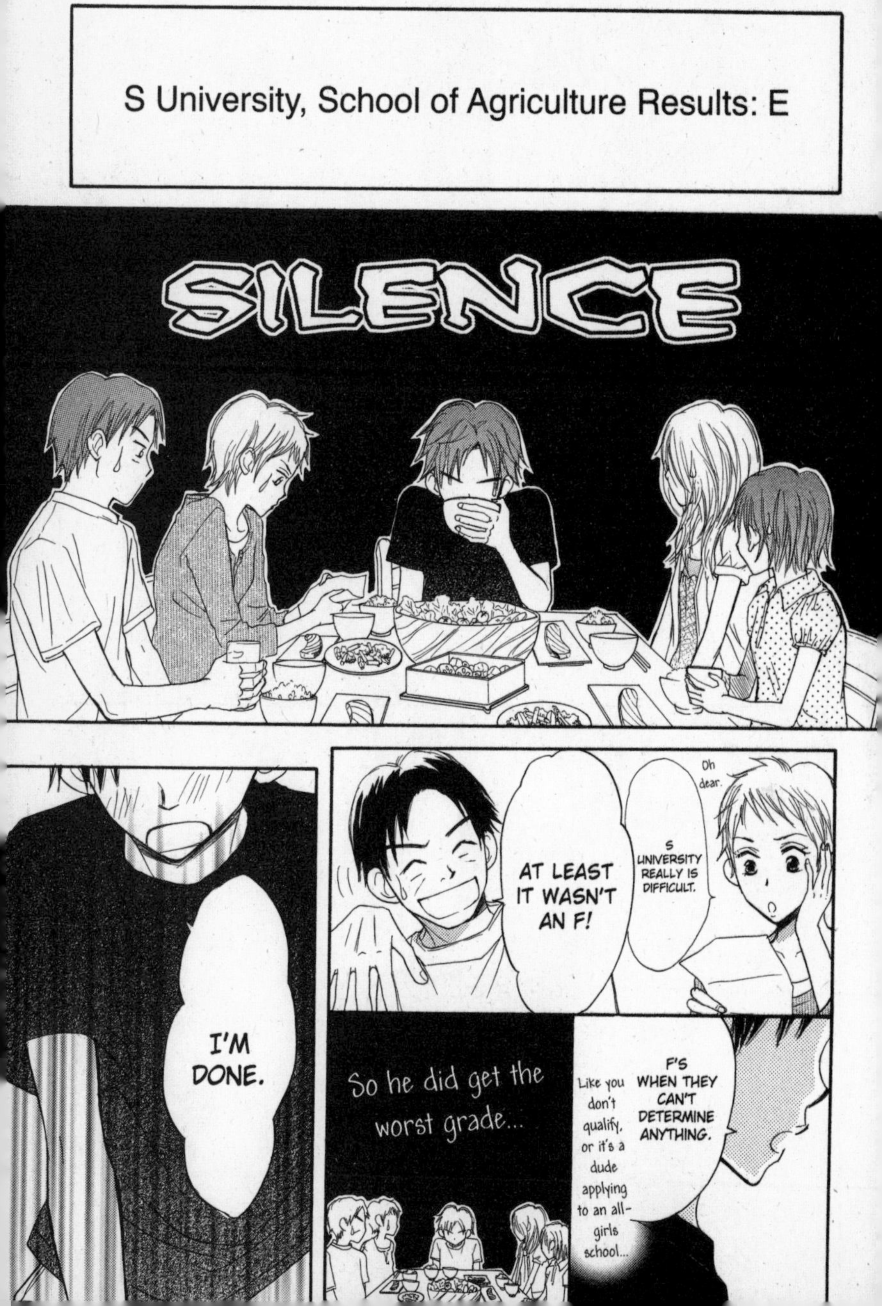
S University, School of Agriculture Results: E
SILENCE
Oh dear.
S UNIVERSITY REALLY IS DIFFICULT.
AT LEAST IT WASN'T AN F!
F'S WHEN THEY CAN'T DETERMINE ANYTHING.
Like you don't qualify, or it's a dude applying to an all-girls school...
So he did get the worst grade...
I'M DONE.

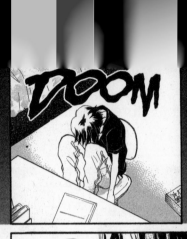

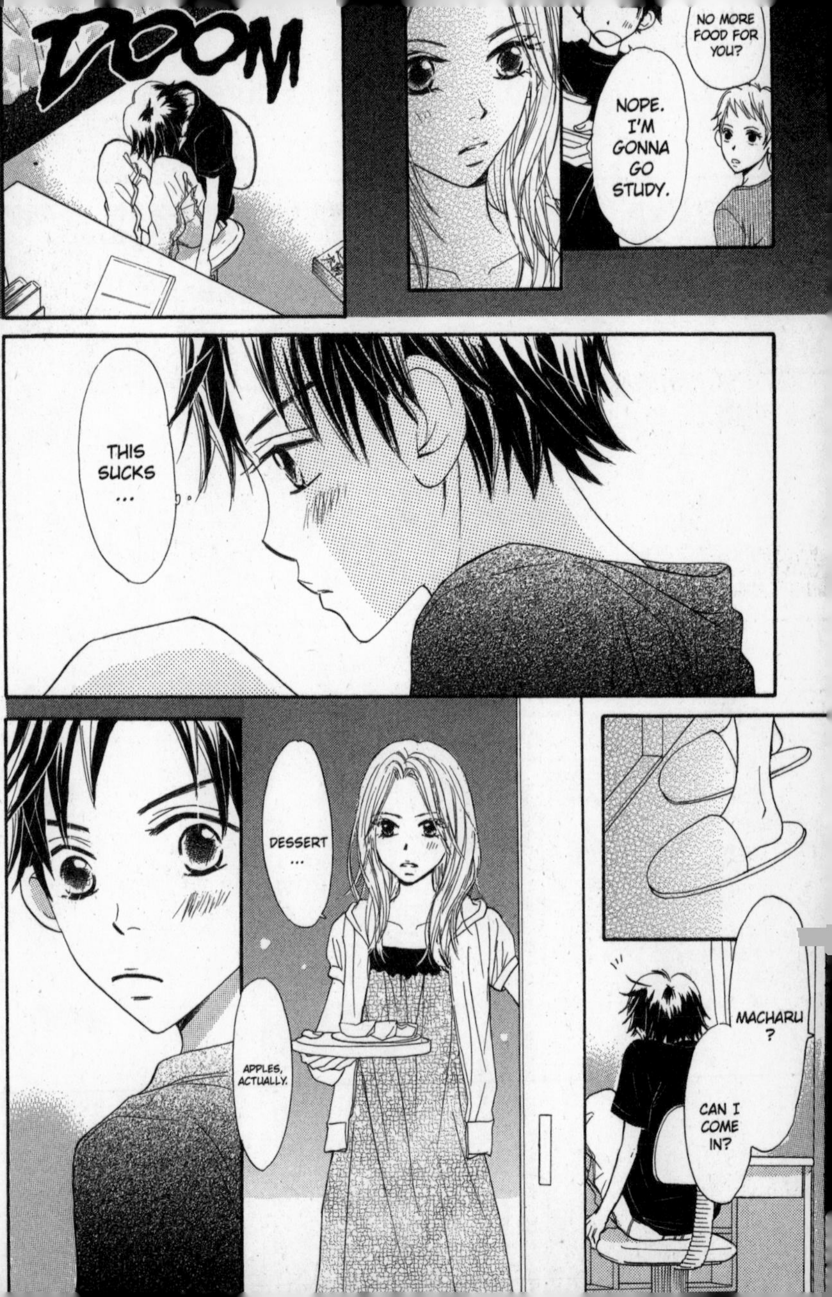
NO MORE FOOD FOR YOU?
NOPE. I'M GONNA GO STUDY.
DOOM
THIS SUCKS...
MACHARU?
CAN I COME IN?
DESSERT...
APPLES, ACTUALLY.

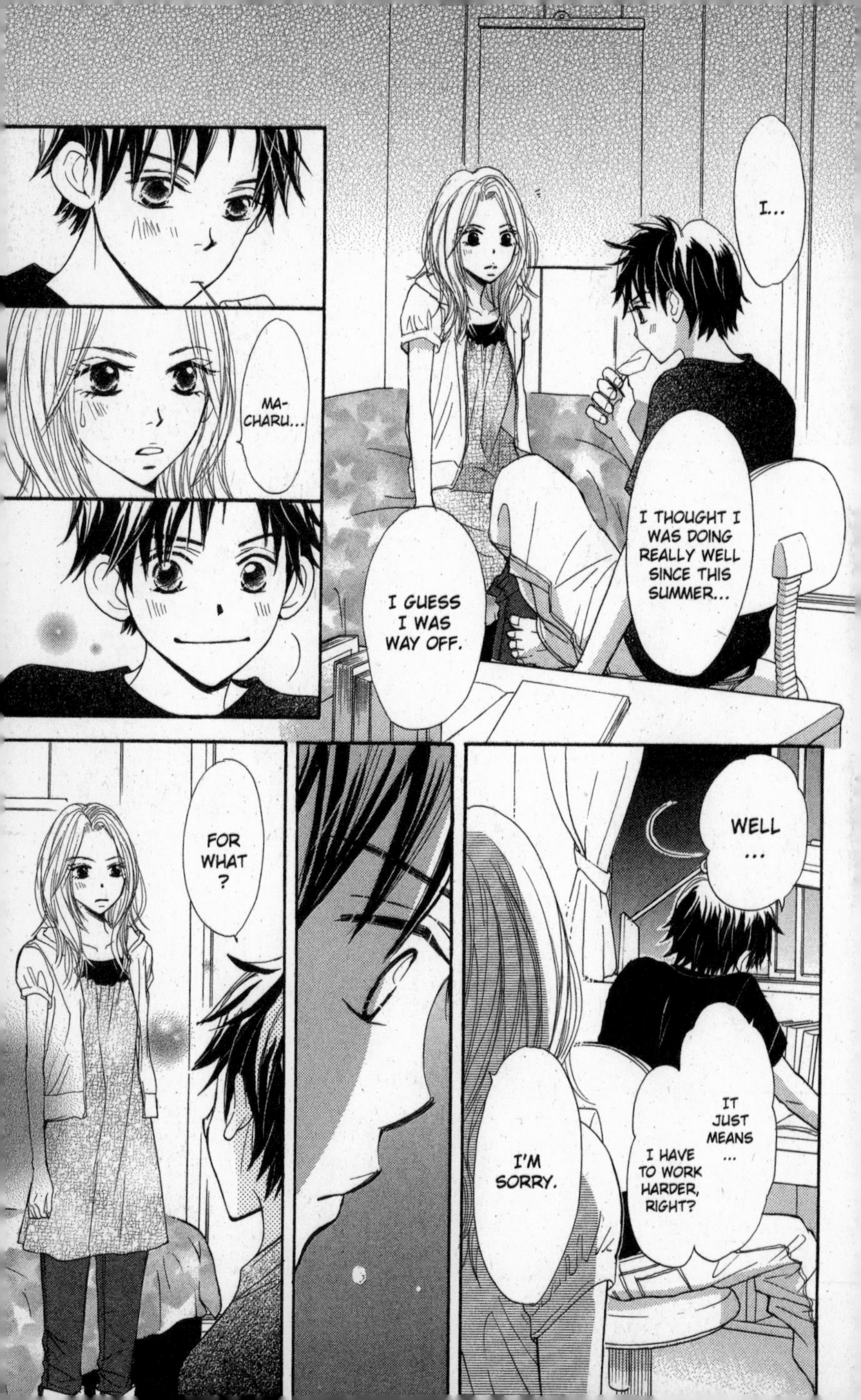
I...
I THOUGHT I WAS DOING REALLY WELL SINCE THIS SUMMER...
I GUESS I WAS WAY OFF.
MA-CHARU...
WELL...
IT JUST MEANS... I HAVE TO WORK HARDER, RIGHT?
I'M SORRY.
FOR WHAT?

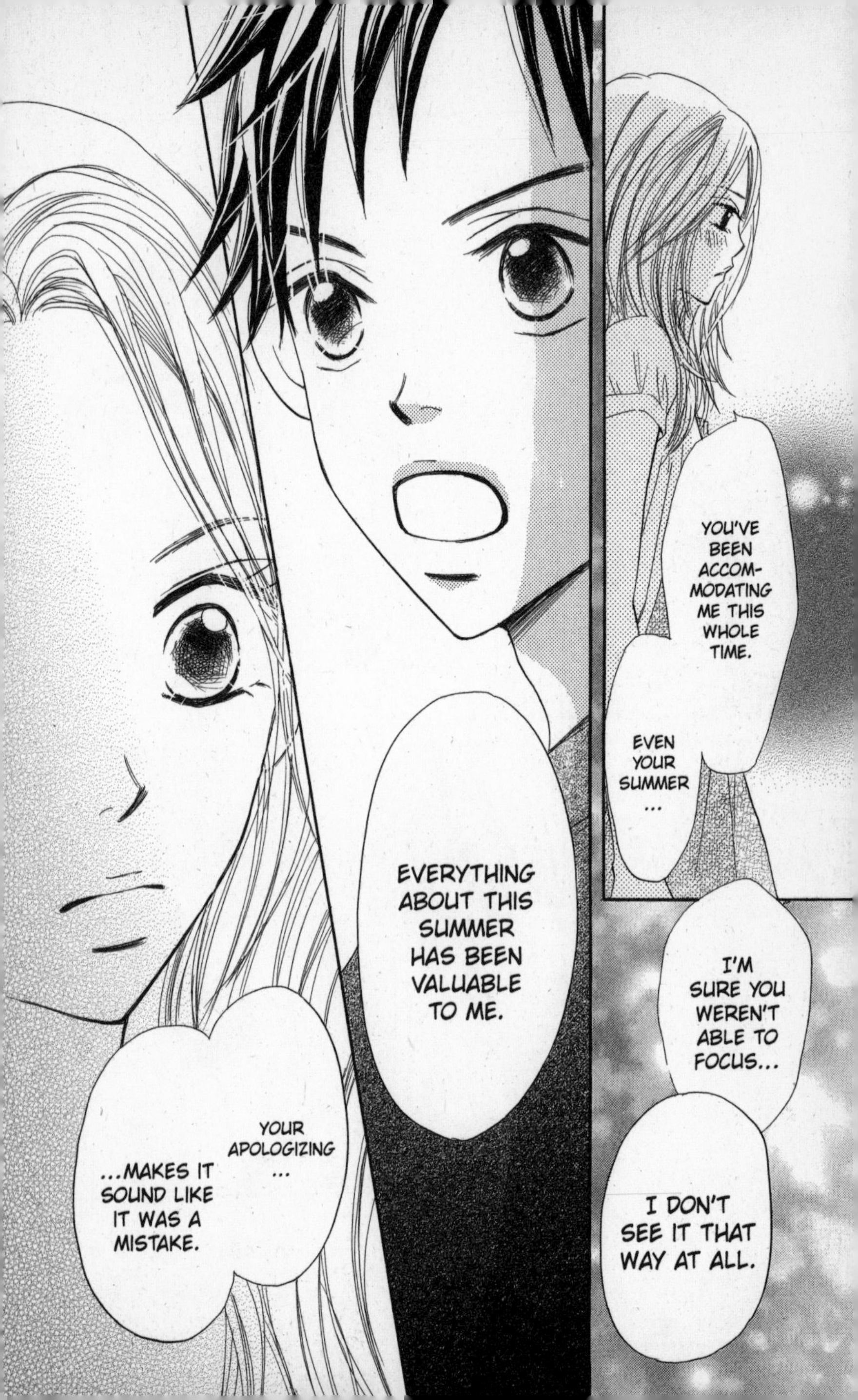
YOU'VE BEEN ACCOM-MODATING ME THIS WHOLE TIME.
EVEN YOUR SUMMER ...
I'M SURE YOU WEREN'T ABLE TO FOCUS...
I DON'T SEE IT THAT WAY AT ALL.
EVERYTHING ABOUT THIS SUMMER HAS BEEN VALUABLE TO ME.
YOUR APOLOGIZING ...
...MAKES IT SOUND LIKE IT WAS A MISTAKE.

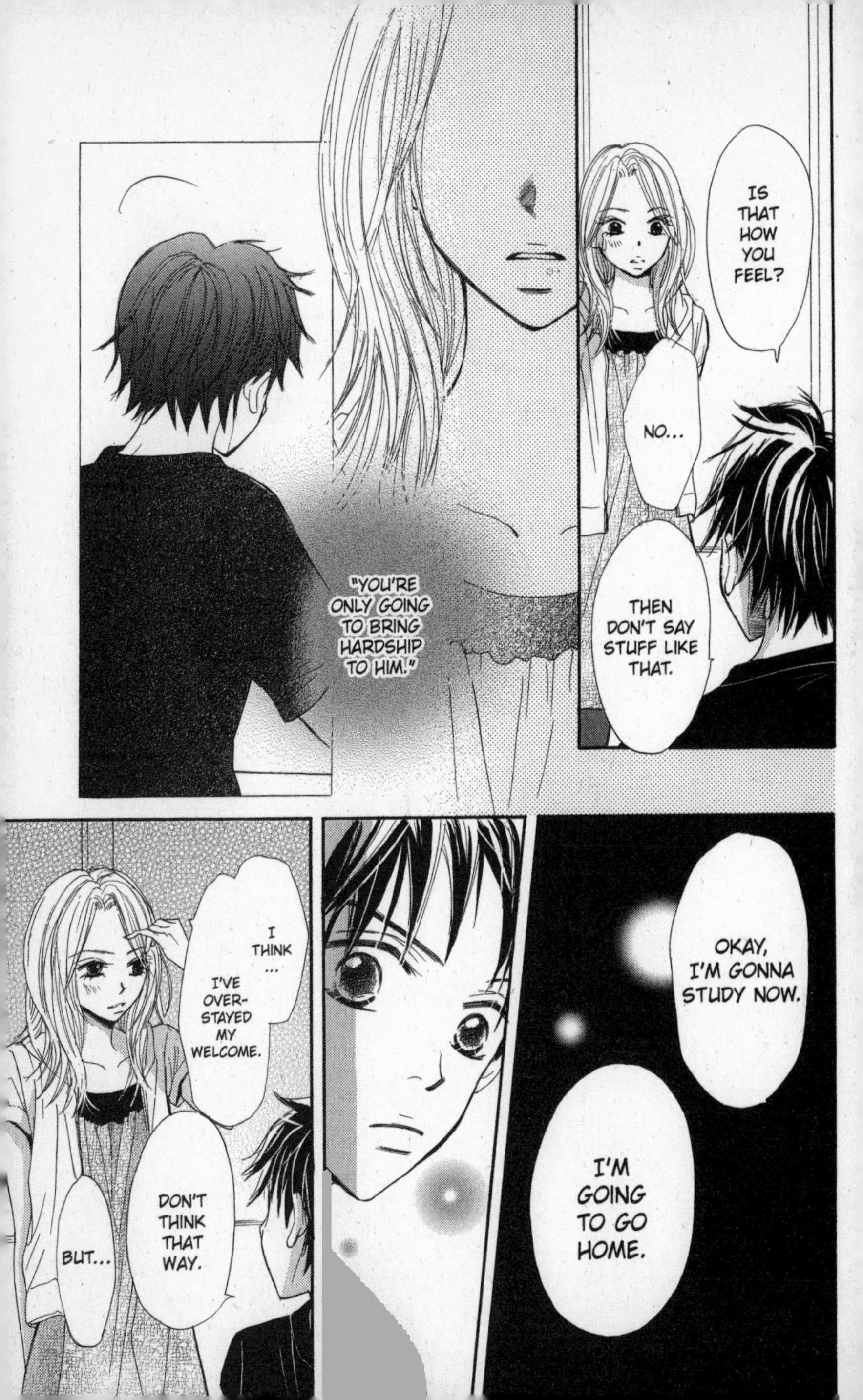
IS THAT HOW YOU FEEL?
NO...
THEN DON'T SAY STUFF LIKE THAT.
"YOU'RE ONLY GOING TO BRING HARDSHIP TO HIM."
OKAY, I'M GONNA STUDY NOW.
I'M GOING TO GO HOME.
I THINK ... I'VE OVER-STAYED MY WELCOME.
DON'T THINK THAT WAY.
BUT...

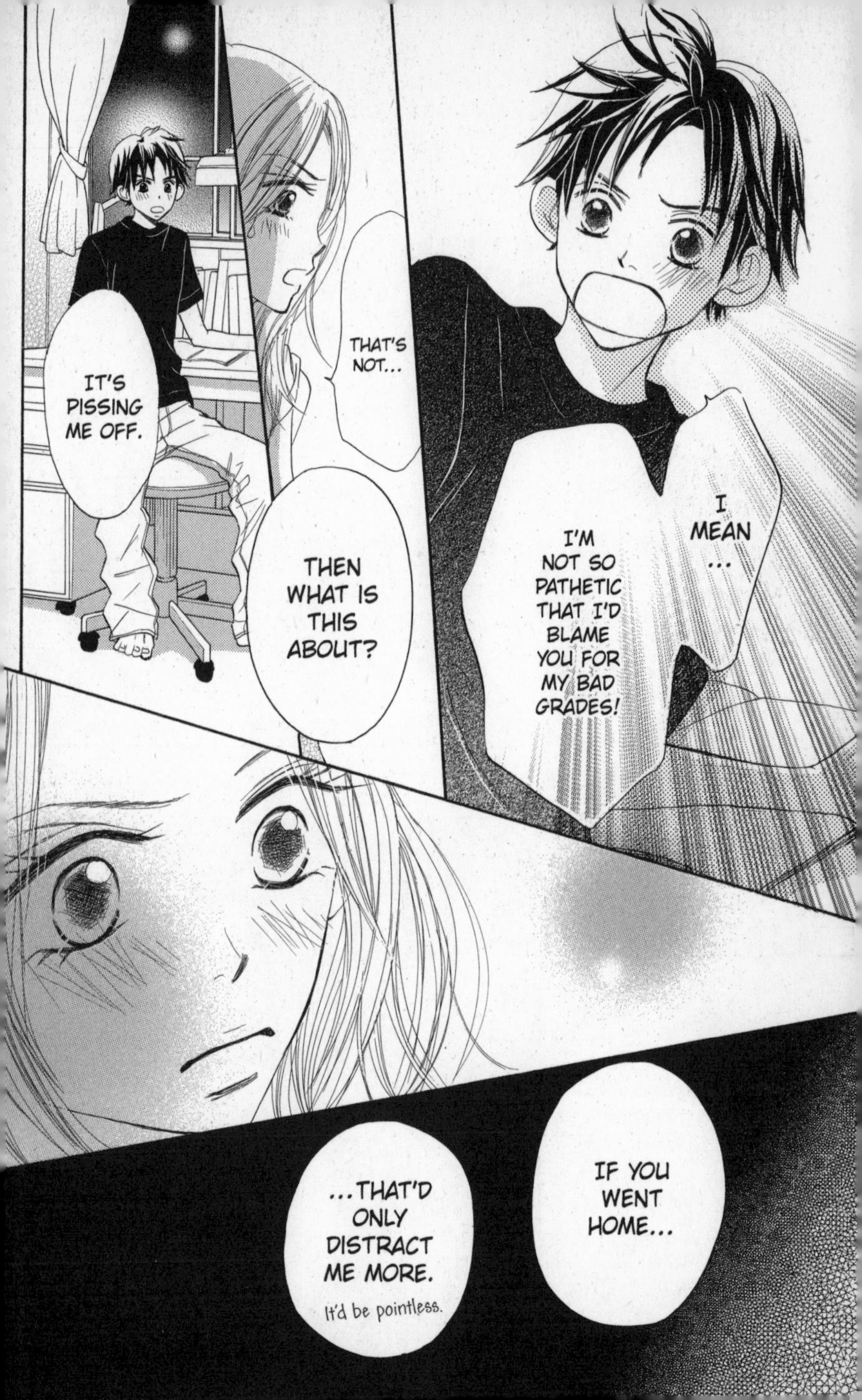
I MEAN...
I'M NOT SO PATHETIC THAT I'D BLAME YOU FOR MY BAD GRADES!
THAT'S NOT...
THEN WHAT IS THIS ABOUT?
IT'S PISSING ME OFF.
IF YOU WENT HOME...
...THAT'D ONLY DISTRACT ME MORE.
It'd be pointless.

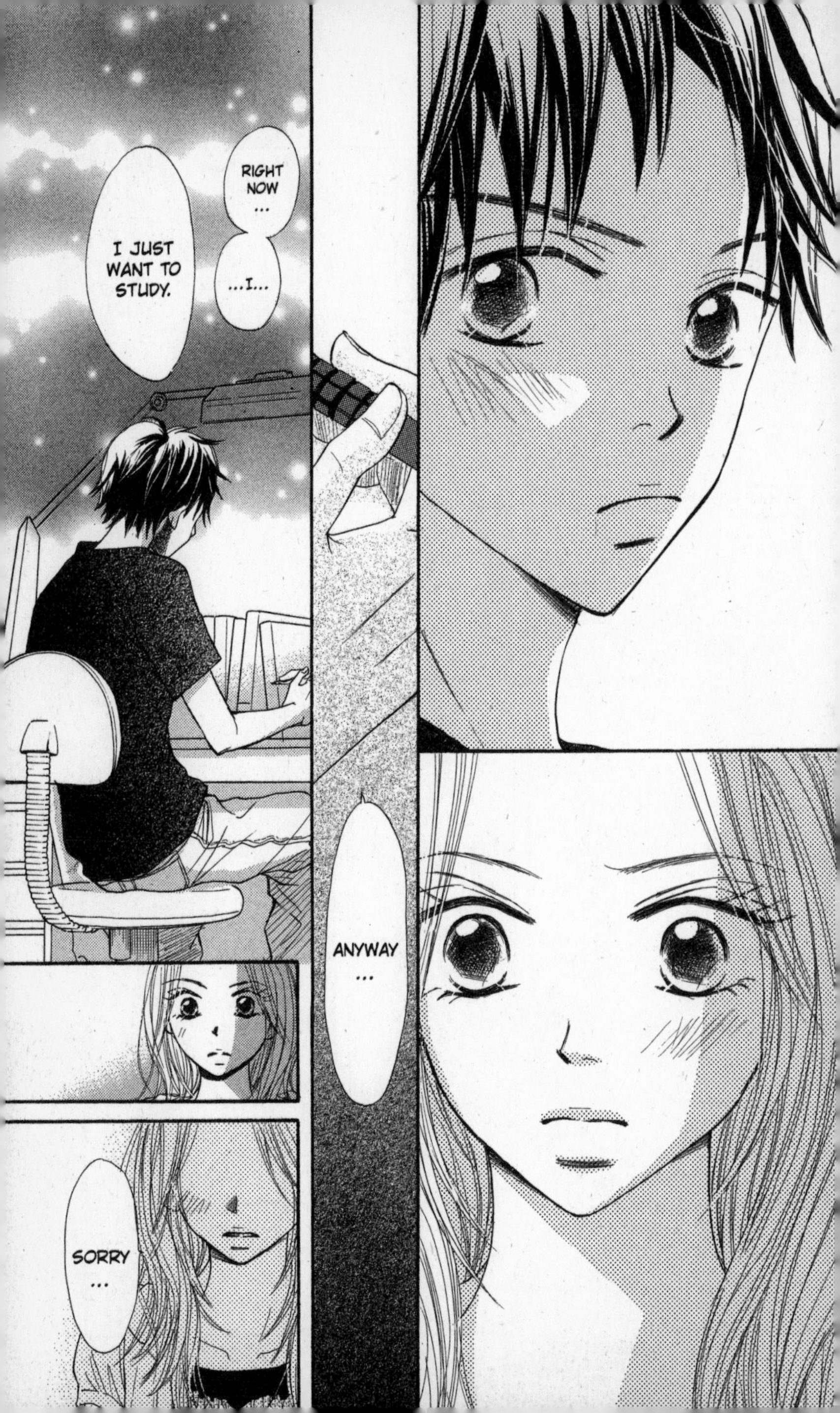
ANYWAY ...
RIGHT NOW ...
...I...
I JUST WANT TO STUDY.
SORRY ...

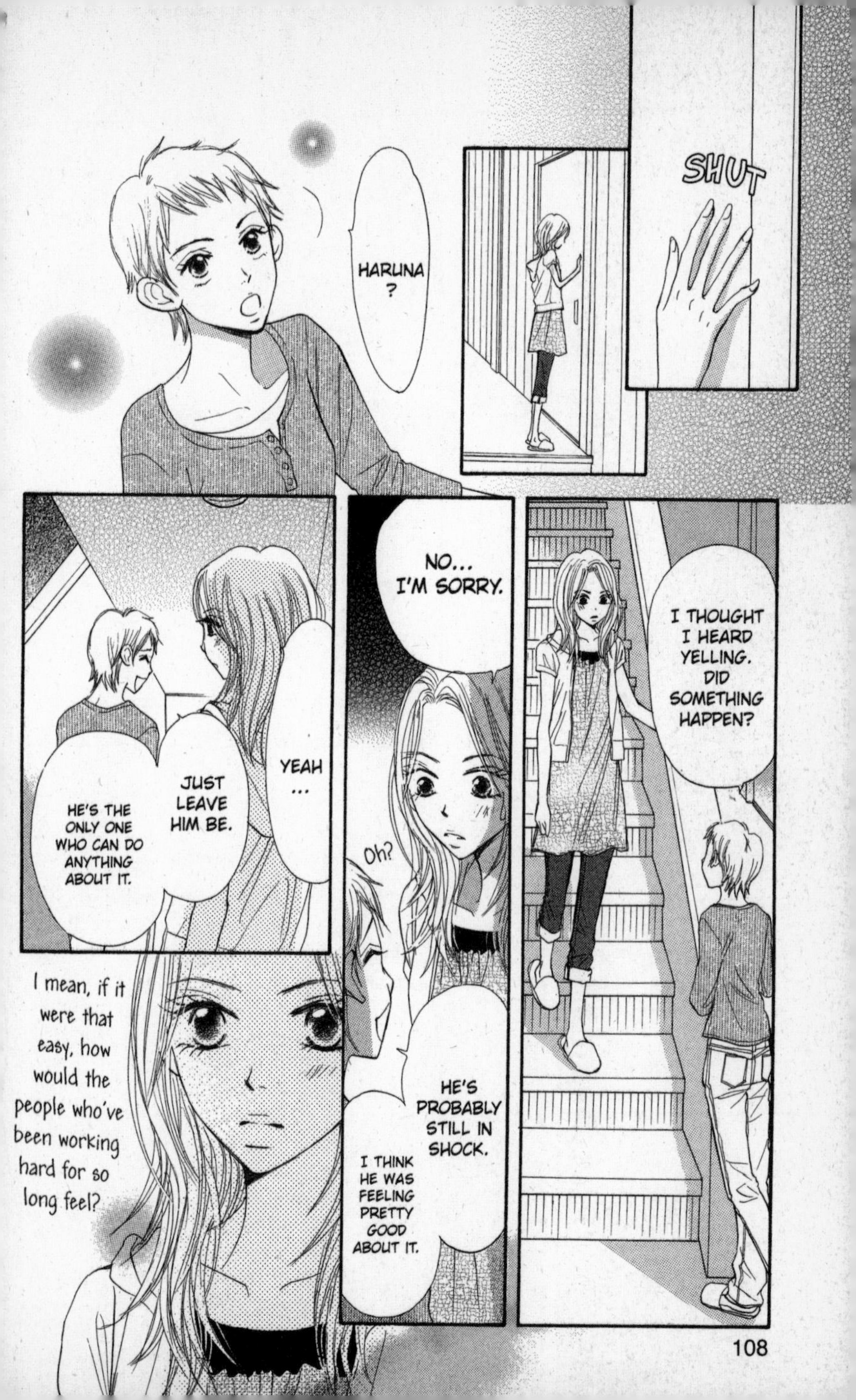
SHUT
HARUNA ?
I THOUGHT I HEARD YELLING. DID SOMETHING HAPPEN?
NO... I'M SORRY.
Oh?
HE'S PROBABLY STILL IN SHOCK.
I THINK HE WAS FEELING PRETTY GOOD ABOUT IT.
YEAH ...
JUST LEAVE HIM BE.
HE'S THE ONLY ONE WHO CAN DO ANYTHING ABOUT IT.
I mean, if it were that easy, how would the people who've been working hard for so long feel?

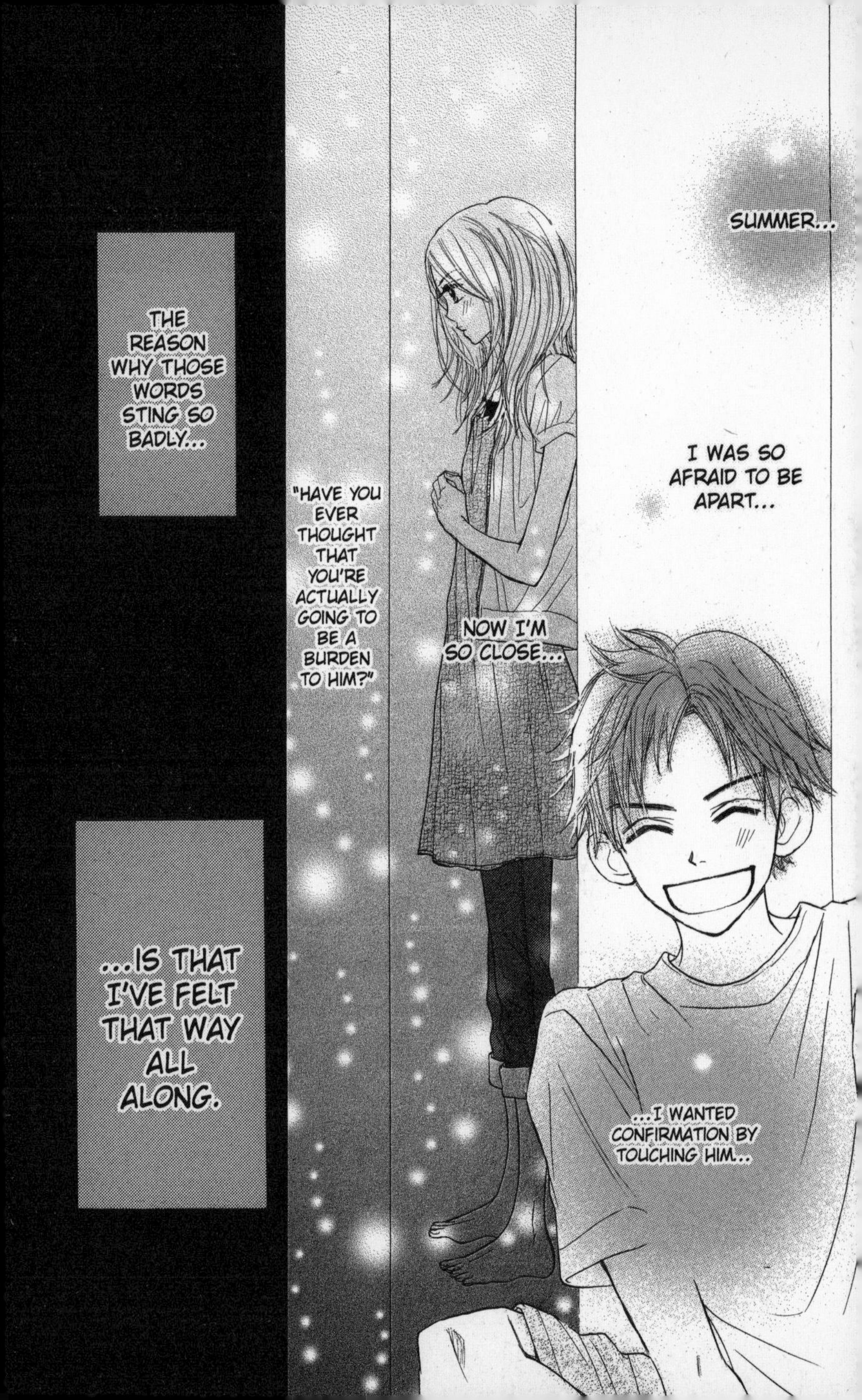
SUMMER...
I WAS SO AFRAID TO BE APART...
...I WANTED CONFIRMATION BY TOUCHING HIM...
NOW I'M SO CLOSE...
"HAVE YOU EVER THOUGHT THAT YOU'RE ACTUALLY GOING TO BE A BURDEN TO HIM?"
THE REASON WHY THOSE WORDS STING SO BADLY...
...IS THAT I'VE FELT THAT WAY ALL ALONG.

KITA HIGH FESTIVAL FINAL!

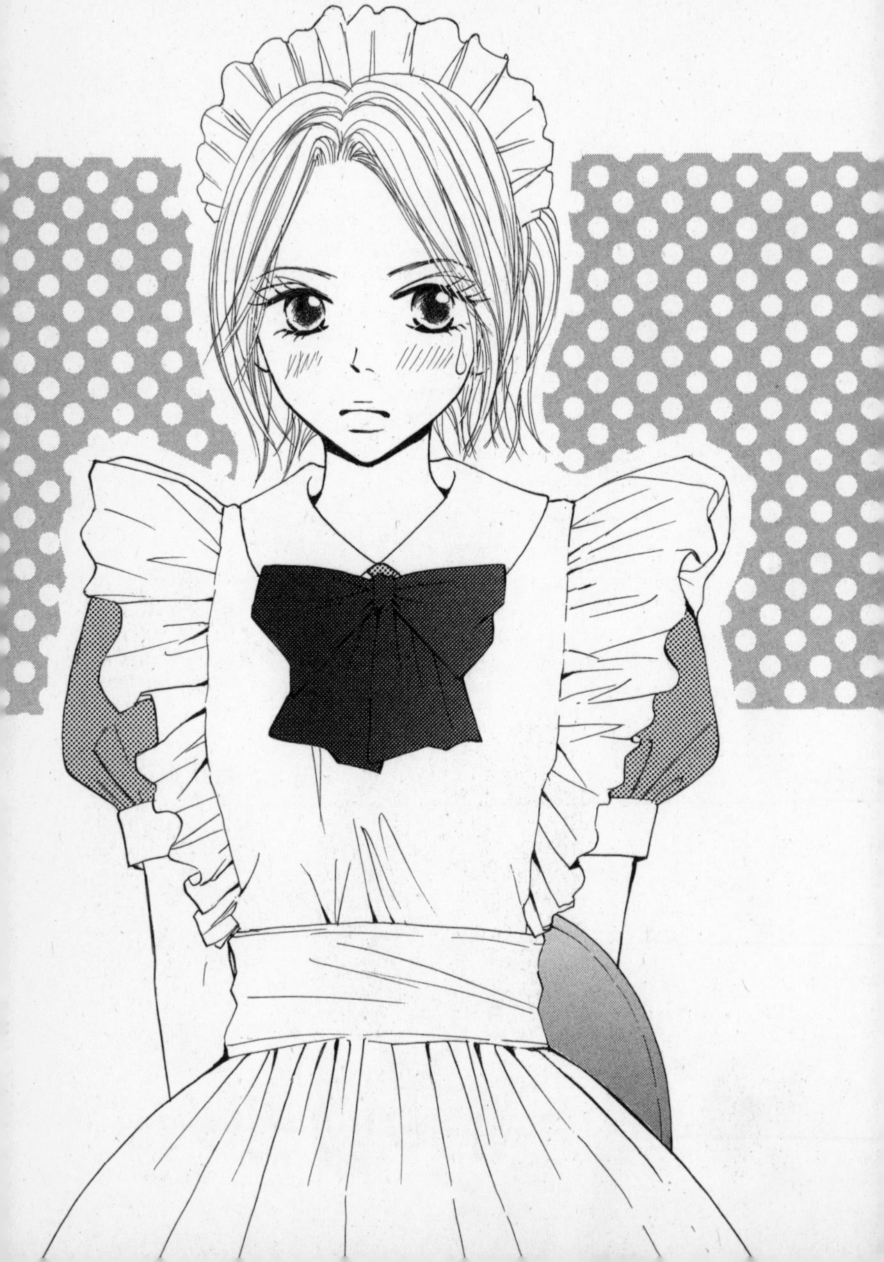

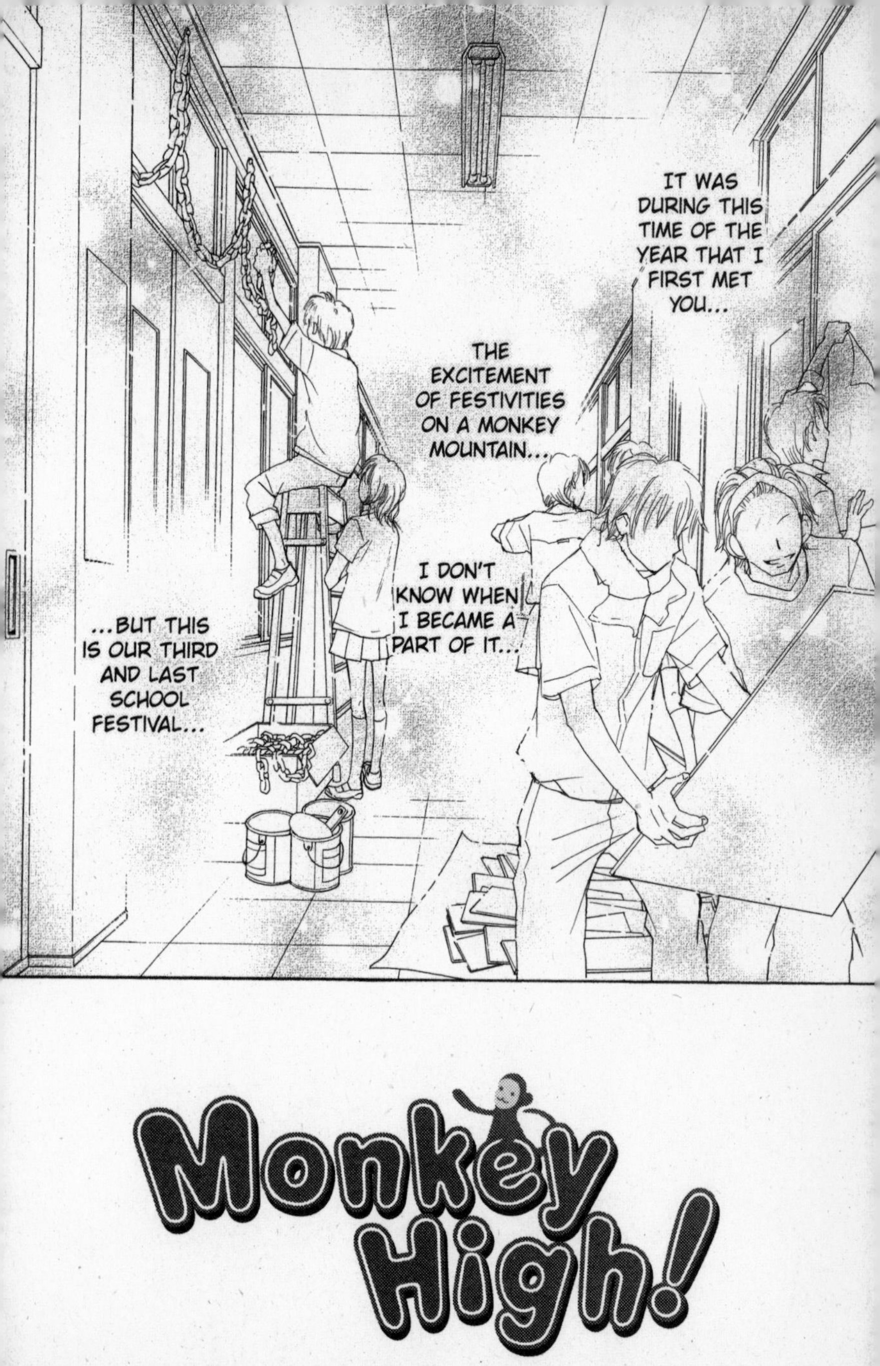
IT WAS DURING THIS TIME OF THE YEAR THAT I FIRST MET YOU...
THE EXCITEMENT OF FESTIVITIES ON A MONKEY MOUNTAIN...
I DON'T KNOW WHEN I BECAME A PART OF IT...
...BUT THIS IS OUR THIRD AND LAST SCHOOL FESTIVAL...

Monkey High!

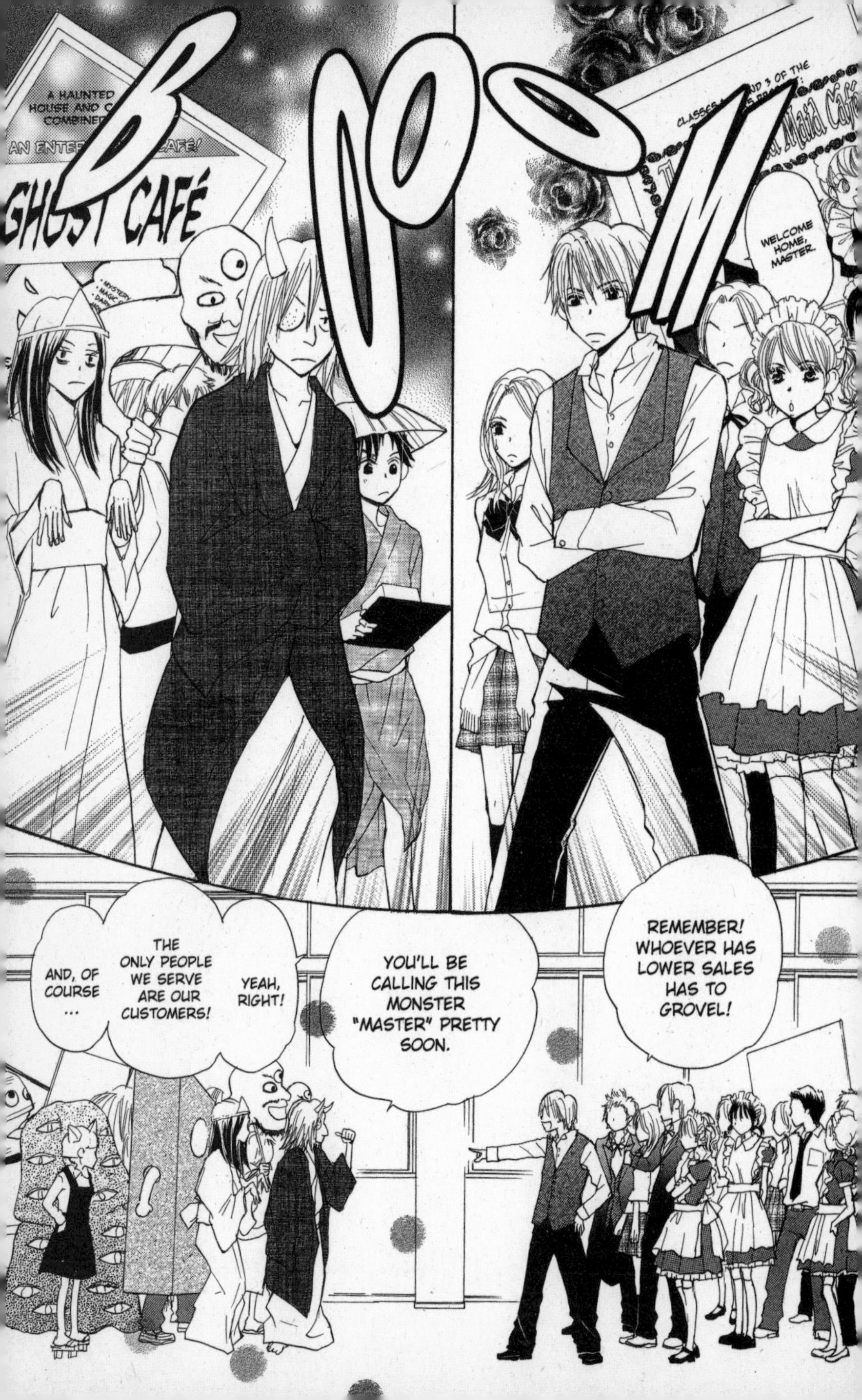
WELCOME HOME, MASTER.
BOOOM
A HAUNTED
GHOST CAFÉ
REMEMBER! WHOEVER HAS LOWER SALES HAS TO GROVEL!
YOU'LL BE CALLING THIS MONSTER "MASTER" PRETTY SOON.
YEAH, RIGHT!
THE ONLY PEOPLE WE SERVE ARE OUR CUSTOMERS!
AND, OF COURSE ...

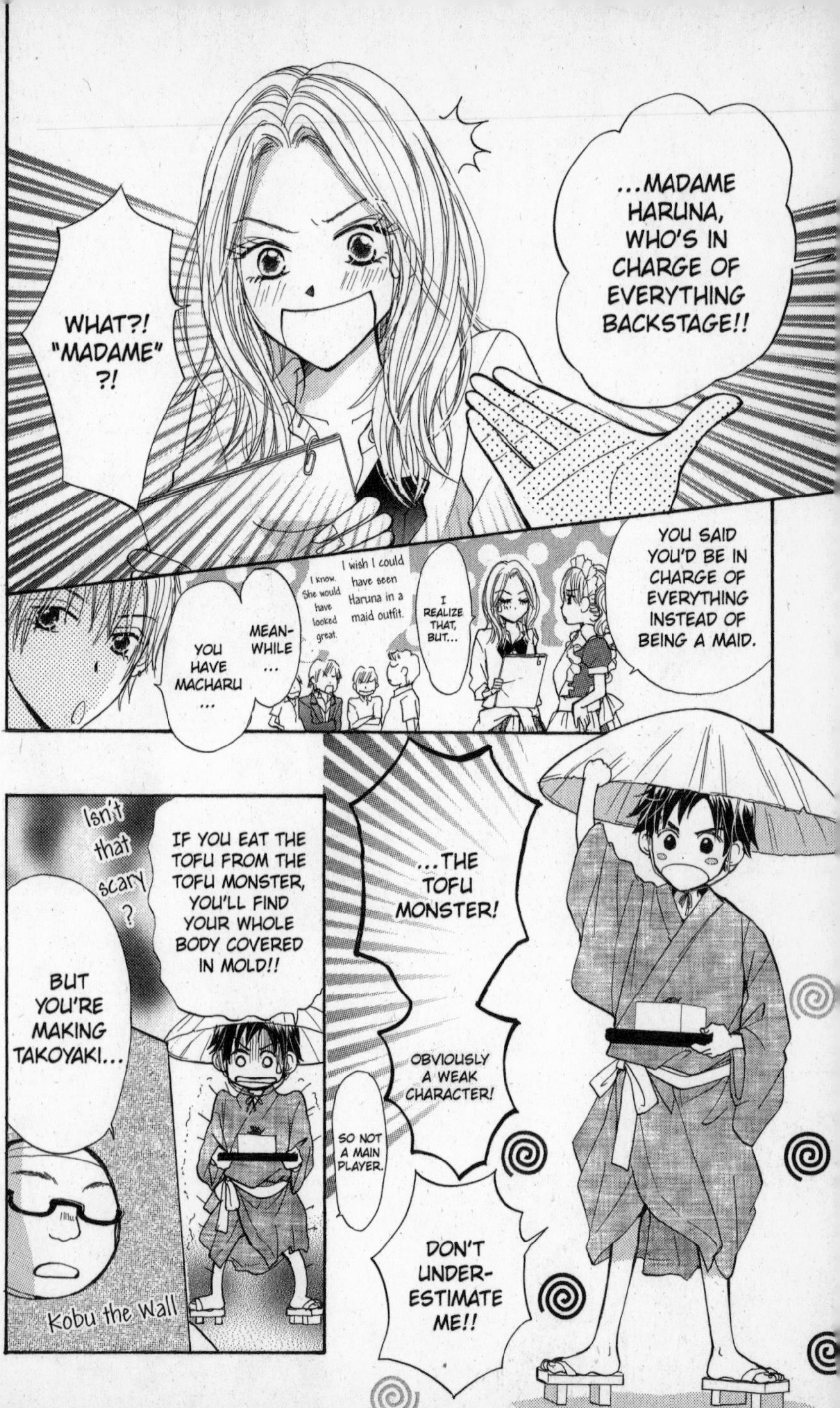
...MADAME HARUNA, WHO'S IN CHARGE OF EVERYTHING BACKSTAGE!!
WHAT?! "MADAME" ?!
YOU SAID YOU'D BE IN CHARGE OF EVERYTHING INSTEAD OF BEING A MAID.
I REALIZE THAT, BUT...
I wish I could have seen Haruna in a maid outfit.
I know. She would have looked great.
MEAN-WHILE...
YOU HAVE MACHARU...
...THE TOFU MONSTER!
OBVIOUSLY A WEAK CHARACTER!
SO NOT A MAIN PLAYER.
DON'T UNDER-ESTIMATE ME!!
IF YOU EAT THE TOFU FROM THE TOFU MONSTER, YOU'LL FIND YOUR WHOLE BODY COVERED IN MOLD!!
Isn't that scary?
BUT YOU'RE MAKING TAKOYAKI...
Kobu the Wall

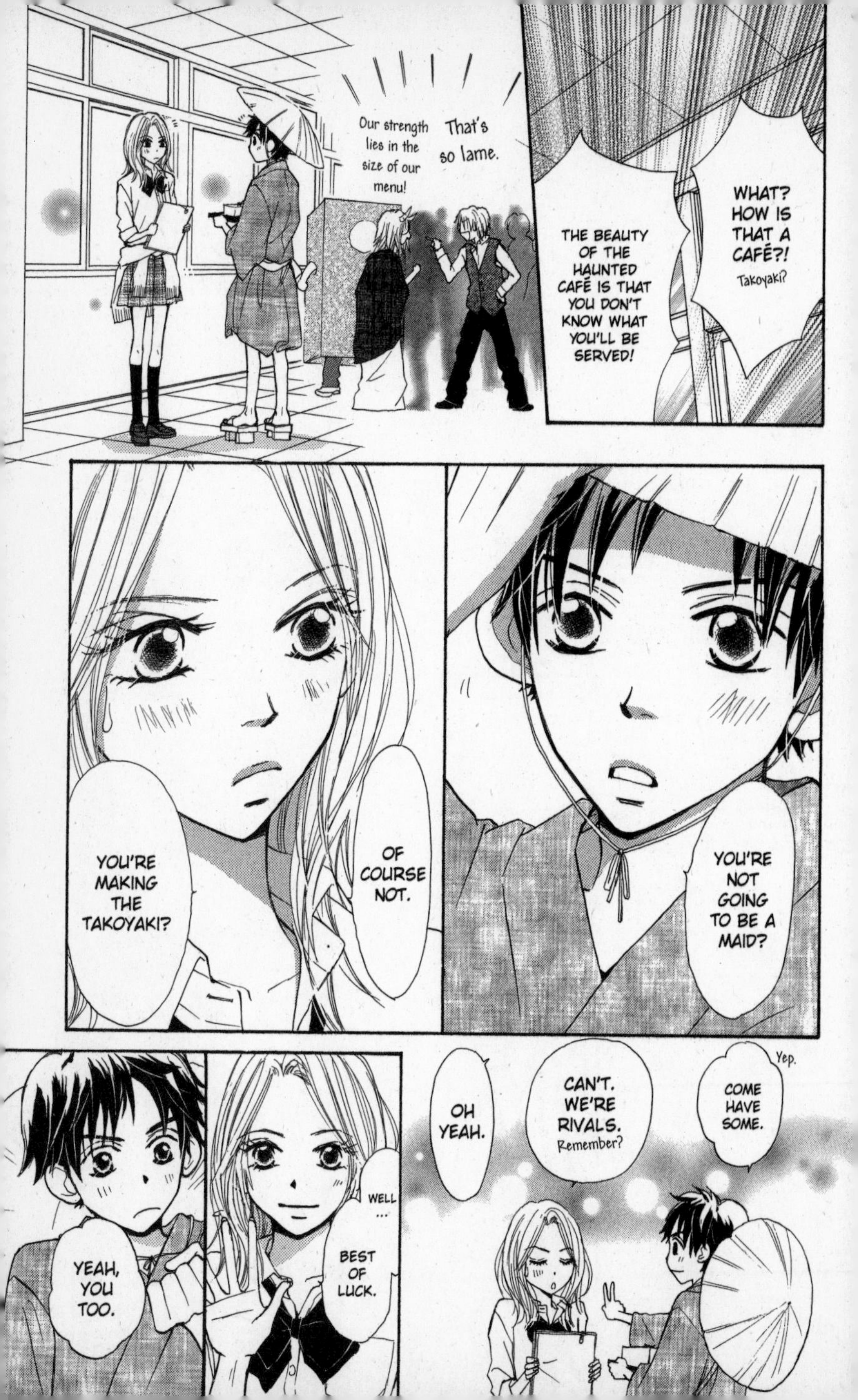
WHAT? HOW IS THAT A CAFÉ?!
Takoyaki?
THE BEAUTY OF THE HAUNTED CAFÉ IS THAT YOU DON'T KNOW WHAT YOU'LL BE SERVED!
That's so lame.
Our strength lies in the size of our menu!
YOU'RE NOT GOING TO BE A MAID?
OF COURSE NOT.
YOU'RE MAKING THE TAKOYAKI?
Yep.
COME HAVE SOME.
CAN'T. WE'RE RIVALS.
Remember?
OH YEAH.
WELL...
BEST OF LUCK.
YEAH, YOU TOO.

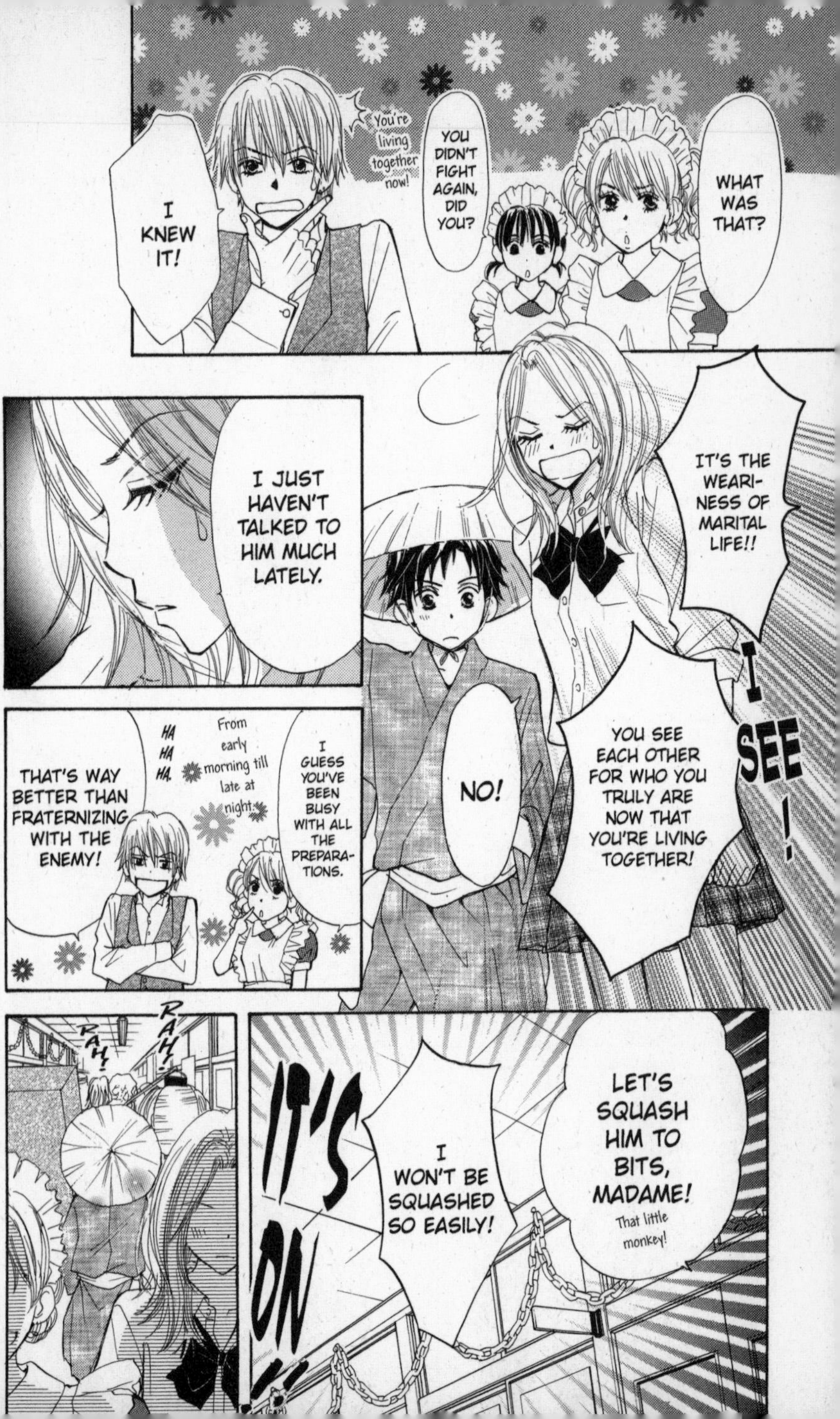
WHAT WAS THAT?
YOU DIDN'T FIGHT AGAIN, DID YOU?
You're living together now!
I KNEW IT!
IT'S THE WEARINESS OF MARITAL LIFE!!
I SEE!
YOU SEE EACH OTHER FOR WHO YOU TRULY ARE NOW THAT YOU'RE LIVING TOGETHER!
NO!
I JUST HAVEN'T TALKED TO HIM MUCH LATELY.
I GUESS YOU'VE BEEN BUSY WITH ALL THE PREPARATIONS.
From early morning till late at night.
HA HA HA.
THAT'S WAY BETTER THAN FRATERNIZING WITH THE ENEMY!
LET'S SQUASH HIM TO BITS, MADAME!
That little monkey!
I WON'T BE SQUASHED SO EASILY!
IT'S ON!!
RAH!
RAH!

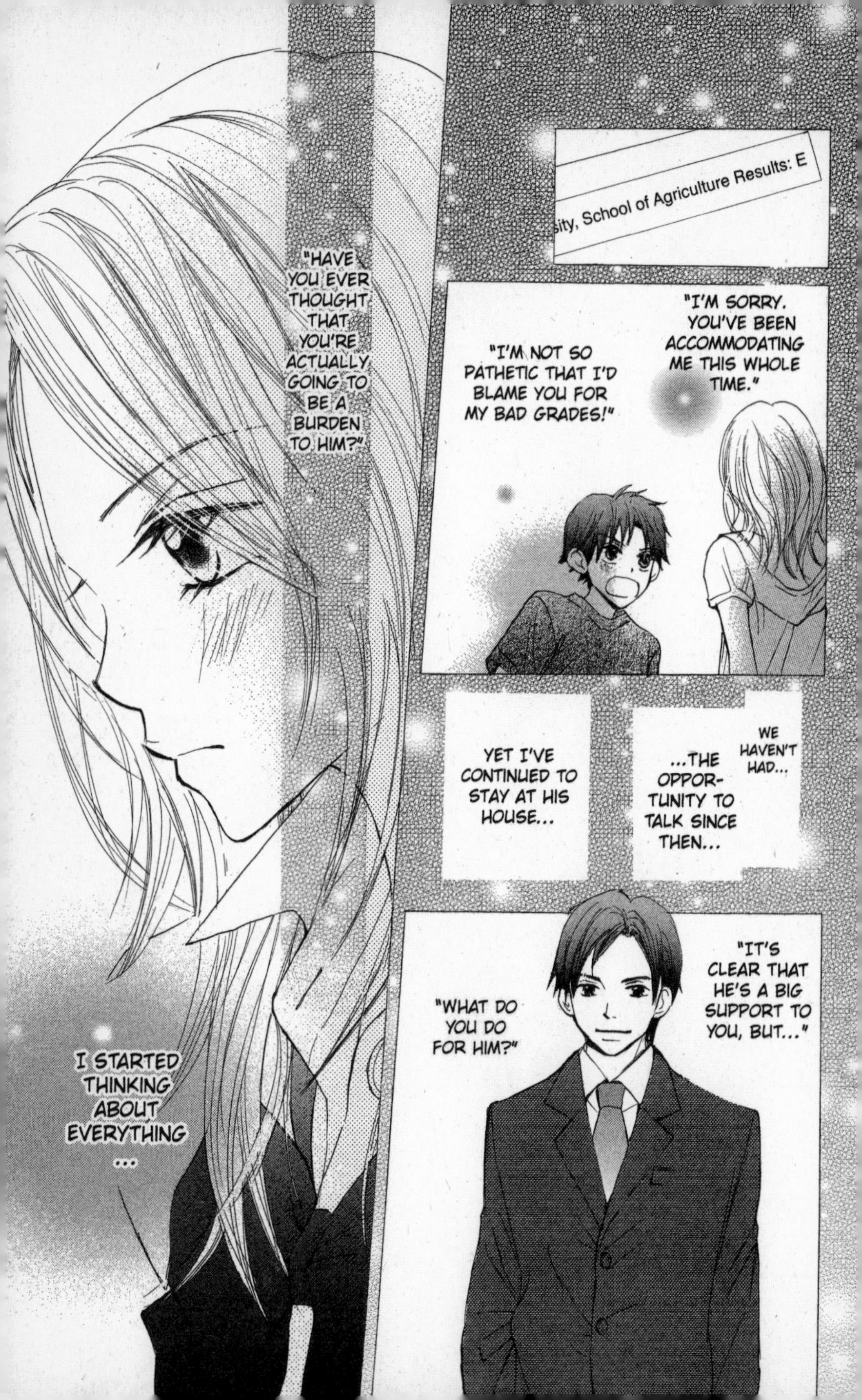
sity, School of Agriculture Results: E
"I'M SORRY. YOU'VE BEEN ACCOMMODATING ME THIS WHOLE TIME."
"I'M NOT SO PATHETIC THAT I'D BLAME YOU FOR MY BAD GRADES!"
WE HAVEN'T HAD...
...THE OPPOR-TUNITY TO TALK SINCE THEN...
YET I'VE CONTINUED TO STAY AT HIS HOUSE...
"IT'S CLEAR THAT HE'S A BIG SUPPORT TO YOU, BUT..."
"WHAT DO YOU DO FOR HIM?"
"HAVE YOU EVER THOUGHT THAT YOU'RE ACTUALLY GOING TO BE A BURDEN TO HIM?"
I STARTED THINKING ABOUT EVERYTHING...

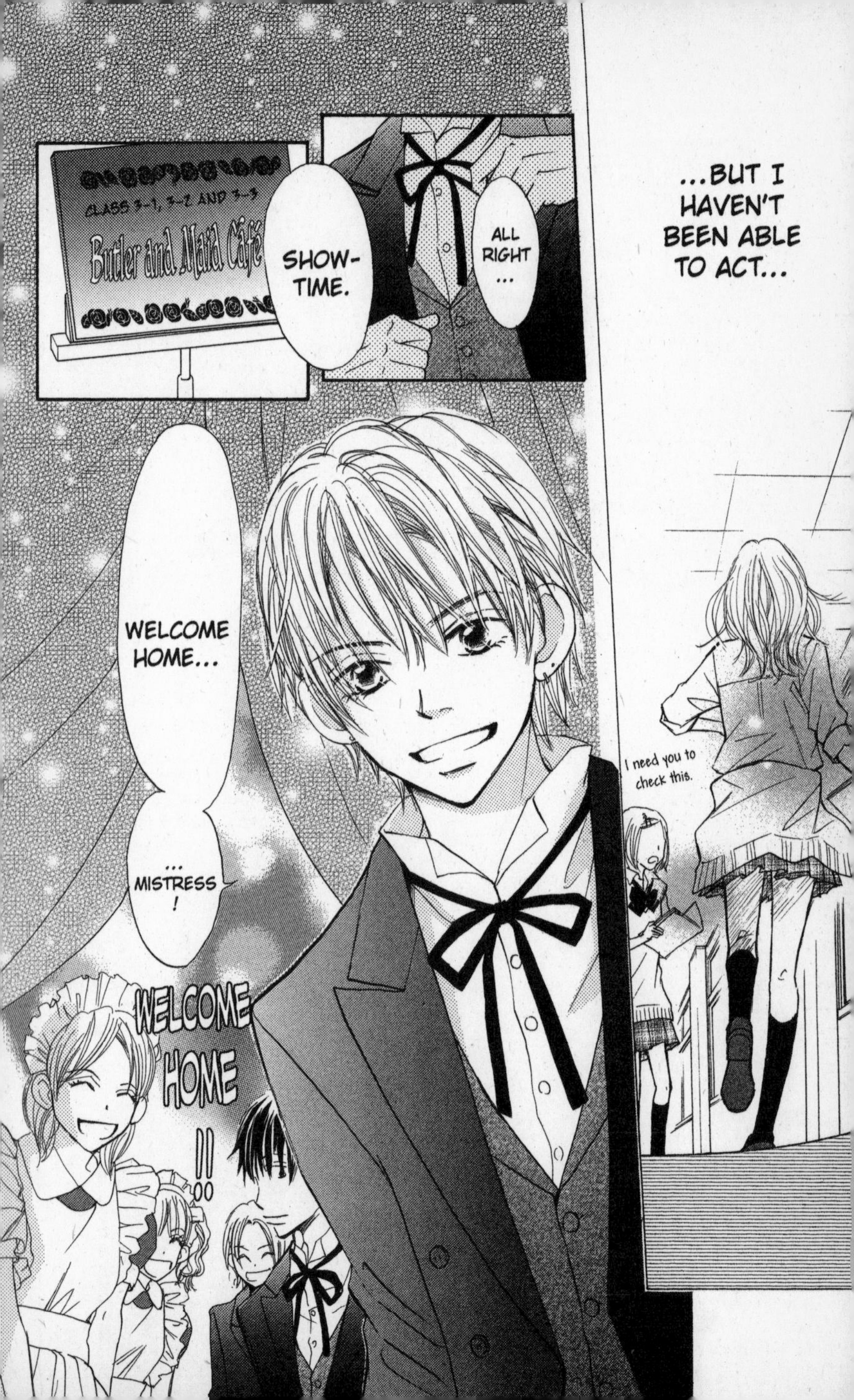
...BUT I HAVEN'T BEEN ABLE TO ACT...
I need you to check this.
ALL RIGHT...
SHOW-TIME.
CLASS 3-1, 3-2 AND 3-3
Butler and Maid Café
WELCOME HOME...
...MISTRESS!
WELCOME HOME!!

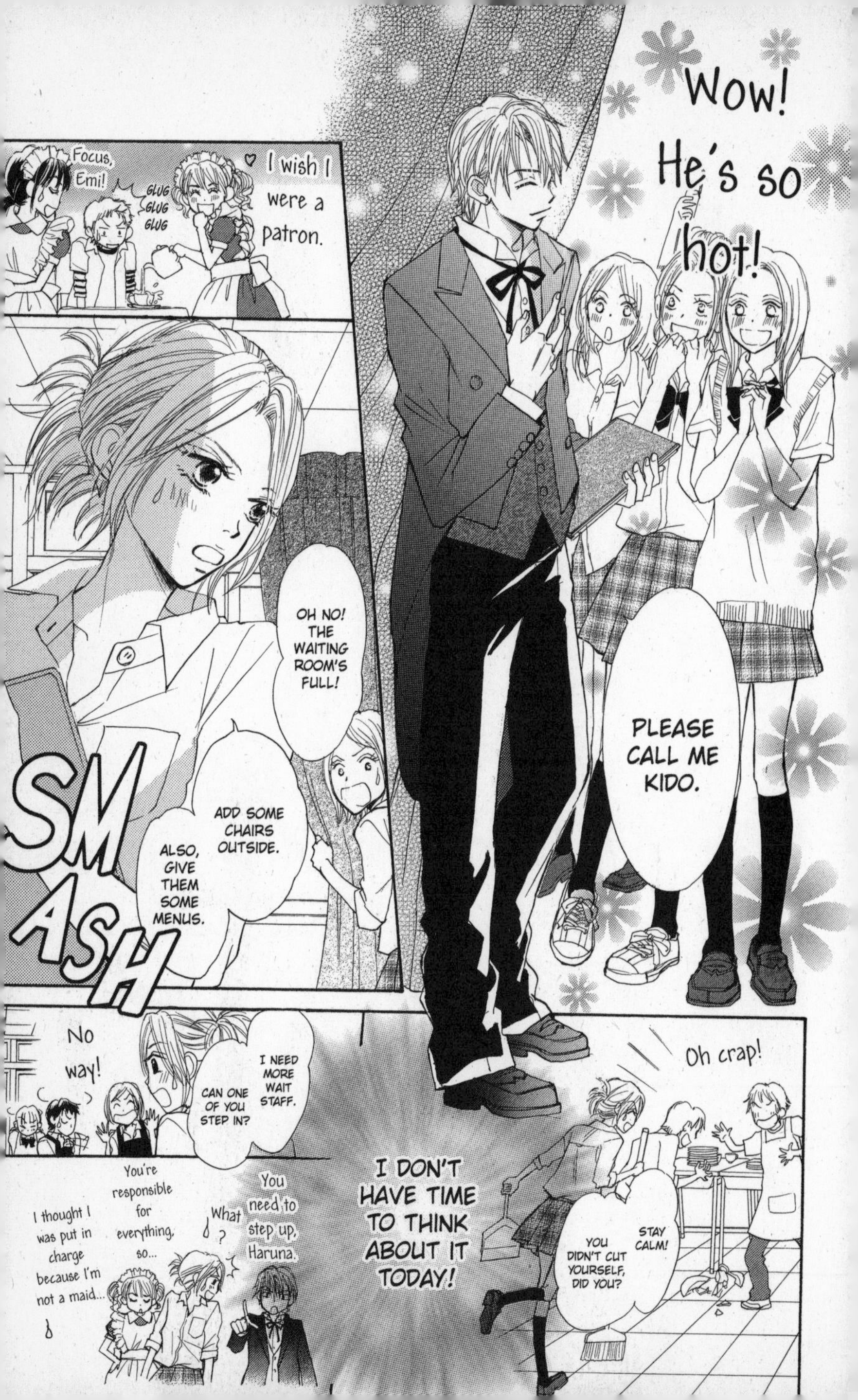
Wow! He's so hot!
PLEASE CALL ME KIDO.
I wish I were a patron.
GLUG GLUG GLUG
Focus, Emi!
OH NO! THE WAITING ROOM'S FULL!
ADD SOME CHAIRS OUTSIDE.
ALSO, GIVE THEM SOME MENUS.
SMASH
Oh crap!
STAY CALM!
YOU DIDN'T CUT YOURSELF, DID YOU?
I NEED MORE WAIT STAFF.
CAN ONE OF YOU STEP IN?
No way!
You need to step up, Haruna.
What?
You're responsible for everything, so...
I thought I was put in charge because I'm not a maid...
I DON'T HAVE TIME TO THINK ABOUT IT TODAY!

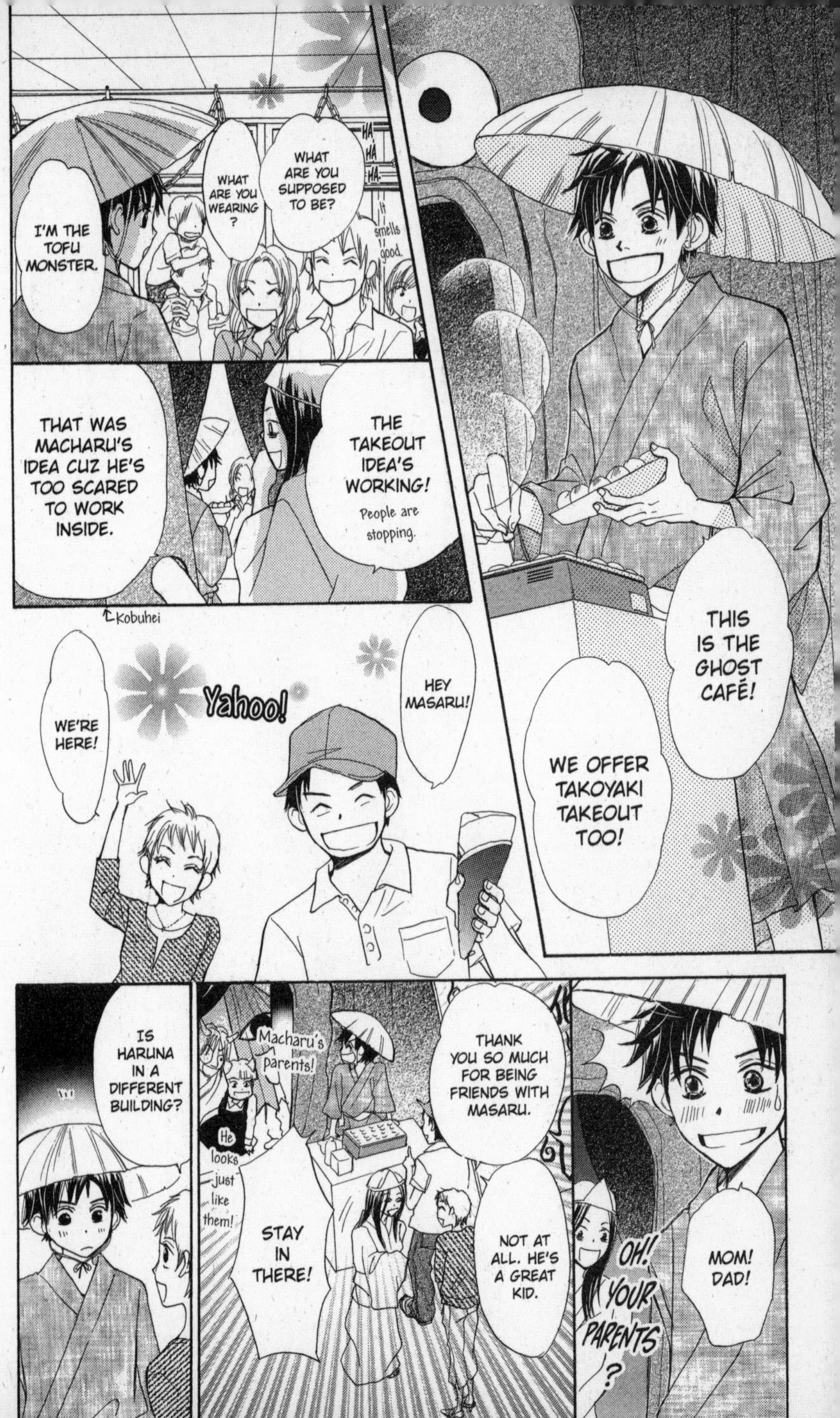

THIS IS THE GHOST CAFÉ!
WE OFFER TAKOYAKI TAKEOUT TOO!
HA HA HA
It smells good.
WHAT ARE YOU SUPPOSED TO BE?
WHAT ARE YOU WEARING?
I'M THE TOFU MONSTER.
THE TAKEOUT IDEA'S WORKING!
People are stopping.
THAT WAS MACHARU'S IDEA CUZ HE'S TOO SCARED TO WORK INSIDE.
Kobuhei
HEY MASARU!
Yahoo!
WE'RE HERE!
MOM! DAD!
OH! YOUR PARENTS?
THANK YOU SO MUCH FOR BEING FRIENDS WITH MASARU.
NOT AT ALL. HE'S A GREAT KID.
Macharu's parents!
He looks just like them!
STAY IN THERE!
IS HARUNA IN A DIFFERENT BUILDING?

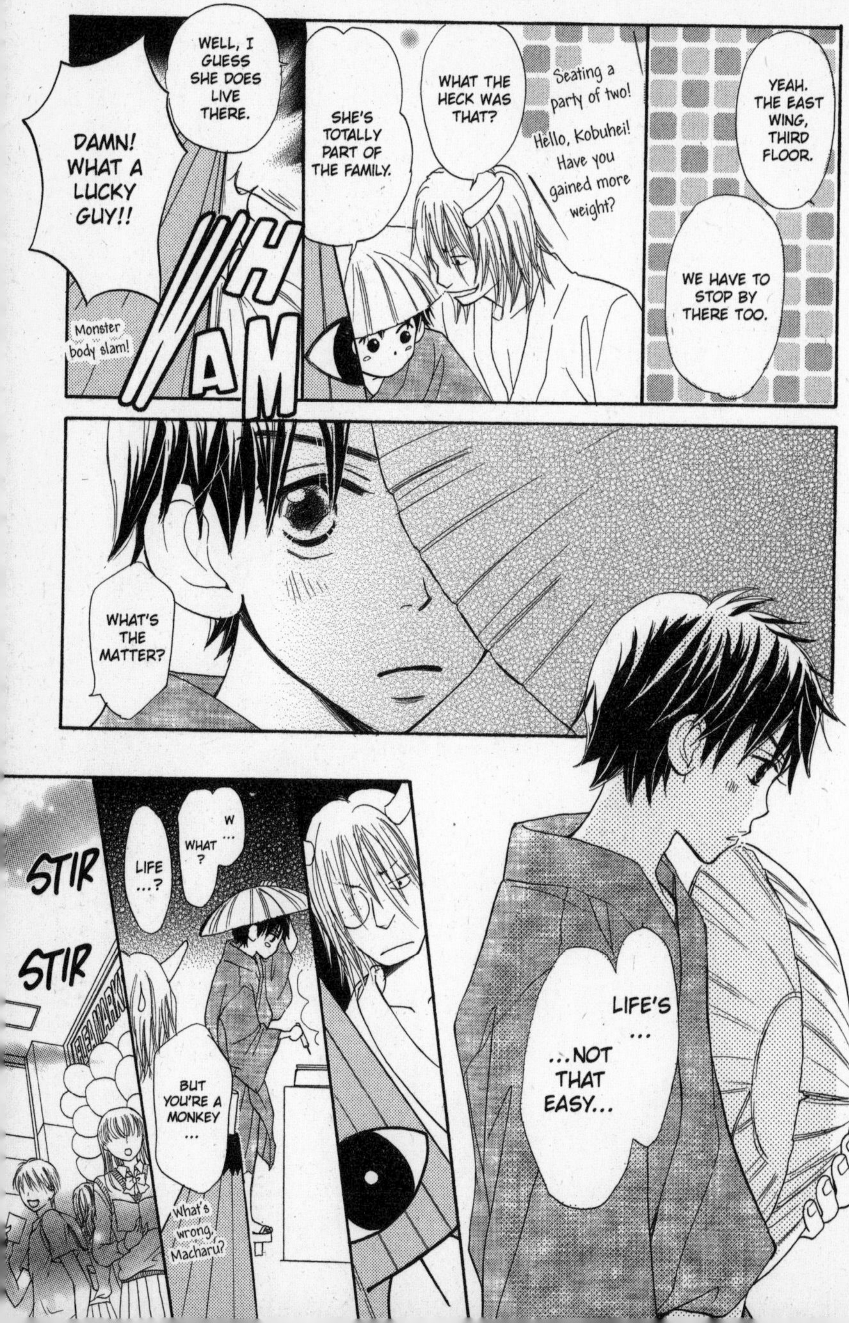
YEAH. THE EAST WING, THIRD FLOOR.
WE HAVE TO STOP BY THERE TOO.
WHAT THE HECK WAS THAT?
Seating a party of two!
Hello, Kobuhei! Have you gained more weight?
SHE'S TOTALLY PART OF THE FAMILY.
WELL, I GUESS SHE DOES LIVE THERE.
DAMN! WHAT A LUCKY GUY!!
WHAM
Monster body slam!
WHAT'S THE MATTER?
LIFE'S ...
...NOT THAT EASY...
W... WHAT?
LIFE...?
BUT YOU'RE A MONKEY...
What's wrong, Macharu?
STIR
STIR

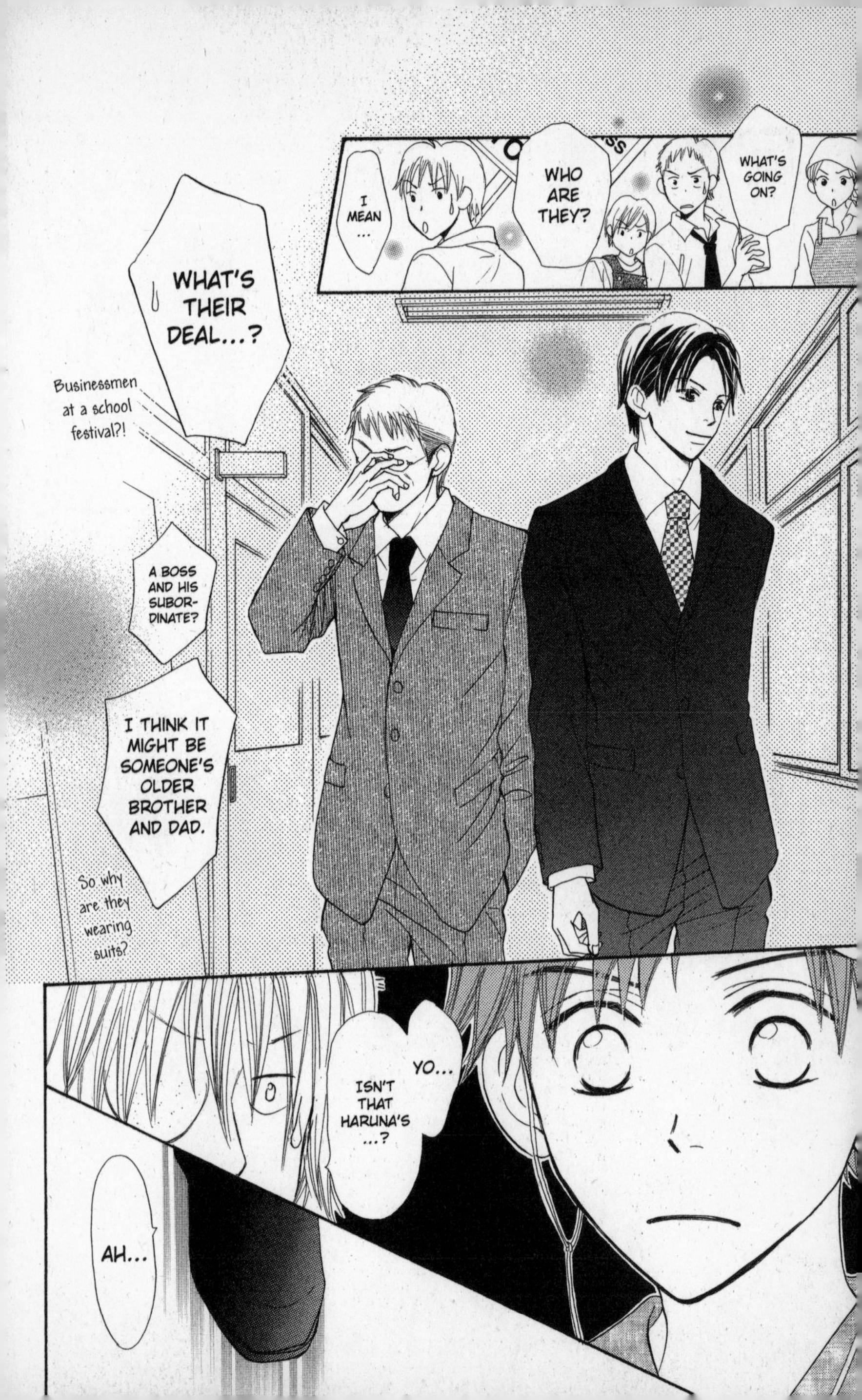
WHAT'S GOING ON?
WHO ARE THEY?
I MEAN ...
WHAT'S THEIR DEAL...?
Businessmen at a school festival?!
A BOSS AND HIS SUBORDINATE?
I THINK IT MIGHT BE SOMEONE'S OLDER BROTHER AND DAD.
So why are they wearing suits?
YO... ISN'T THAT HARUNA'S ...?
AH...

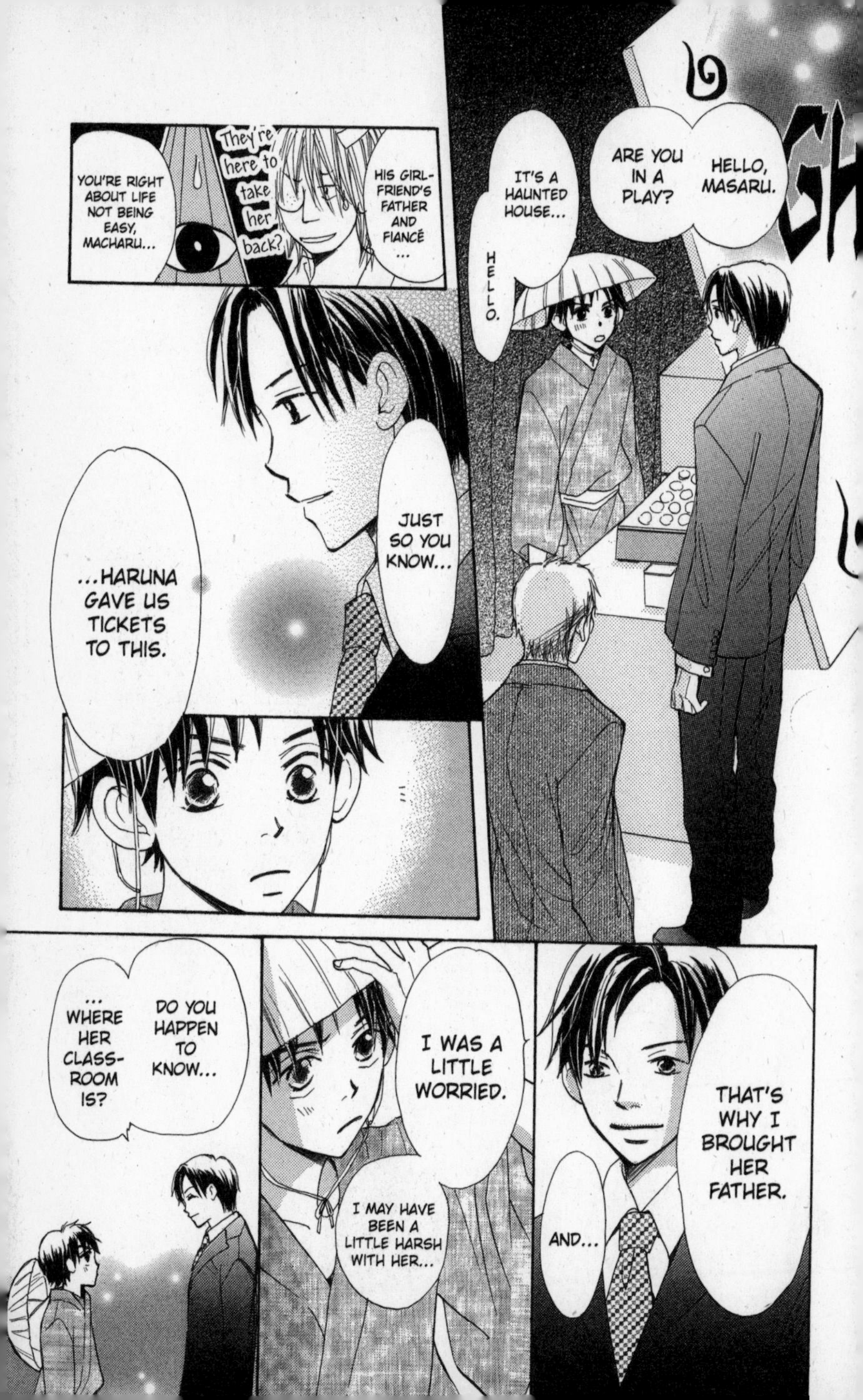
HELLO, MASARU.
ARE YOU IN A PLAY?
IT'S A HAUNTED HOUSE...
HELLO.
HIS GIRL-FRIEND'S FATHER AND FIANCÉ...
They're here to take her back?
YOU'RE RIGHT ABOUT LIFE NOT BEING EASY, MACHARU...
JUST SO YOU KNOW...
...HARUNA GAVE US TICKETS TO THIS.
THAT'S WHY I BROUGHT HER FATHER.
AND...
I WAS A LITTLE WORRIED.
I MAY HAVE BEEN A LITTLE HARSH WITH HER...
DO YOU HAPPEN TO KNOW...
...WHERE HER CLASS-ROOM IS?

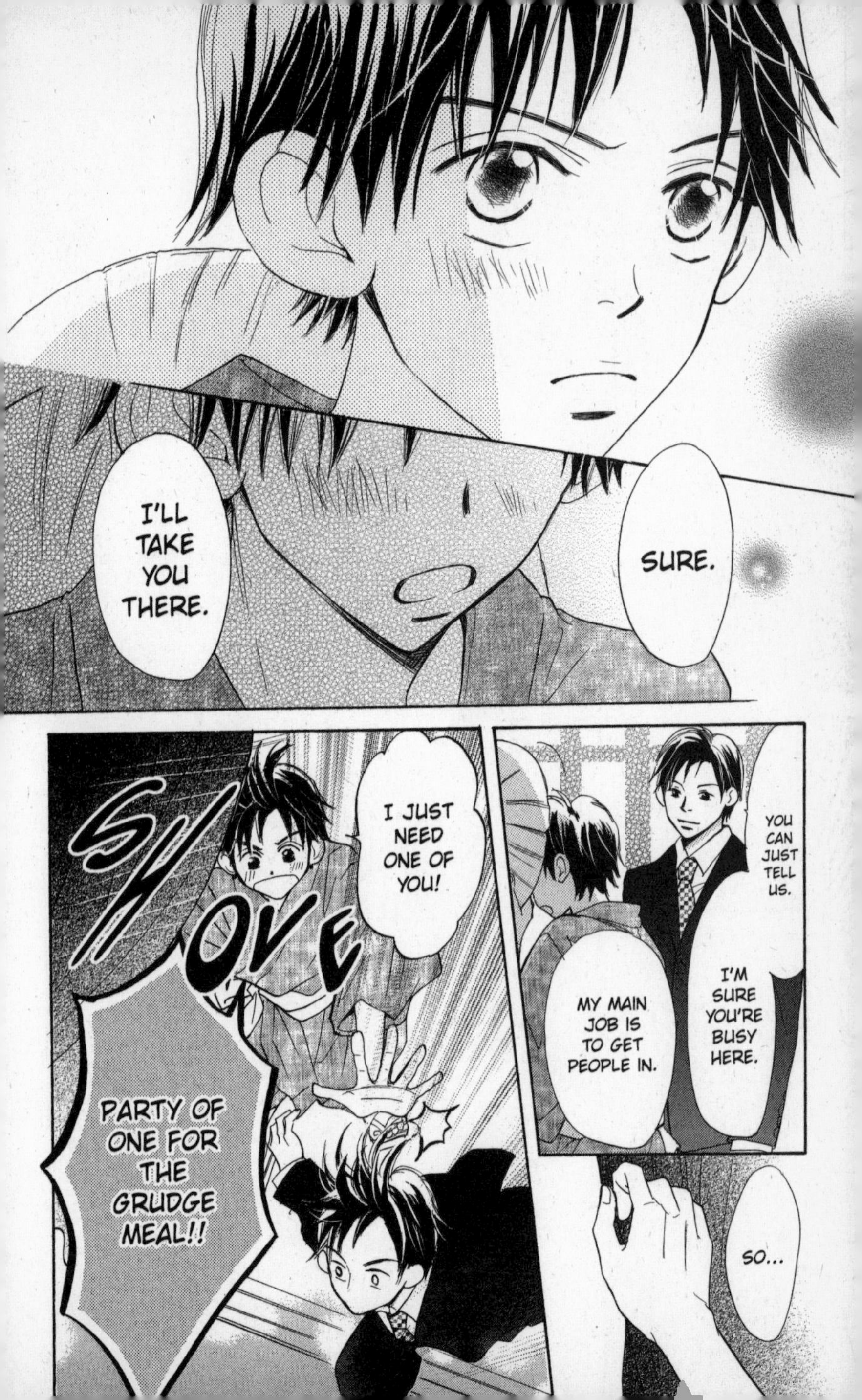
SURE.
I'LL TAKE YOU THERE.
YOU CAN JUST TELL US.
I'M SURE YOU'RE BUSY HERE.
MY MAIN JOB IS TO GET PEOPLE IN.
SO...
I JUST NEED ONE OF YOU!
SHOVE
PARTY OF ONE FOR THE GRUDGE MEAL!!

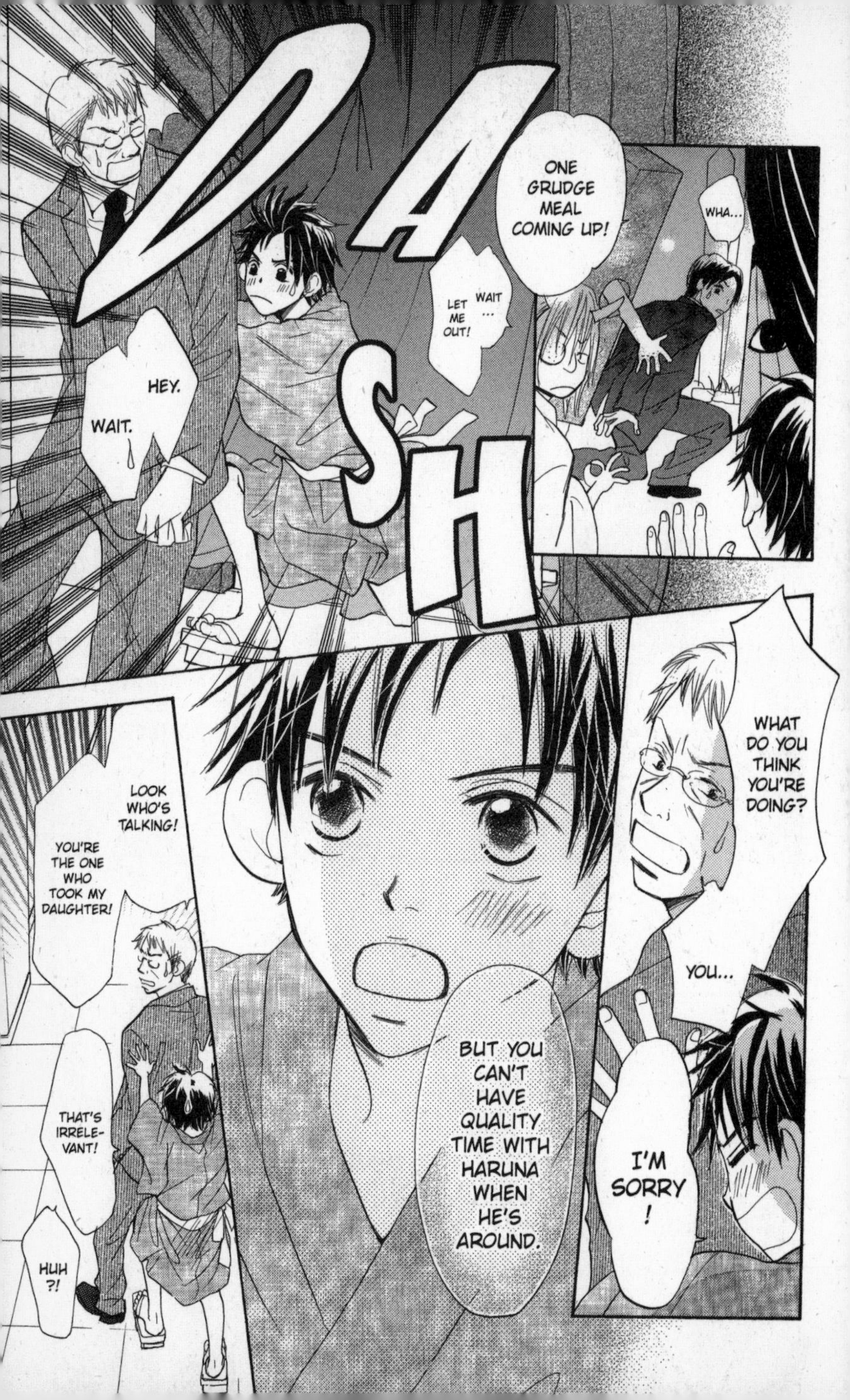
ONE GRUDGE MEAL COMING UP!
WHA...
WAIT ...
LET ME OUT!
DASH
HEY.
WAIT.
WHAT DO YOU THINK YOU'RE DOING?
YOU...
I'M SORRY!
BUT YOU CAN'T HAVE QUALITY TIME WITH HARUNA WHEN HE'S AROUND.
LOOK WHO'S TALKING!
YOU'RE THE ONE WHO TOOK MY DAUGHTER!
THAT'S IRRELEVANT!
HUH?!

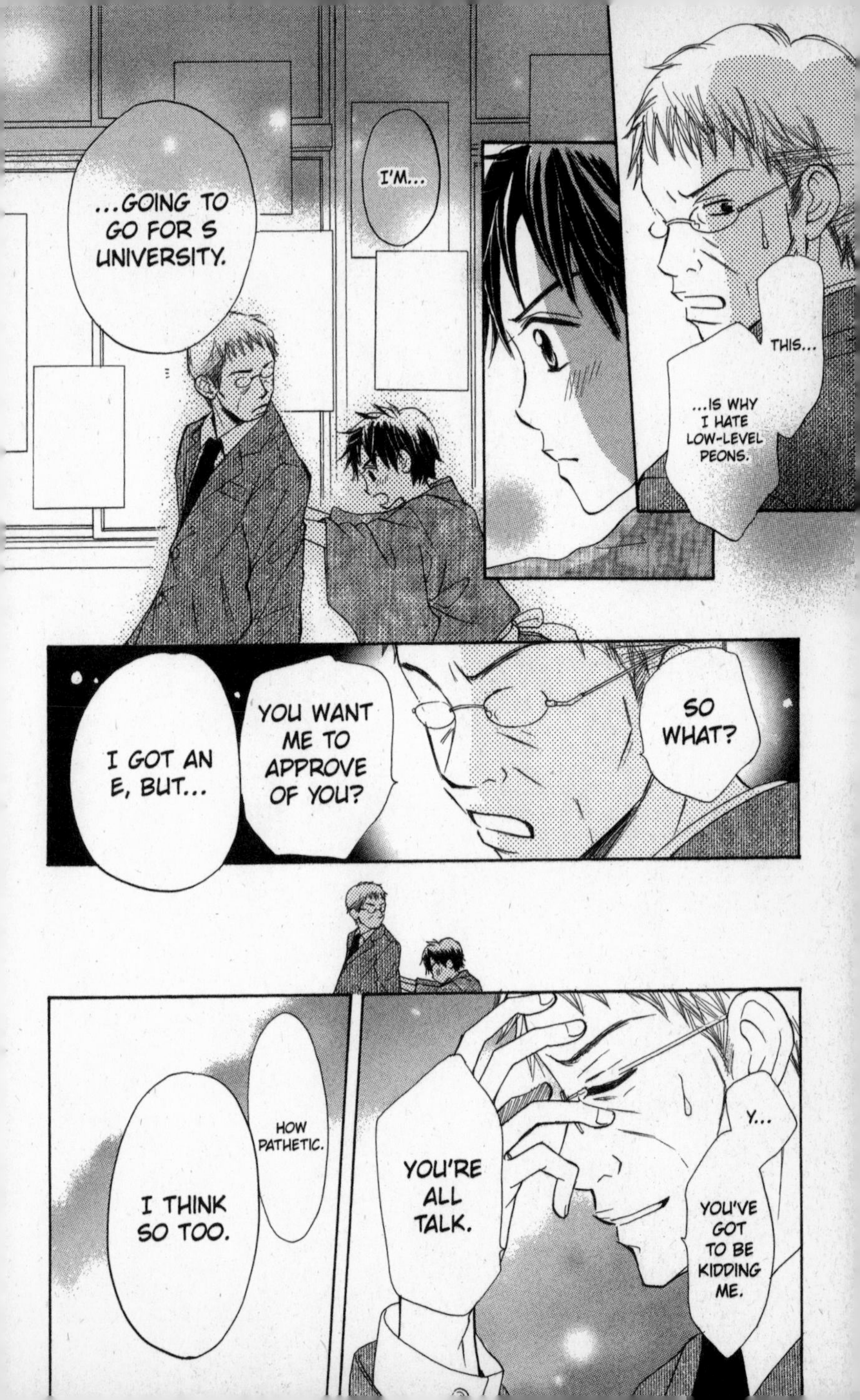
THIS...
...IS WHY I HATE LOW-LEVEL PEONS.
I'M...
...GOING TO GO FOR S UNIVERSITY.
SO WHAT?
YOU WANT ME TO APPROVE OF YOU?
I GOT AN E, BUT...
Y...
YOU'VE GOT TO BE KIDDING ME.
YOU'RE ALL TALK.
HOW PATHETIC.
I THINK SO TOO.

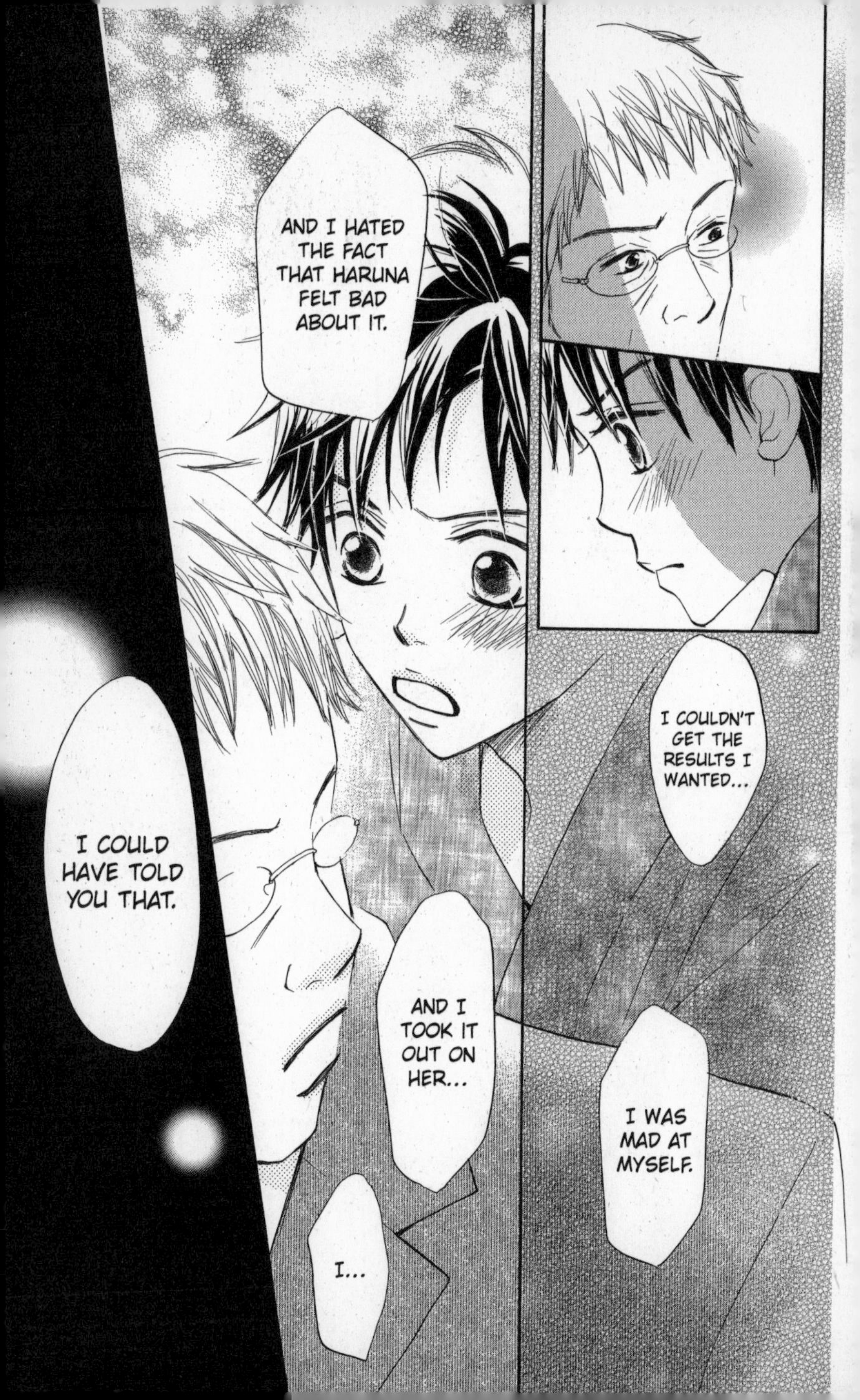
I COULDN'T GET THE RESULTS I WANTED...
I WAS MAD AT MYSELF.
AND I HATED THE FACT THAT HARUNA FELT BAD ABOUT IT.
AND I TOOK IT OUT ON HER...
I...
I COULD HAVE TOLD YOU THAT.

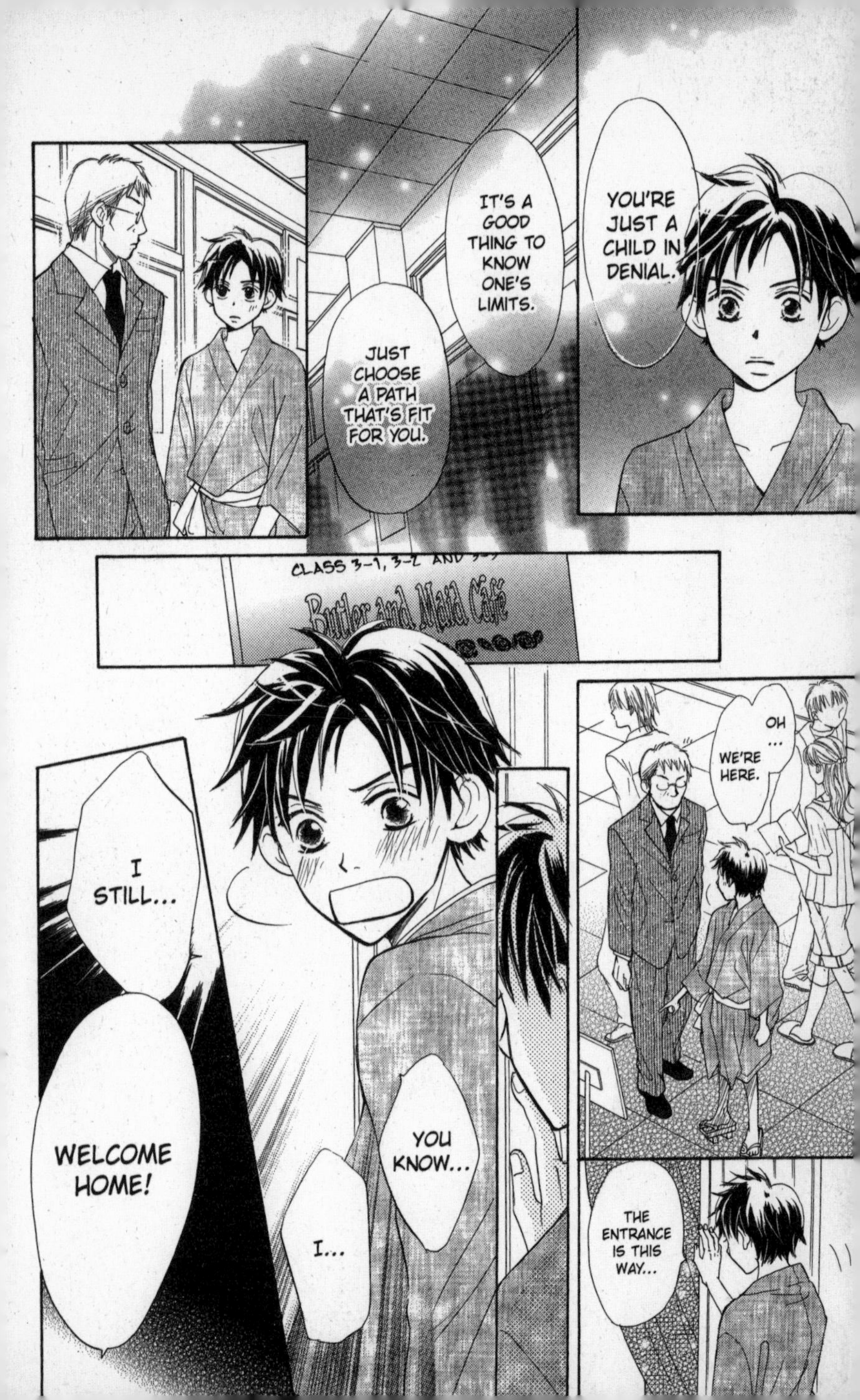
YOU'RE JUST A CHILD IN DENIAL.
IT'S A GOOD THING TO KNOW ONE'S LIMITS.
JUST CHOOSE A PATH THAT'S FIT FOR YOU.
CLASS 3-1, 3-2 AND
Butler and Maid Café
OH... WE'RE HERE.
THE ENTRANCE IS THIS WAY...
YOU KNOW...
I...
I STILL...
WELCOME HOME!

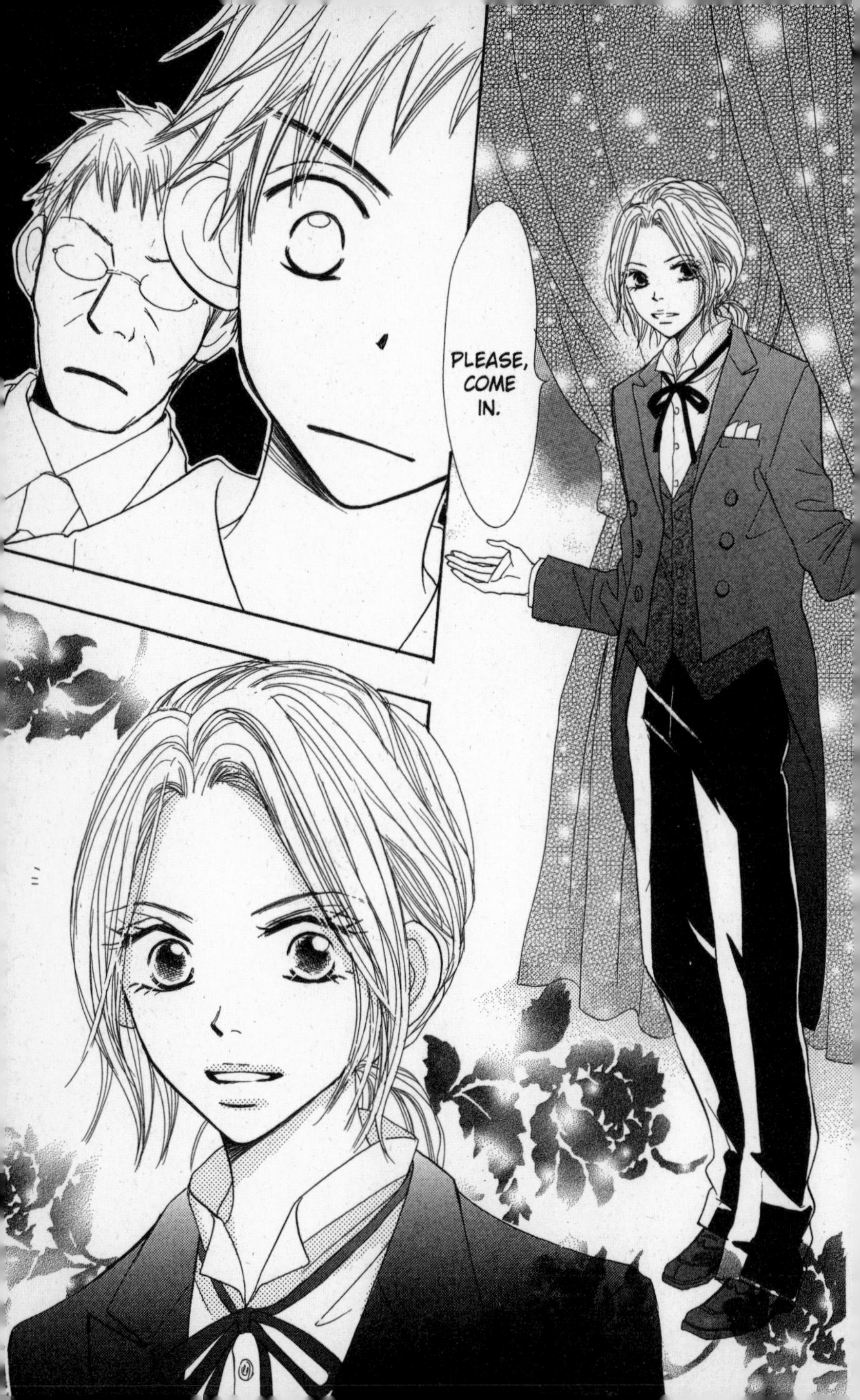
PLEASE, COME IN.

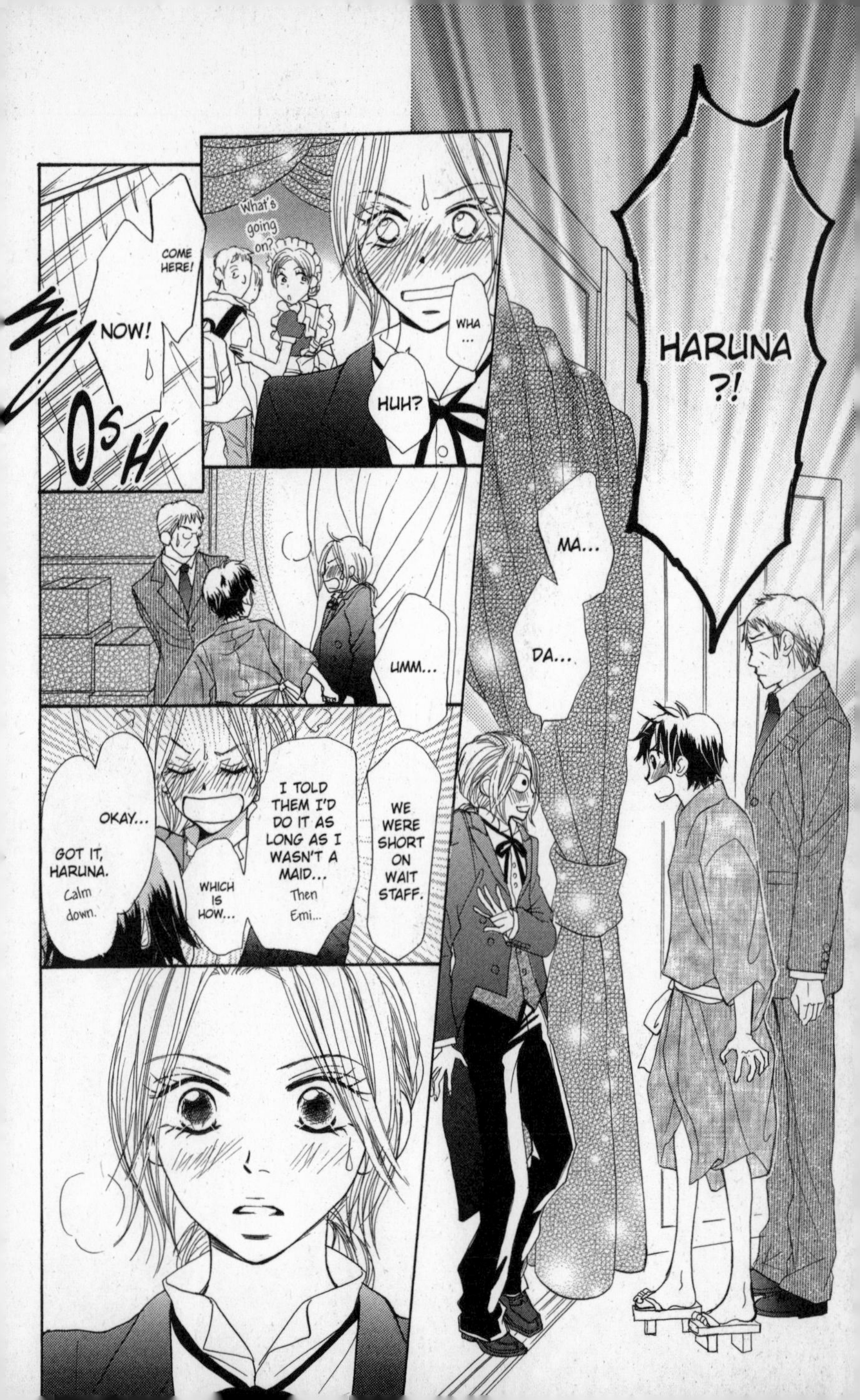
HARUNA ?!
MA...
DA...
WHA...
HUH?
What's going on?
COME HERE!
NOW!
WHOOSH
UMM...
WE WERE SHORT ON WAIT STAFF.
I TOLD THEM I'D DO IT AS LONG AS I WASN'T A MAID...
Then Emi...
WHICH IS HOW...
OKAY... GOT IT, HARUNA.
Calm down.

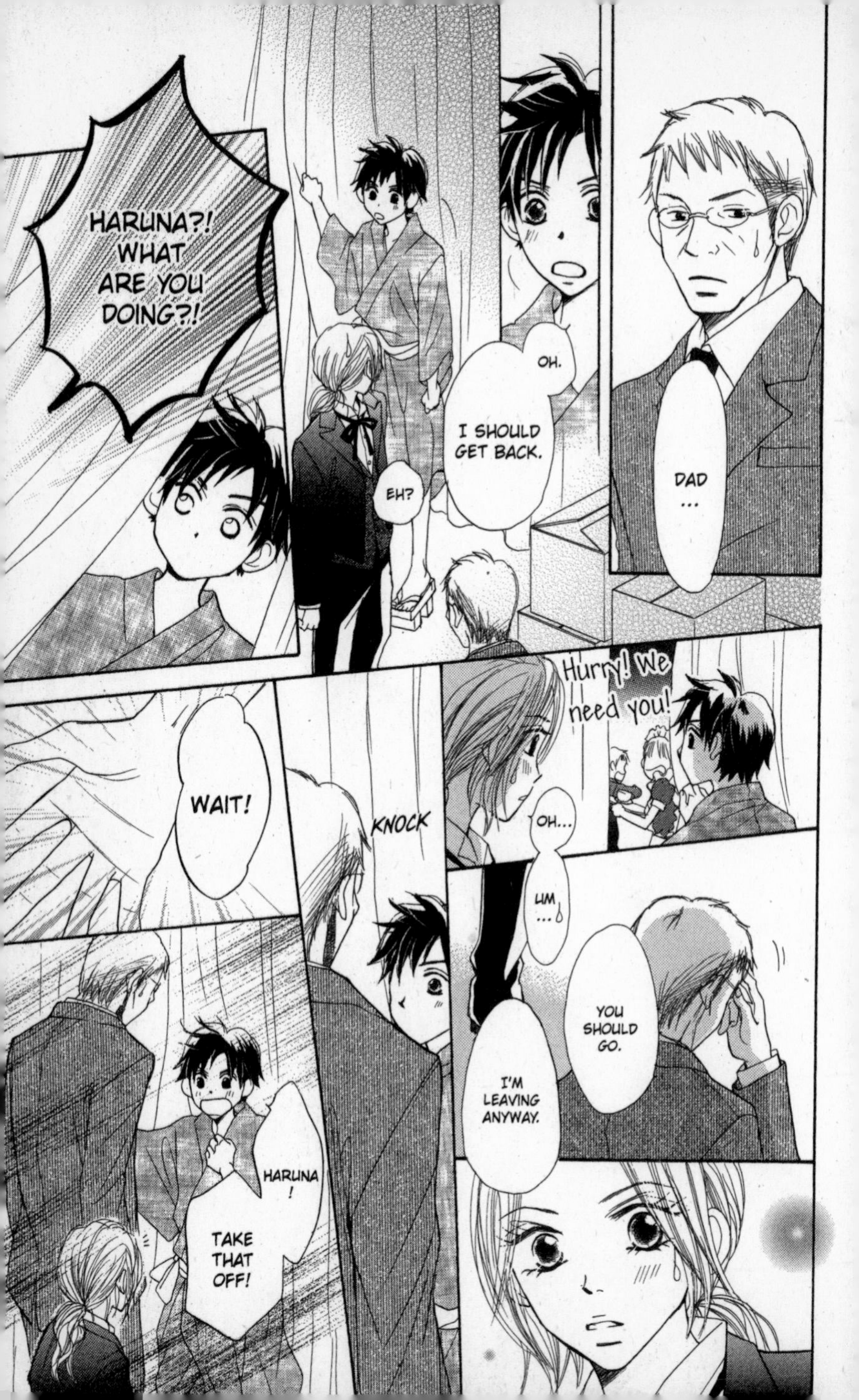
DAD ...
OH.
I SHOULD GET BACK.
EH?
HARUNA?! WHAT ARE YOU DOING?!
Hurry! We need you!
OH...
UM ...
YOU SHOULD GO.
I'M LEAVING ANYWAY.
KNOCK
WAIT!
HARUNA!
TAKE THAT OFF!

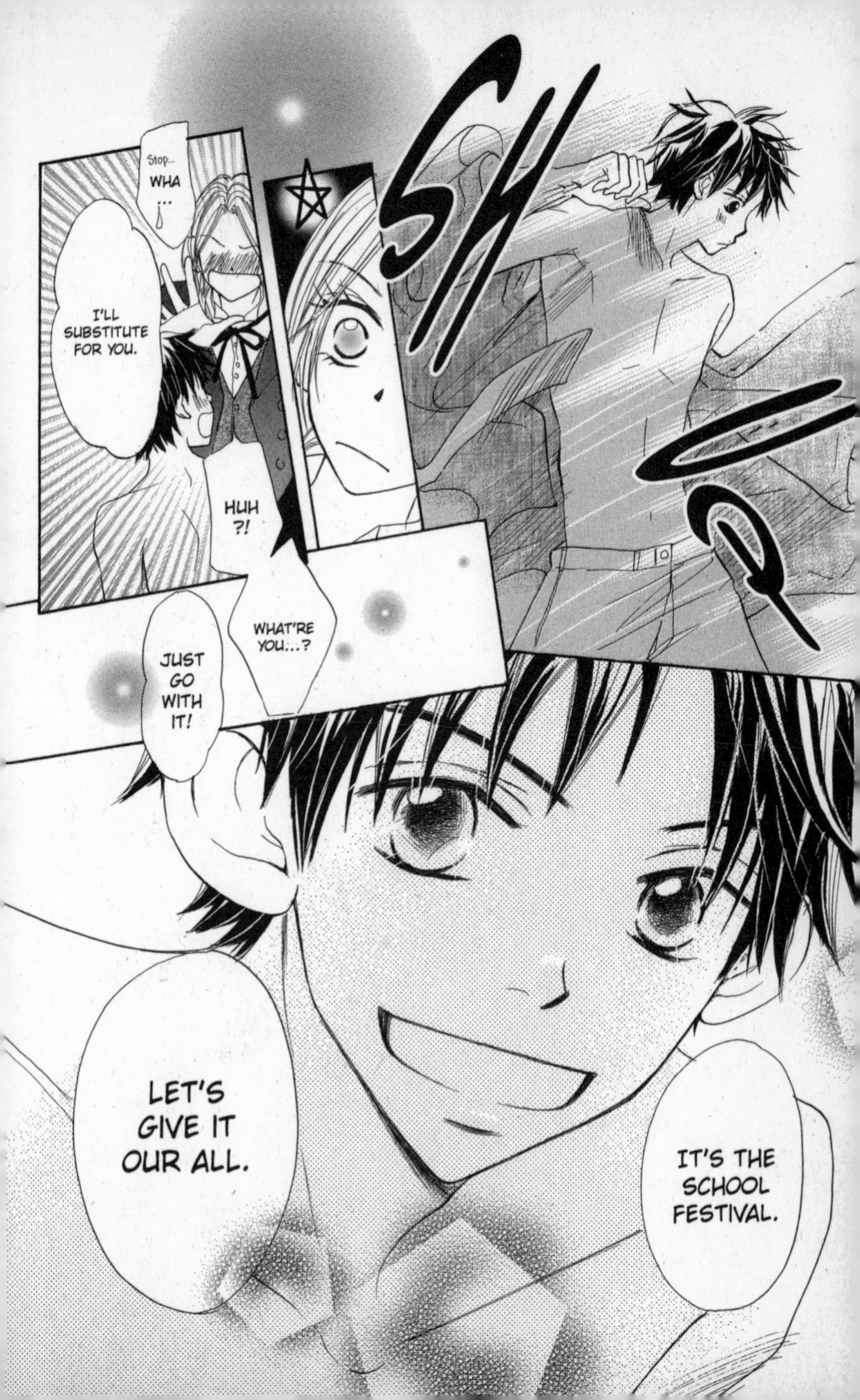
SHUP
Stop... WHA...?
I'LL SUBSTITUTE FOR YOU.
HUH?!
WHAT'RE YOU...?
JUST GO WITH IT!
IT'S THE SCHOOL FESTIVAL.
LET'S GIVE IT OUR ALL.

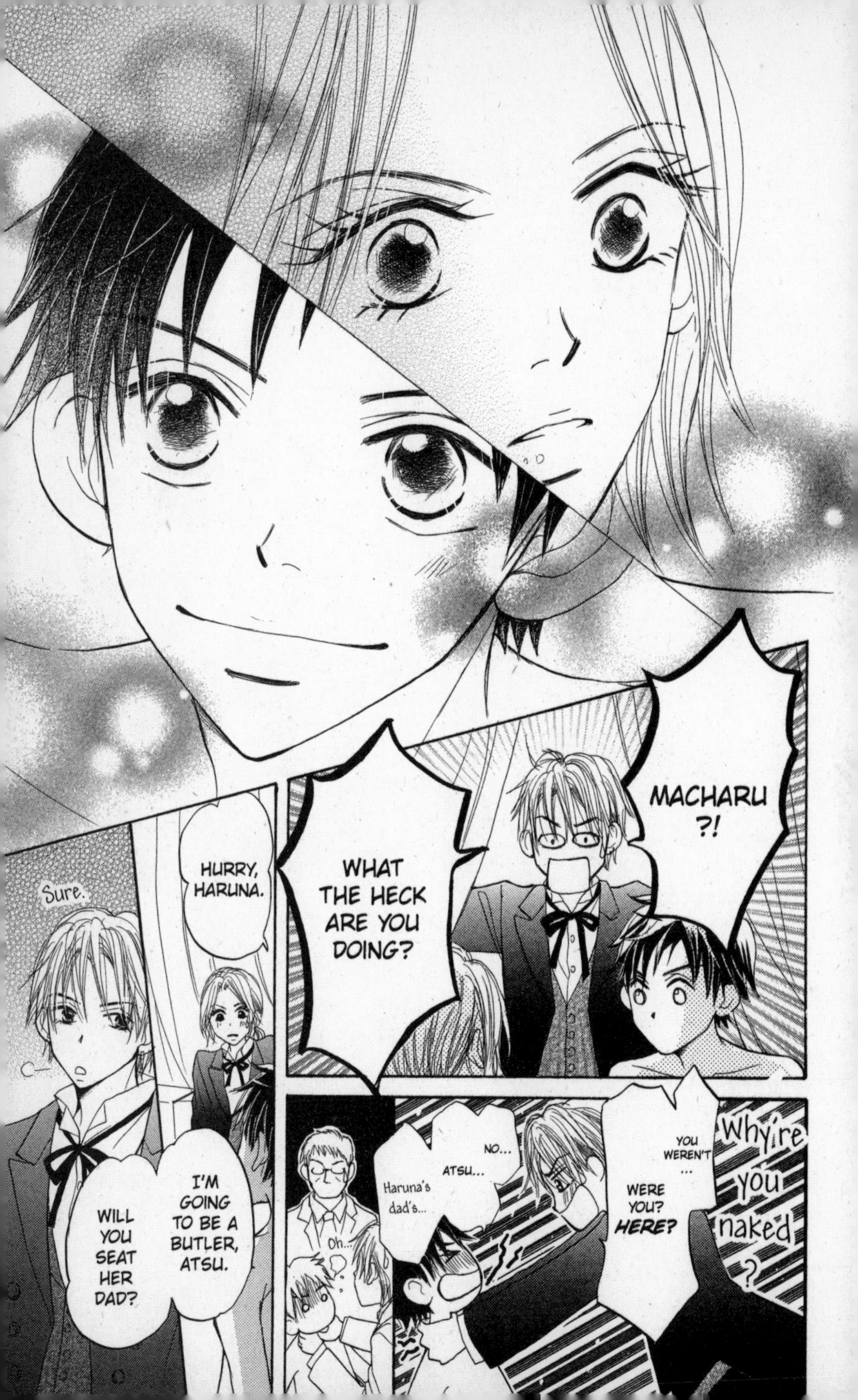
MACHARU ?!
WHAT THE HECK ARE YOU DOING?
Why're you naked?
YOU WEREN'T ... WERE YOU? HERE?
NO... ATSU...
Haruna's dad's...
Oh...
HURRY, HARUNA.
Sure.
I'M GOING TO BE A BUTLER, ATSU.
WILL YOU SEAT HER DAD?

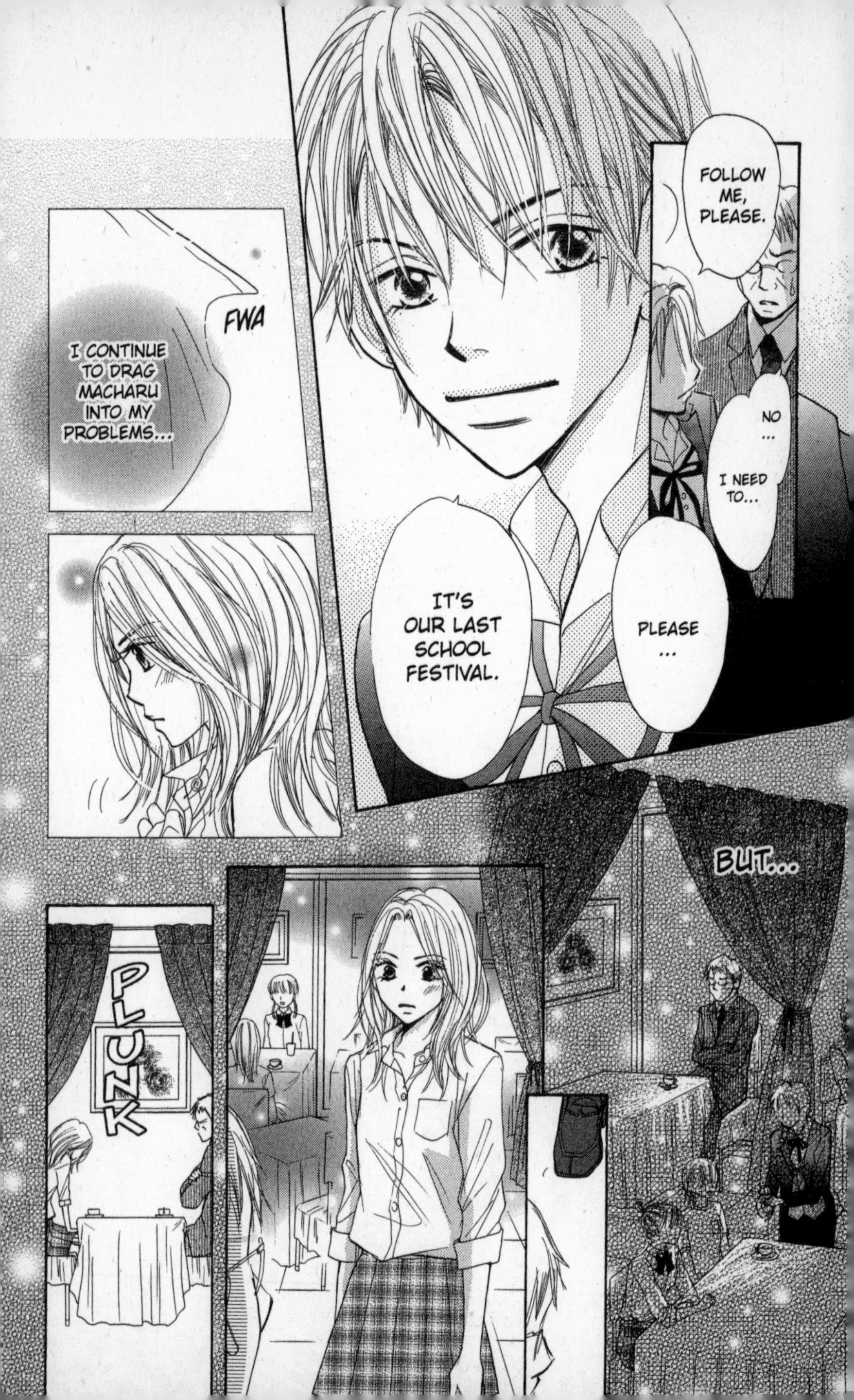
FOLLOW ME, PLEASE.
NO ... I NEED TO...
PLEASE ...
IT'S OUR LAST SCHOOL FESTIVAL.
FWA
I CONTINUE TO DRAG MACHARU INTO MY PROBLEMS...
BUT...
PLUNK

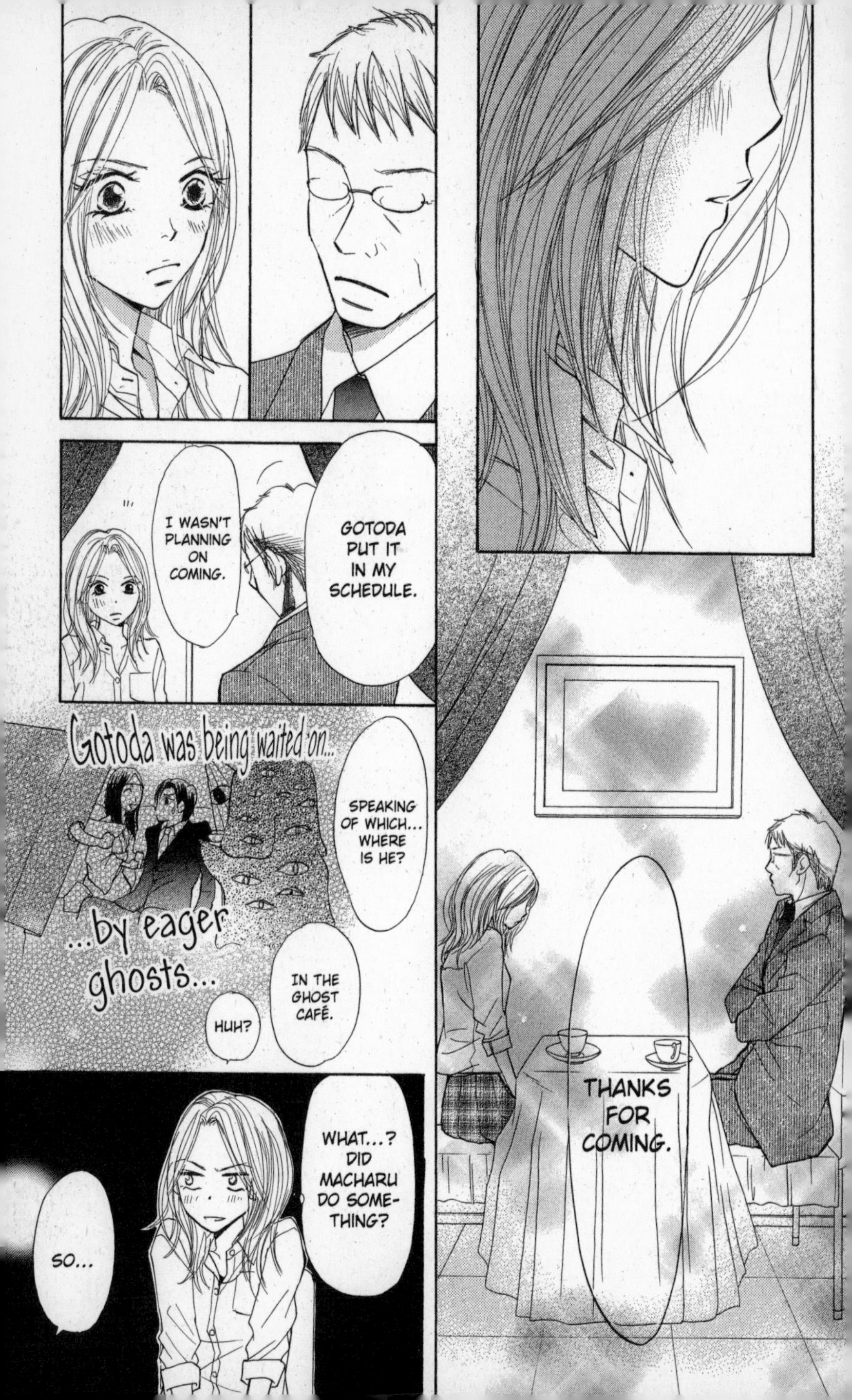
THANKS FOR COMING.
GOTODA PUT IT IN MY SCHEDULE.
I WASN'T PLANNING ON COMING.
SPEAKING OF WHICH... WHERE IS HE?
IN THE GHOST CAFÉ.
HUH?
Gotoda was being waited on...
...by eager ghosts...
WHAT...? DID MACHARU DO SOME-THING?
SO...

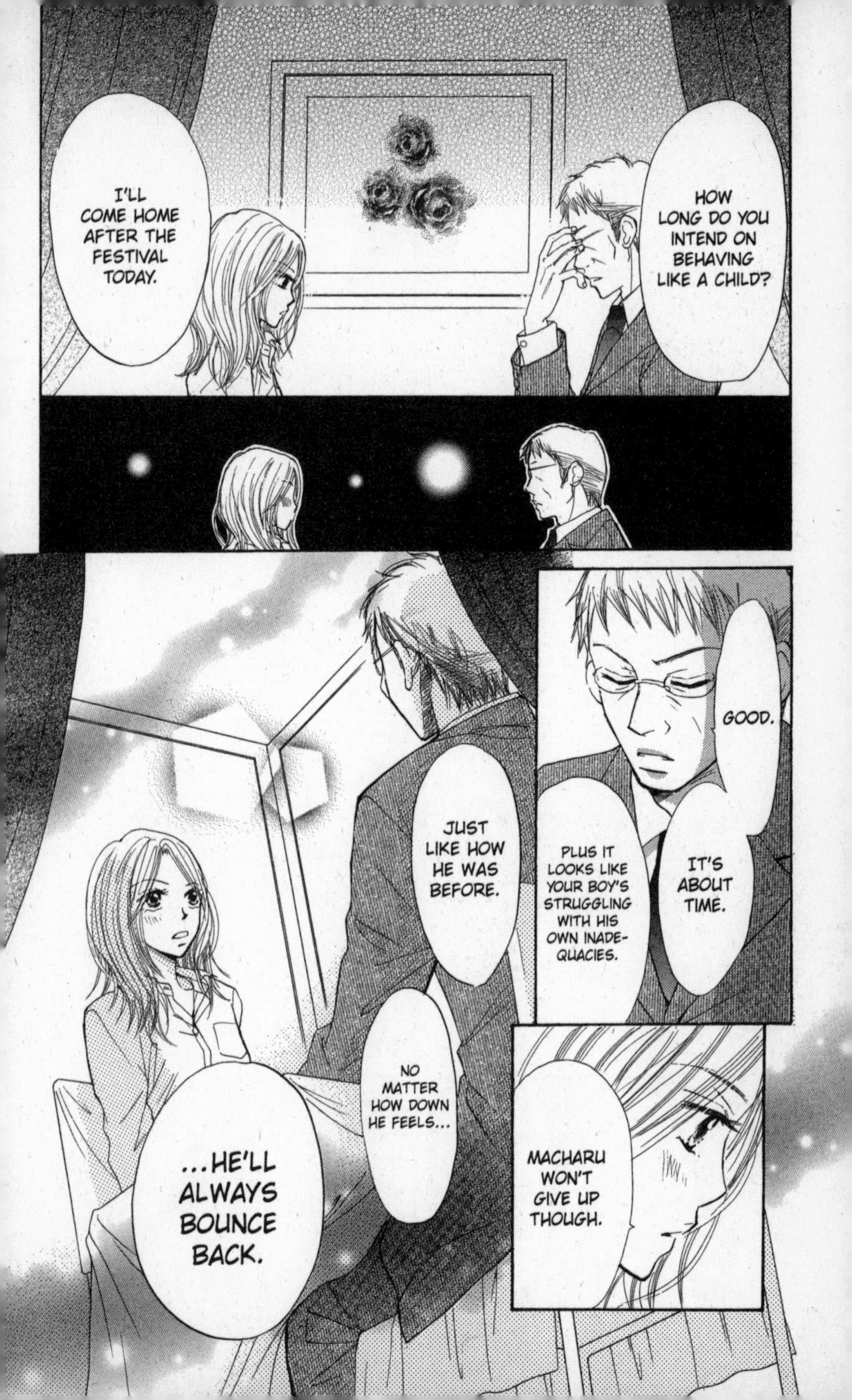
HOW LONG DO YOU INTEND ON BEHAVING LIKE A CHILD?
I'LL COME HOME AFTER THE FESTIVAL TODAY.
GOOD.
IT'S ABOUT TIME.
PLUS IT LOOKS LIKE YOUR BOY'S STRUGGLING WITH HIS OWN INADE-QUACIES.
MACHARU WON'T GIVE UP THOUGH.
JUST LIKE HOW HE WAS BEFORE.
NO MATTER HOW DOWN HE FEELS...
...HE'LL ALWAYS BOUNCE BACK.

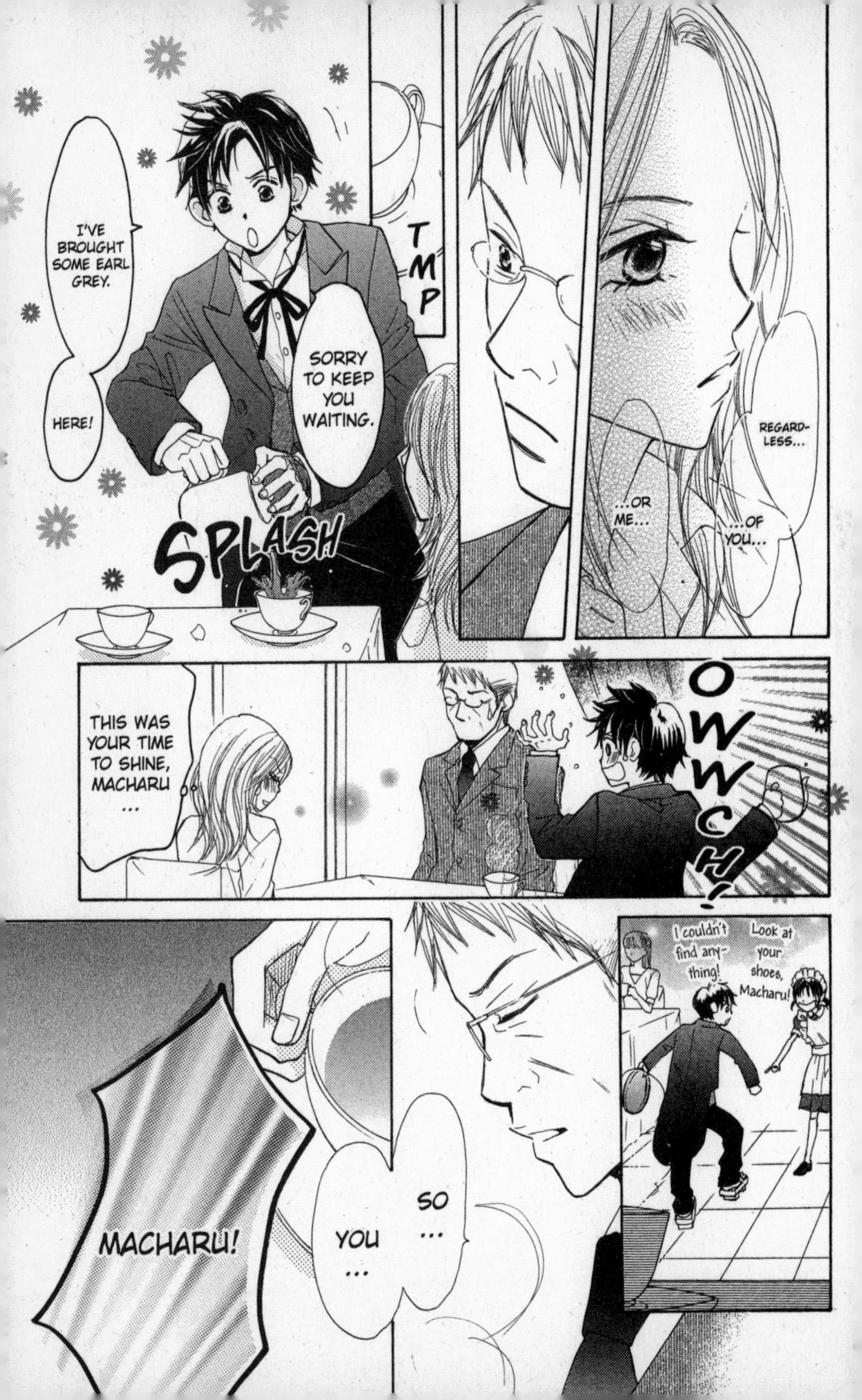
REGARDLESS...
...OF YOU...
...OR ME...
TMP
SORRY TO KEEP YOU WAITING.
I'VE BROUGHT SOME EARL GREY.
HERE!
SPLASH
OWWCH!
THIS WAS YOUR TIME TO SHINE, MACHARU...
Look at your shoes, Macharu!
I couldn't find anything!
SO...
YOU...
MACHARU!

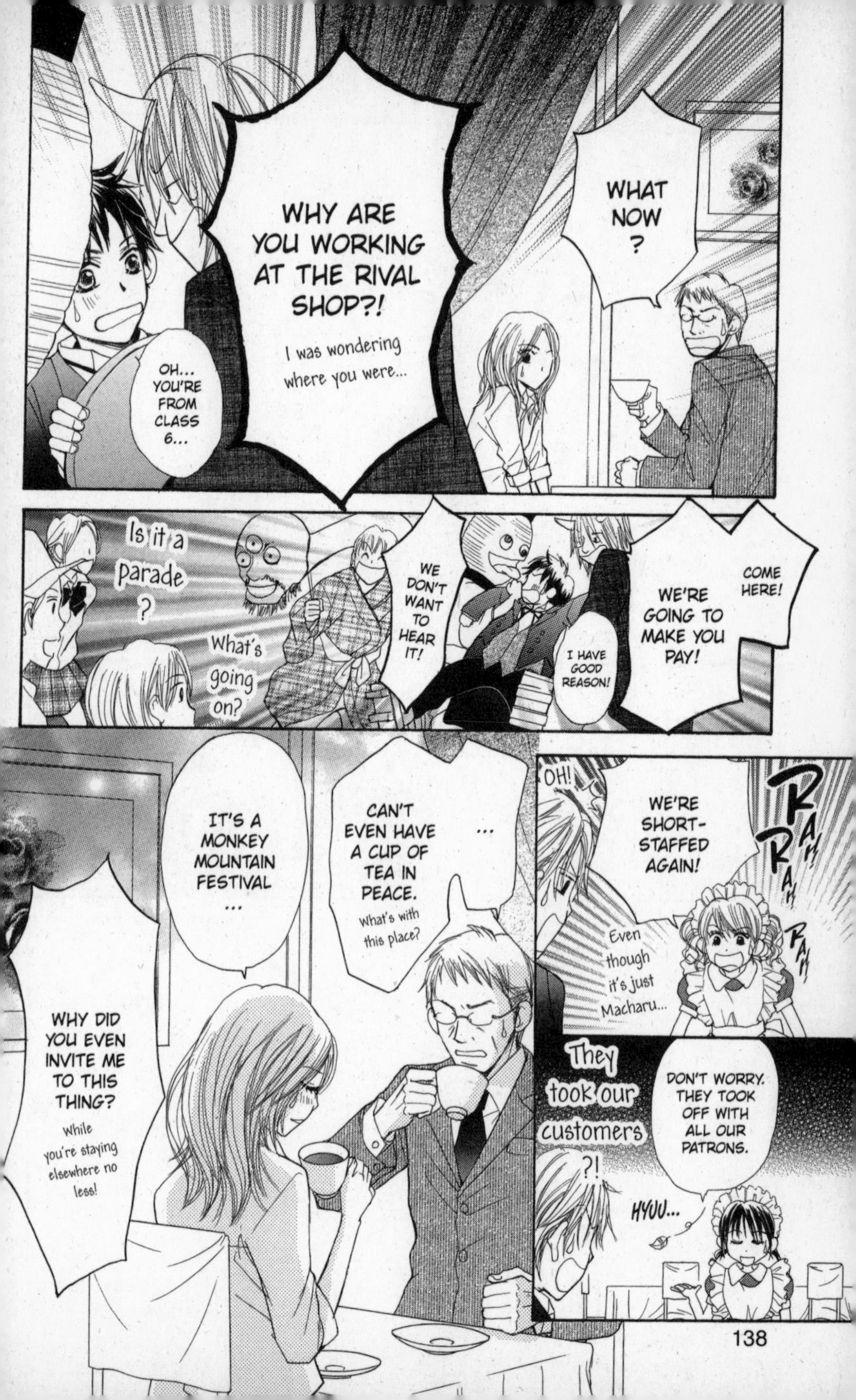
WHAT NOW ?
WHY ARE YOU WORKING AT THE RIVAL SHOP?!
I was wondering where you were...
OH... YOU'RE FROM CLASS 6...
COME HERE!
WE'RE GOING TO MAKE YOU PAY!
I HAVE GOOD REASON!
WE DON'T WANT TO HEAR IT!
Is it a parade ?
What's going on?
RAH RAH RAH RAH
WE'RE SHORT-STAFFED AGAIN!
OH!
Even though it's just Macharu...
DON'T WORRY. THEY TOOK OFF WITH ALL OUR PATRONS.
HYUU...
They took our customers ?!
...
CAN'T EVEN HAVE A CUP OF TEA IN PEACE.
What's with this place?
IT'S A MONKEY MOUNTAIN FESTIVAL ...
WHY DID YOU EVEN INVITE ME TO THIS THING?
While you're staying elsewhere no less!

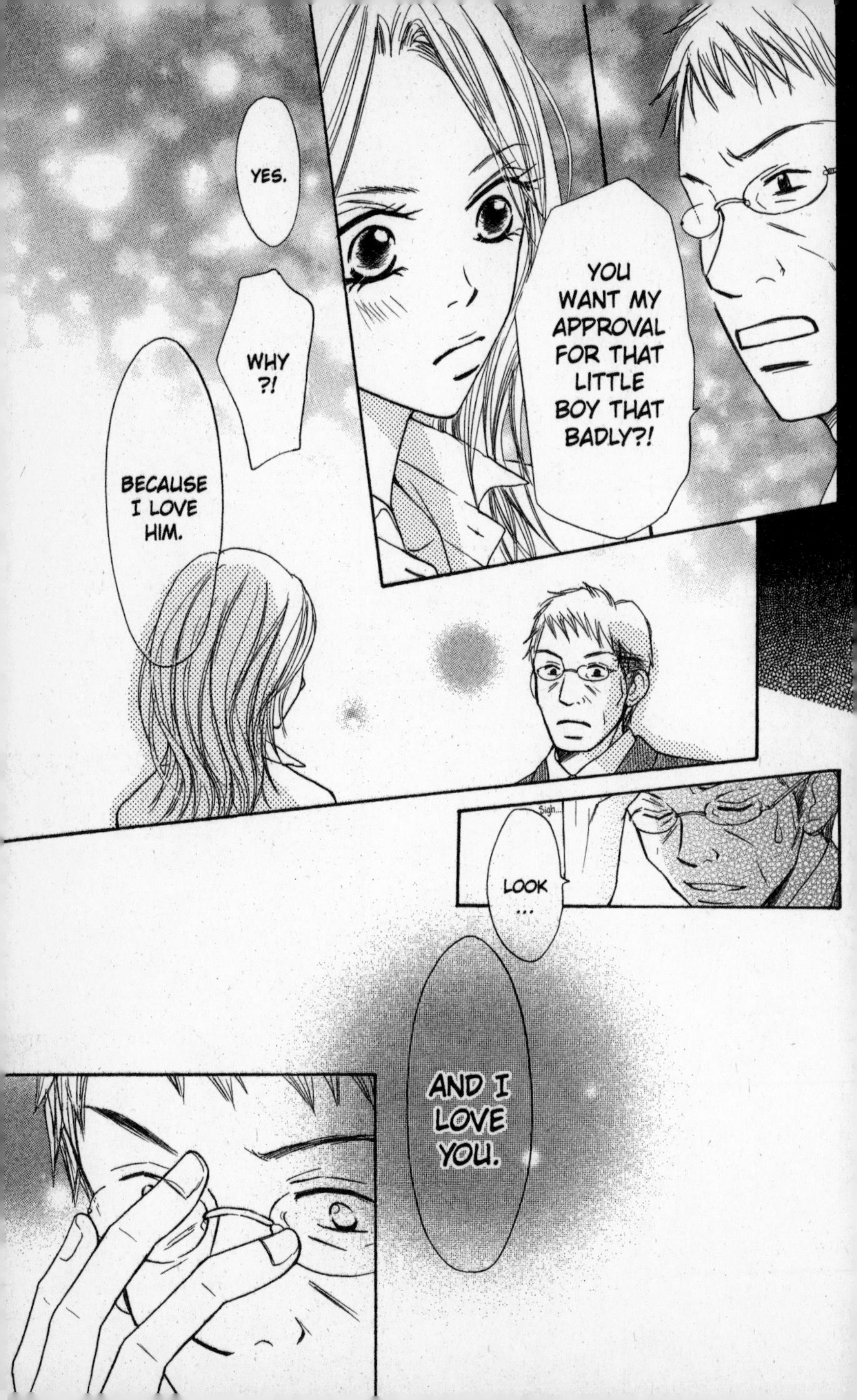
YOU WANT MY APPROVAL FOR THAT LITTLE BOY THAT BADLY?!
YES.
WHY?!
BECAUSE I LOVE HIM.
Sigh...
LOOK...
AND I LOVE YOU.

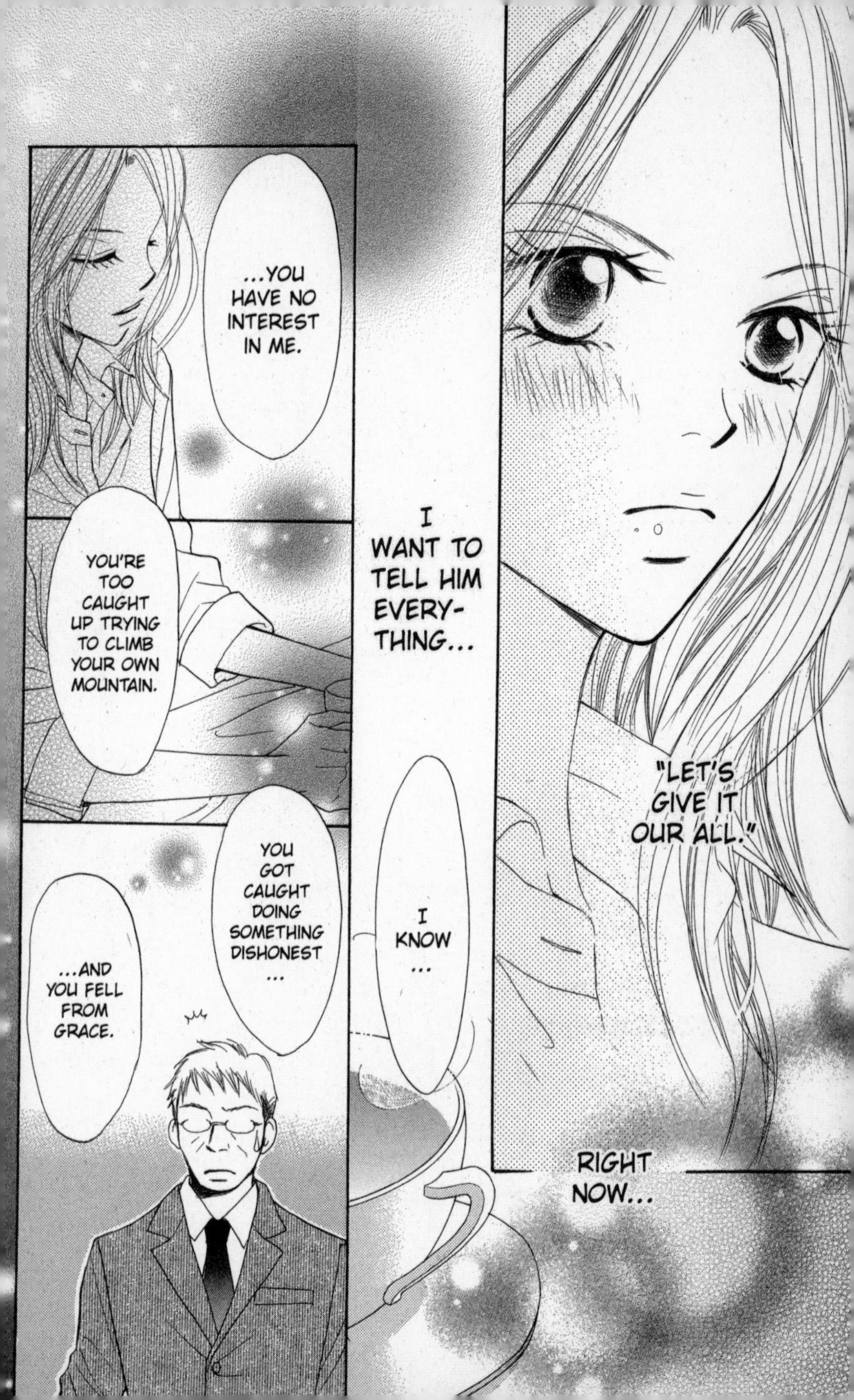
"LET'S GIVE IT OUR ALL."
I WANT TO TELL HIM EVERYTHING...
RIGHT NOW...
...YOU HAVE NO INTEREST IN ME.
YOU'RE TOO CAUGHT UP TRYING TO CLIMB YOUR OWN MOUNTAIN.
I KNOW...
YOU GOT CAUGHT DOING SOMETHING DISHONEST...
...AND YOU FELL FROM GRACE.

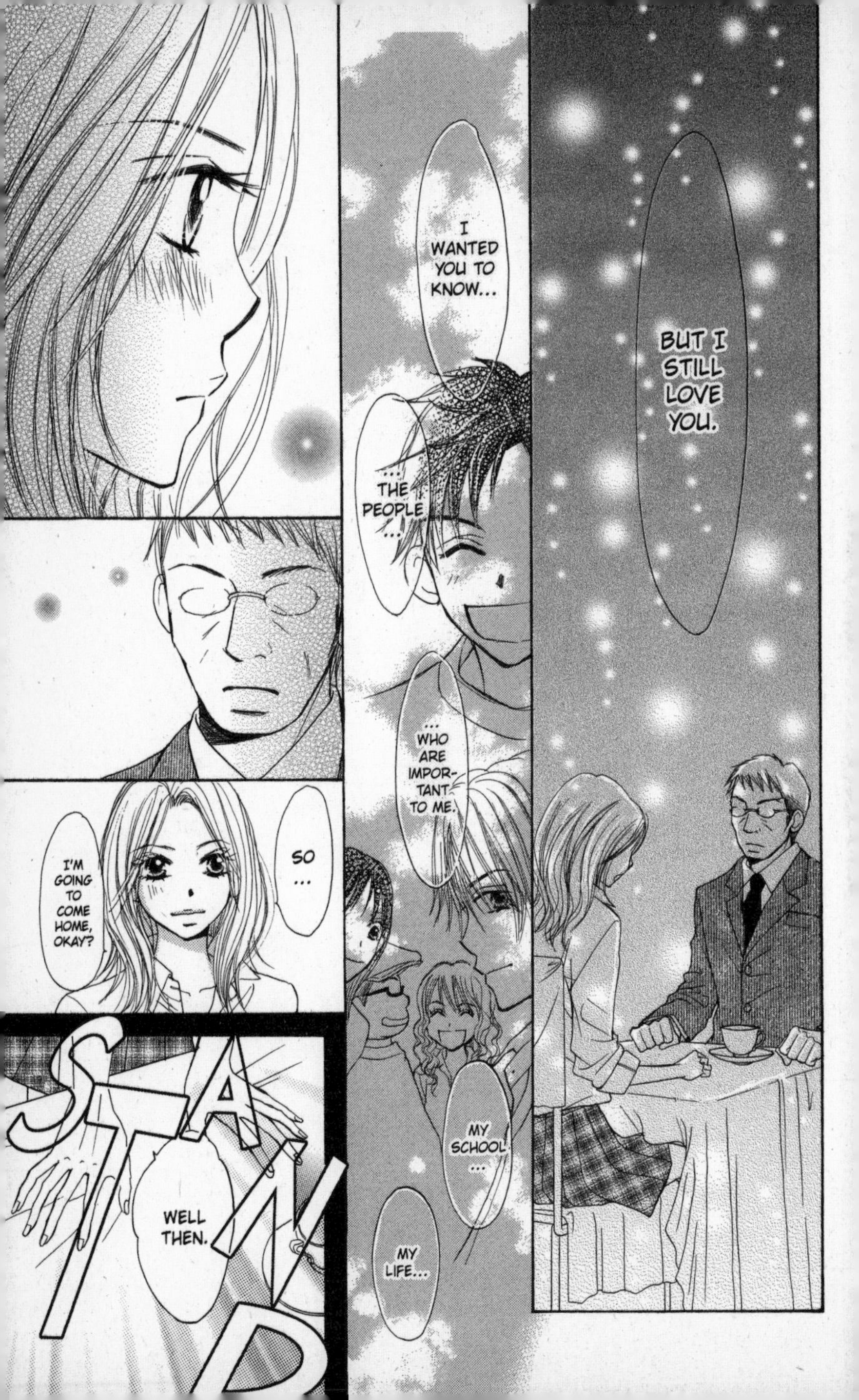
BUT I STILL LOVE YOU.
I WANTED YOU TO KNOW...
...THE PEOPLE...
...WHO ARE IMPORTANT TO ME.
MY SCHOOL...
MY LIFE...
SO...
I'M GOING TO COME HOME, OKAY?
STAND
WELL THEN.

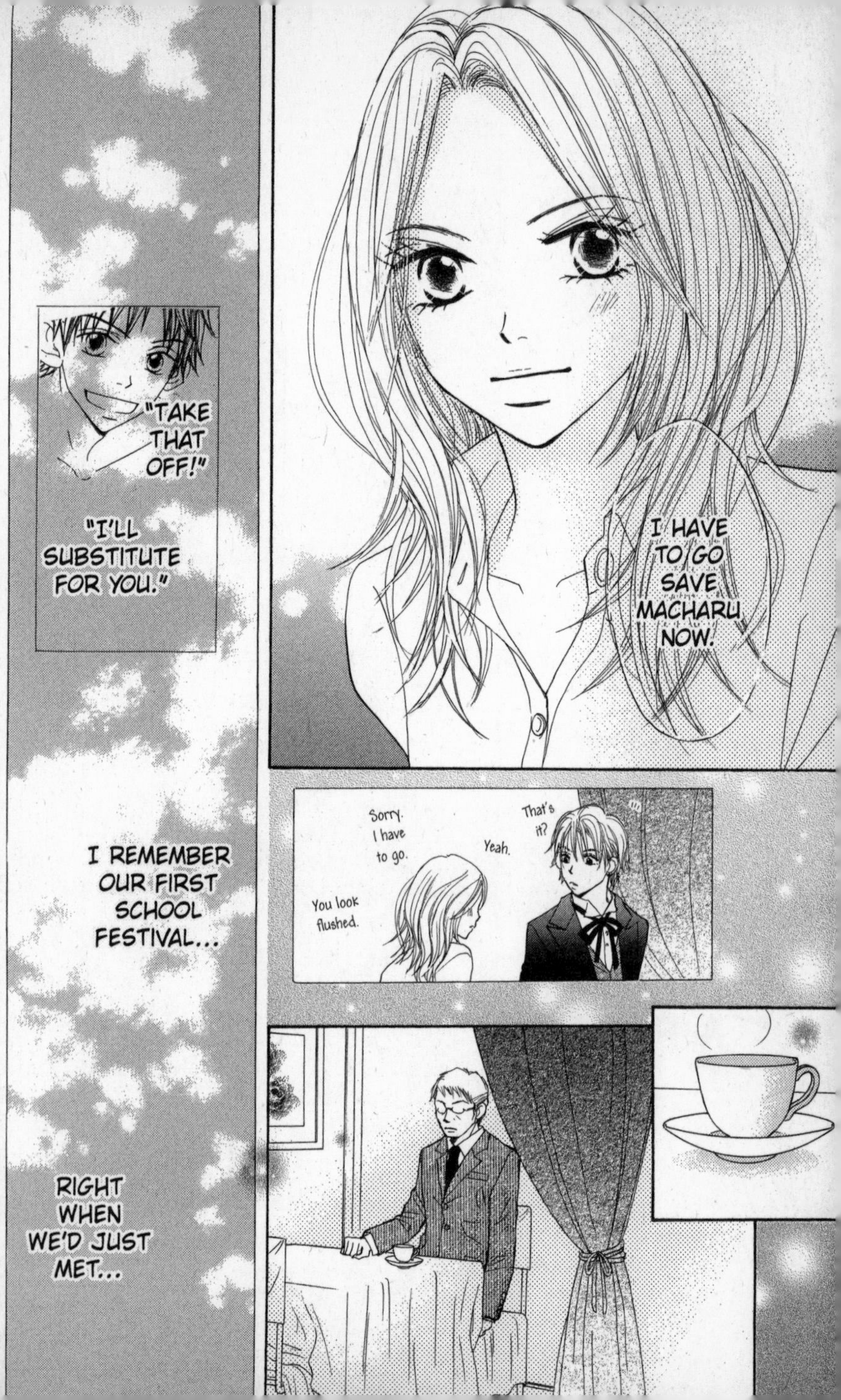
I HAVE TO GO SAVE MACHARU NOW.
That's it?
Yeah.
Sorry. I have to go.
You look flushed.
"TAKE THAT OFF!"
"I'LL SUBSTITUTE FOR YOU."
I REMEMBER OUR FIRST SCHOOL FESTIVAL...
RIGHT WHEN WE'D JUST MET...

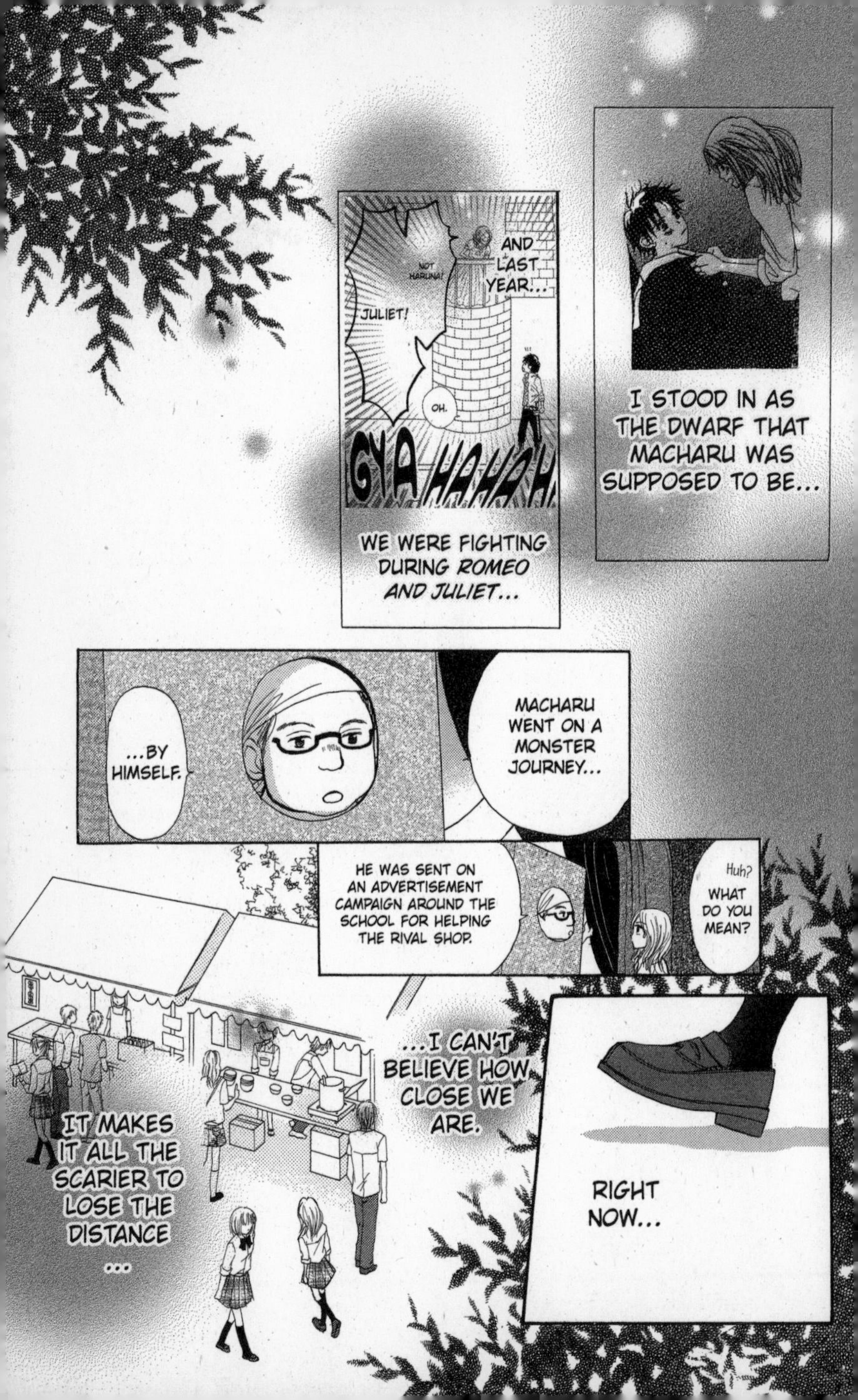
I STOOD IN AS THE DWARF THAT MACHARU WAS SUPPOSED TO BE...
AND LAST YEAR...
NOT HARUNA!
JULIET!
OH.
GYAHAHAH
WE WERE FIGHTING DURING *ROMEO AND JULIET*...
MACHARU WENT ON A MONSTER JOURNEY...
...BY HIMSELF.
Huh? WHAT DO YOU MEAN?
HE WAS SENT ON AN ADVERTISEMENT CAMPAIGN AROUND THE SCHOOL FOR HELPING THE RIVAL SHOP.
RIGHT NOW...
...I CAN'T BELIEVE HOW CLOSE WE ARE.
IT MAKES IT ALL THE SCARIER TO LOSE THE DISTANCE...

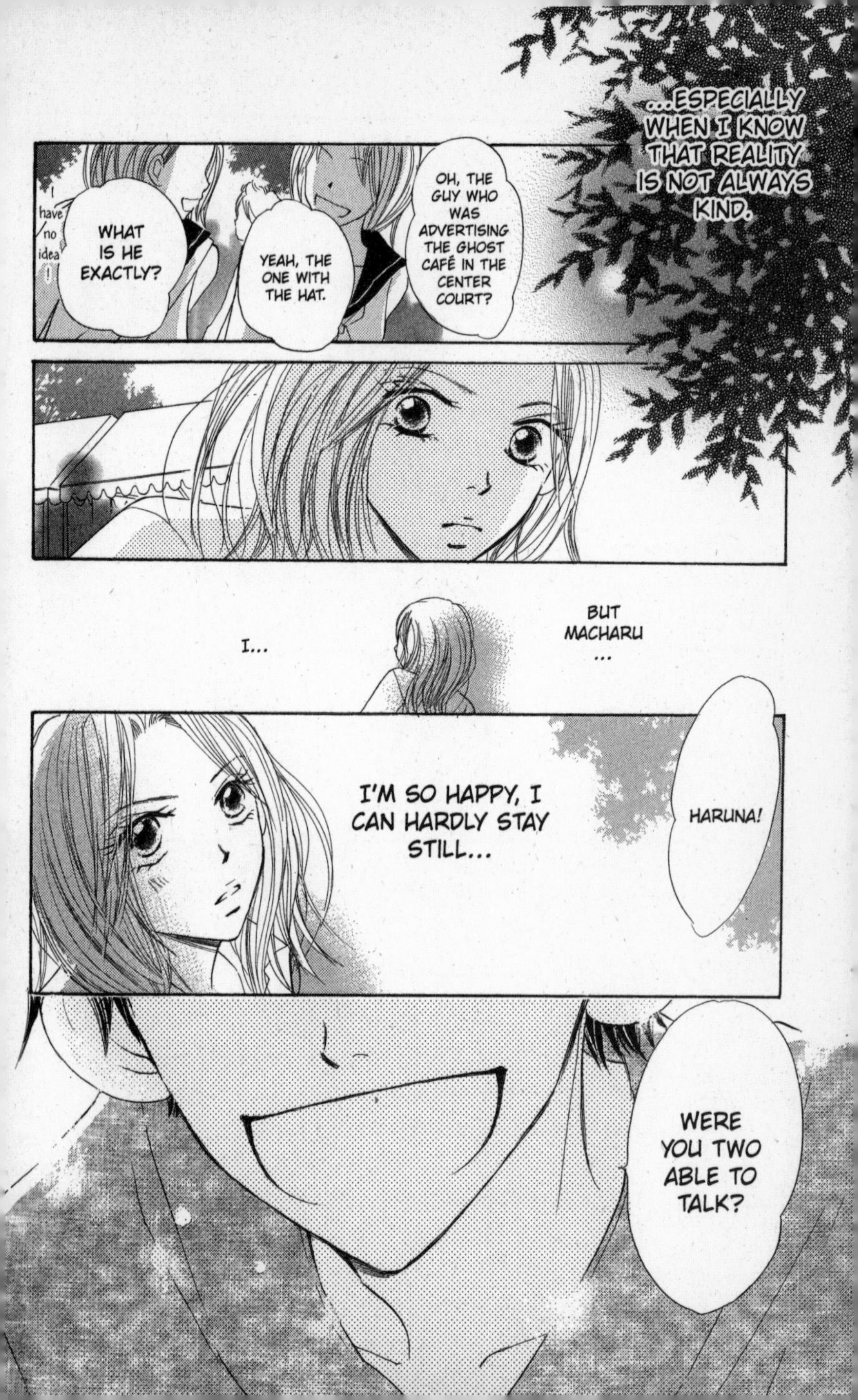
...ESPECIALLY WHEN I KNOW THAT REALITY IS NOT ALWAYS KIND.
OH, THE GUY WHO WAS ADVERTISING THE GHOST CAFÉ IN THE CENTER COURT?
YEAH, THE ONE WITH THE HAT.
WHAT IS HE EXACTLY?
I have no idea!
BUT MACHARU...
I...
HARUNA!
I'M SO HAPPY, I CAN HARDLY STAY STILL...
WERE YOU TWO ABLE TO TALK?

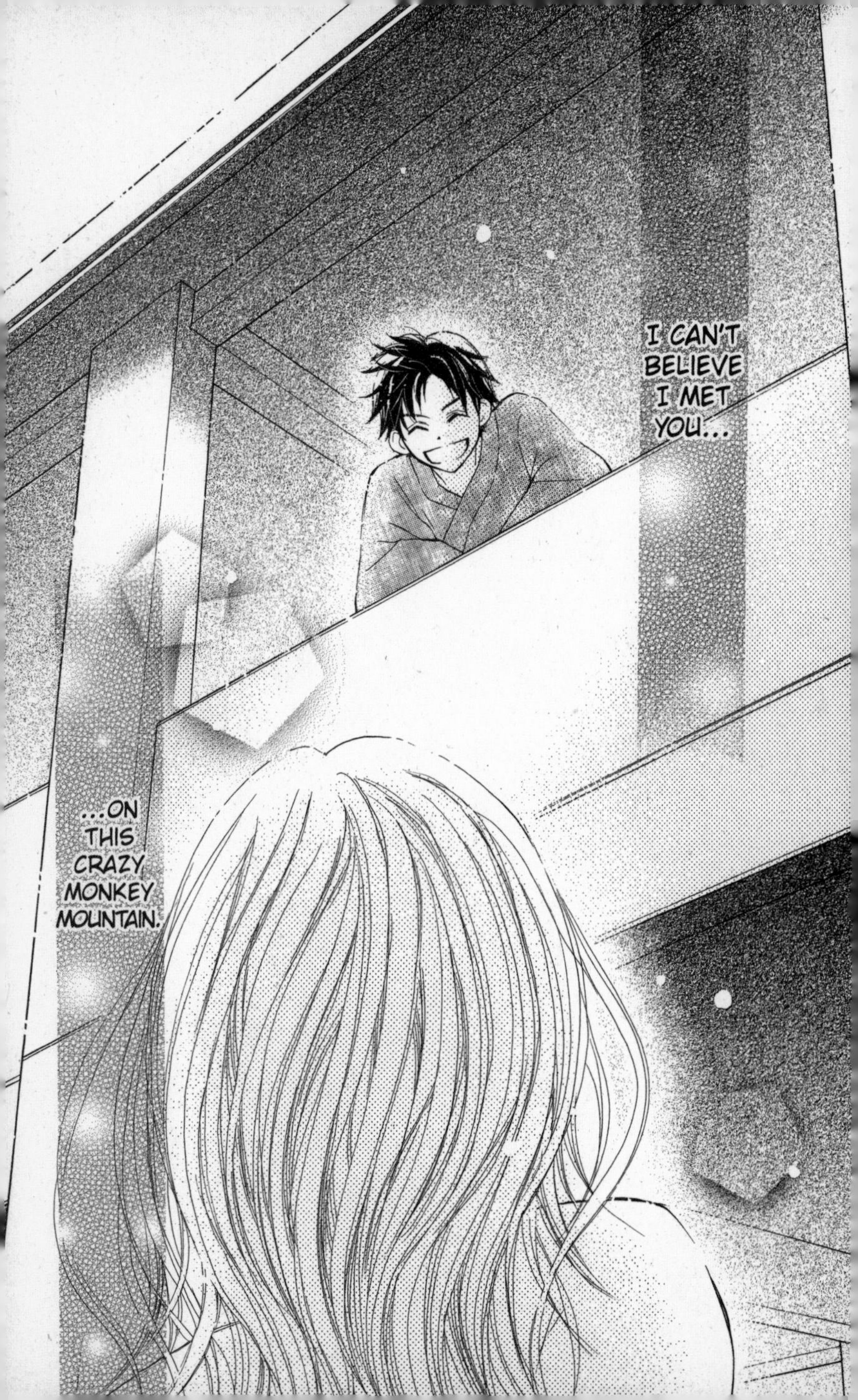
I CAN'T BELIEVE I MET YOU...
...ON THIS CRAZY MONKEY MOUNTAIN.

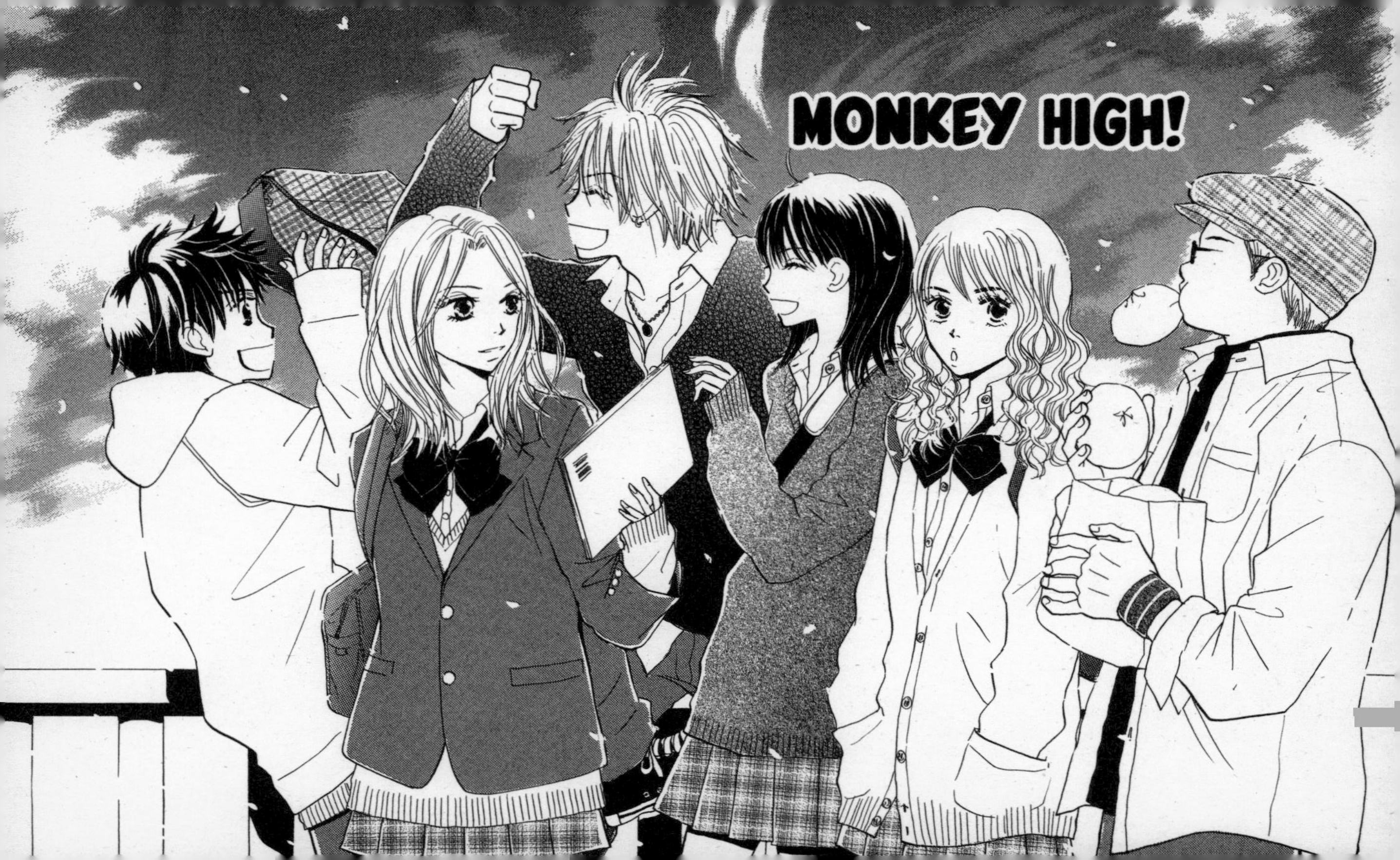
MONKEY HIGH!

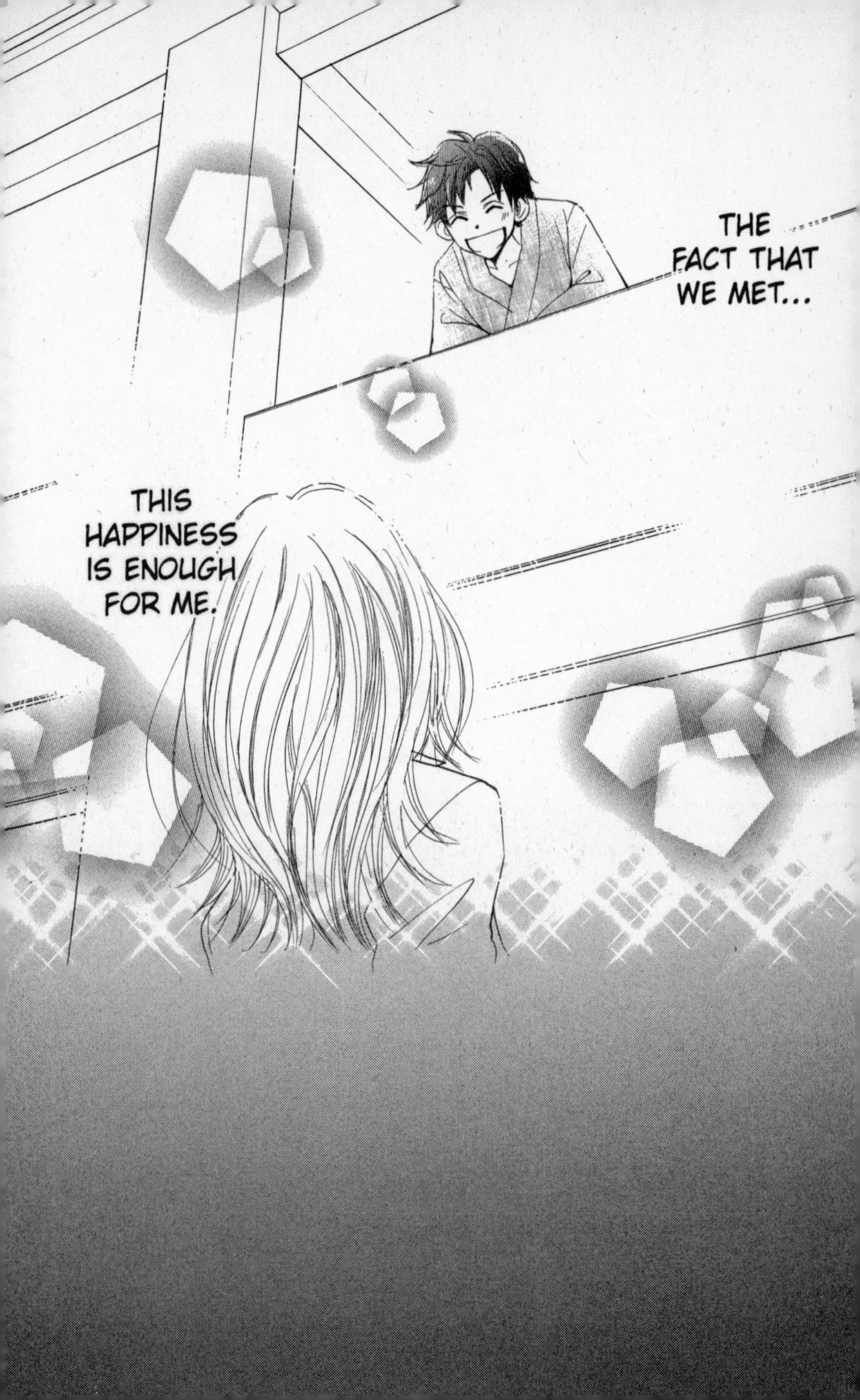
THE FACT THAT WE MET...
THIS HAPPINESS IS ENOUGH FOR ME.

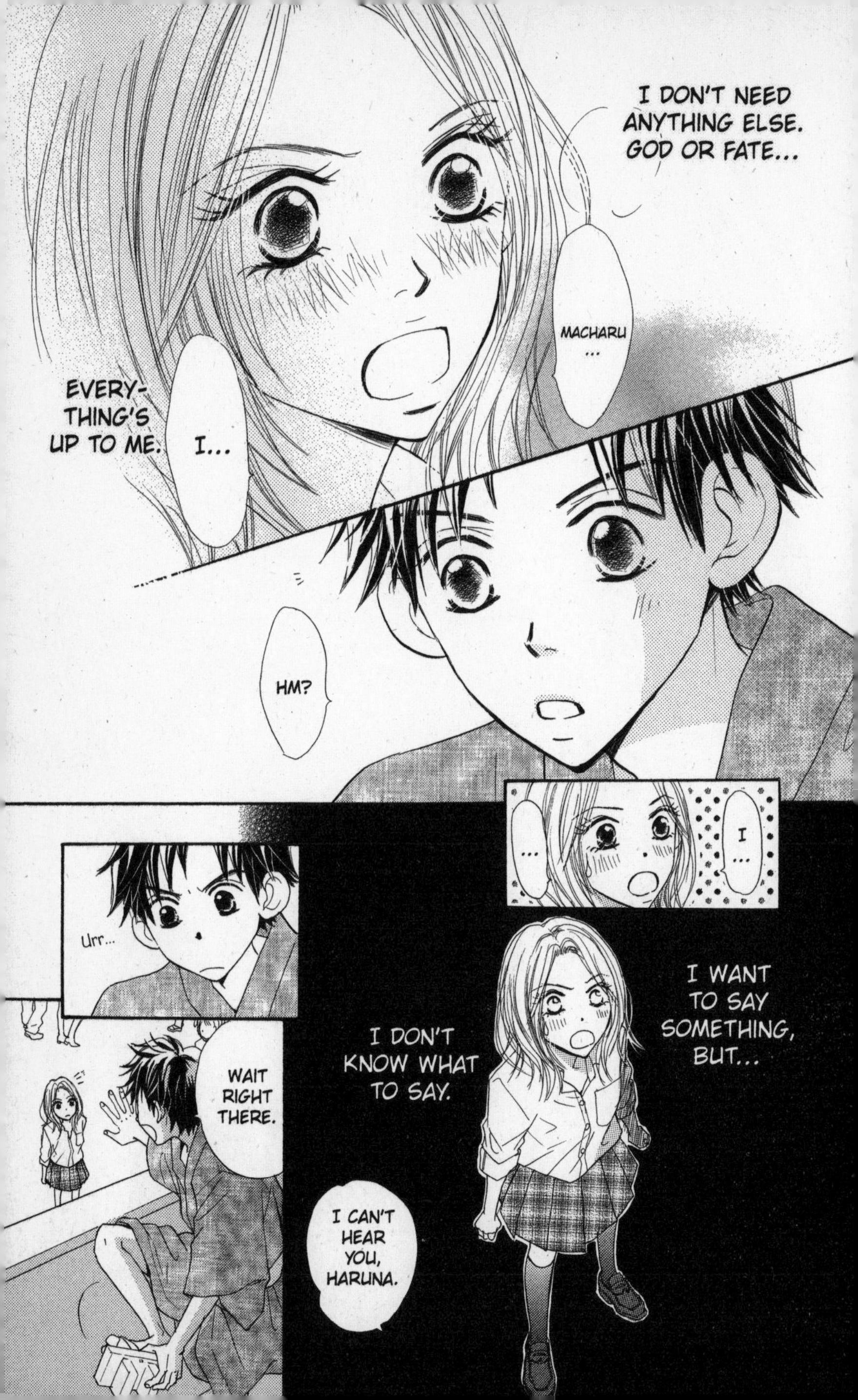

I DON'T NEED ANYTHING ELSE. GOD OR FATE...
MACHARU...
I...
EVERY-THING'S UP TO ME.
HM?
I...
...
I WANT TO SAY SOMETHING, BUT...
I DON'T KNOW WHAT TO SAY.
I CAN'T HEAR YOU, HARUNA.
Urr...
WAIT RIGHT THERE.

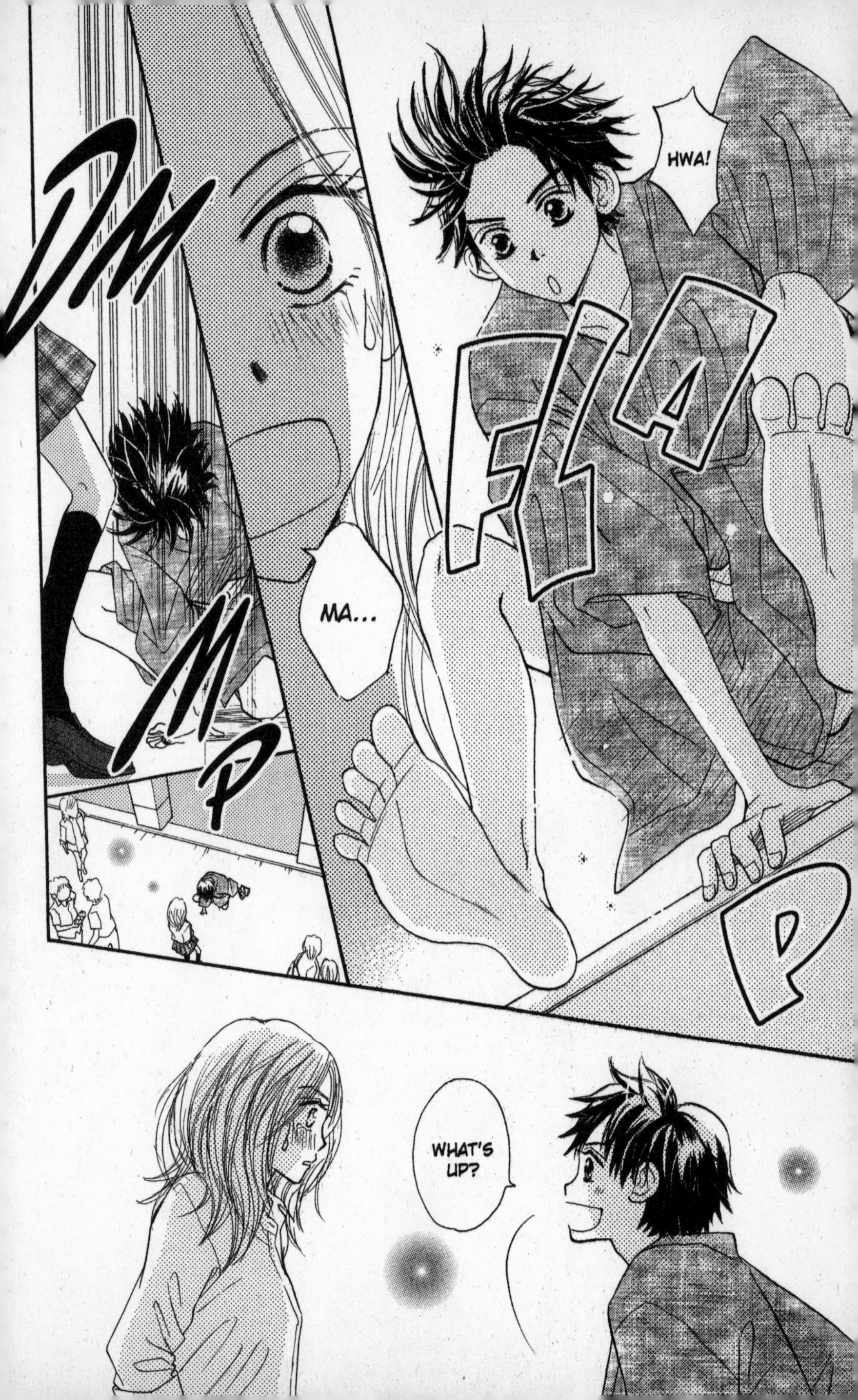
HWA!
FLAP
MA...
DMMP
WHAT'S UP?

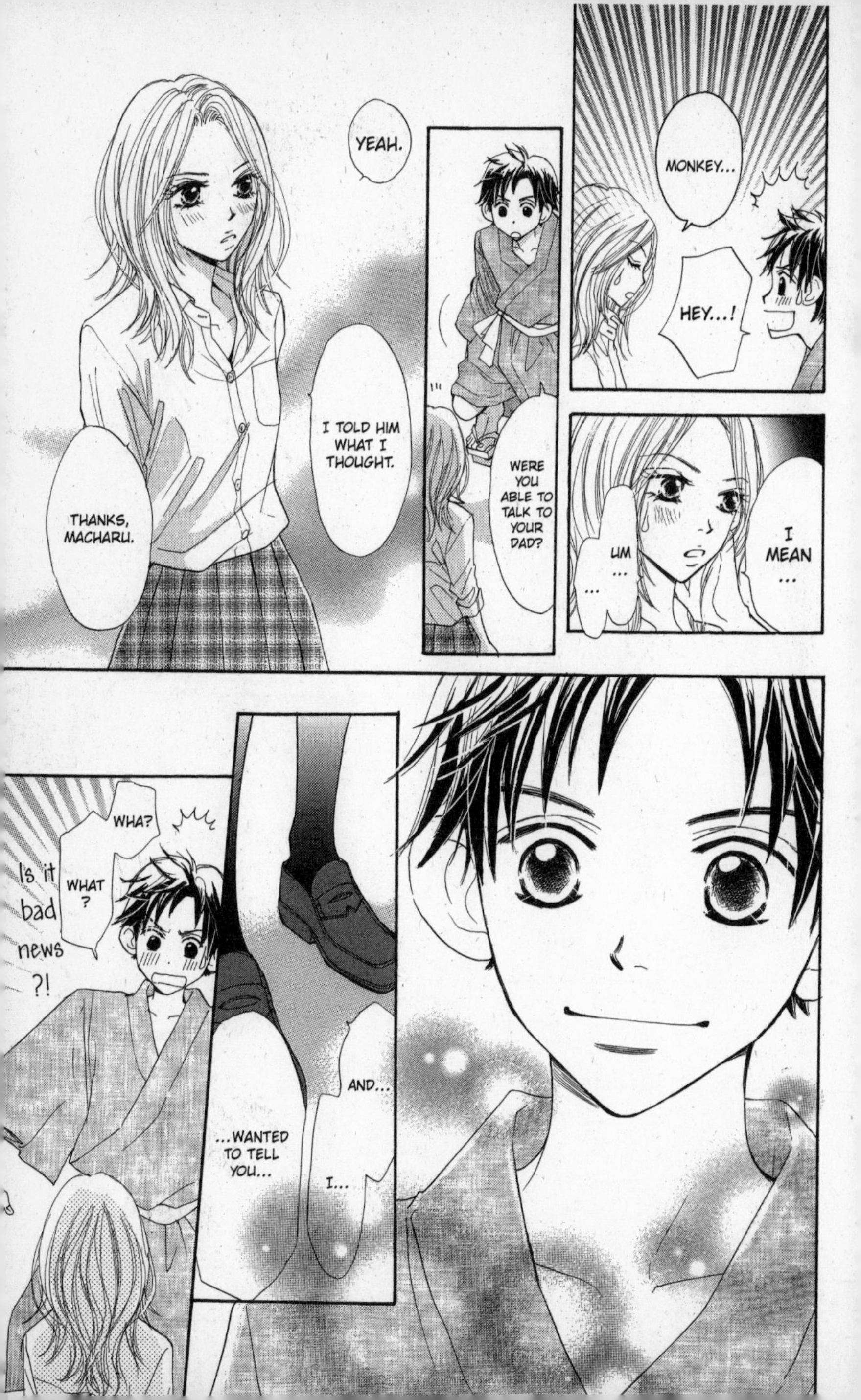

MONKEY...
HEY...!
I MEAN...
UM...
...
WERE YOU ABLE TO TALK TO YOUR DAD?
YEAH.
I TOLD HIM WHAT I THOUGHT.
THANKS, MACHARU.
AND...
I...
...WANTED TO TELL YOU...
WHA?
WHAT?
Is it bad news?!

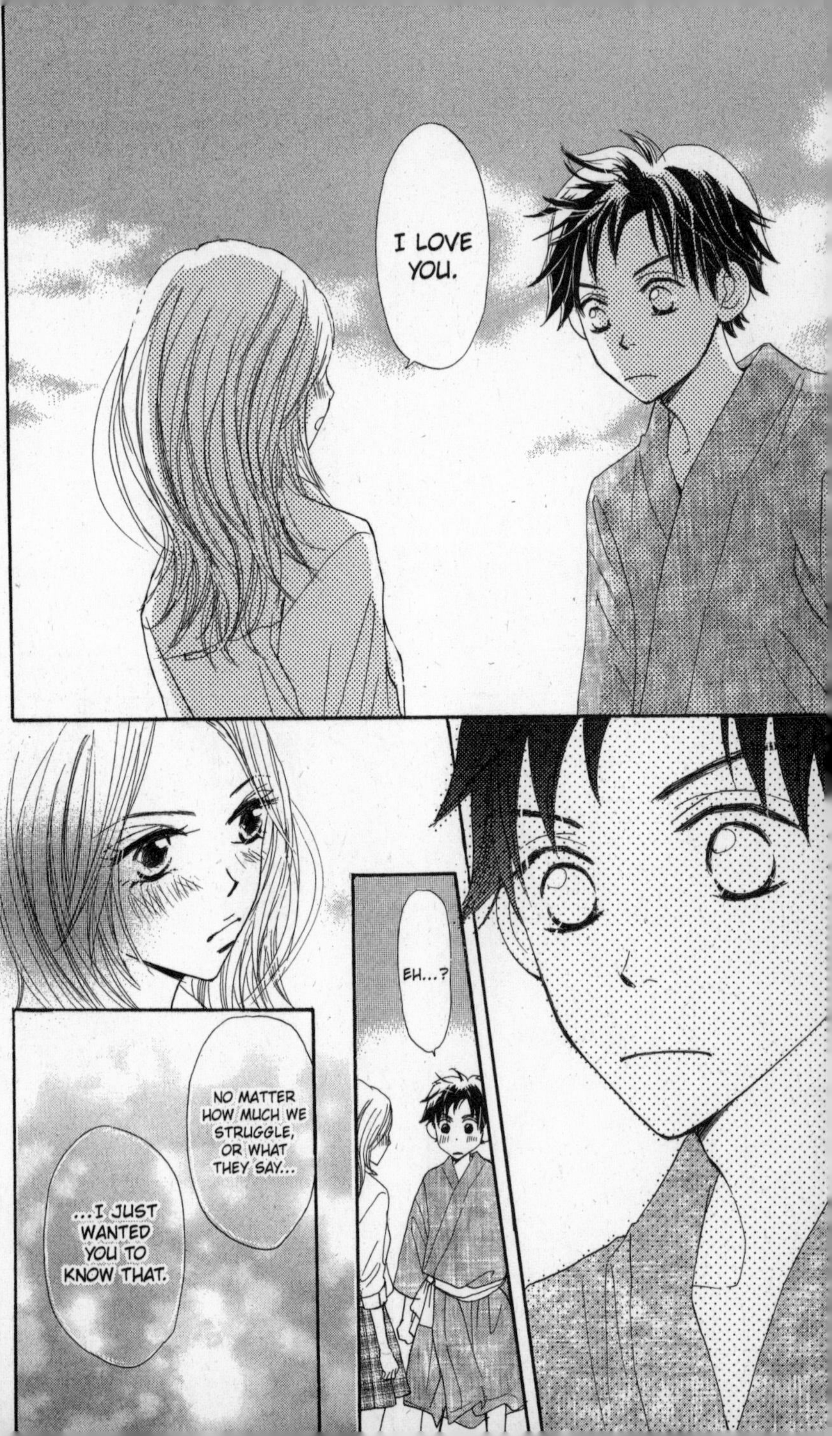
I LOVE YOU.
EH...?
NO MATTER HOW MUCH WE STRUGGLE, OR WHAT THEY SAY...
...I JUST WANTED YOU TO KNOW THAT.

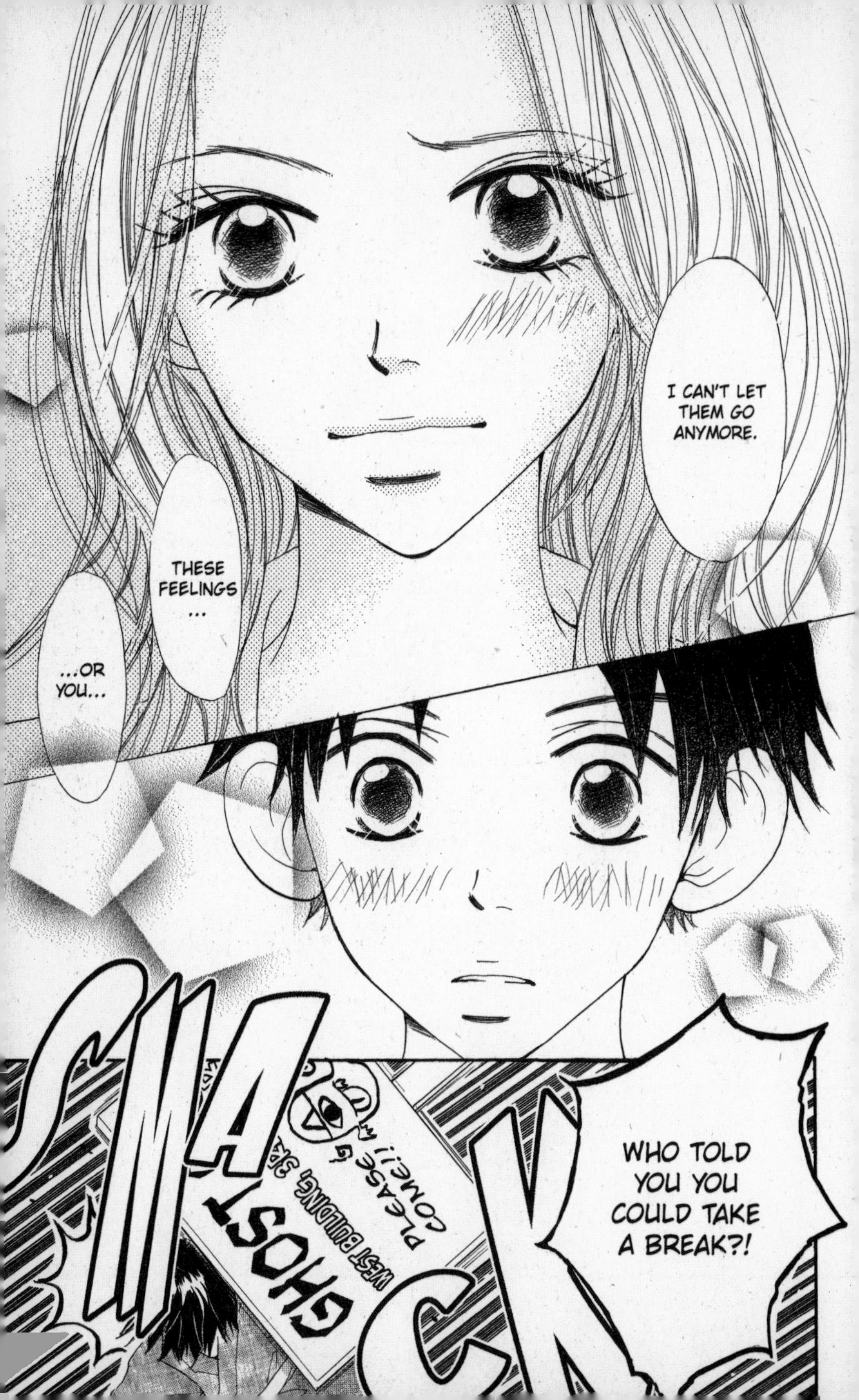
I CAN'T LET THEM GO ANYMORE.
THESE FEELINGS...
...OR YOU...
WHO TOLD YOU YOU COULD TAKE A BREAK?!
GHOST
WEST BUILDING, 3RD
PLEASE COME!!

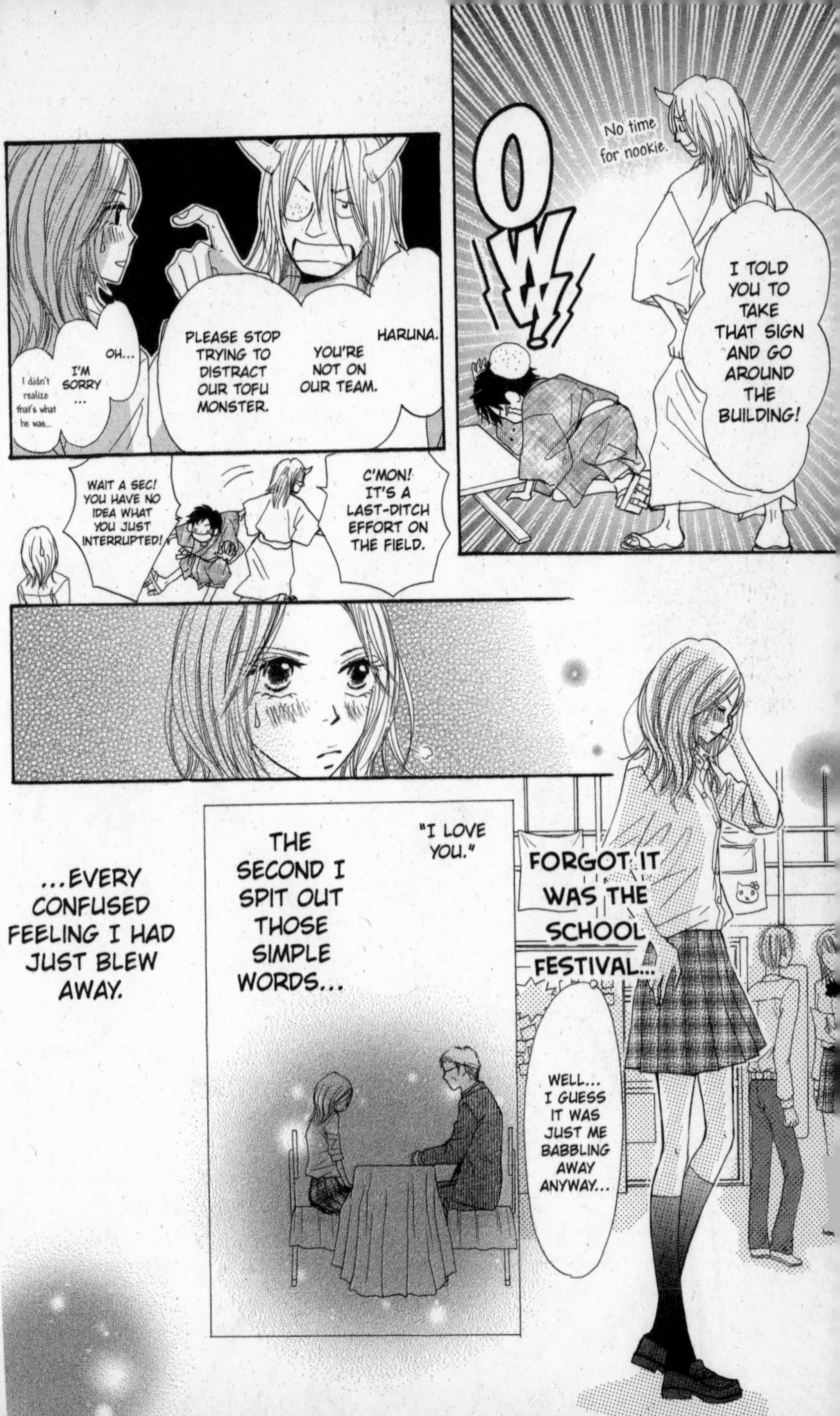

No time for nookie.
I TOLD YOU TO TAKE THAT SIGN AND GO AROUND THE BUILDING!
OW!
HARUNA.
YOU'RE NOT ON OUR TEAM.
PLEASE STOP TRYING TO DISTRACT OUR TOFU MONSTER.
OH... I'M SORRY...
I didn't realize that's what he was...
C'MON! IT'S A LAST-DITCH EFFORT ON THE FIELD.
WAIT A SEC! YOU HAVE NO IDEA WHAT YOU JUST INTERRUPTED!
FORGOT IT WAS THE SCHOOL FESTIVAL...
WELL... I GUESS IT WAS JUST ME BABBLING AWAY ANYWAY...
"I LOVE YOU."
THE SECOND I SPIT OUT THOSE SIMPLE WORDS...
...EVERY CONFUSED FEELING I HAD JUST BLEW AWAY.

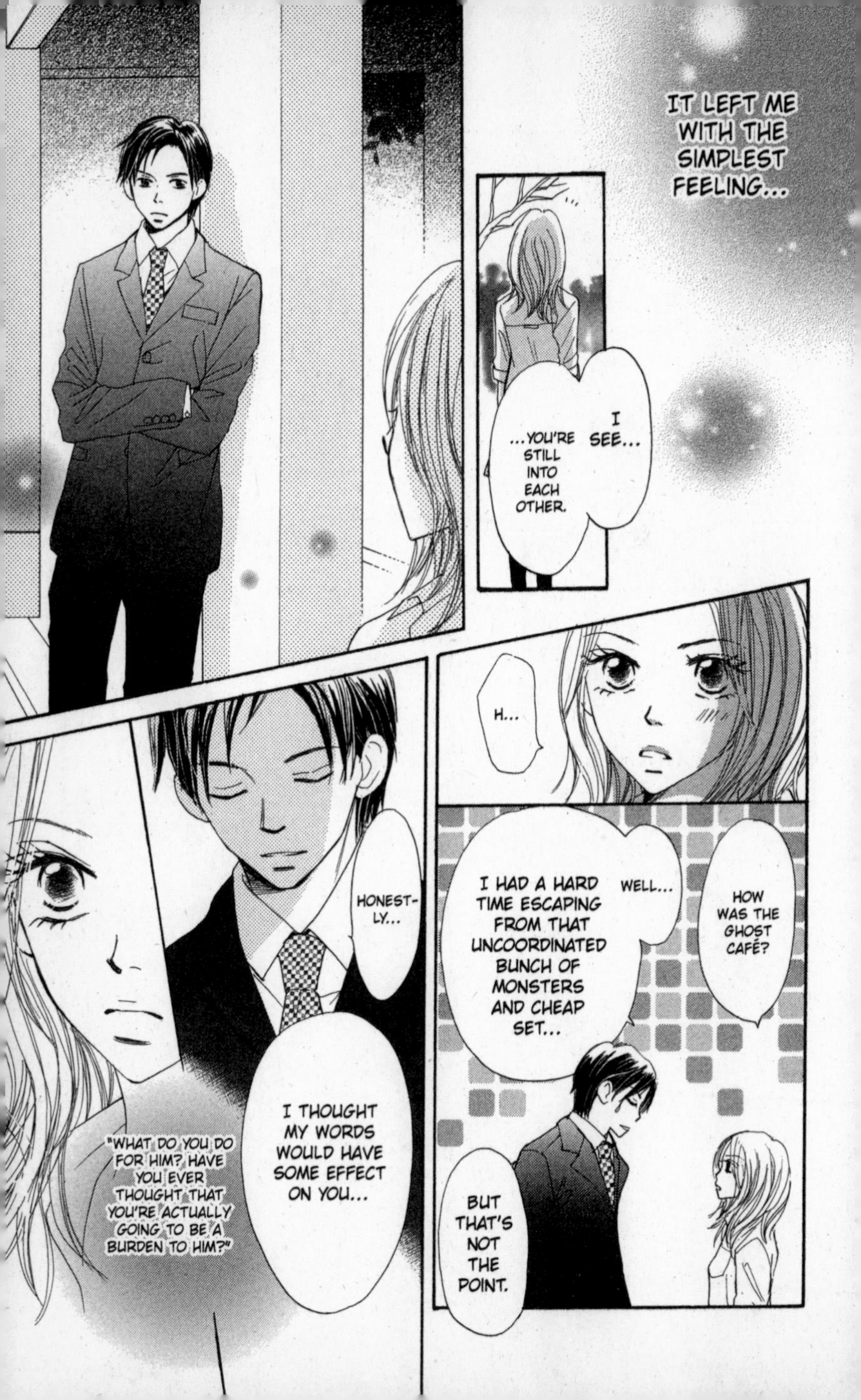
IT LEFT ME WITH THE SIMPLEST FEELING...
I SEE...
...YOU'RE STILL INTO EACH OTHER.
H...
HOW WAS THE GHOST CAFÉ?
WELL...
I HAD A HARD TIME ESCAPING FROM THAT UNCOORDINATED BUNCH OF MONSTERS AND CHEAP SET...
BUT THAT'S NOT THE POINT.
HONESTLY...
I THOUGHT MY WORDS WOULD HAVE SOME EFFECT ON YOU...
"WHAT DO YOU DO FOR HIM? HAVE YOU EVER THOUGHT THAT YOU'RE ACTUALLY GOING TO BE A BURDEN TO HIM?"

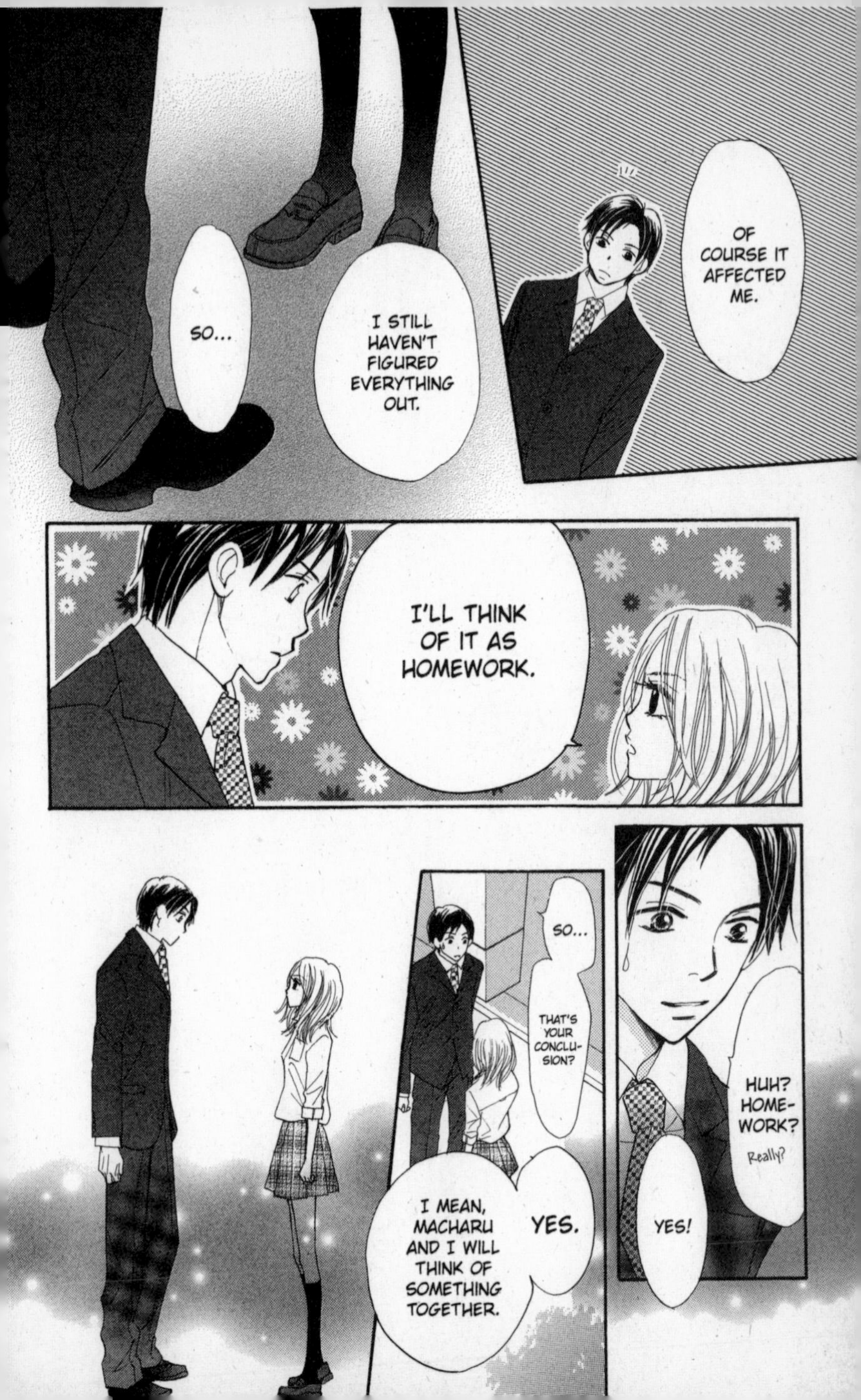
OF COURSE IT AFFECTED ME.
I STILL HAVEN'T FIGURED EVERYTHING OUT.
SO...
I'LL THINK OF IT AS HOMEWORK.
HUH? HOME-WORK?
Really?
YES!
SO...
THAT'S YOUR CONCLU-SION?
YES.
I MEAN, MACHARU AND I WILL THINK OF SOMETHING TOGETHER.

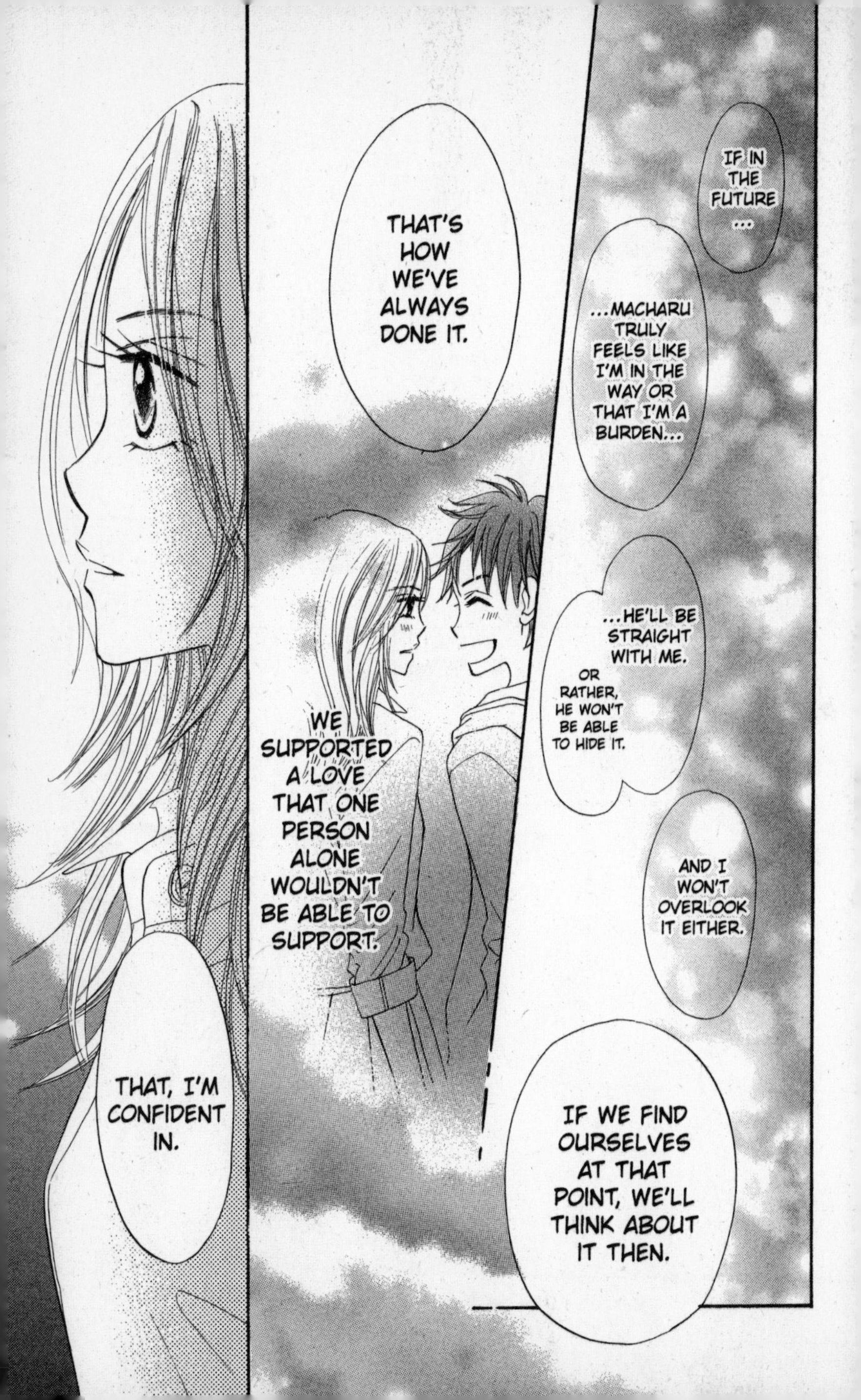
IF IN THE FUTURE...
...MACHARU TRULY FEELS LIKE I'M IN THE WAY OR THAT I'M A BURDEN...
...HE'LL BE STRAIGHT WITH ME.
OR RATHER, HE WON'T BE ABLE TO HIDE IT.
AND I WON'T OVERLOOK IT EITHER.
IF WE FIND OURSELVES AT THAT POINT, WE'LL THINK ABOUT IT THEN.
THAT'S HOW WE'VE ALWAYS DONE IT.
WE SUPPORTED A LOVE THAT ONE PERSON ALONE WOULDN'T BE ABLE TO SUPPORT.
THAT, I'M CONFIDENT IN.

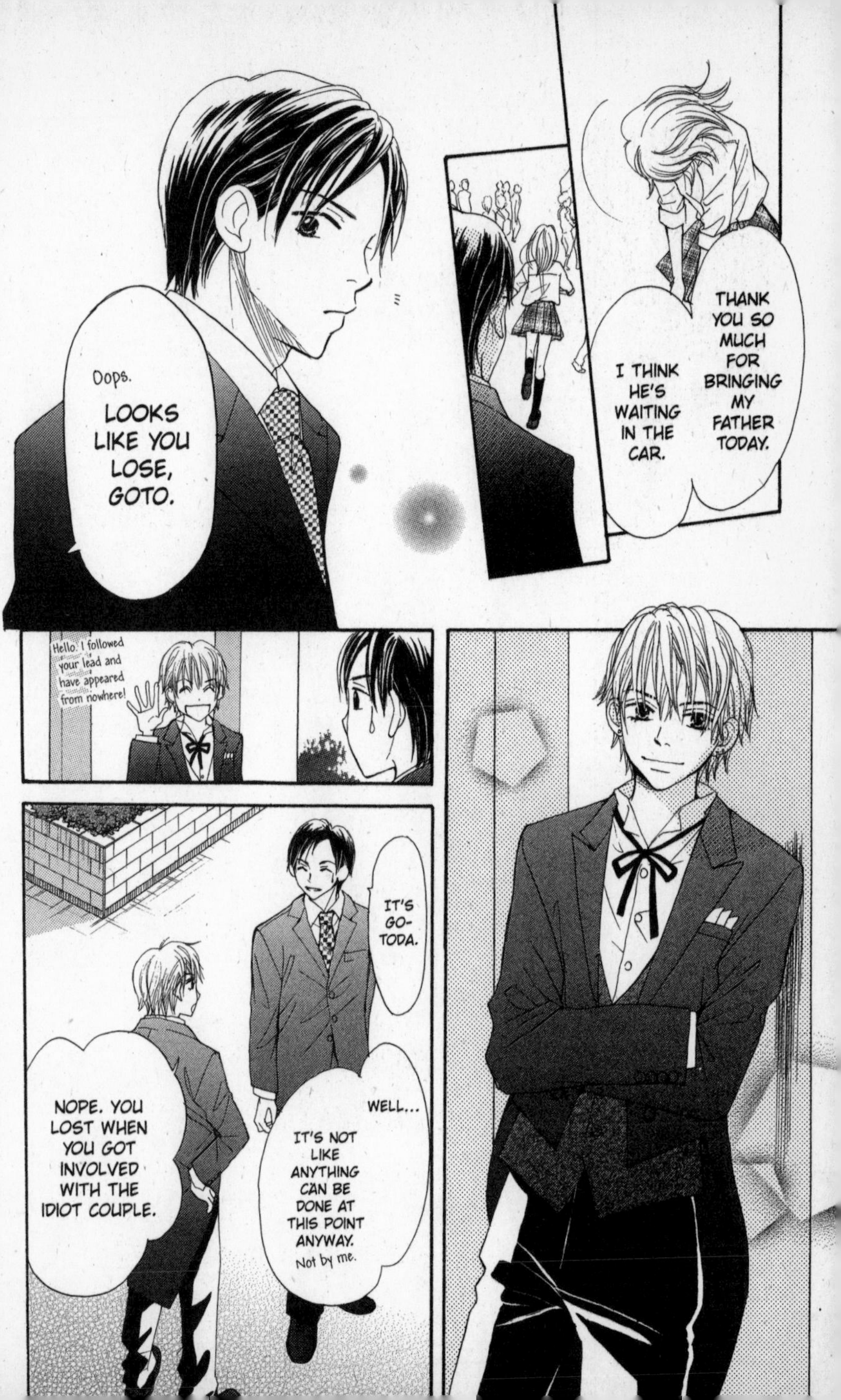
THANK YOU SO MUCH FOR BRINGING MY FATHER TODAY.
I THINK HE'S WAITING IN THE CAR.
Oops.
LOOKS LIKE YOU LOSE, GOTO.
Hello. I followed your lead and have appeared from nowhere!
IT'S GO-TODA.
WELL...
IT'S NOT LIKE ANYTHING CAN BE DONE AT THIS POINT ANYWAY.
Not by me.
NOPE. YOU LOST WHEN YOU GOT INVOLVED WITH THE IDIOT COUPLE.

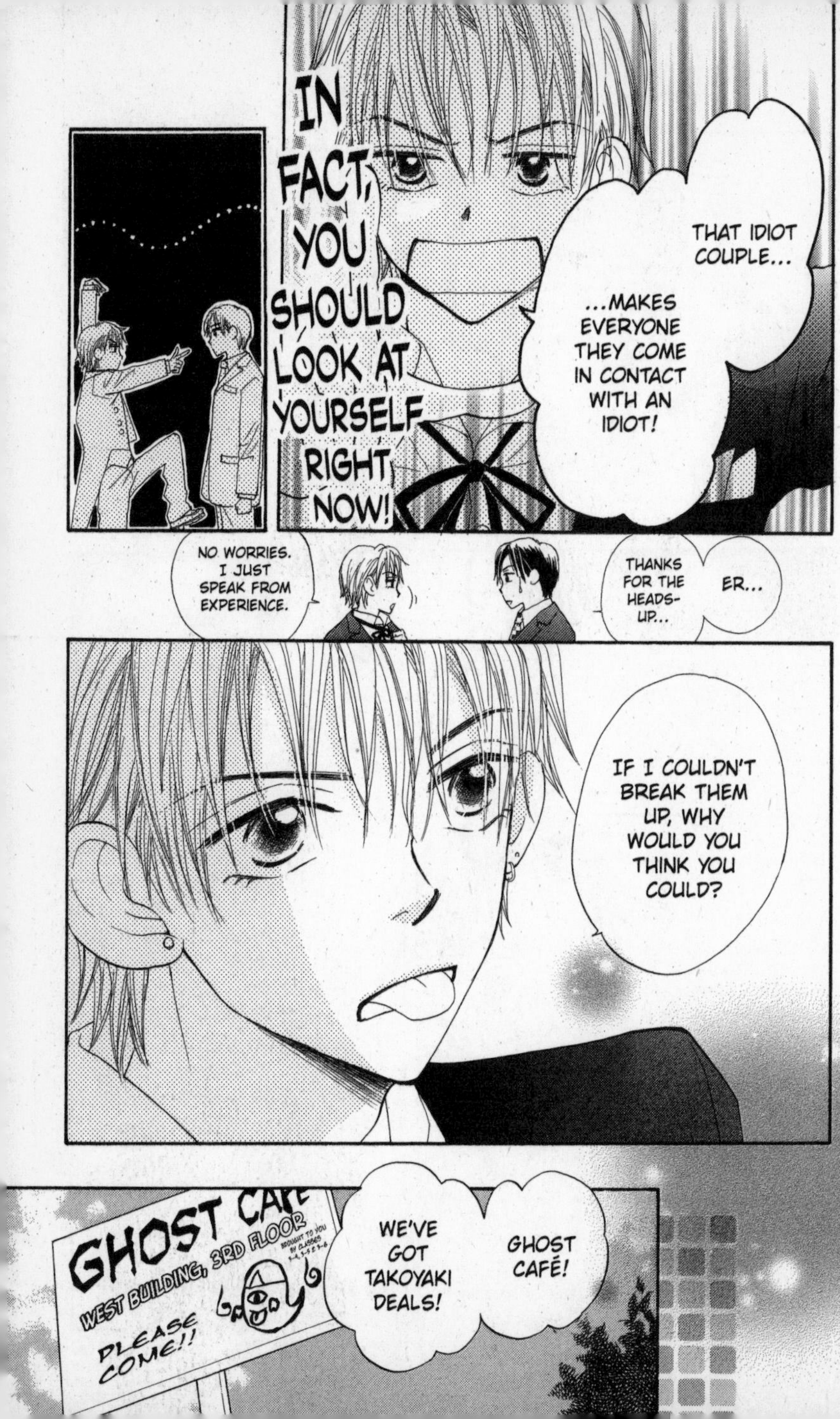
THAT IDIOT COUPLE...
...MAKES EVERYONE THEY COME IN CONTACT WITH AN IDIOT!
IN FACT, YOU SHOULD LOOK AT YOURSELF RIGHT NOW!
ER...
THANKS FOR THE HEADS-UP...
NO WORRIES. I JUST SPEAK FROM EXPERIENCE.
IF I COULDN'T BREAK THEM UP, WHY WOULD YOU THINK YOU COULD?
GHOST CAFÉ!
WE'VE GOT TAKOYAKI DEALS!
GHOST CAFE
WEST BUILDING, 3RD FLOOR
BROUGHT TO YOU BY CLASSES 3-4, 3-5 & 3-6
PLEASE COME!!

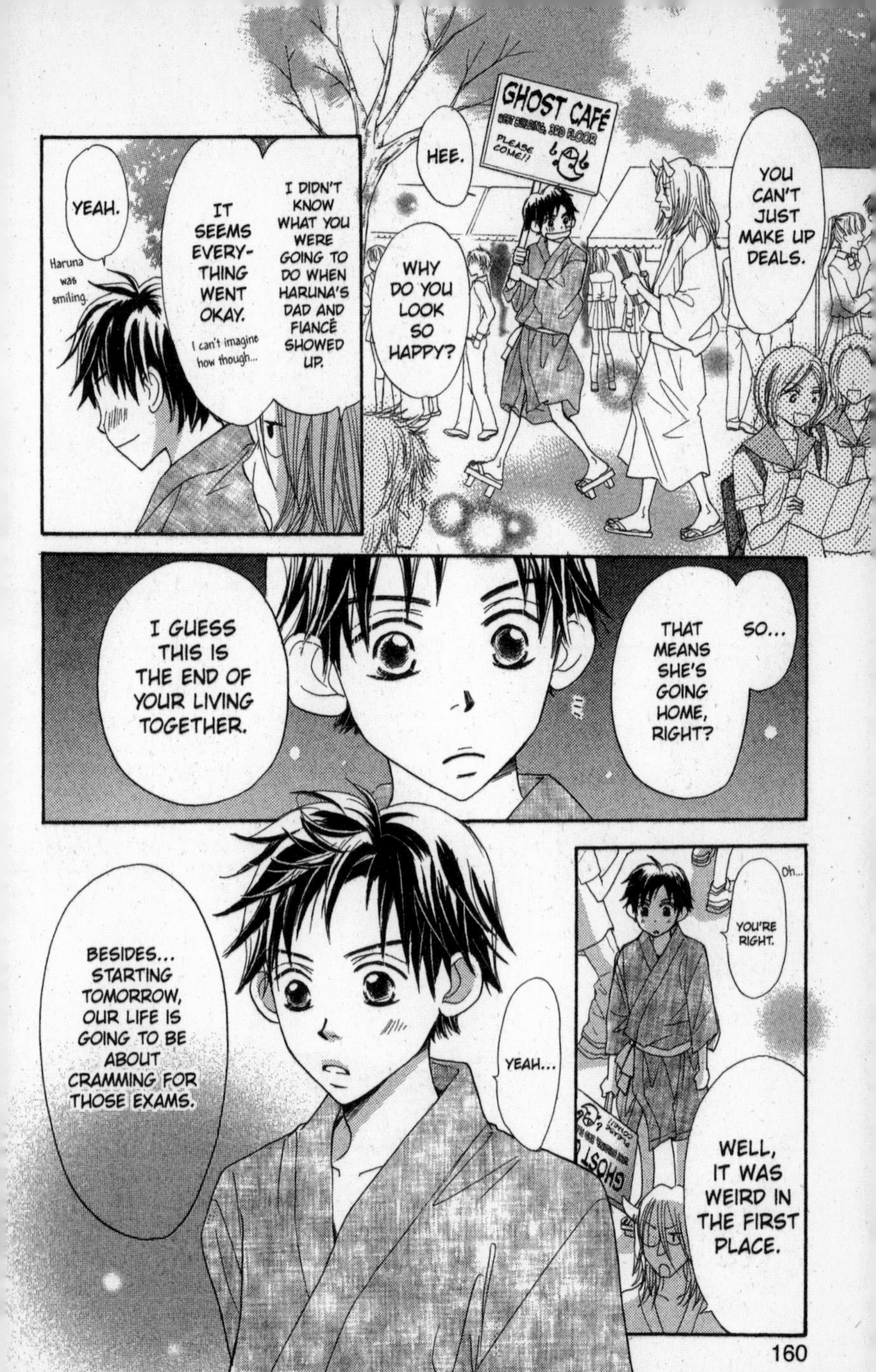
YOU CAN'T JUST MAKE UP DEALS.
GHOST CAFÉ
WEST BUILDING, 3RD FLOOR
PLEASE COME!!
HEE.
WHY DO YOU LOOK SO HAPPY?
I DIDN'T KNOW WHAT YOU WERE GOING TO DO WHEN HARUNA'S DAD AND FIANCÉ SHOWED UP.
IT SEEMS EVERYTHING WENT OKAY.
I can't imagine how though...
YEAH.
Haruna was smiling.
SO...
THAT MEANS SHE'S GOING HOME, RIGHT?
I GUESS THIS IS THE END OF YOUR LIVING TOGETHER.
Oh...
YOU'RE RIGHT.
WELL, IT WAS WEIRD IN THE FIRST PLACE.
YEAH...
BESIDES... STARTING TOMORROW, OUR LIFE IS GOING TO BE ABOUT CRAMMING FOR THOSE EXAMS.

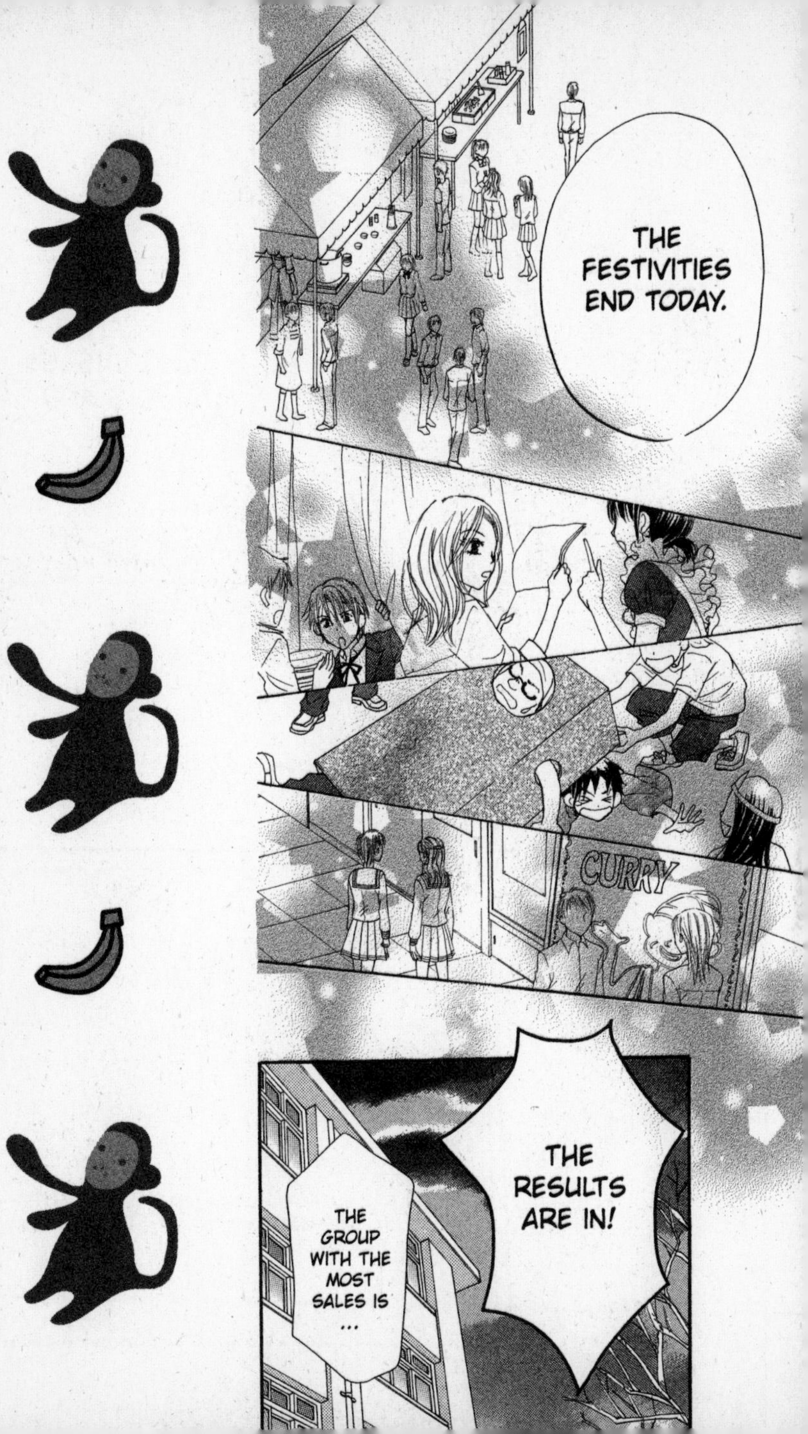
THE FESTIVITIES END TODAY.
CURRY
THE RESULTS ARE IN!
THE GROUP WITH THE MOST SALES IS ...

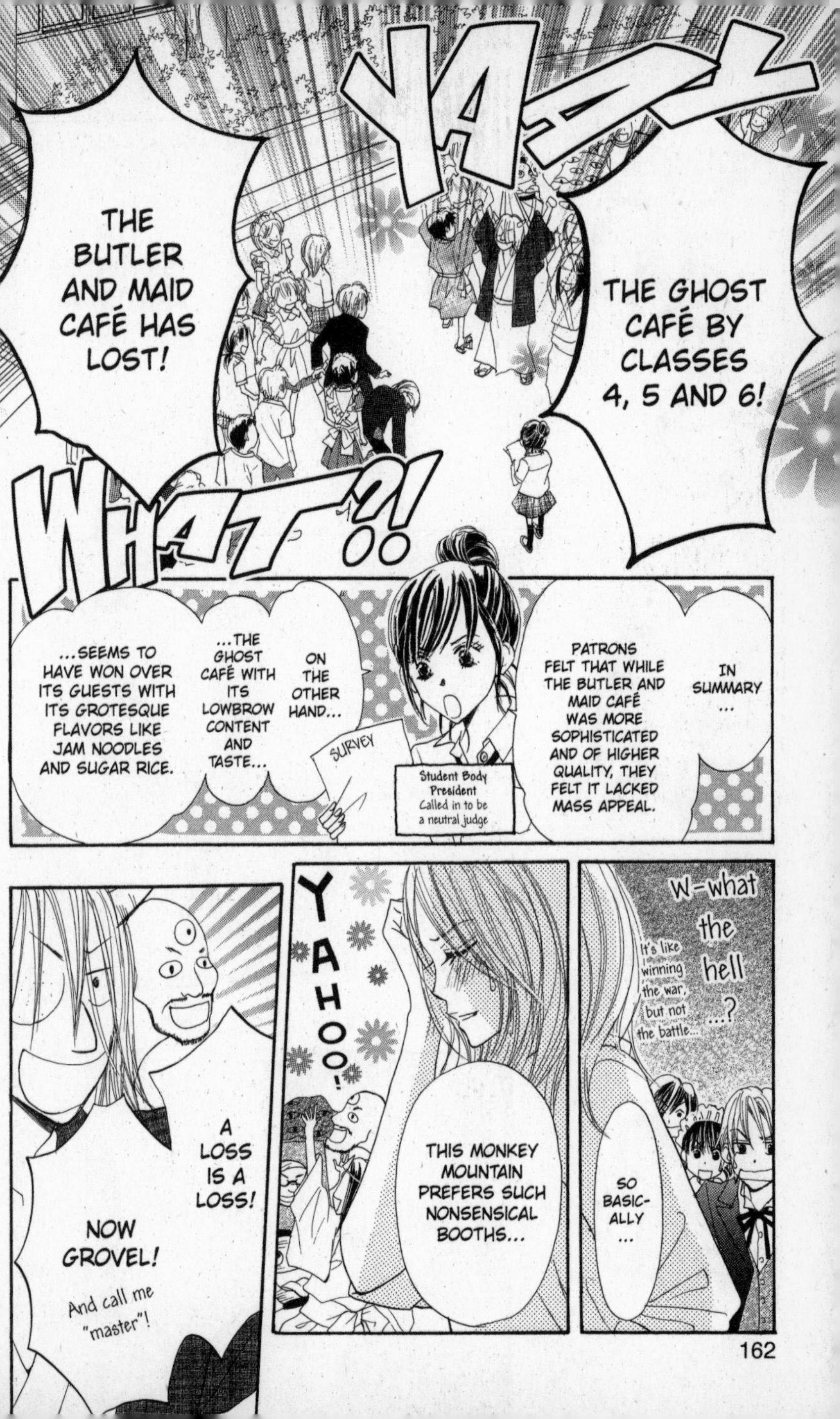
THE GHOST CAFÉ BY CLASSES 4, 5 AND 6!
YAAAY
THE BUTLER AND MAID CAFÉ HAS LOST!
WHAT?!
IN SUMMARY...
PATRONS FELT THAT WHILE THE BUTLER AND MAID CAFÉ WAS MORE SOPHISTICATED AND OF HIGHER QUALITY, THEY FELT IT LACKED MASS APPEAL.
Student Body President Called in to be a neutral judge
SURVEY
ON THE OTHER HAND...
...THE GHOST CAFÉ WITH ITS LOWBROW CONTENT AND TASTE...
...SEEMS TO HAVE WON OVER ITS GUESTS WITH ITS GROTESQUE FLAVORS LIKE JAM NOODLES AND SUGAR RICE.
W-what the hell...?
It's like winning the war, but not the battle...
SO BASICALLY...
THIS MONKEY MOUNTAIN PREFERS SUCH NONSENSICAL BOOTHS...
YAHOO!
A LOSS IS A LOSS!
NOW GROVEL!
And call me "master"!

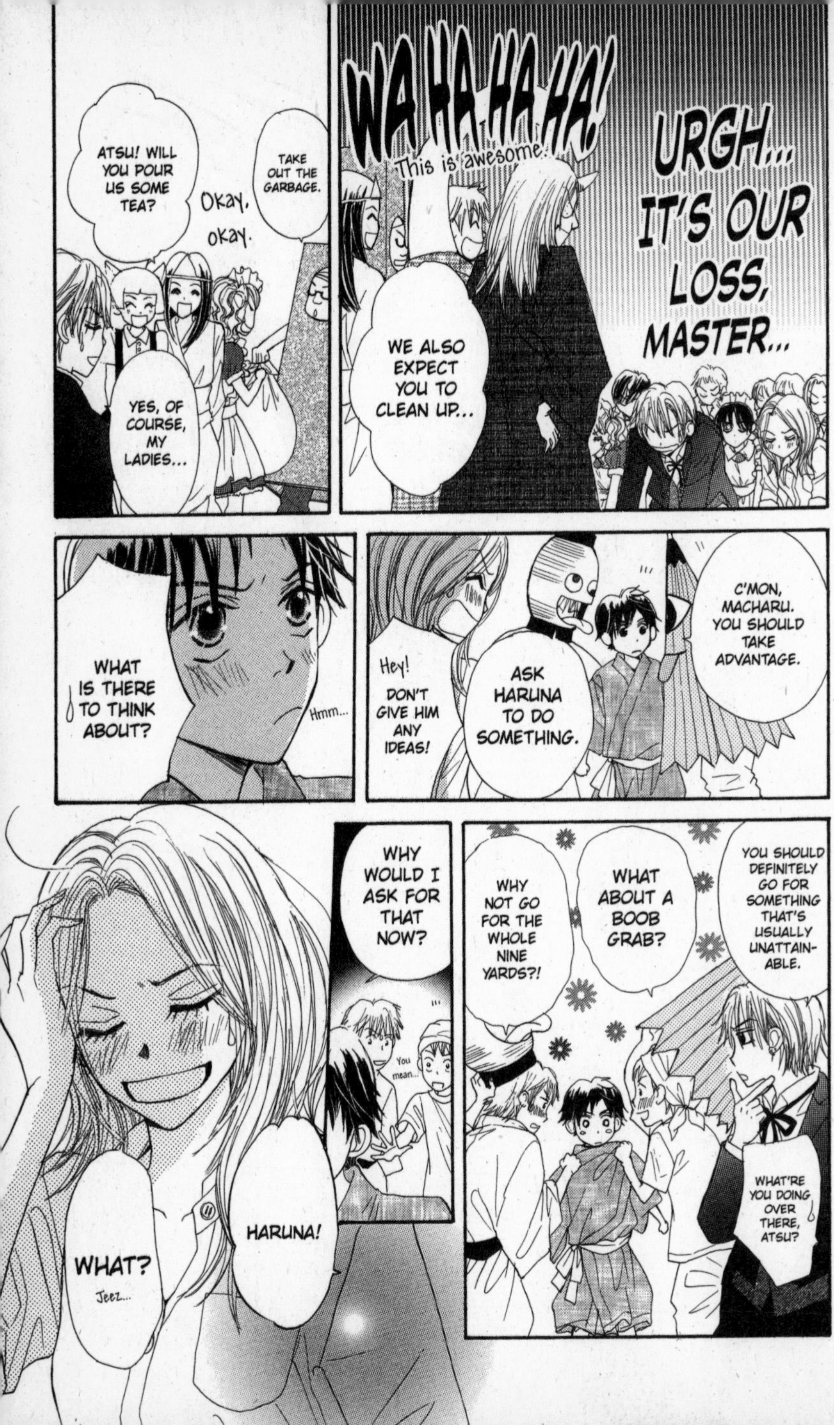
WA HA HA HA!
This is awesome!
URGH... IT'S OUR LOSS, MASTER...
WE ALSO EXPECT YOU TO CLEAN UP...
TAKE OUT THE GARBAGE.
ATSU! WILL YOU POUR US SOME TEA?
Okay, okay.
YES, OF COURSE, MY LADIES...
C'MON, MACHARU. YOU SHOULD TAKE ADVANTAGE.
ASK HARUNA TO DO SOMETHING.
Hey! DON'T GIVE HIM ANY IDEAS!
WHAT IS THERE TO THINK ABOUT?
Hmm...
YOU SHOULD DEFINITELY GO FOR SOMETHING THAT'S USUALLY UNATTAIN-ABLE.
WHAT ABOUT A BOOB GRAB?
WHY NOT GO FOR THE WHOLE NINE YARDS?!
WHAT'RE YOU DOING OVER THERE, ATSU?
WHY WOULD I ASK FOR THAT NOW?
You mean...
HARUNA!
WHAT?
Jeez...

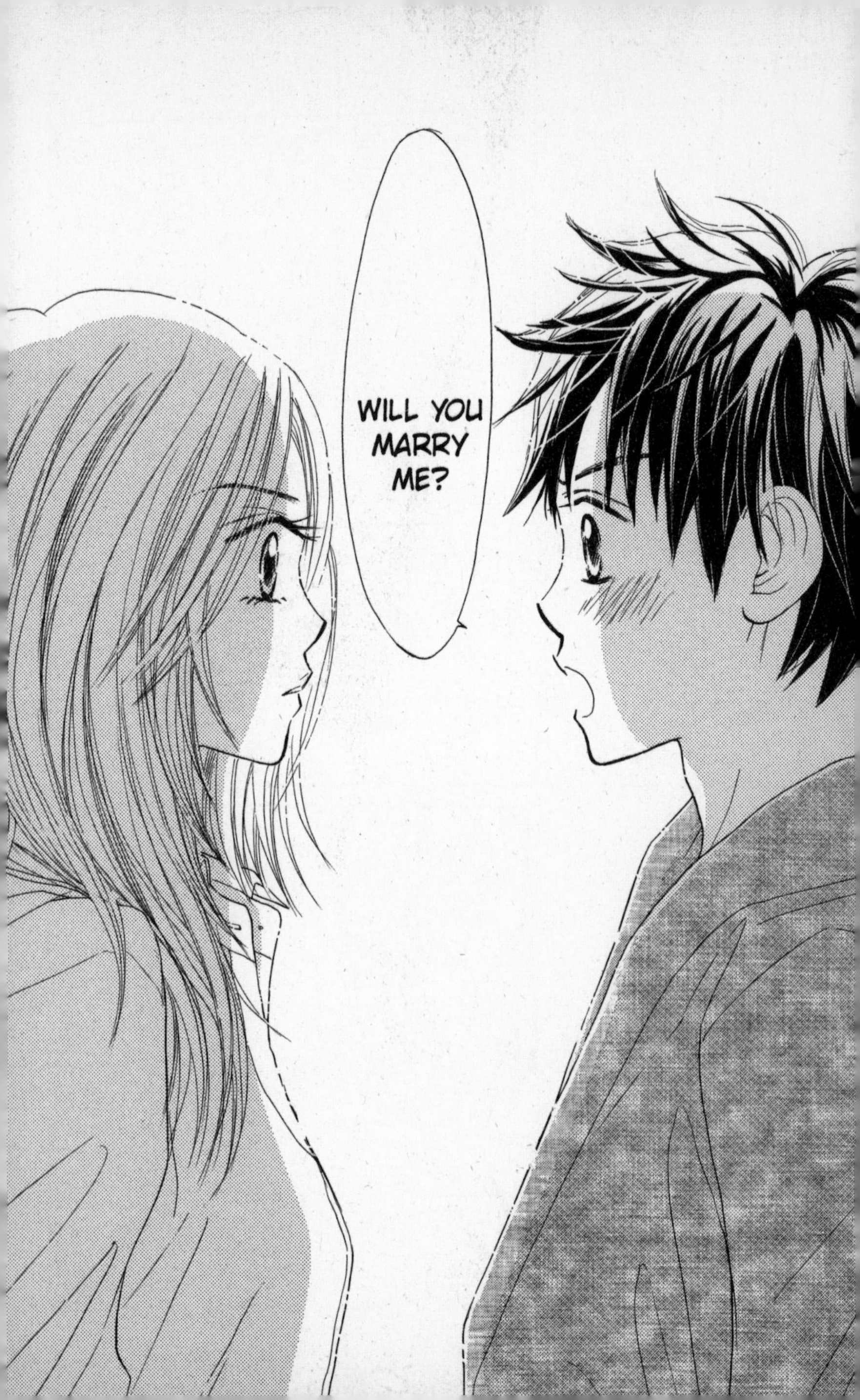
WILL YOU MARRY ME?

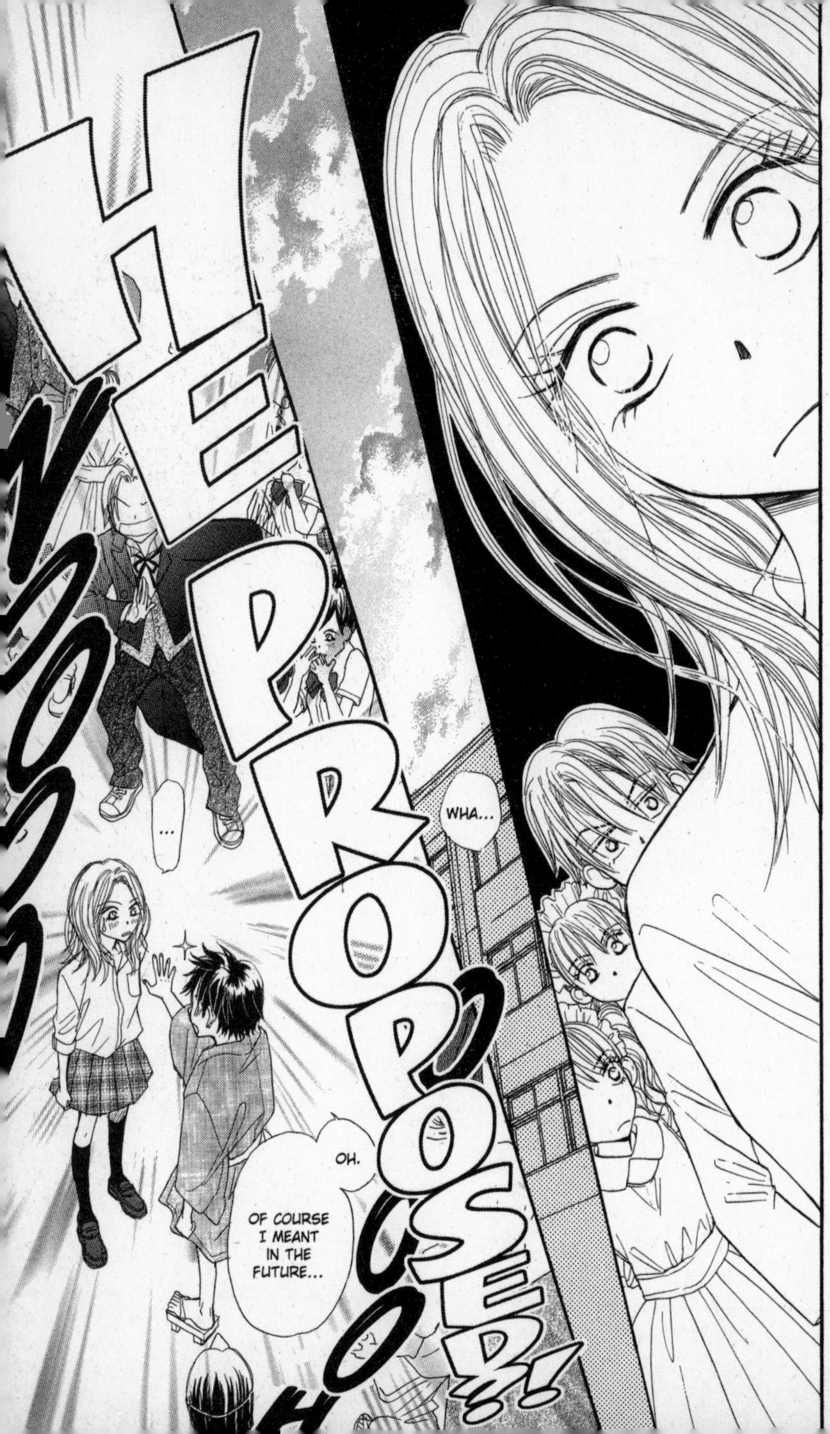
WHA...
HE PROPOSED!!
...
OH.
OF COURSE I MEANT IN THE FUTURE...
GOOOH

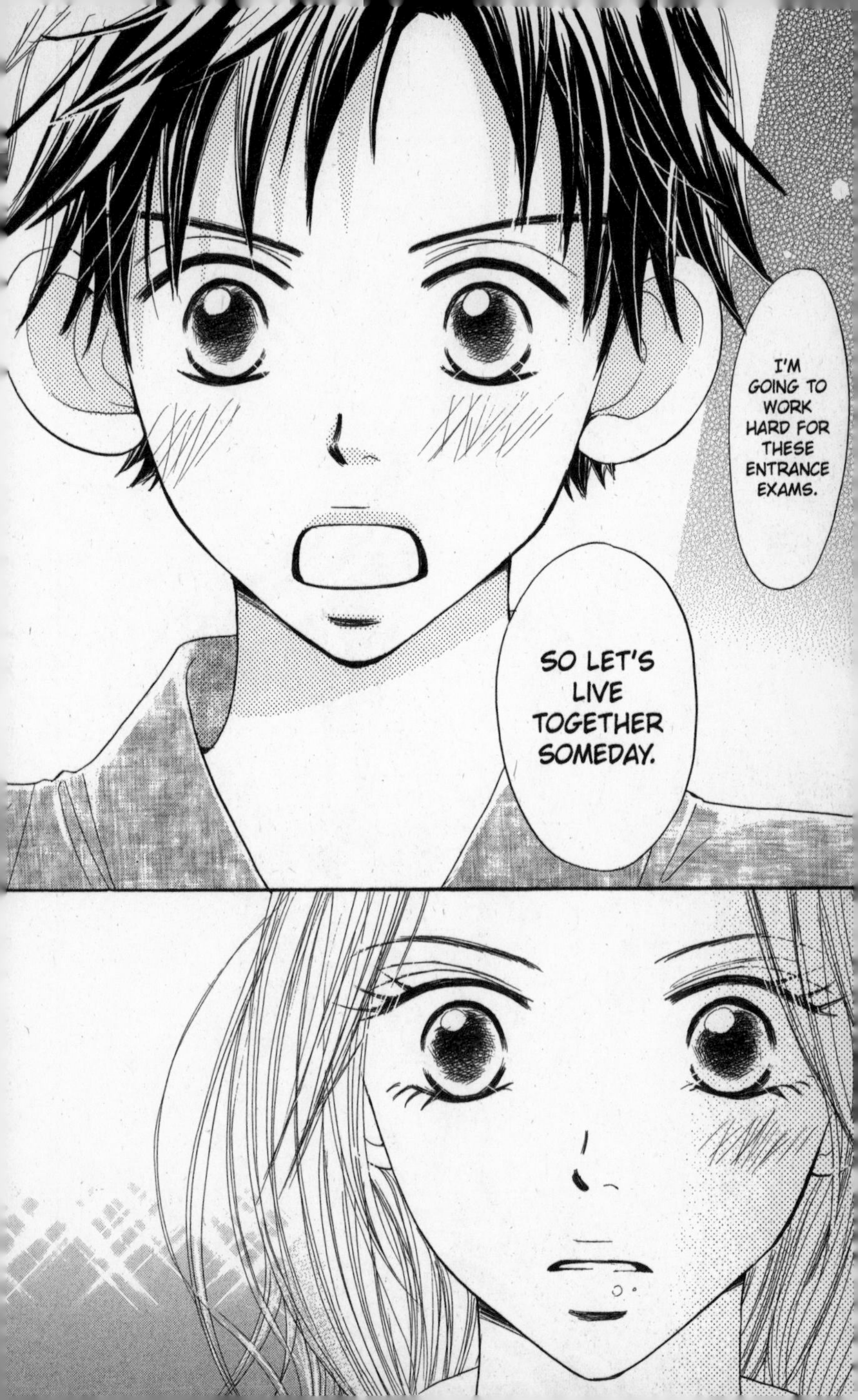
I'M GOING TO WORK HARD FOR THESE ENTRANCE EXAMS.
SO LET'S LIVE TOGETHER SOMEDAY.

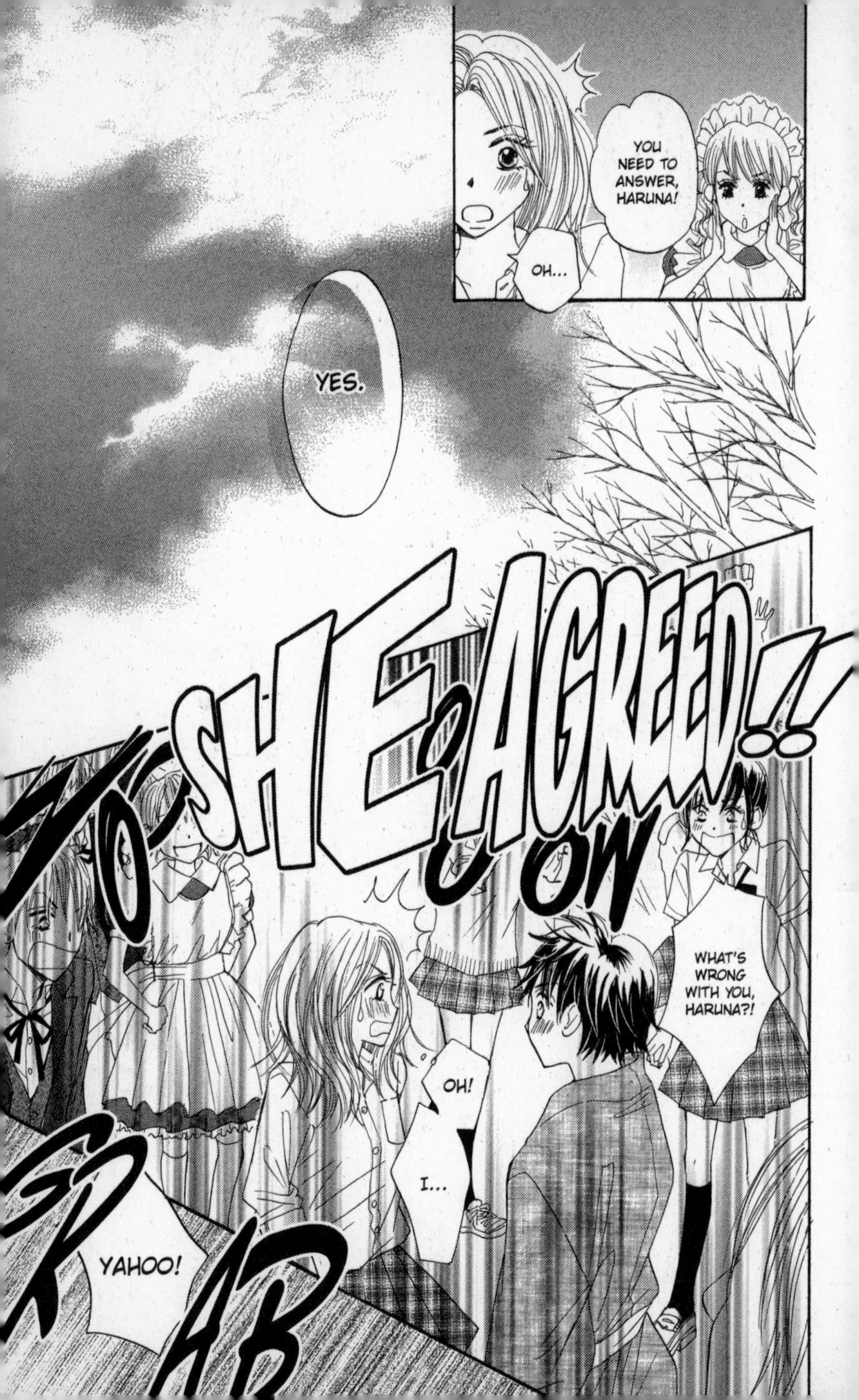
YOU NEED TO ANSWER, HARUNA!
OH...
YES.
SHE AGREED!!
WOOOW
WHAT'S WRONG WITH YOU, HARUNA?!
OH!
I...
YAHOO!
GRAB

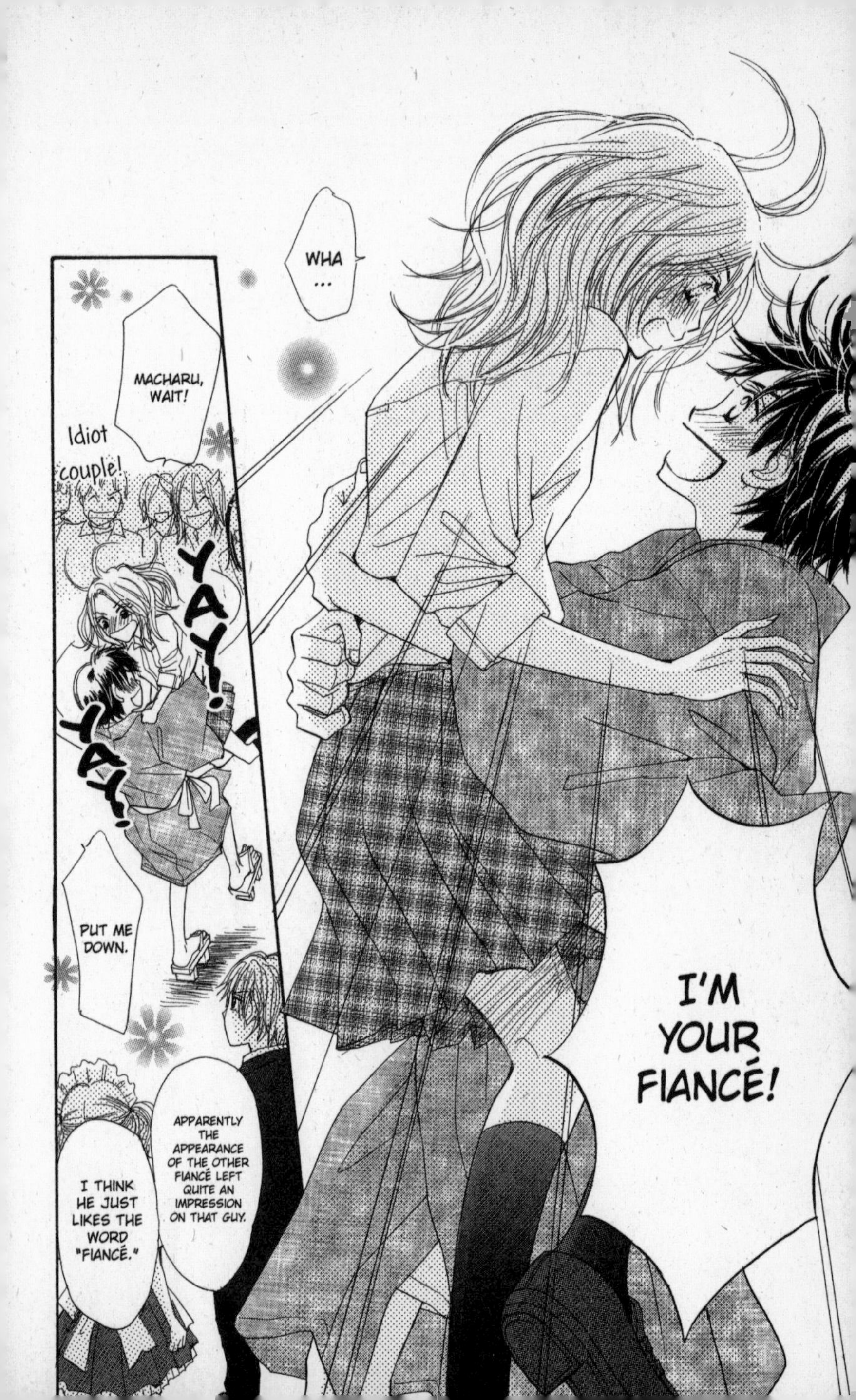
WHA ...
I'M YOUR FIANCÉ!
MACHARU, WAIT!
Idiot couple!
YAY!
YAY!
PUT ME DOWN.
APPARENTLY THE APPEARANCE OF THE OTHER FIANCÉ LEFT QUITE AN IMPRESSION ON THAT GUY.
I THINK HE JUST LIKES THE WORD "FIANCÉ."

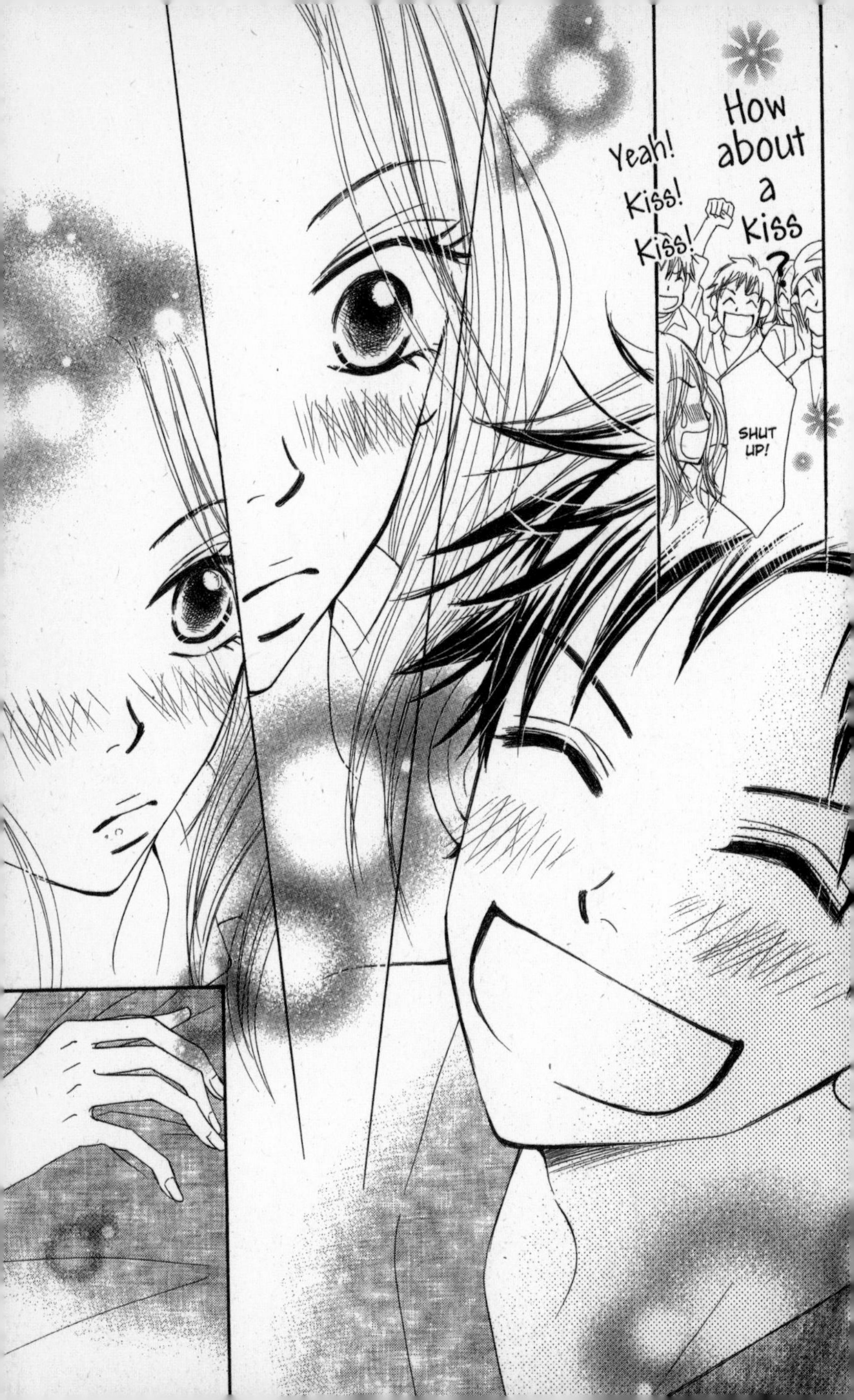
How about a kiss?
Yeah! Kiss! Kiss!
SHUT UP!

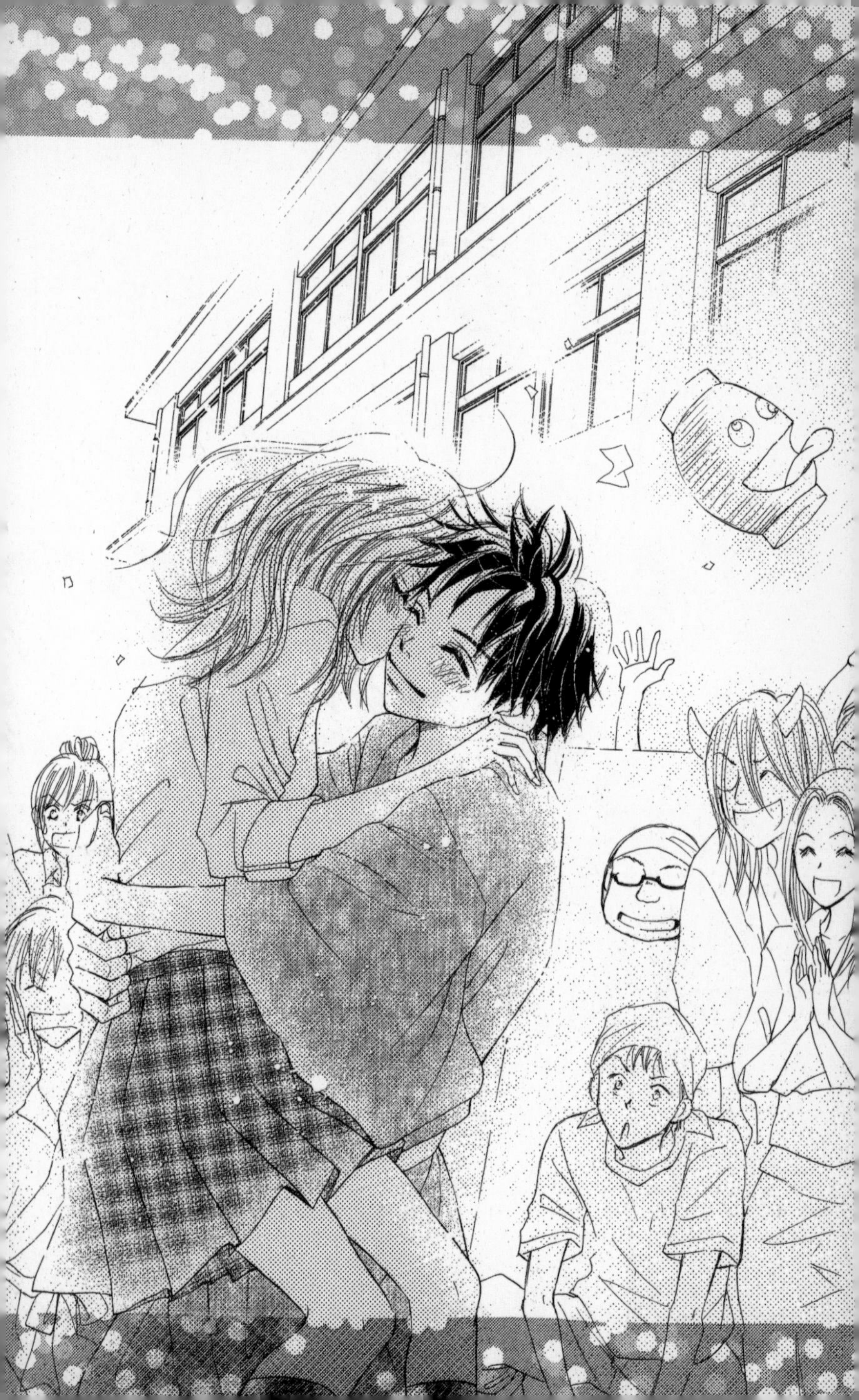

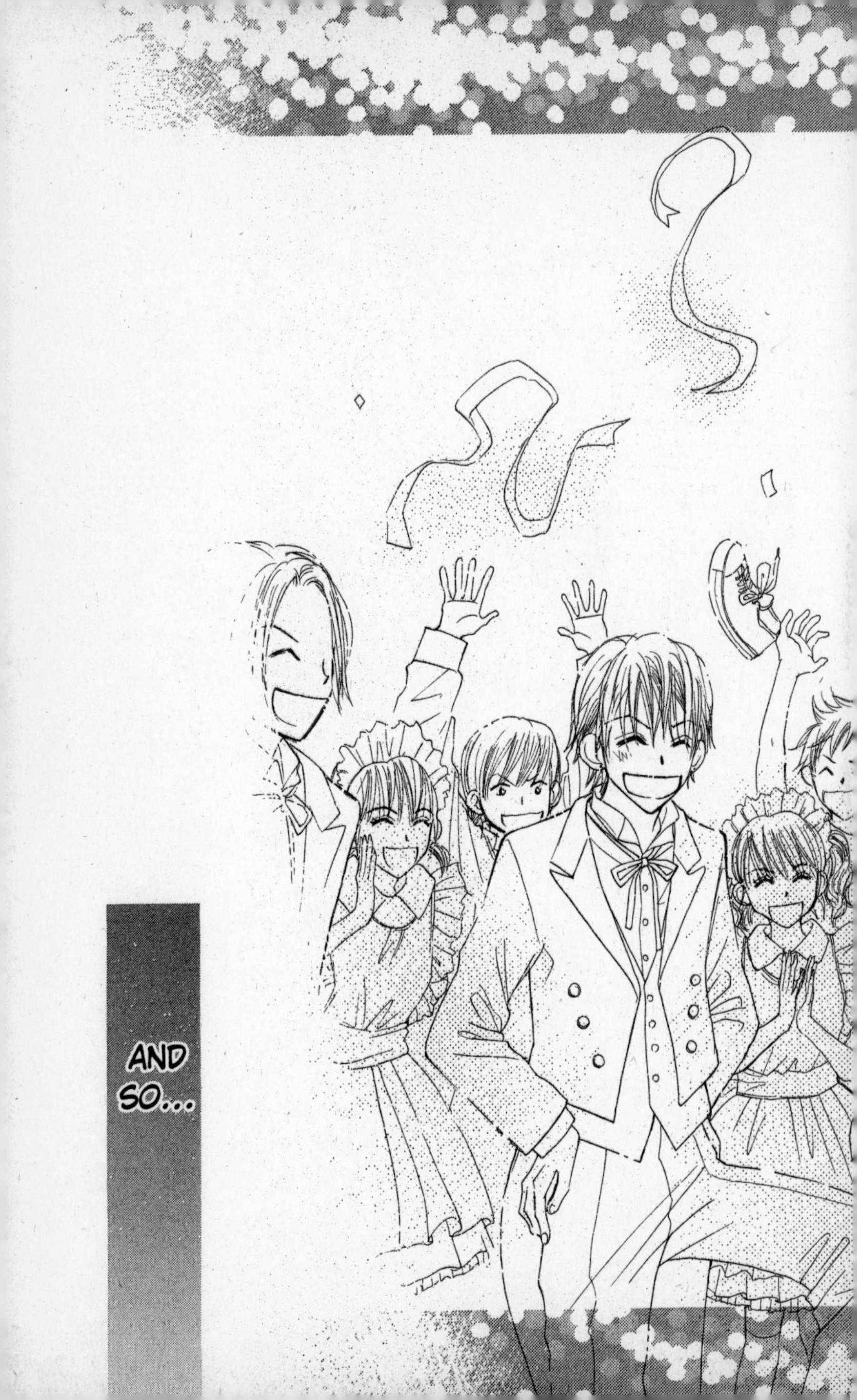
AND SO...

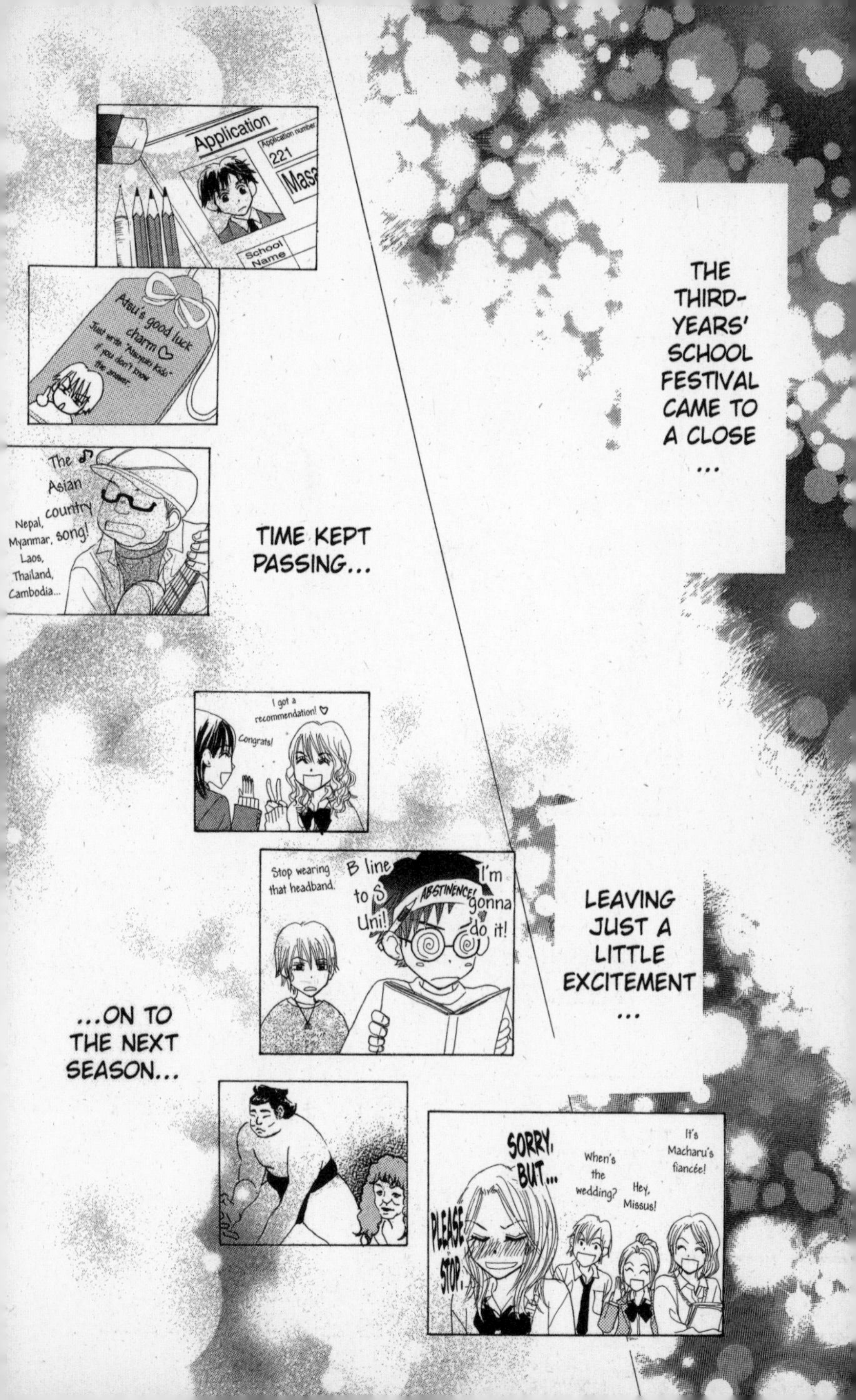
THE THIRD-YEARS' SCHOOL FESTIVAL CAME TO A CLOSE...
Application
Application number
221
Masa
School Name
Atsu's good luck charm ♡
Just write "Atsuyuki Kido" if you don't know the answer.
TIME KEPT PASSING...
The Asian country song! ♪
Nepal, Myanmar, Laos, Thailand, Cambodia...
I got a recommendation! ♡
Congrats!
I'm gonna do it!
ABSTINENCE!
B line to S Uni!
Stop wearing that headband.
LEAVING JUST A LITTLE EXCITEMENT...
...ON TO THE NEXT SEASON...
It's Macharu's fiancée!
Hey, Missus!
When's the wedding?
SORRY, BUT...
PLEASE STOP.

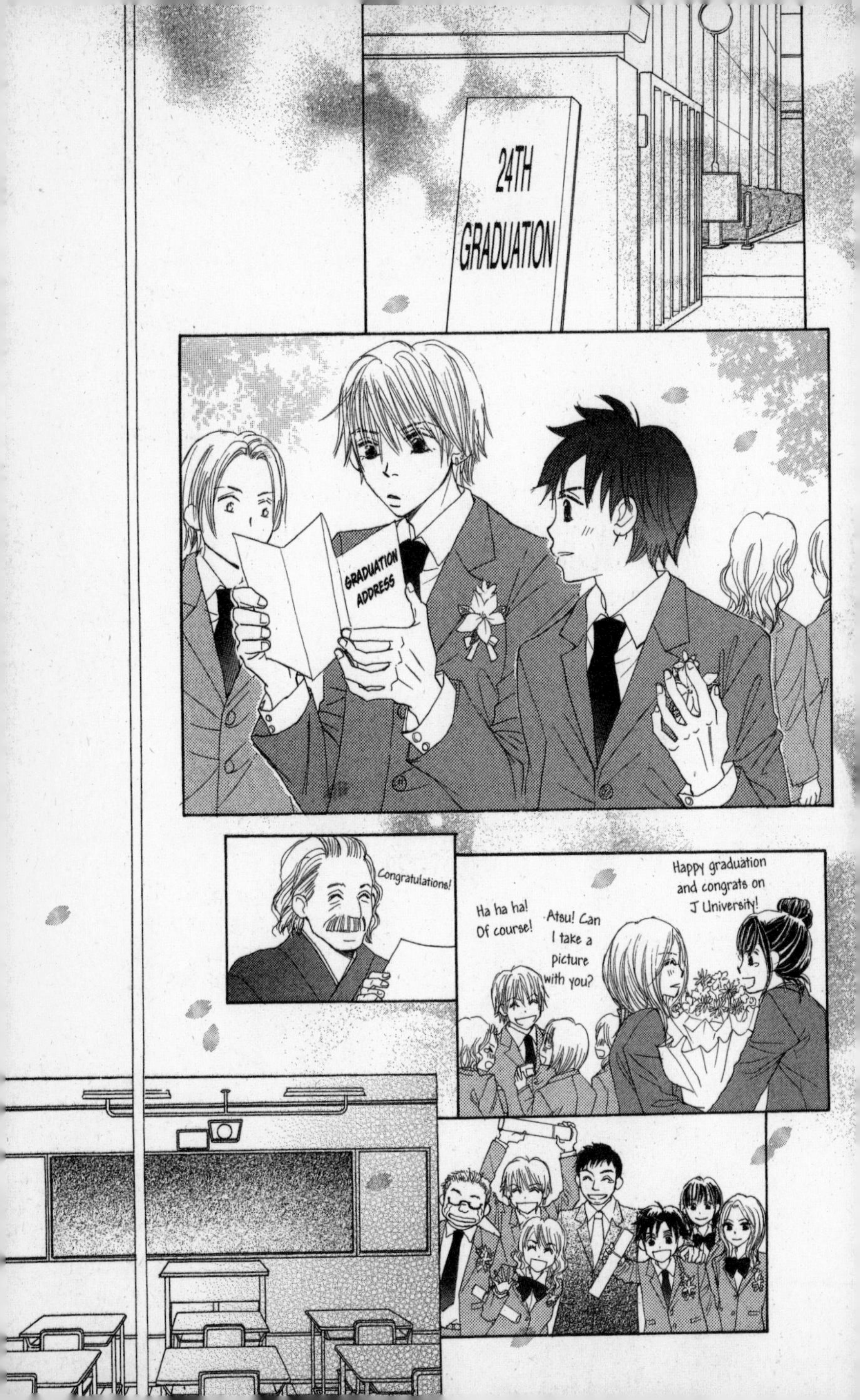
24TH GRADUATION
GRADUATION ADDRESS
Happy graduation and congrats on J University!
Atsu! Can I take a picture with you?
Ha ha ha! Of course!
Congratulations!

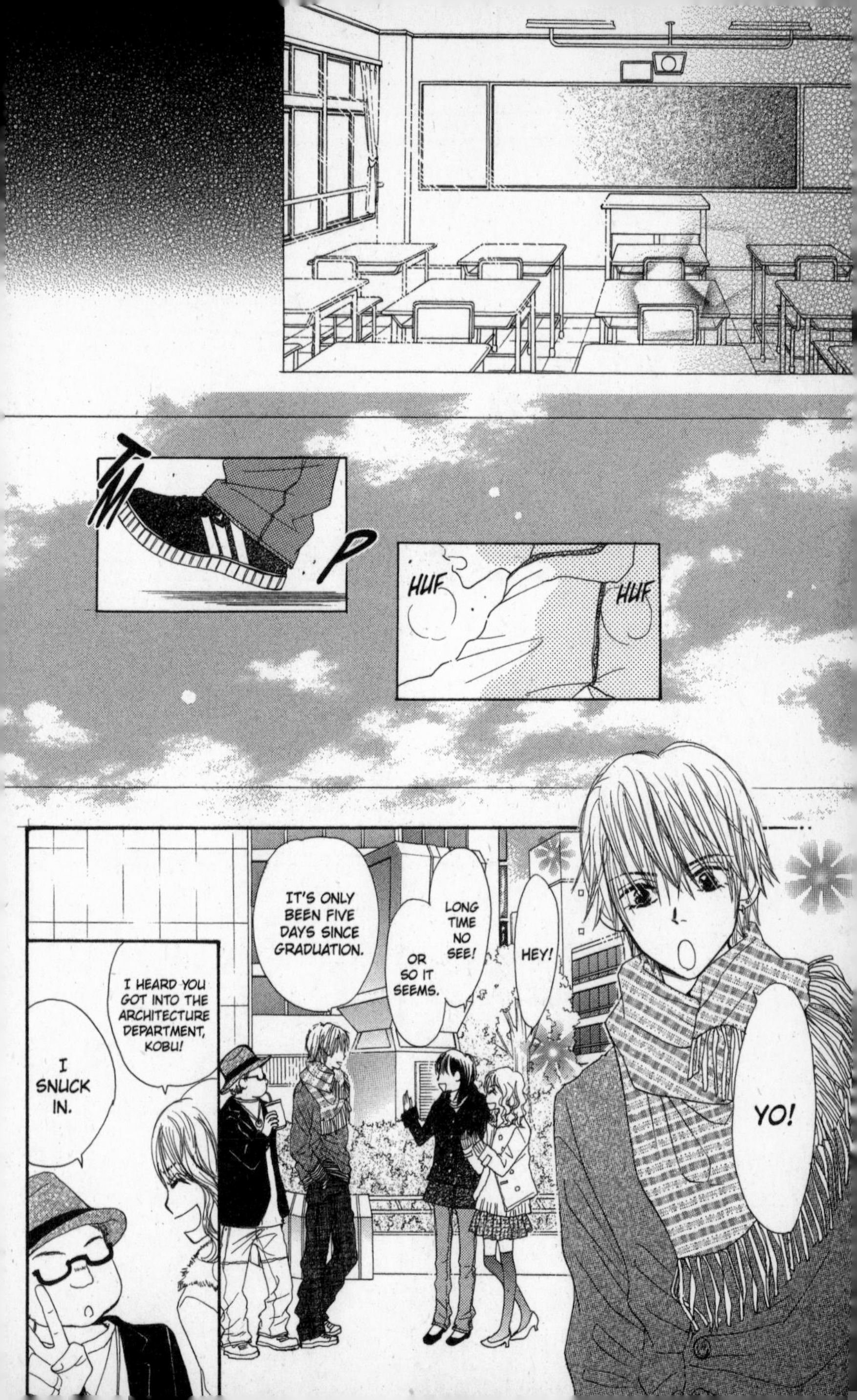

TMP
HUF
HUF
YO!
HEY!
LONG TIME NO SEE!
OR SO IT SEEMS.
IT'S ONLY BEEN FIVE DAYS SINCE GRADUATION.
I HEARD YOU GOT INTO THE ARCHITECTURE DEPARTMENT, KOBU!
I SNUCK IN.

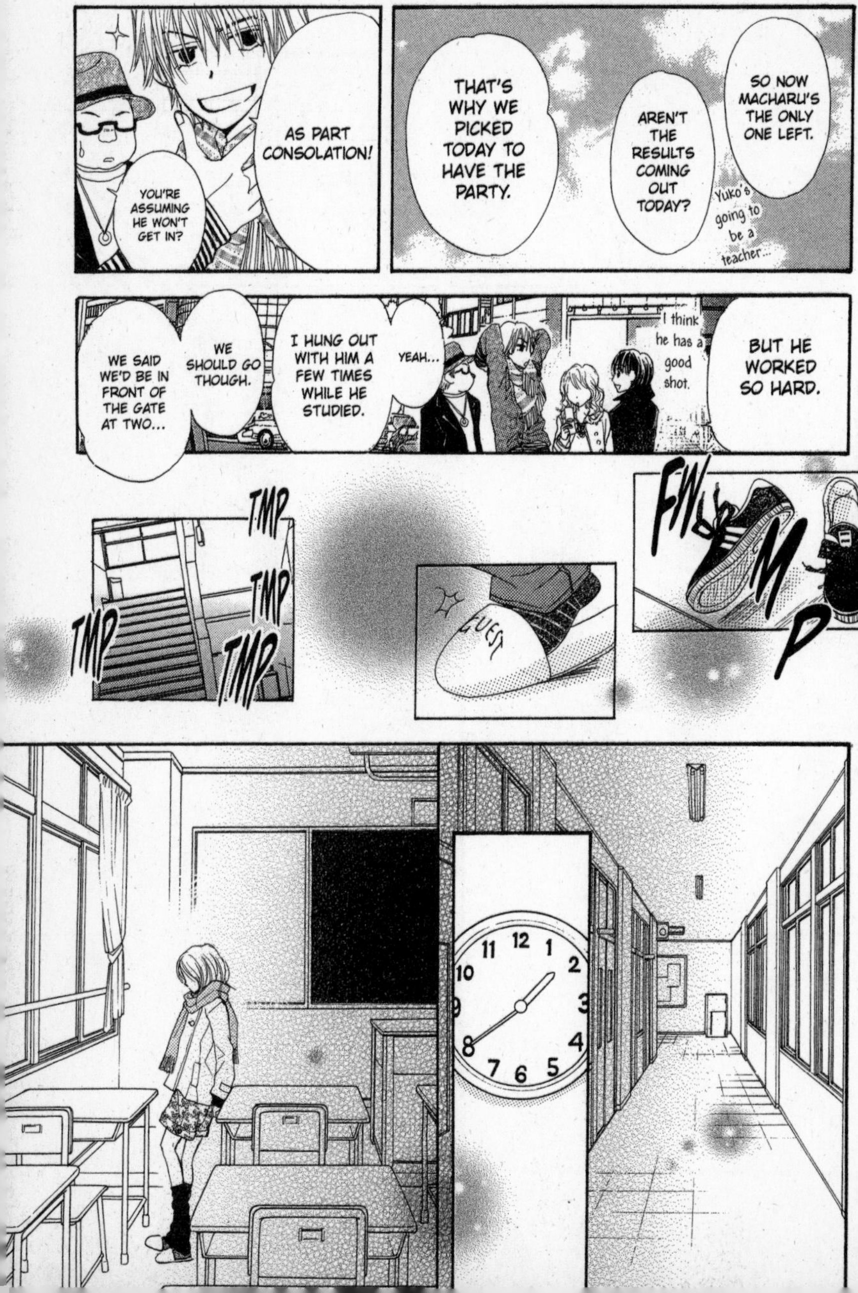
SO NOW MACHARU'S THE ONLY ONE LEFT.
Yuko's going to be a teacher...
AREN'T THE RESULTS COMING OUT TODAY?
THAT'S WHY WE PICKED TODAY TO HAVE THE PARTY.
AS PART CONSOLATION!
YOU'RE ASSUMING HE WON'T GET IN?
BUT HE WORKED SO HARD.
I think he has a good shot.
YEAH...
I HUNG OUT WITH HIM A FEW TIMES WHILE HE STUDIED.
WE SHOULD GO THOUGH.
WE SAID WE'D BE IN FRONT OF THE GATE AT TWO...
FWUMP
GUEST
TMP
TMP
TMP
TMP

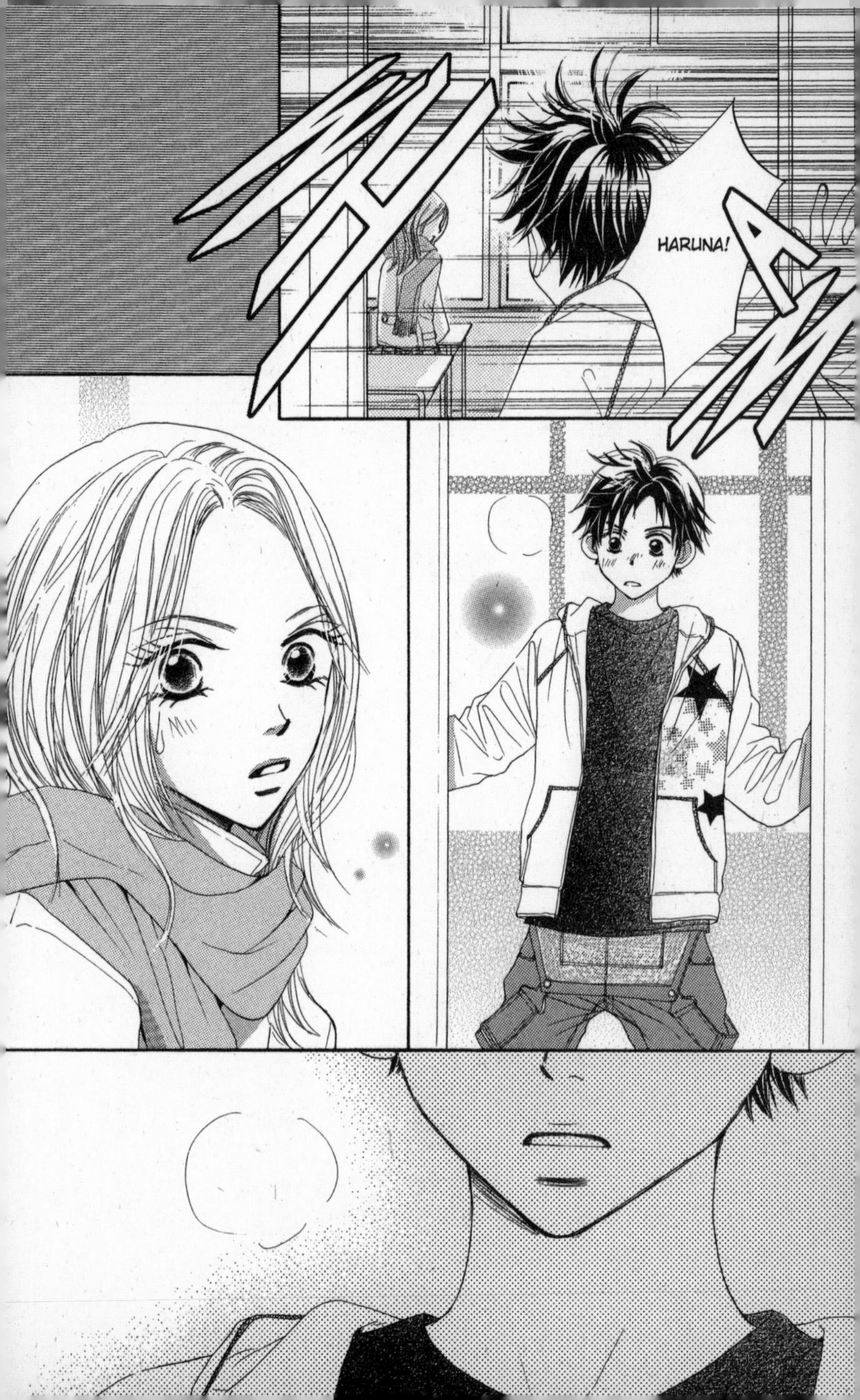
WHAM
HARUNA!

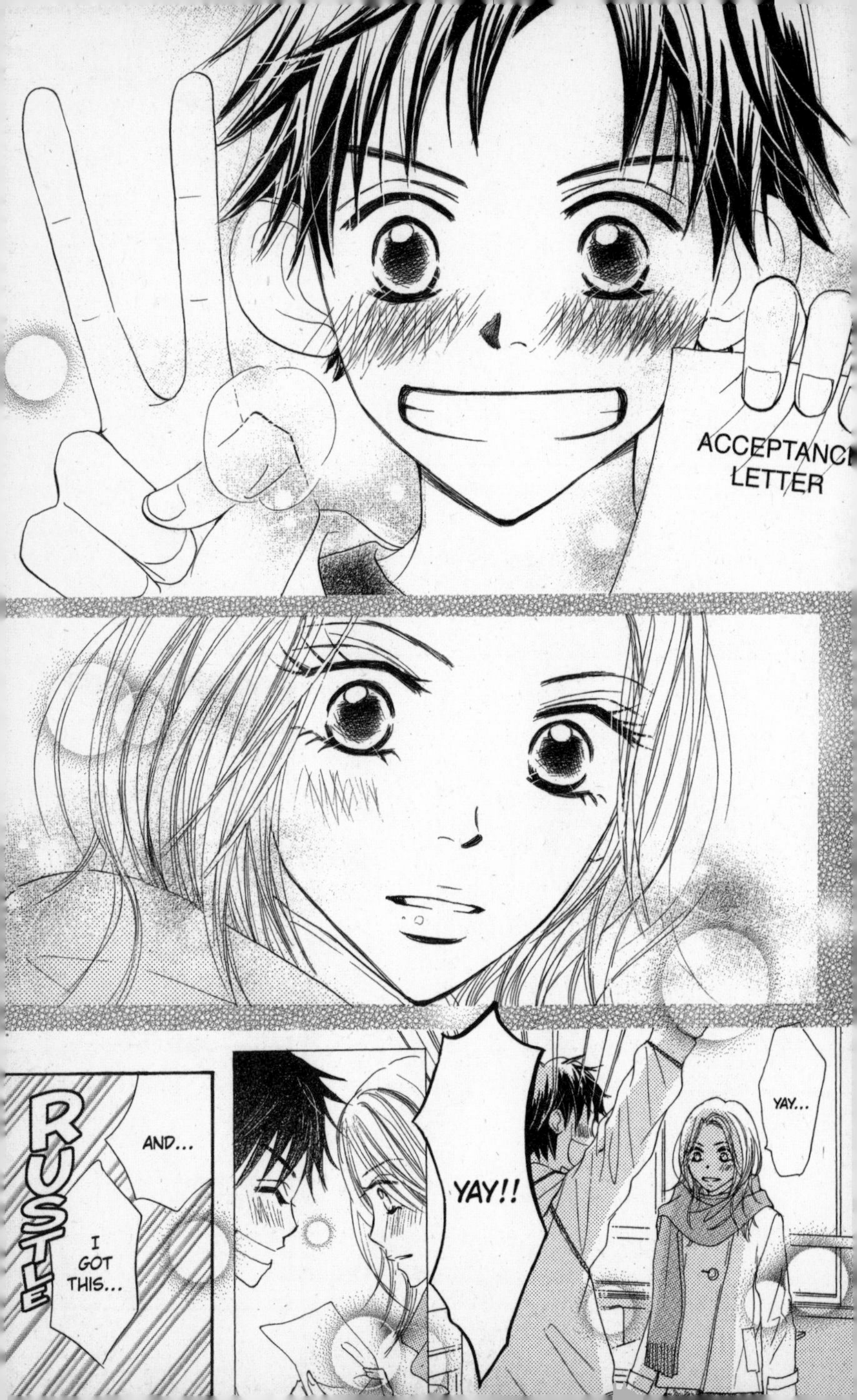
ACCEPTANC
LETTER
YAY...
YAY!!
AND...
RUSTLE
I GOT THIS...

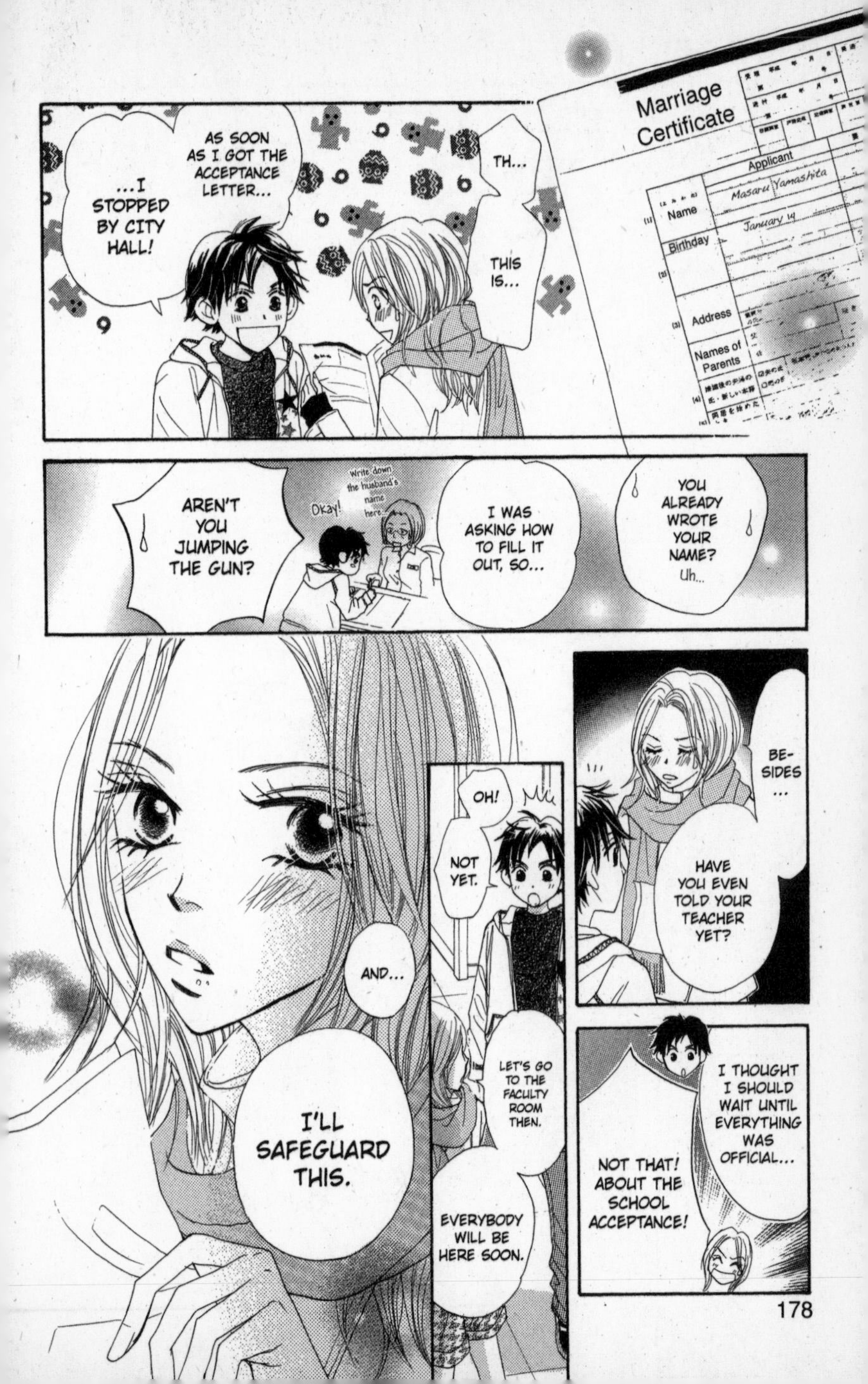
Marriage Certificate
Applicant
Name
Masaru Yamashita
Birthday
January 14
Address
Names of Parents
TH...
THIS IS...
AS SOON AS I GOT THE ACCEPTANCE LETTER...
...I STOPPED BY CITY HALL!
YOU ALREADY WROTE YOUR NAME? Uh...
I WAS ASKING HOW TO FILL IT OUT, SO...
Write down the husband's name here...
Okay!
AREN'T YOU JUMPING THE GUN?
BESIDES...
HAVE YOU EVEN TOLD YOUR TEACHER YET?
I THOUGHT I SHOULD WAIT UNTIL EVERYTHING WAS OFFICIAL...
NOT THAT! ABOUT THE SCHOOL ACCEPTANCE!
OH!
NOT YET.
LET'S GO TO THE FACULTY ROOM THEN.
EVERYBODY WILL BE HERE SOON.
AND...
I'LL SAFEGUARD THIS.

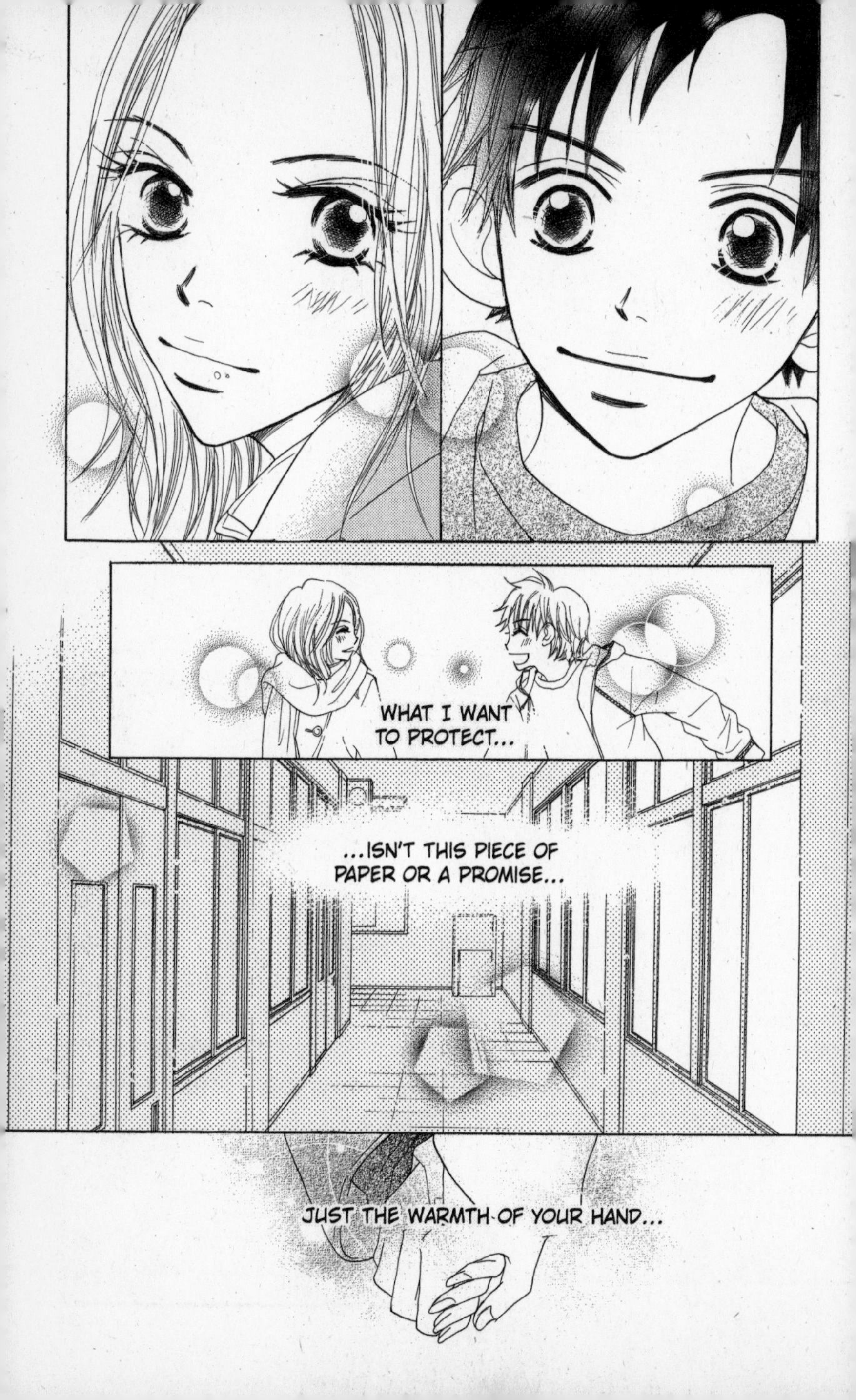
WHAT I WANT TO PROTECT...
...ISN'T THIS PIECE OF PAPER OR A PROMISE...
JUST THE WARMTH OF YOUR HAND...

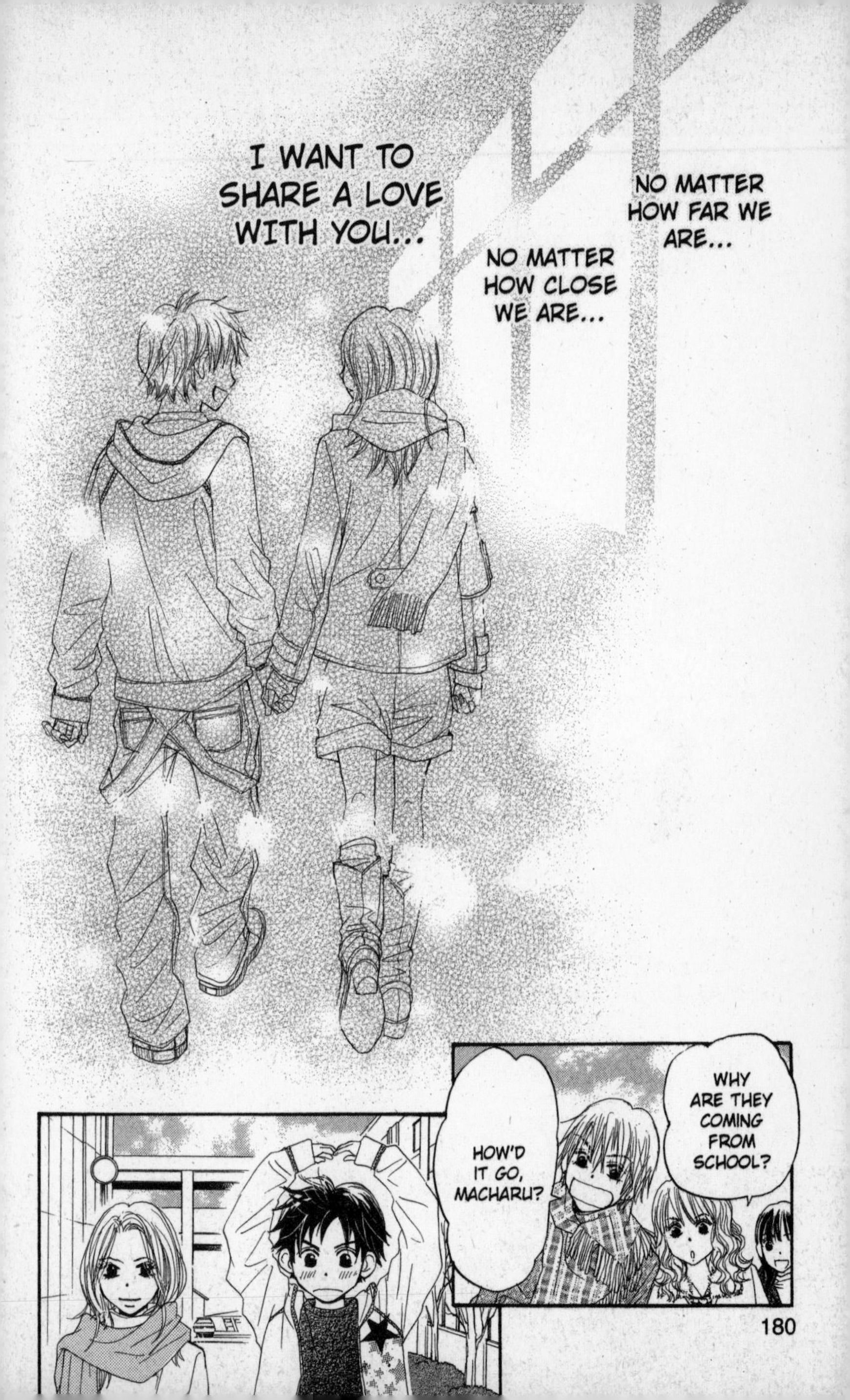
NO MATTER HOW FAR WE ARE...
NO MATTER HOW CLOSE WE ARE...
I WANT TO SHARE A LOVE WITH YOU...
WHY ARE THEY COMING FROM SCHOOL?
HOW'D IT GO, MACHARU?

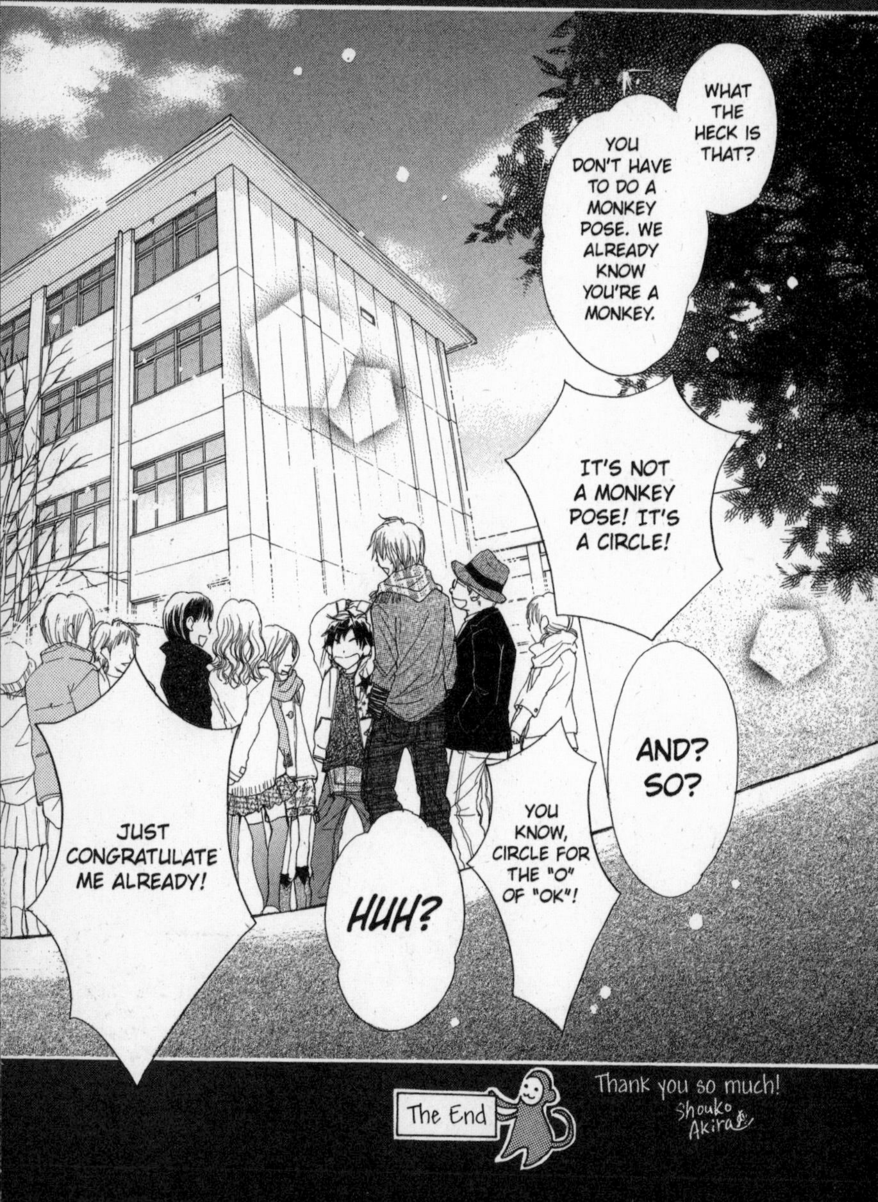
WHAT THE HECK IS THAT?
YOU DON'T HAVE TO DO A MONKEY POSE. WE ALREADY KNOW YOU'RE A MONKEY.
IT'S NOT A MONKEY POSE! IT'S A CIRCLE!
AND? SO?
YOU KNOW, CIRCLE FOR THE "O" OF "OK"!
HUH?
JUST CONGRATULATE ME ALREADY!
Thank you so much!
Shouko Akira
The End

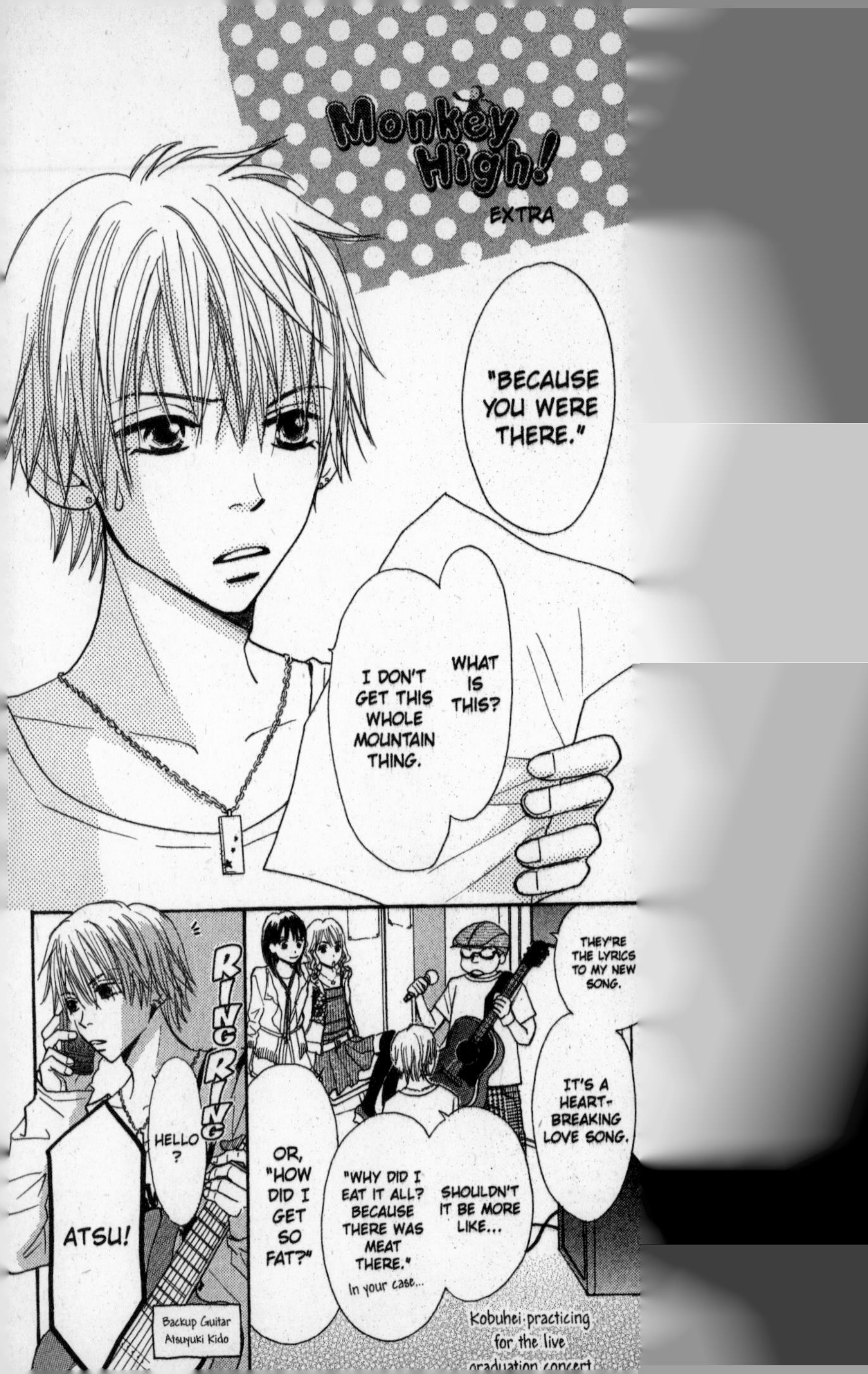
Monkey High!
EXTRA
"BECAUSE YOU WERE THERE."
WHAT IS THIS?
I DON'T GET THIS WHOLE MOUNTAIN THING.
THEY'RE THE LYRICS TO MY NEW SONG.
IT'S A HEART-BREAKING LOVE SONG.
SHOULDN'T IT BE MORE LIKE...
"WHY DID I EAT IT ALL? BECAUSE THERE WAS MEAT THERE."
In your case...
OR, "HOW DID I GET SO FAT?"
Kobuhei practicing for the live graduation concert
RING RING
HELLO?
ATSU!
Backup Guitar Atsuyuki Kido

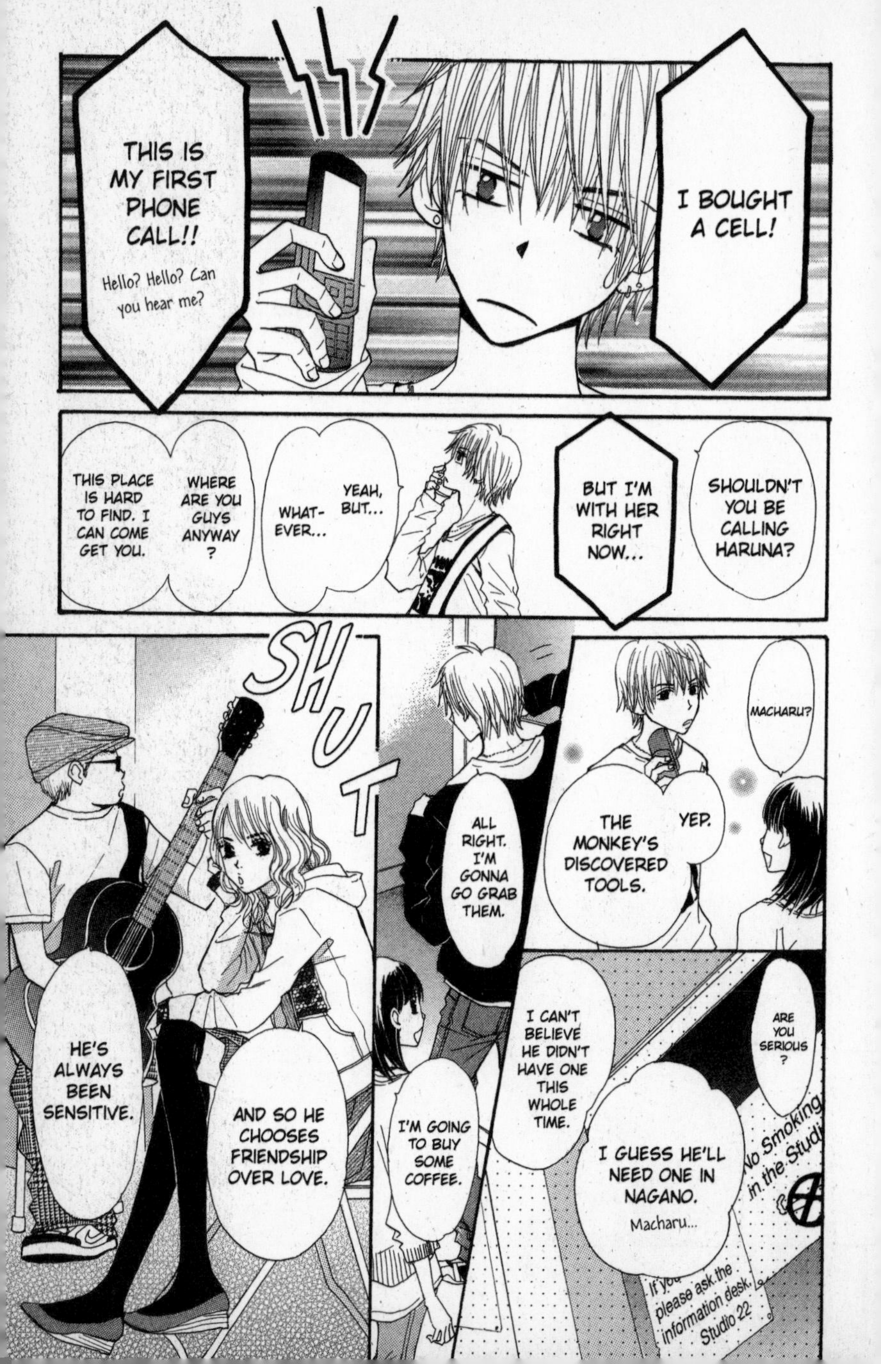
I BOUGHT A CELL!
THIS IS MY FIRST PHONE CALL!!
Hello? Hello? Can you hear me?
SHOULDN'T YOU BE CALLING HARUNA?
BUT I'M WITH HER RIGHT NOW...
YEAH, BUT...
WHAT-EVER...
WHERE ARE YOU GUYS ANYWAY?
THIS PLACE IS HARD TO FIND. I CAN COME GET YOU.
MACHARU?
YEP.
THE MONKEY'S DISCOVERED TOOLS.
ALL RIGHT. I'M GONNA GO GRAB THEM.
SHUT
ARE YOU SERIOUS?
I CAN'T BELIEVE HE DIDN'T HAVE ONE THIS WHOLE TIME.
I GUESS HE'LL NEED ONE IN NAGANO.
Macharu...
No Smoking in the Studi
please ask the information desk. Studio 22
I'M GOING TO BUY SOME COFFEE.
AND SO HE CHOOSES FRIENDSHIP OVER LOVE.
HE'S ALWAYS BEEN SENSITIVE.

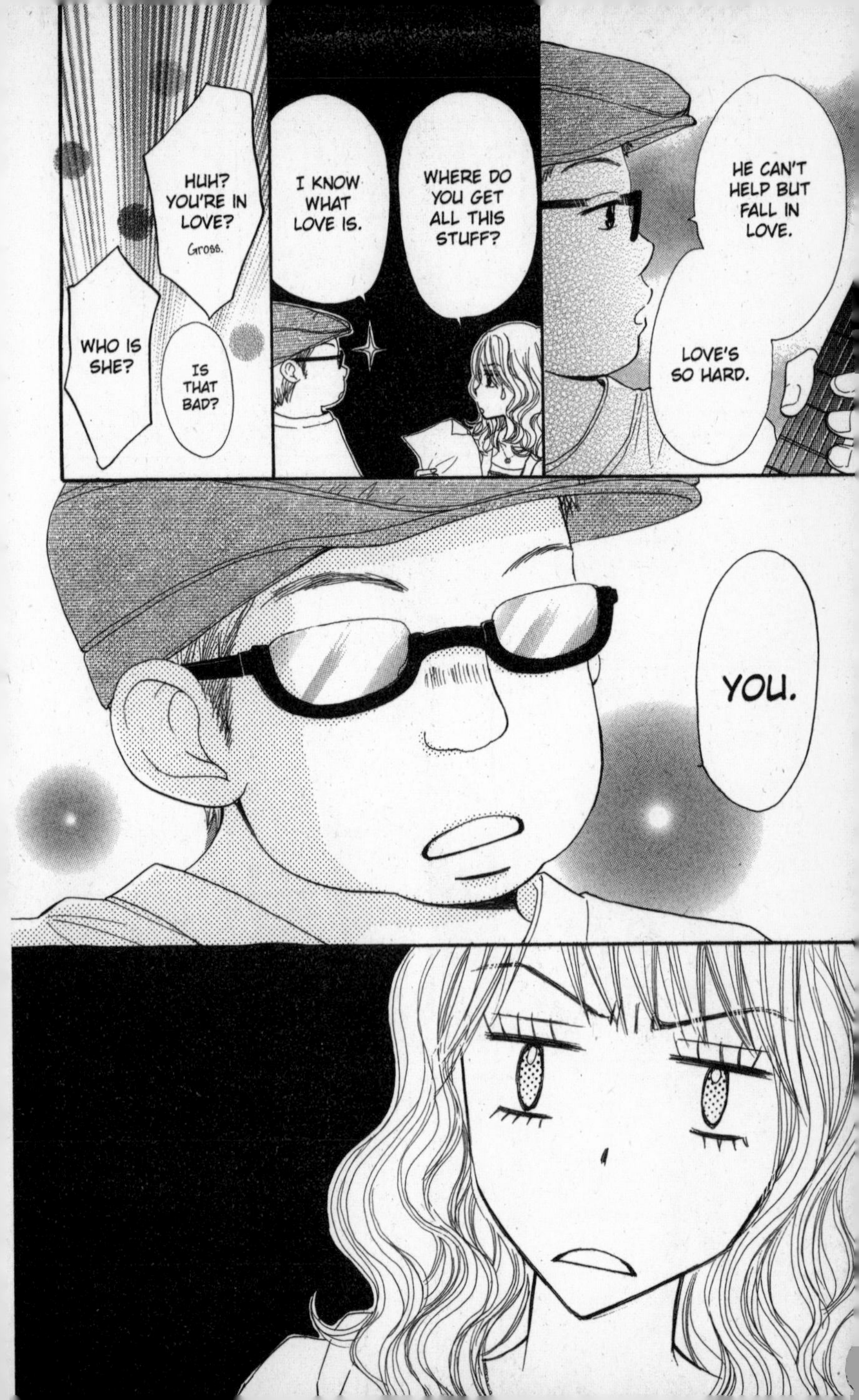

HE CAN'T HELP BUT FALL IN LOVE.
LOVE'S SO HARD.
WHERE DO YOU GET ALL THIS STUFF?
I KNOW WHAT LOVE IS.
HUH? YOU'RE IN LOVE?
Gross.
IS THAT BAD?
WHO IS SHE?
YOU.

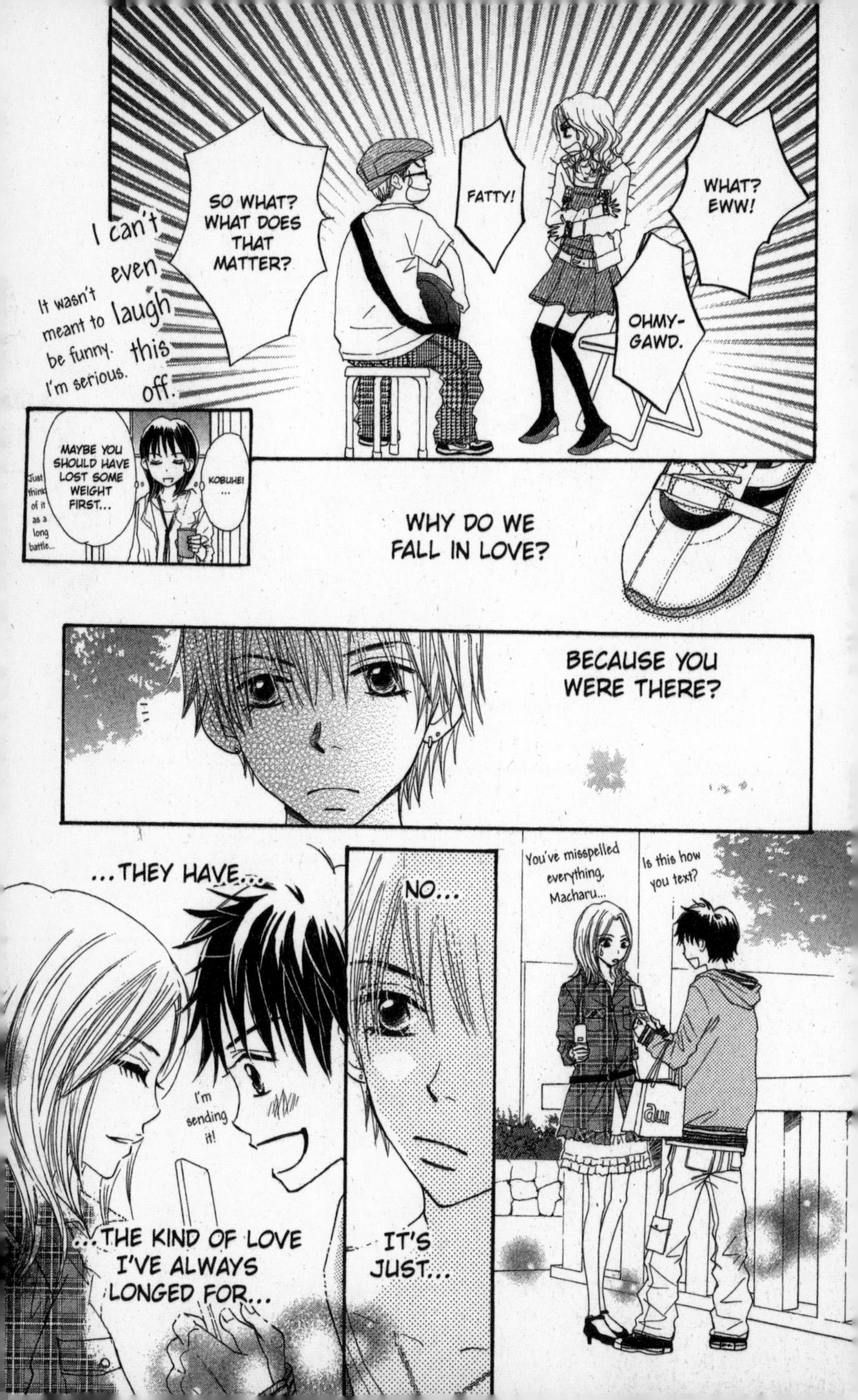
WHAT? EWW!
OHMY-GAWD.
FATTY!
SO WHAT? WHAT DOES THAT MATTER?
I can't even laugh this off.
It wasn't meant to be funny. I'm serious.
WHY DO WE FALL IN LOVE?
KOBUHEI...
MAYBE YOU SHOULD HAVE LOST SOME WEIGHT FIRST...
Just think of it as a long battle...
BECAUSE YOU WERE THERE?
Is this how you text?
You've misspelled everything, Macharu...
NO...
IT'S JUST...
...THEY HAVE...
I'm sending it!
...THE KIND OF LOVE I'VE ALWAYS LONGED FOR...

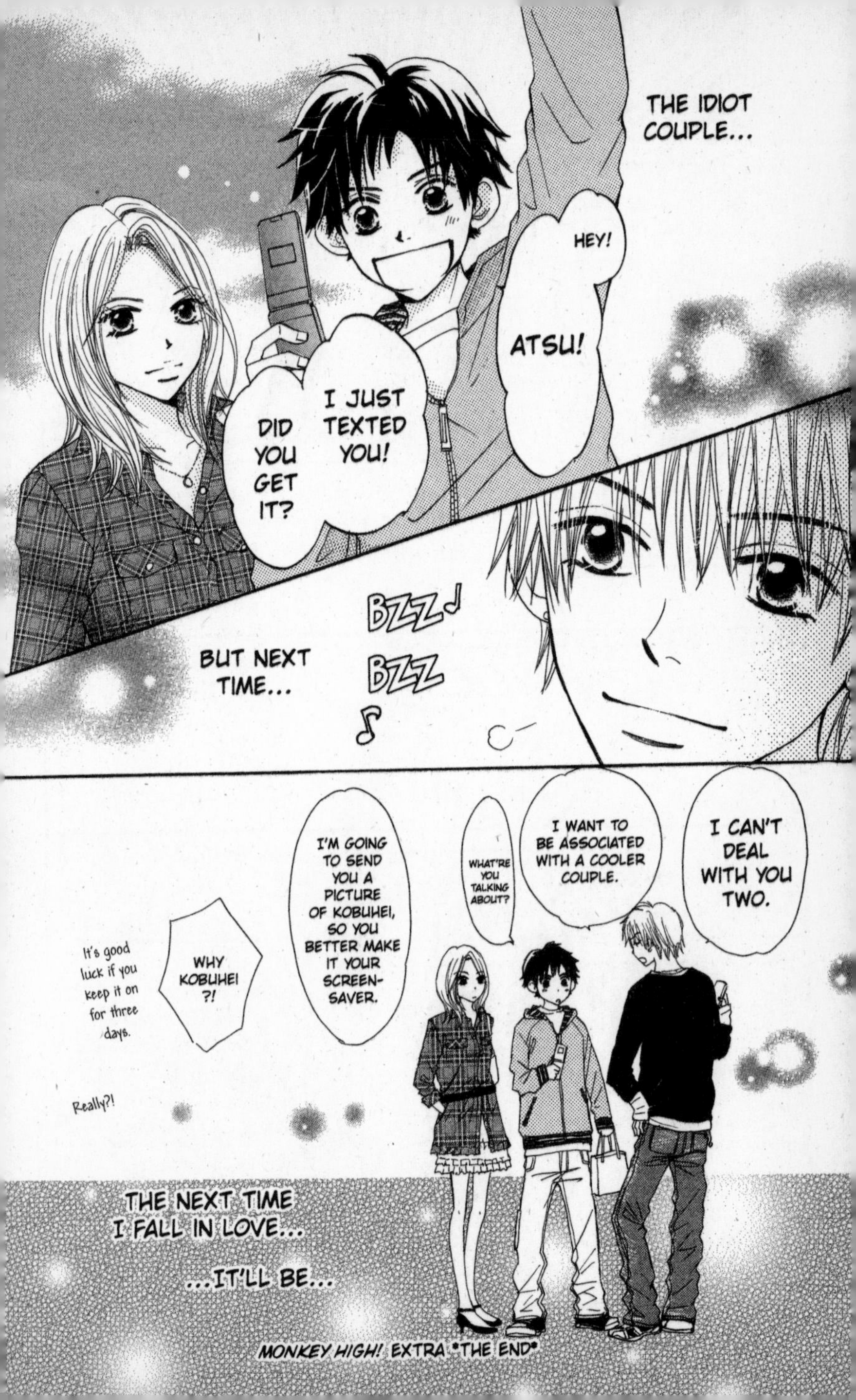
THE IDIOT COUPLE...
HEY! ATSU!
I JUST TEXTED YOU! DID YOU GET IT?
BZZ♩ BZZ ♪
BUT NEXT TIME...
I CAN'T DEAL WITH YOU TWO.
I WANT TO BE ASSOCIATED WITH A COOLER COUPLE.
WHAT'RE YOU TALKING ABOUT?
I'M GOING TO SEND YOU A PICTURE OF KOBUHEI, SO YOU BETTER MAKE IT YOUR SCREEN-SAVER.
WHY KOBUHEI?!
It's good luck if you keep it on for three days.
Really?!
THE NEXT TIME I FALL IN LOVE...
...IT'LL BE...
MONKEY HIGH! EXTRA *THE END*

POSTSCRIPT

THANK YOU SO MUCH FOR SEEING THIS THROUGH. I'M SHOUKO AKIRA. VOLUME 8... THE FINAL VOLUME. EIGHT'S A GOOD NUMBER TO END ON, I THINK. I'D LIKE TO REFLECT ON THE STORIES FOR THE LAST TIME.

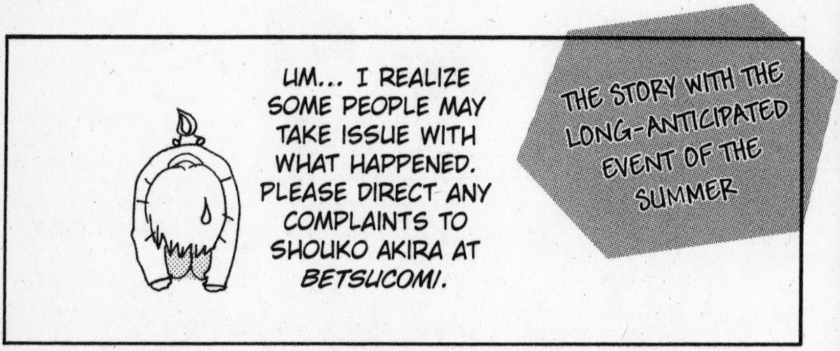
THE STORY WITH THE LONG-ANTICIPATED EVENT OF THE SUMMER
UM... I REALIZE SOME PEOPLE MAY TAKE ISSUE WITH WHAT HAPPENED. PLEASE DIRECT ANY COMPLAINTS TO SHOUKO AKIRA AT *BETSUCOMI*.

BUT SINCE *MONKEY HIGH!* HAS BEEN A STORY OF THE TWO DEVELOPING AS A COUPLE, I WONDERED IF IT WOULD BE APPROPRIATE TO SKIP THIS.

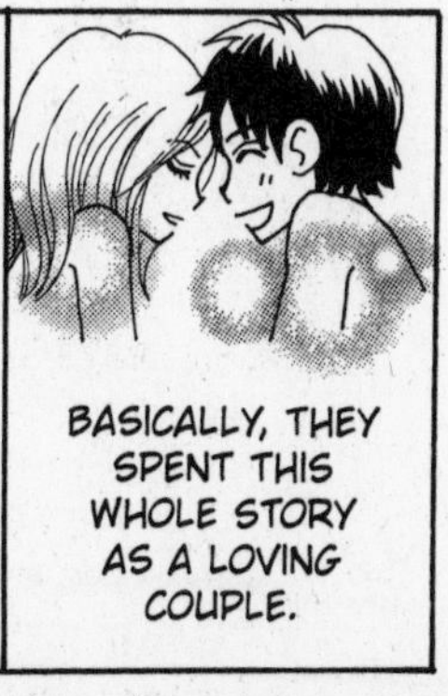
BASICALLY, THEY SPENT THIS WHOLE STORY AS A LOVING COUPLE.

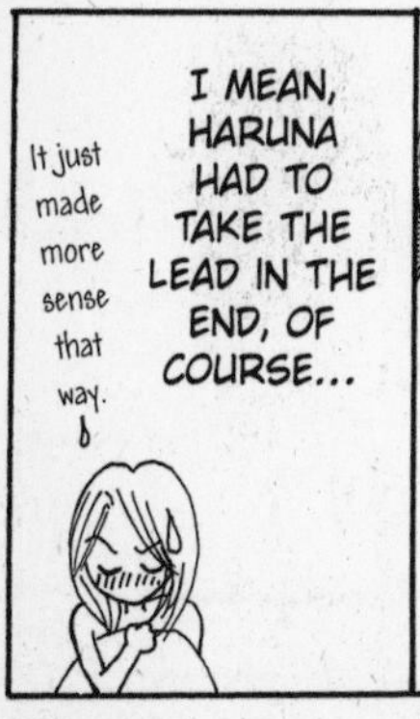
I MEAN, HARUNA HAD TO TAKE THE LEAD IN THE END, OF COURSE...
It just made more sense that way.

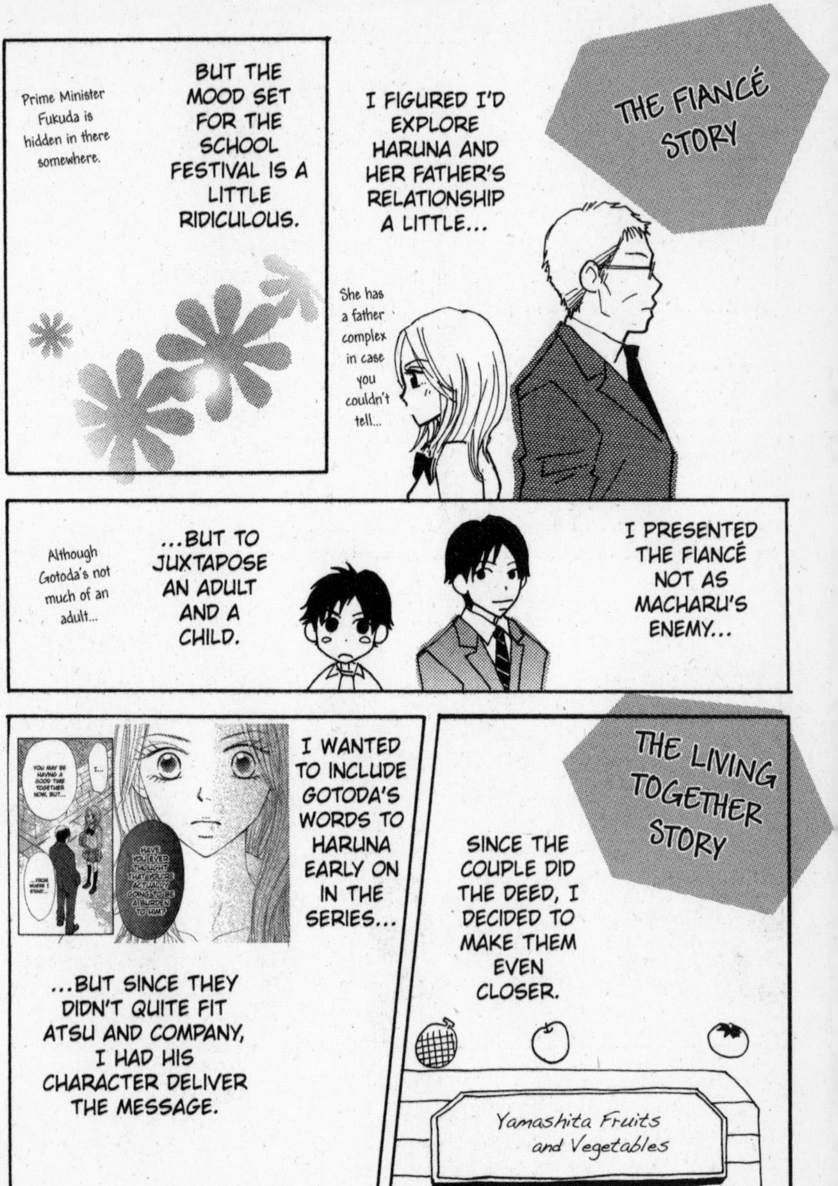
THE FIANCÉ STORY
I FIGURED I'D EXPLORE HARUNA AND HER FATHER'S RELATIONSHIP A LITTLE...
She has a father complex in case you couldn't tell...
BUT THE MOOD SET FOR THE SCHOOL FESTIVAL IS A LITTLE RIDICULOUS.
Prime Minister Fukuda is hidden in there somewhere.
I PRESENTED THE FIANCÉ NOT AS MACHARU'S ENEMY...
...BUT TO JUXTAPOSE AN ADULT AND A CHILD.
Although Gotoda's not much of an adult...
THE LIVING TOGETHER STORY
SINCE THE COUPLE DID THE DEED, I DECIDED TO MAKE THEM EVEN CLOSER.
Yamashita Fruits and Vegetables
I WANTED TO INCLUDE GOTODA'S WORDS TO HARUNA EARLY ON IN THE SERIES...
YOU MAY BE HAVING A GOOD TIME TOGETHER NOW, BUT...
...FROM WHERE I STAND...
I...
HAVE YOU EVER THOUGHT THAT YOU'RE ACTUALLY GOING TO BE A BURDEN TO HIM?
...BUT SINCE THEY DIDN'T QUITE FIT ATSU AND COMPANY, I HAD HIS CHARACTER DELIVER THE MESSAGE.

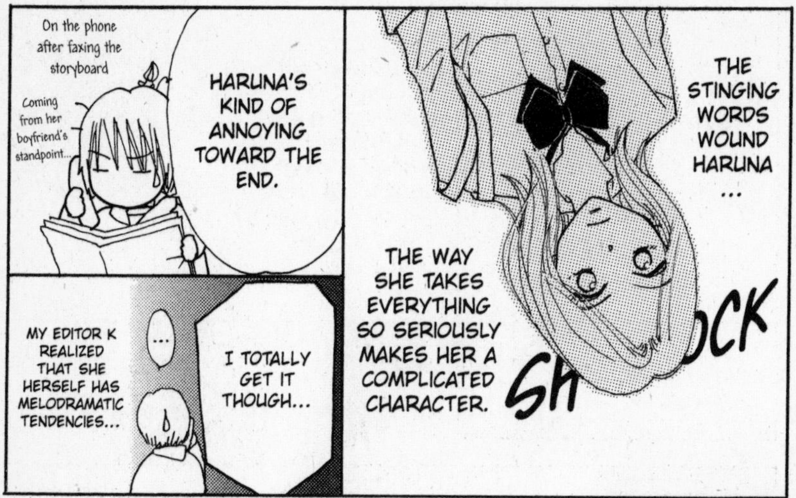
THE STINGING WORDS WOUND HARUNA...
SHOCK
THE WAY SHE TAKES EVERYTHING SO SERIOUSLY MAKES HER A COMPLICATED CHARACTER.
On the phone after faxing the storyboard
HARUNA'S KIND OF ANNOYING TOWARD THE END.
Coming from her boyfriend's standpoint...
I TOTALLY GET IT THOUGH...
...
MY EDITOR K REALIZED THAT SHE HERSELF HAS MELODRAMATIC TENDENCIES...

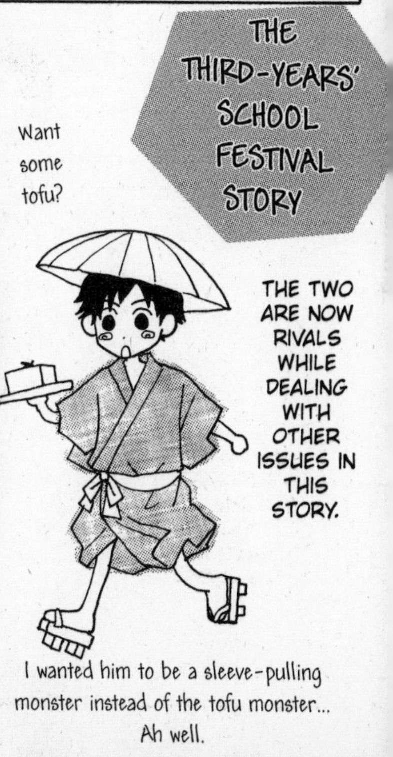
THE THIRD-YEARS' SCHOOL FESTIVAL STORY
THE TWO ARE NOW RIVALS WHILE DEALING WITH OTHER ISSUES IN THIS STORY.
Want some tofu?
I wanted him to be a sleeve-pulling monster instead of the tofu monster... Ah well.

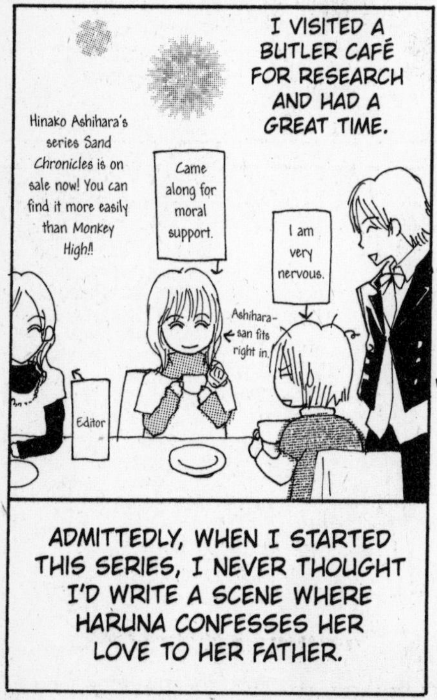
I VISITED A BUTLER CAFÉ FOR RESEARCH AND HAD A GREAT TIME.
Hinako Ashihara's series Sand Chronicles is on sale now! You can find it more easily than Monkey High!!
I am very nervous.
Came along for moral support.
Ashihara-san fits right in.
Editor
ADMITTEDLY, WHEN I STARTED THIS SERIES, I NEVER THOUGHT I'D WRITE A SCENE WHERE HARUNA CONFESSES HER LOVE TO HER FATHER.

FINAL STORY!

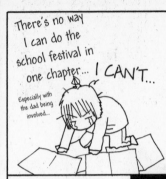

I WAS ACTUALLY PLANNING ON FINISHING UP THE SCHOOL FESTIVAL IN THE PREVIOUS STORYLINE AND SAVING THE FINAL STORY FOR THE TIME AROUND GRADUATION...

There's no way I can do the school festival in one chapter... I CAN'T...

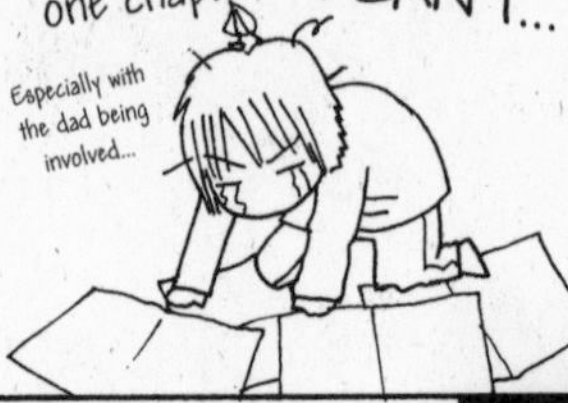

Especially with the dad being involved...

BUT I FIGURED IT WAS GOOD TO COME FULL CIRCLE BY ENDING WITH THE THIRD-YEAR FESTIVAL SINCE WE STARTED WITH THEIR FIRST-YEAR SCHOOL FESTIVAL.

I sobbed the last three times because I couldn't fit everything in.

MY LITTLE SISTER WAS WATCHING A VARIETY SHOW AND WAS STRUCK BY THE STORY OF SCREENWRITER MAKIKO UCHIDATE GOING TO SEE ASASHORYU'S FIRST SUMO MATCH BACK AFTER HIS RECOVERY, SO THAT'S BEEN INCORPORATED.

I INTRODUCED *MONKEY HIGH!* AS A LIGHTHEARTED HIGH SCHOOL LOVE DRAMA, BUT OVER TIME THE LOVE TAKES PLACE AT SCHOOL.

THE EXTRA STORY

KOBUHEI'S CONFESSION WAS ACTUALLY SUPPOSED TO BE INCORPORATED INTO THE MAIN STORY NUMEROUS TIMES, BUT IT KEPT GETTING DENIED BECAUSE IT WOULD RUIN THE MAIN STORYLINE.

For the record, it's unlikely that their relationship would change anyway...

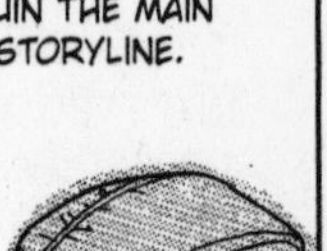

EVEN THOUGH ATSU IS SO POPULAR, HE SPENT HIS HIGH SCHOOL CAREER WITHOUT A GIRLFRIEND.

HIS PROBLEM IS THAT HE LIKES MACHARU MORE THAN HARUNA, AND THAT SHE IS FULLY AWARE OF THAT.

Also, he knows that Haruna is way more into Macharu between the two. So sad...

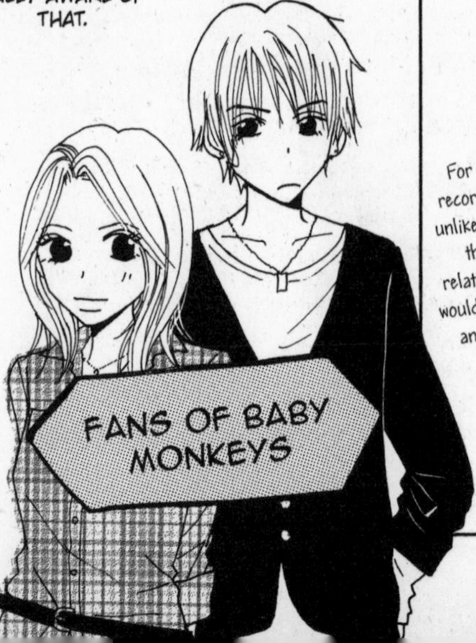
FANS OF BABY MONKEYS

I like the interactions between these two... They're very similar...

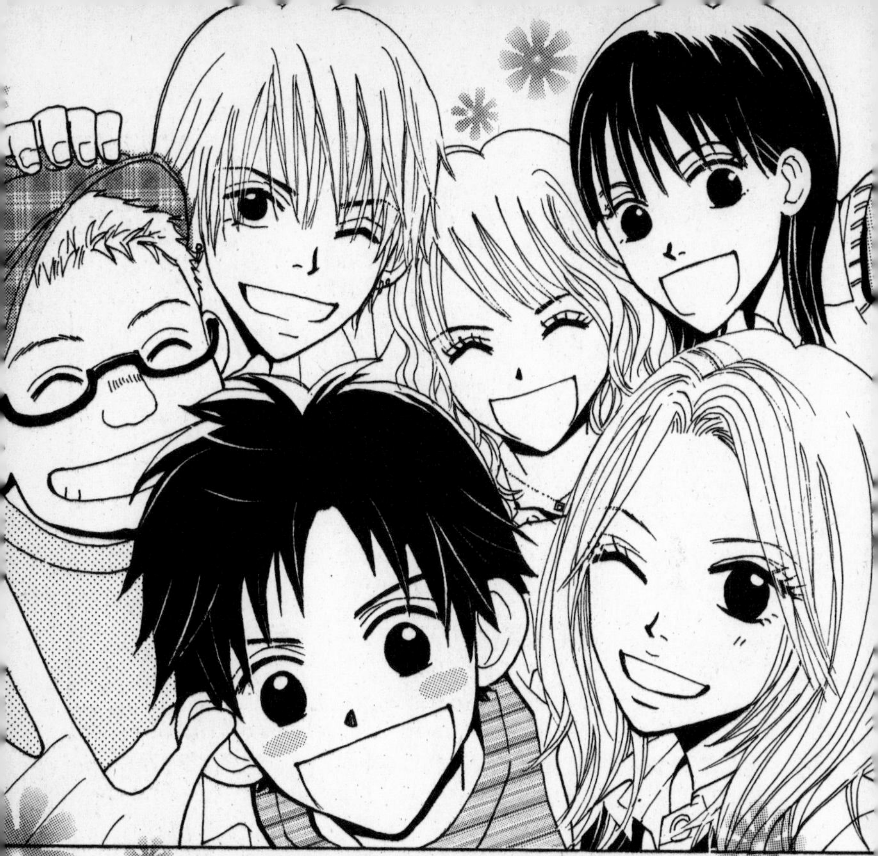

THIS IS MY FINAL NOTE FOR THE *MONKEY HIGH!* SERIES.
I'M NOT ONE TO GET TOO ATTACHED TO MY CHARACTERS, BUT WITH THIS MUCH TIME SPENT TOGETHER, I CAN'T HELP BUT FEEL A LITTLE SENTIMENTAL.

I AM SO GRATEFUL FOR ALL THE SUPPORT THAT ALLOWED ME TO DO THIS. I MADE A LOT OF MISTAKES BUT WAS ALWAYS FORGIVEN FOR THEM.

TO MY EDITORS H, Y, S AND K... TO NAKUI-SAN FOR THE CUTE MONKEY LOGO AND COVER DESIGN... TO THE DESIGN PEOPLE, MY ASSISTANTS AND MY FAMILY... THANK YOU SO MUCH.

AND TO ALL MY READERS OF COURSE! THANK YOU FOR ALL THE LETTERS! I'M GOING TO CONTINUE TO WORK HARD, SO YOUR CONTINUED SUPPORT IS MUCH APPRECIATED.

IF YOU HAVE ANY OPINIONS OR REVIEWS ABOUT THE FINAL VOLUME, PLEASE SEND THEM TO:

SHOUKO AKIRA
C/O *MONKEY HIGH!* EDITOR
VIZ MEDIA
P.O. BOX 77010
SAN FRANCISCO, CA 94107

See you again soon!

March 2008
Shouko Akira

Slightly confused by all the monkeying around? Here are some notes to help you out!

Page 2: Masaru
Even though everyone refers to him by his nickname, Macharu's real name is "Masaru," which means "superior" in Japanese. Interestingly enough, *saru* by itself means "monkey."

Page 2: Nagano Prefecture
Nagano Prefecture is located in the central region of the island Honshu in Japan.

Page 59, panel 2: Maid Café
A theme café where the servers dress up as maids and treat the customers as masters. There are also butler cafés, where the servers dress up as butlers instead of maids.

Page 59, panel 5: Takoyaki
Takoyaki are dough balls with pieces of octopus in them. They are made using a hot plate and are often sold at Japanese festivals. *Tako* means "octopus" in Japanese.

Page 78, panel 2: Sukiyaki
A hot-pot dish where meat and vegetables are simmered in a mixture of soy sauce, sugar and *mirin* (a type of rice wine).

Page 187, panel 2: *Betsucomi*
A monthly Japanese shojo manga magazine published by Shogakukan.

We've finally come to volume 8—the last volume. Eight volumes are just the right number to have on your bookshelf! It's an easy-to-collect series!! Even for those of you who read the series by borrowing books from your friends... In any case, thank you.

—Shouko Akira

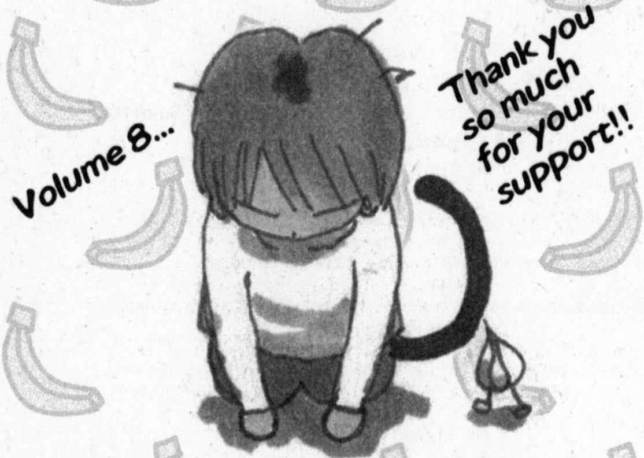
Volume 8...
Thank you so much for your support!!

Shouko Akira was born on September 10th and grew up in Kyoto. She currently lives in Tokyo and loves soccer, cycling, and Yoshimoto Shin Kigeki (a comedy stage show based out of Osaka). Most of her works revolve around school life and love, including *Times Two*, a collection of five romantic short stories.

MONKEY HIGH!
VOL. 8
Shojo Beat Manga Edition

STORY AND ART BY
SHOUKO AKIRA

Translation & Adaptation/Mai Ihara
Touch-up Art & Lettering/John Hunt
Design/Hidemi Dunn
Editor/Amy Yu

VP, Production/Alvin Lu
VP, Publishing Licensing/Rika Inouye
VP, Sales & Product Marketing/Gonzalo Ferreyra
VP, Creative/Linda Espinosa
Publisher/Hyoe Narita

SARUYAMA! 8 by Shouko AKIRA © 2008 Shouko AKIRA
All rights reserved.
Original Japanese edition published in 2008 by Shogakukan Inc., Tokyo.

Printed in the U.S.A.

Published by VIZ Media, LLC
P.O. Box 77010
San Francisco, CA 94107

10 9 8 7 6 5 4 3 2 1
First printing, December 2009

www.viz.com

PARENTAL ADVISORY
MONKEY HIGH! is rated T+ for Older Teen
and is recommended for ages 16 and up.
This volume contains sexual themes.
ratings.viz.com

www.shojobeat.com

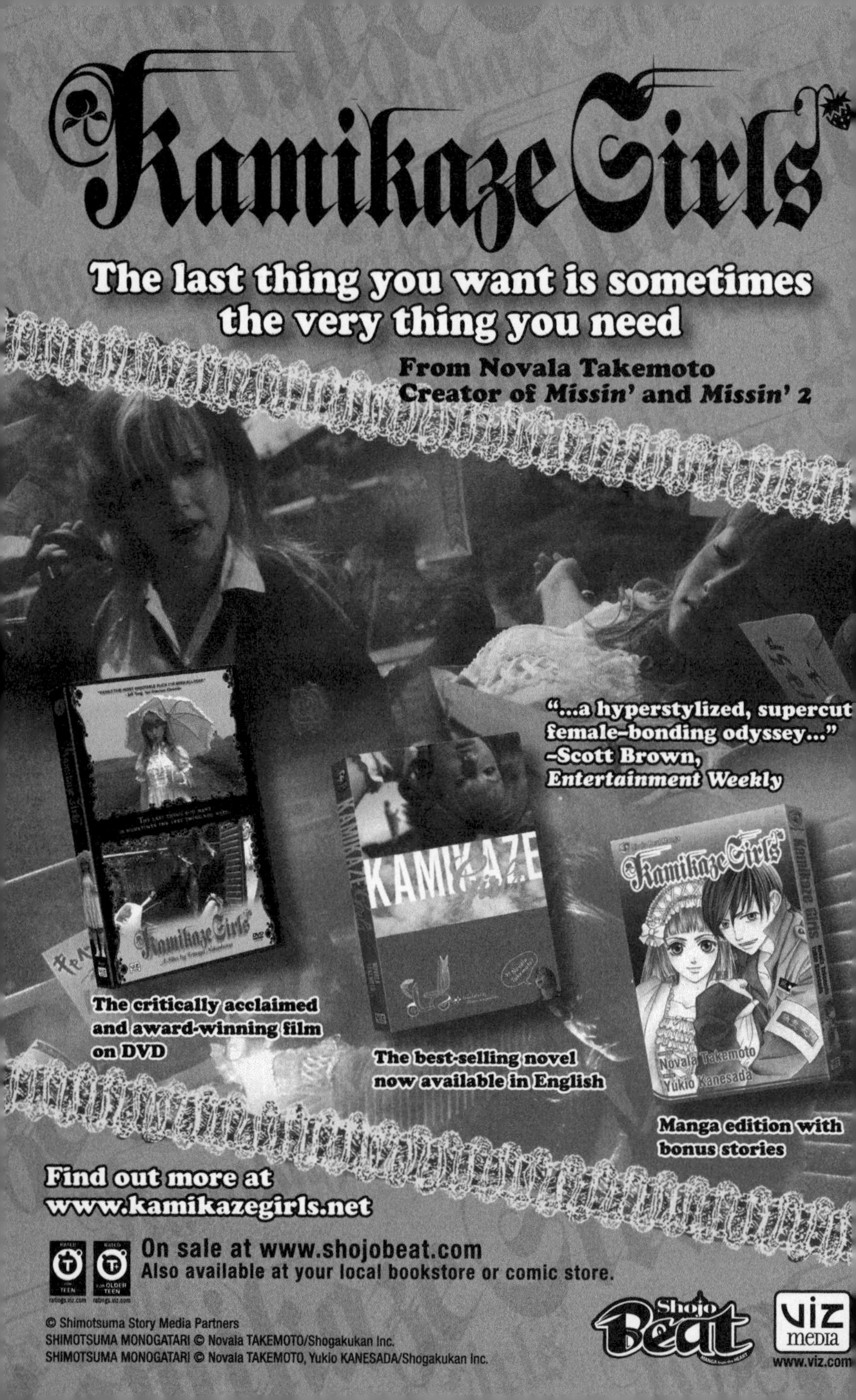
Kamikaze Girls
The last thing you want is sometimes the very thing you need
From Novala Takemoto
Creator of Missin' and Missin' 2
"...a hyperstylized, supercut female-bonding odyssey..."
–Scott Brown, Entertainment Weekly
The critically acclaimed and award-winning film on DVD
The best-selling novel now available in English
Manga edition with bonus stories
KAMIKAZE
Kamikaze Girls
Novala Takemoto
Yukio Kanesada
Find out more at www.kamikazegirls.net
On sale at www.shojobeat.com
Also available at your local bookstore or comic store.
© Shimotsuma Story Media Partners
SHIMOTSUMA MONOGATARI © Novala TAKEMOTO/Shogakukan Inc.
SHIMOTSUMA MONOGATARI © Novala TAKEMOTO, Yukio KANESADA/Shogakukan Inc.
Shojo Beat
viz media
www.viz.com

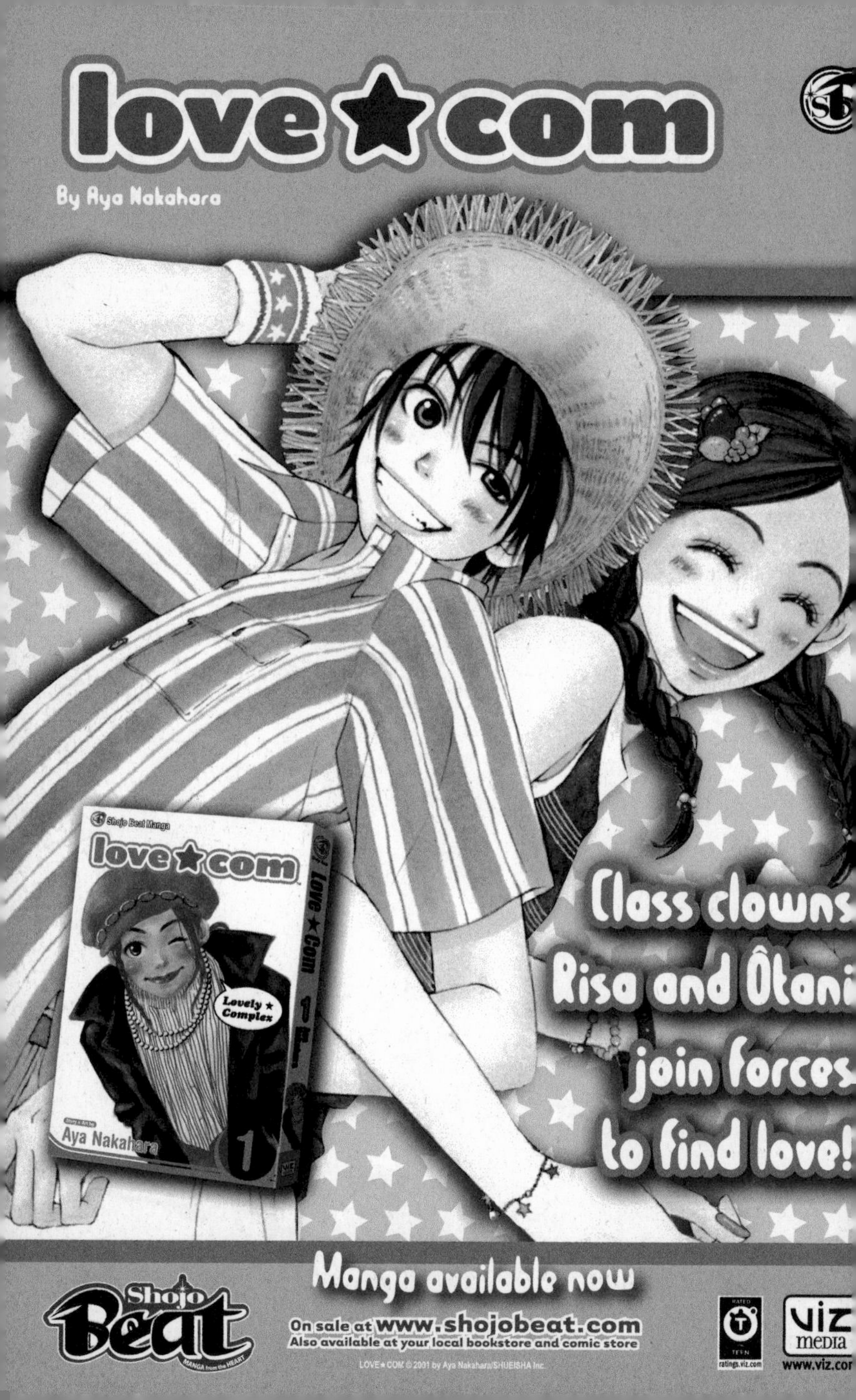

love★com
By Aya Nakahara
Shojo Beat Manga
love★com
Lovely ★ Complex
Aya Nakahara
1
Class clowns
Risa and Ôtani
join forces
to find love!
Manga available now
Shojo Beat
MANGA from the HEART
On sale at www.shojobeat.com
Also available at your local bookstore and comic store
LOVE★COM © 2001 by Aya Nakahara/SHUEISHA Inc.
RATED
T
TEEN
ratings.viz.com
VIZ media
www.viz.co